AFGHAN MODERN

AFGHAN
MODERN

THE HISTORY OF A GLOBAL NATION

Robert D. Crews

THE BELKNAP PRESS *of*
HARVARD UNIVERSITY PRESS

Cambridge, Massachusetts
London, England

2015

First printing

Library of Congress Cataloging-in-Publication Data
is available from the Library of Congress

ISBN 978-0-674-28609-2

For Christopher and Reina

CONTENTS

AFGHAN MODERN

INTRODUCTION

"BIGGER THAN DUBAI" was how my Afghan neighbor on the flight from Kabul to the shimmering Gulf emirate dreamily envisioned the future of his country. Over miniature bottles of scotch and lukewarm cans of beer—a number of passengers having suspended certain public mores upon reaching cruising altitude—my companion breathlessly enthused about how Afghanistan could replace Dubai as the most dynamic and modern hub of global transportation and commerce. Ideally situated between Europe and Asia, it could become fabulously wealthy, he explained, as a broker of all kinds of global flows. Afghanistan was destined to be a luminous center, not a grim and destitute periphery, of our world.

Such talk was much more than the bravado of an ambitious banker in his late twenties who was confidently buying up real estate in Kabul just when other Afghans were sending hundreds of millions of dollars in search of safe havens abroad, and foreigners were poised to turn off the spigot of billions of dollars in aid and investment following the withdrawal of a significant number of foreign troops in 2014. Considering his observations in the context of my historical research, it struck me that his conviction was grounded in a cosmopolitan sensibility that I had encountered before, in archives and in interviews with Afghans in a half dozen countries. His perspective drew strength from an intellectual tradition that has long imagined Afghans as central to global politics. This way of thinking also reflected a sense, built up by the collective memories of millions of Afghan families, of a shared past stamped by various kinds of diaspora experience, of inhabiting all parts of the globe far beyond the borders of their country. This conversation with my savvy banker acquaintance helped to crystallize a new way to think about the experiences of Afghans in the world.

The result is this book, which puts Afghan globalism at the heart of a reinterpretation of the history of Afghanistan. By *globalism* I mean the myriad ways in which Afghans engaged and connected with a wider world, how they came to participate in our modern, globalized age. On the one hand, globalism is about physical mobility. For centuries before Afghans became the world's largest refugee community in the 1980s, they were on the move across the globe. Among the characters we will meet are Afghan traders in Africa, poets in Iran, scholars in Iraq, pilgrims in Jerusalem, seafarers in India, entrepreneurs in Australia, carpenters in California, students in Turkey, workers in London, and a writer in Denmark.

On the other hand, globalism here encompasses other varieties of connectivity. Afghans became integrated in the global flows of migrants and commodities that have been the focus of so many recent global histories. They were, at the same time, intensely engaged with intellectual currents that transcended national or regional boundaries. In a vast range of historical sources, we find men and women, often with very little formal education, connected to global events and with very sophisticated knowledge of the world. Further up the social hierarchy, Afghan educated elites may have been few in number. Yet they have played an outsized role in the history of the country. Remarkably multilingual and adept at navigating among diverse intellectual canons, the Afghan thinkers whom we will encounter were more than cosmopolitans coming to terms with a modernity framed by their foreign interlocutors. For many, Afghan answers to global questions were not provincial adaptations. They were universal. In this strand of Afghan globalism, the country was fated to serve at once as a refuge and a beacon for humanity.

My approach is intended as a broad challenge to current thinking about Afghanistan. It starts from the premise that how we conceptualize the country, in our journalism and public-policy debates and in much of our scholarly work, remains intractably mired in tropes that bear little resemblance to historical reality. Pervading all of these genres, the most enduring image of Afghanistan evokes a desolate, inward-looking, and isolated place. Numerous twentieth-century writers mythologized this "hermit kingdom" over and over, claiming that its ostensibly primitive inhabitants have remained immobilized in time and space in a morass only made worse, for all parties, by repeated foreign invasions. In this "graveyard of empires," everything is different. Ancient tribes reign supreme, undergirded by patriarchy and xenophobic religious authority. Ethnic chauvinism trumps ideas. And loyalty goes to the highest bidder. A French ethnologist sketched out most of this forbidding picture already in the late nineteenth century when he wrote, "The Afghans do not have a history, because anarchy has none."[1]

The question of scale is central to this problem. If one embraces the view that we are dealing with a hopelessly archaic and insular society in Afghanistan, then adopting an optic designed for small-scale phenomena would seem fitting. A lens built for fine-grained analysis might reveal a great deal about a particular locale or group. Indeed, much of the most insightful research on the country was carried out by Western anthropologists in the 1960s and 1970s at a moment when, for a variety of methodological and ethical reasons, the discipline tended to highlight the distinctiveness and isolation of localized cultures. Social scientists and historians working on Afghanistan employed a somewhat larger scale. They focused on the nation-state, a perspective that inclined its practitioners toward treating subjects such as modernization and high politics as if they were largely contained by national boundaries. In the field of area studies, given institutional form by the U.S. government and its partners in American universities, Afghanistan did not belong properly to the "Middle East" or "South Asia." It seemed sui generis, a world apart from everywhere else.[2]

Another gargantuan obstacle to a deeper understanding of Afghanistan has been the fighting that has gripped some or all of the country more or less continuously since 1978. Melding a toxic mix of elements of civil war and foreign occupation, war-time conditions have had several glaring effects on research, in addition to interrupting the productive fieldwork of the 1970s. This violence shifted research priorities. The great powers who intervened in the country dictated what kinds of questions have been asked. As in other colonial settings, this meant that what the foreigners wanted to know was first and foremost supposed to be useful in ruling the place as cheaply as possible. This dynamic, rather than the unchanging character of Afghans or Afghanistan, accounts for why the British in the nineteenth and early twentieth centuries and the Soviets in the late twentieth century and the Americans in the twenty-first century would invest so much in devising highly racialized typologies of tribes and ethnic types. It also explains why the "graveyard of empires" narrative would have such staying power. Since 2001, nearly all American research on the subject (including some of my own) has been addressed, if sometimes only indirectly, to U.S. and NATO war policy making.

The war has also been so crucial because it has made the task of distinguishing causes from effects far more difficult. For instance, are tribal and ethnic identities or Taliban religious ideologies the underlying roots of perennial conflict, or are they the more recent products of the past three decades of violence? And for all but a few intrepid, mostly European scholars (and among them, Germans, Dutch, British, and French in particular), the fog of war has been compounded by the real dangers of fieldwork. All of these factors have made it plausible for observers to see today's Afghan society as unchanging for centuries, if not millennia, and not one whose features are effects of the ongoing war and its global context.

A focus on Afghan globalism yields a very different story. Viewed as an expansive space that accommodated varying kinds of networks that crisscrossed the region and the globe, rather than a static collection of tribes or ethnic groups, Afghanistan can no longer be understood as isolated from the global circulation of modern politics. The national lens is imperfect everywhere. But in the case of Afghanistan it has obscured diverse interconnections that linked Afghans to a wider modernity.

Meanwhile, many of the assumptions that underlay anthropological and historical writing a half century ago have shifted. Outside of the community of social scientists and anthropologists working for the American military in the field of counterinsurgency studies, scholars are now far more skeptical about claims about rigidly bounded cultures. They are more inclined to see entities like tribes and ethnic groups as social constructs, as the products of contingent and contested histories. In Afghanistan, as in other parts of the globe, such identities are situational and malleable, not immutable and all-encompassing.[3]

Consider the state of African studies, which was once dominated by similar categories. Tribes, villages, and even ethnic groups, scholars have shown, were essential to narratives that justified foreign rule. But they were frequently little more than invented mechanisms of hierarchical control. As the historian Trevor Getz reminds us, "the story we often tell of African tribes, chiefs, and villages tells us more about how Europeans thought of themselves in the period of colonization than of the realities in Africa prior to their coming." Rejecting the notion that "the local" is somehow more "authentic," scholars of

Africa and other parts of the globe are more likely to explore the inter-play of local, regional, national, and global settings and to appreciate that human mobility forces us to think through different spatial frameworks. Taking all of this into account, the Afghan past must be reimagined on a much broader canvas.[4]

The chapters that follow trace this global history. The story be-gins in the early modern period, an era when there were Afghans and others inhabiting this space, but no Afghanistan. Rather than treat this period as a brief interlude in the inevitable rise of an Af-ghan nation-state, Chapter 1 explores the inhabitants of this area as imperial cosmopolitans, the subjects of sprawling empires with far-flung centers of gravity in Iran, Central Asia, and north India. In this setting, the Mughal, Safavid, and Uzbek polities were more than empires of conquest. They simultaneously forged linkages across vast distances, drawing their subjects into various networks by cultivating commerce, spurring migration, and recruiting elites and servitors. It was as subjects of empire that residents of places such as Kabul and Kandahar came into contact with cosmopolitan court cultures in Is-fahan, Delhi, Agra, Samarkand, and elsewhere.

These imperial contexts proved fertile ground for the state-building projects, examined in Chapter 2, which Afghans launched across a space that extended from the frontiers of the Caucasus moun-tain range to deep in the Indian subcontinent. Only one of these survived in the eighteenth century, its success largely owed to its im-perial inheritance. These empires left another indelible mark on the course of Afghan history in that their patronage of writing by and about the Afghans formed a canon of imagery that Europeans—and Afghans themselves—would carry into the modern era. It was in this setting that the opponents of these Afghan political movements began to circulate narratives about the supposedly "wild," "unruly," and "warlike" Afghan, an idea that subsequent observers would take up and apply to very different contexts, even in the face of considerable evidence to the contrary.

Chapter 3 analyzes the making of the Afghan nation-state both within and beyond the borders as they exist today. By exploring interactions between a sizable Afghan diaspora abroad and the rulers of the kingdom in the late nineteenth and early twentieth centuries, this chapter shows how Afghan nation-making was, at multiple levels, part of a series of global processes. More and more Afghans were on the move across the globe, capitalizing on rail and steamship networks that began at the frontiers of the kingdom. Here, too, empire was central to how Afghans and others imagined this nation. By 1919, Afghanistan was among the last independent Muslim states, and its amir, Amanullah, boldly offered his leadership to the faithful everywhere, as we shall see in Chapter 4. To Moscow, though, Afghanistan looked like a potential leader to rally all "the East" in anticolonial revolution. A host of Indians, from Pan-Islamists to socialists and anarchists, looked to Kabul during the 1920s as well. For these activists, and for Afghan nationalist circles, events in Afghanistan had global significance, and it was from there, they hoped, that these varied revolutionary projects would spread, challenging European empires and forging unity among Asians and Muslims.

In Chapter 5, I take up the pivotal period of the 1930s and 1940s, in which Afghanistan became deeply embedded in global financial networks and the pace of Afghan interaction with the rest of the world dramatically increased. Not limited to the elites who studied abroad or interacted with foreigners in major cities, the effects of these changes rippled throughout society. From herders in northern Afghanistan raising karakul skins for the fur industry in New York to workers in the new textile factories built with aid from Germany and know-how from North Carolina, increasing numbers of Afghan men and women owed their livelihoods to distant markets and sources of technology. The Second World War played a key role, too, ultimately opening up a space for the United States to displace Germany as the leading donor underwriting Afghan development projects.

With the onset of the Cold War, the focus of Chapter 6, Afghanistan was awash with foreign advisers and experts eager to turn the Afghan rush toward the industrial era to the advantage of one of the superpowers. For intellectuals and political leaders—and soon for many other strata of society—the influx of hundreds of millions of dollars in foreign aid and thousands of foreigners sharpened controversies about the political order. The Afghan monarchy had conjured the spirit of capitalism. Calls for socialism and a democratic order followed. On the right, this all smelled like godless materialism, a realization strengthened by contact with Muslim thinkers in Egypt, Pakistan, and Iran who were busy with their own answers to the ideological questions of the day. In their eyes, it did not help matters that Kabul was becoming a thoroughly international city. By the early 1970s, tens of thousands of foreign tourists visited from Pakistan, Europe, and the United States. Elvis Presley played on Kabul's movie screens, and miniskirts abounded. Western hippies bought—and exported—tons and tons of Afghan dope. Afghanistan was by the mid-1970s thoroughly saturated with technocrats from East and West, local socialists, Muslim radicals, Peace Corps volunteers, family planning experts, multinational corporate bosses, spies, drug dealers, agricultural specialists, and even astronauts and cosmonauts who visited the country to tout the achievements of the superpowers.

The crisis unleashed by the seizure of power in 1978 by an underground Afghan socialist party, whose leaders included several students who had studied in the United States and numerous military officers trained in the Soviet Union, is the subject of Chapter 7. This chapter surveys the revolutionary projects that upended and remade Afghan society. To the communists, the revolution presented an opportunity to liberate Afghan society and to force Afghans to be modern, all in a manner that would teach the world how to build a progressive society. In response, Muslim fighters from around the world joined the anti-Soviet fray, later spawning al-Qaeda and other revolutionary movements. Although they differed from their Arab allies, many of the Afghan mujahidin saw their struggle not just as a defense of the Afghan nation and Islam but of humanity writ large. Anticommunists such as President Ronald Reagan shared a similar view. With Afghanistan at its very center, the American-led "crusade" against the Soviets, as one of his advisers put it, was a gift to the entire world. Against this backdrop, the flight of some seven million refugees, coupled with the wholesale transition by thousands of Afghan farmers to opium and cannabis production, meant that, from geographically remote mountain villages to the diaspora in Europe, Pakistan, Iran, Russia, Central Asia, the United States, Australia, and elsewhere, Afghan lives were interconnected more than ever with the world beyond the borders of Afghanistan.

Chapter 8 investigates how the American intervention against the Taliban in 2001 opened up yet another distinctive era in the history of Afghan globalism. Afghans became the object of an American-led humanitarian mission that was, simultaneously, a campaign to remake Afghans in the name of American security. By 2014, facing stalemate with the Taliban movement, Washington had abandoned many of its earlier ambitions. However, the global flows unleashed by war and occupation had taken on a life of their own. The drug trade flourished, and consumption expanded around the globe. At the same time, though, several states erected new boundaries to the movement of Afghans and closed their doors to Afghan refugees. Human mobility proved to be more vulnerable to interdiction by American, European, Iranian, Australian, and other authorities. Having waged a war to free Afghans, NATO countries increasingly threw up barriers to Afghan migration, even denying visas to those who had served in their military units as translators and guides. In this, too, Afghans could claim for themselves many of the essential, if lamentable, attributes of global citizenship.

In sum, this book calls for new approaches to Afghanistan, to how we imagine its past and act in the present. It shows how Afghan history is intertwined with that of its neighbors and the great powers. It is, at once, Indian, Iranian, Central Asian, Chinese, British, and Russian history. From the 1940s, it is also American history. Cutting across all of these national stories, is, of course, an overarching global narrative. Viewed from this interpretive angle, and through a variety of archival and secondary sources and oral histories, the history of Afghanistan emerges into view, then, as a new kind of subject, less the object of an anthropological fascination with the exotic—or as an archaic threat to be contained in a security sense—than as one of the many stories that can enrich our understanding of the complexity of our modern times.

1 | IMPERIAL COSMOPOLITANS

AFGHANS HAVE RARELY imagined themselves as peripheral to the rest of the world. One of the first histories of the Afghans placed them at the center of a universal history. Composed in the seventeenth century, Nimatullah's *History of the Afghans (Makhzan-i Afghānī)* mapped their past onto a sacred landscape. It followed the contours of the geography of both the Bible and the Quran and portrayed Afghans in dynamic contact with these holy places. Their history began with Adam and Eve and their descendant, the prophet Yaqub Israel. Their progeny included the original Israelites, and they ruled at Jerusalem, where one of them, Afghana, constructed the al-Aqsa Mosque.

Nimatullah's history accounted for the later geography of the Afghans by narrating a story of divinely inspired mass migration. Under King Suleiman, a figure named Bokhtnasser subjugated the area. He was responsible for "carrying away the Israelites, whom he settled in the mountainous districts of Ghor, Ghazneen, Kabul, Candahar, Koh Firozeh, and the parts lying within the fifth and sixth climates; where they, especially those descended of Asif and Afghana, fixed their habitations, continually increasing in number, and incessantly making war on the infidels around them."[1]

Their leader, Qais, was summoned to Medina to receive the blessings of the Prophet Muhammad and to fight alongside him against the army of Mecca. There he received a momentous prophecy: God would make Qais's offspring "so numerous, that they, with respect to the establishment of the Faith, would outvie all other people." At Medina, the angel Gabriel also revealed "that their attachment to the Faith would, in strength, be like the wood upon which they lay the keel when constructing a ship, which wood the seaman call Pathan [Pashtun]."

Thus it was the Prophet himself that conferred the title of *Pathan,* or *Pashtun,* upon Qais and his people. They then returned to the region of Ghor to spread Islam and to pledge loyalty to Sultan Mahmud Ghaznavi (r. 998–1030), who had recently laid claim to territories from Iraq to the Sind River. Following the collapse of this dynasty in the twelfth century, a new ruler enticed the Afghans to migrate again. They journeyed farther to the east to another "Kohistan," or "land of mountains." The Afghans were to serve as "the guardians of the seat of the empire, and check the infidels about Hindustan." Having recounted their trek from Arabia to the "Kohistan of Ghor" and then on to their present-day Kohistan, the *History of the Afghans* turned to a description of their military might. In the Indian subcontinent, they established themselves as sultans, "who sat on the throne in the principal provinces of Hindustan, and practised the right of having the Khotba [sermon] read, and money coined in their name; who carried the ball of justice and equity; and perpetuated their fame in this perishable world."[2]

Nimatullah's compilation of prophetic genealogy and epic migrations serves as a reminder that the history of the Afghans—and their thinking about their place in the world—did not begin with the state whose borders took form in the late nineteenth and early twentieth centuries. Before the modern era, the space that would become Afghanistan belonged to very different political geographies. The largest of these territories was known as Khorasan. It was an ancient fixture in the writings of Arab, Armenian, and Iranian geographers. Khorasan was an elastic and often expansive construct, and writers imagined it as the eastern part of the Iranian lands. But they differed on whether it covered all of the Hindu Kush and reached to the

Indus River and how far it extended beyond the Amu Darya (Oxus River). This latter region geographers regarded as a separate entity, Mawarannahr, or Transoxiana. It was anchored in long-standing urban centers such as Bukhara and Samarkand. These sites had been fertile ground for Buddhists, Zoroastrians, Manicheans, Jews, and Nestorian Christians before the Arab conquests and conversion to Islam. Whereas Mashhad and Herat were the two urban pillars of Khorasan, Kandahar had long faced the east. A former outpost of the Gandhara empire in India, the site of important Buddhist temples, and the seat of governors who spoke Aramaic and Greek, Kandahar tended to belong, according to early Arabic geographers, to the province of Sind. However, rulers from Khorasan and western Iran would challenge this association, waging campaign after campaign to seize the town and the valuable trade routes that passed through it. Kabul, once synonymous with utter remoteness in a saying favored by Arabic geographers, had occupied a more intermediate position, shaped at different moments by Hellenic and, later, Indic rulers and traditions. At the source of the Oxus, Badakhshan was yet another entity with its own history and politics. It was described by Chinese and Arab writers and widely known for the Badakhshani rubies that earned the praise of Marco Polo and became a stock image of Persian poetry.[3]

Other regions bore the name of peoples: Turan and Turkestan were inhabited by Turks, the Hazarajat by the Hazaras, and Baluchistan by the Baluch (though Baluch chronicles recounted their migration from an ancient homeland in Syria). Between the tenth and seventeenth centuries, a succession of imperial dynasties would also leave their mark. Besides the Ghaznavids and the dynasties of the Delhi Sultanate, the Timurids, Shibanids, and Mughals as well as smaller states based in Badakhshan and Baluchistan would seek to integrate parts of this territory along with its resources and populations in their respective imperial projects.

In short, the inhabitants of this space were for centuries the subjects of competing empires, princely realms, and city-states oriented toward cultural and political centers of gravity beyond the region. At the same time, though, there was much to connect the inhabitants of this space. People were mobile, and boundaries fluid. Moreover, different kinds of networks—commercial, diplomatic, religious, literary, and artistic—sustained connections among the major urban centers, while linking them to other parts of the world.

To Europeans writing about the country later, Afghanistan seemed to be a prisoner of this past, one that they mistook for an endless stream of marauding invaders and savage conquests. A British eyewitness to the Anglo-Afghan War of 1838–1842 painted a typical portrait of the Afghans: "The people are a fine race, tall, athletic, and handsome; in Affghanistan they are remarkably fair, many of them scarcely darker than Europeans; they are accustomed to war from their childhood, and the history of their country, so far as we know it, presents a continual struggle between rival competitors for power—a series, with scarcely an intermission, of anarchy, blood, and confusion." When Americans became involved in Afghanistan after the Second World War, they adopted a similar perspective. "For ages, the arid, twisted mountain masses of Afghanistan have formed the vortex for countless whirlpools of human migrations which have swept through Asia," wrote Waldo Drake in the *Los Angeles Times* in 1947. "Invariably," he claimed, "these invasions have been attended by wholesale massacres of populations, by the ravishment of great cities which housed the transplanted cultures of Iran, of Greece, of India." These contradictory images of a timeless country that was at once landlocked and isolated and simultaneously an ancient crossroads for invading armies have doggedly persisted into the present.[4]

As an alternative to these enduring clichés, texts such as Nimatullah's *History of the Afghans* open up the possibility of exploring interpretations that are more carefully grounded in historical evidence. As with all such texts, the context for his imaginative invocation of distant Jerusalem and Mecca was crucial. The setting for its compilation was, after all, an imperial court in India: Nimatullah took up his pen under the patronage of an Afghan nobleman at the court of the Mughal emperor Jahangir (r. 1605–1627). In the north Indian palaces and courtyards of Delhi, Agra, and elsewhere, we encounter figures such as Nimatullah who were molded by vibrant and cosmopolitan imperial worlds, not merely as the hapless victims of "foreign invasions" or passive bystanders at some mythic "crossroads" of civilizations but as actors who engaged in complicated ways with imperial societies and institutions.[5]

Empire, in this setting as in others, was about more than occupying territory. It was an adaptive form of governance that projected power over vast distances and forged distinctive forms of connectivity among far-flung locales. It established hierarchies based on cultural, religious, and other distinctions and integrated diverse populations to varying degrees. The deep imperial imprint on the history of the region should not be taken for some uniquely Afghan pathology marked by a relentless cycle of imperial subjugation and resistance, however. The peoples who inhabited this space shared the experience of imperial rule with most other humans on this planet for lengthy periods of our recorded history. From the Romans to the Mongols, the Chinese, the British, and the Americans, empires seized territories and exploited subject populations. At the same time, though, they built new connections and facilitated exchange across regions and around the globe.[6]

Before the rise of Afghanistan and other nation-states in the nineteenth and twentieth centuries, inhabitants of the assorted polities that dotted and traversed this space were linked in innumerable ways to distant parts of the planet. Dynastic states of varying sizes jostled for authority over this space, continuously creating new political and social geographies that differ dramatically from those of modern maps. In the mid-seventh century, for example, the Chinese Tang dynasty (618–906) stretched all the way to Kabul and Herat. Other global connections would emerge not through conquest but via trade relations made possible by the web of early modern empires that spread across the region. The arrival of silver and tobacco, among the most important commodities exported by Europeans from the New World, attests to the global scale of these connections.

Migration was another factor. Beginning with traders, agriculturalists, and mercenaries who had moved to the east from at least the tenth century, groups calling themselves *Afghan*, or labeled such by those around them, became a diaspora of sorts. From the mid-fifteenth century Afghans who migrated from the eastern ranges of the Hindu Kush to the north Indian plains established dynasties there. Their descendants spread to nearly every corner of the subcontinent, with many of their number maintaining a sense of connection to the mythical territory mapped by Nimatullah. They would be called *Afghan, Pathan,* or *Pashtun,* depending on the setting. Yet they are not the only actors in this story.

The history of this area is also about the interaction of diverse populations. In analyzing events of this and later time periods, we will follow the practice of the historical sources in utilizing the names of groups as the authors of these accounts do, though with the proviso that they are sometimes deceptively modern sounding. Thus, in the eighteenth century we might encounter an "Afghan" on the Bay of Bengal, but this term does not have the same meaning as the word used with increasing frequency in the second half of the twentieth century to denote subjects of the state of Afghanistan. From the outset, we should note that labels such as "Afghan," "Hazara," "Qizilbash," "Uzbek" were never fixed permanently; nor did they neatly bind political or social groups in any time period. Group identities—even those asserting detailed genealogical narratives as evidence of an unchanging "tribal" condition—emerged and continuously shifted in relation to imperial politics and institutions.

Throughout this space then, empires put people, goods, and ideas into motion. Imperial institutions, mentalities, and sociabilities in turn left profound legacies for the making of Afghanistan and the worldview of its elites. It was in the dynamic political context of imperial power, and the global connections that it enabled, that particular identities crystallized. Modern Afghans were formed in the cauldron of empire, and their state would retain many of its central characteristics long after the imperial polities that gave birth to it had faded.

The writing of the history of the communities that inhabit Afghanistan has long been about the search for their origins. In the nineteenth century, Europeans, especially those who dreamed of sowing the seeds of Christianity among them, were enthralled by the assertion, like that made by Nimatullah, that the Afghans descended from the ancient Jews. Were they one of the fabled "lost tribes of Israel"? Bernhard Dorn, a German philologist in Russian service who translated Nimatullah's work in the late 1820s, rejected an Afghan tie to the Jews. But he added other important elements to their mythic history. Dorn traced their origins to the seventh century, "when, about 682 A.D., they issued from their mountainous habitations, and caused desolation and destruction in the contiguous countries." In addition to their "pretended origin from the Jews," the Afghans merited further study, Dorn continued, because their many tribes and clans, "which, according to Historians, amount to three hundred and fifty-nine," gave them "a great resemblance to the ancient Scottish clans."

What truly distinguished the Afghans from among "all other Asiatic nations," though, was for Dorn "their indelible love of freedom and liberty." "They never submitted," he insisted, "to a despotic government; but, at every time, succeeded in maintaining their natural right: and the present King of Kabul is little more than the first citizen of the empire."[7] Writing a half century later, H. W. Bellew, a British military officer, relied on linguistic speculation to identify "certain tribes now inhabiting Afghanistan" as "the representatives of the posterity of the Greeks who anciently ruled in that country." "The country now called Afghanistan is the Ariana of the ancient Greeks," he concluded. He went on to offer a scheme allowing observers "to recognise in many of the existing tribes of Afghanistan the modern representatives of the ancient nations of Ariana" and "to form an accurately founded distinction between the old possessors and the later settlers; between the remains of subsequent dynastic invaders and the stragglers of transitory plunderers."[8]

The quest for the discovery of Afghan origins has had relevance far beyond speculative musing about a foggy past. Whether Afghans had affinities with Jews, Greeks, or independent Scots, and whether some of Afghanistan's peoples were "invaders" or "stragglers," would have political implications far into the future. The trope of the Afghans' "indelible love of freedom and liberty" would persist as a staple of commentary on Afghanistan; and from the 1930s, Afghan elites would make a claim to descent from the Aryans a foundation of Afghan nationalist ideology. What all of these conceptions of the Afghan past shared was the idea that it had been stamped by an ancient migration followed by a period of static immobility continuing into the present. Shifting our focus from the quest for origins to reconstructing connections between Afghans and the wider world distances us from these racialized and nationalist categories and reveals a more dynamic picture of mobility and exchange.

Whatever ruling dynasties may have prevailed in the towns that now dot the Afghan landscape, it was the steady stream of commerce that more or less continuously linked their inhabitants—and their rural hinterlands—to distant trading centers. The history of trade networks tying the region to faraway places dates back long before the caravan routes linking the Roman Empire and Han China, a network of corridors for the movement of all manner of commodities, later referred to as the "Silk Road." At Ai Khanum, a Greek city (now in northeastern Afghanistan), archaeologists have found objects that include a silver medallion likely brought from Syria depicting the goddess Cybele on a lion-drawn chariot. Excavations at Bagram uncovered glassware and other objects from Alexandria. Lapis lazuli from the famed mines of Badakhshan had been among the luxury commodities sought out by the Greeks. Traders brought the precious stones to Kabul, where they were passed on via Peshawar to Karachi and then by sea to markets elsewhere. A Chinese visitor to Herat in 1414 discovered that "the people have abundant quantities of gold, silver, gems, coral, amber, crystal, diamonds, cinnabar, chopping stones, pearls, and green jade," which, he added, had "come from other places, but no one knows where." Dating back to the Tang dynasty, the horse trade continued to link these towns and their pastoralist hinterlands to the Timurids (1370–1506) in Central Asia and the Ming dynasty (1368–1644) in China. In the sixteenth century, traders from Kabul transported their goods to China via the towns of Central Asia. At Yarkand, the Italian Jesuit Matteo Ricci observed a caravan of merchants arriving from Kabul whose goods were dispatched in another caravan bound for China. In Kabul, where he would begin to establish his Mughal empire in 1504, Zahir-ud-Din Muhammad Babur encountered goods from "Khurasan, Iraq, Anatolia, and China." It was "the entrepôt between Hindustan and Khurasan," where traders "who go to Cathay and Anatolia do no greater business."

Kabuli merchants, he marveled "would not be satisfied with a 300 to 400 percent profit." Thousands of horses were brought annually to Kabul, he observed, where they met "caravans of ten, fifteen, twenty thousand pack animals" carrying "slaves, textiles, rock sugar, refined sugar, and spices" from India.[9]

The detailed descriptions left behind by the likes of Babur remind us that trade routes were constantly changing. Some of them carried Alexander the Great, Genghis Khan, Marco Polo, and many other lesser-known and anonymous travelers, missionaries, pilgrims, merchants, soldiers, explorers, and adventurers on their voyages from Asia to the West and from Europe and the Middle East to China and India. This road system evolved over time: the paths followed by Buddhist pilgrims from China in the seventh century would differ from those of Arab travelers in later centuries. War, politics, disease, and migration had an impact. Shifts in technology, consumption patterns, and the environment all played a role. Travel routes were seasonal; snow and high waters made passageways through the Hindu Kush impassable during the winter months.

Like most empires elsewhere, these were commercial enterprises. Profits from trade in horses, silk, cotton textiles, silver, lapis lazuli, rubies, and even tobacco, together with agrarian revenues, filled their treasuries. Road maintenance and security were thus among the chief priorities of imperial rule. Powerful dynasties like the Abbasids (749–1258) redirected the flow of travelers and goods from their capital at Baghdad by constructing new roads and favoring certain towns over others. Shifting trade routes and political changes led to the depopulation of some areas and the growth of others. In the early thirteenth century, the Mongols brought devastation. However, when they turned to consolidating their vast empire by promoting commerce and communication, Herat joined a dense network of roads that linked Merv, Balkh, Shiraz, Hamadan, Isfahan, Baghdad, and other trading towns. In the fourteenth century, the famed Arab traveler Ibn Battuta passed through Herat on his way to India. Later, Babur followed a less-traveled route via the Koh-i Baba mountain range when he journeyed eastward from Herat to Kabul. Competition among the Mughals, Shibanid Uzbeks, and Safavids for control of trade routes disrupted commerce during periods of warfare. However, their peacetime investments in commercial infrastructure, roads, and caravansaries boosted trade in the late sixteenth and seventeenth centuries.[10]

The circulation of information about these ever-changing routes was essential to commerce and imperial control alike. Travelers shared information at guesthouses, bazaars, mosques, and shrines along the way. In the mid-sixteenth century, a shipwrecked Ottoman admiral, Seydi 'Ali Reis, presented to the sultan a description of the lands that he encountered on his overland journey home, praising Kabul as "a beautiful city" filled with pleasures and entertainments and admiring the happy people he saw there. An assortment of such guides in Latin, Arabic, Persian, and Chinese ranged from the sixteenth-century atlas, *Theatrum Orbis Terrarum,* to chronicles composed at the Mughal court.[11] Later, European travelers, newswriters, and intelligence gatherers diligently sketched reports with the latest information about road conditions and the movement of people.

As part of an increasingly global system, developments in other parts of the world could have far-reaching consequences. In the wake of Christopher Columbus's voyage to the New World, much European trade shifted to oceanic shipping. Nonetheless, commerce continued to flow through these towns, not just from east to west and back, but also, increasingly between north and south. From the sixteenth century, a multiethnic and multireligious Indian merchant diaspora played a central role in the commerce of the region, joining trading and moneylending activities and linking urban and rural clients. Originally based in Multan, later Shikarpur, the Indian family firm knitted together a vast space from Bandar Abbas and Isfahan to Astrakhan, Kandahar, Bukhara, and Kabul. Allowing timely transactions over these vast distances, bills of exchange (*hundis*) cemented relations of trust and reputation. They formed the crucial mechanism that held this system together. While some commodities moved across the Indian Ocean in the sixteenth century, caravan trade between India and Iran by way of Kandahar (and with alternate routes through Kabul and Herat) intensified for much of the sixteenth and seventeenth centuries. Indian demand for horses from the Central Asian steppe and Turkestan was insatiable. In exchange, Indian traders offered textiles, dyes, cotton, Kashmiri shawls, and other commodities. Along with the textiles from India and Spanish pesos and German coins from Persia, the caravans brought news to communities along the way. An event in 1586 points to the scale of the trade that passed from Central Asia through Kabul and the Khyber Pass to markets in India: a fire at the Peshawar fort damaged one thousand camel-loads of goods, likely including precious metals, fruits, porcelains, silks, and other items. In the early seventeenth century, New World tobacco arrived as well. Locals began cultivating it around Kandahar and elsewhere.[12]

The expansion of the Russian Empire and its demand for Asian commodities was another engine of growth for trade. The Russians were intensely interested in the lands that lay between them and the fabled riches of India and China. From the late sixteenth century, merchants from Central Asia traded in Russian towns. They frequented Moscow, Astrakhan, Nizhnii Novgorod, Kolomna, Iaroslavl', Samara, and even Arkhangelsk in the north. Russian merchants and emissaries also visited Bukhara and Balkh, gathering intelligence about routes to India. Muscovy had the most direct contact with

Balkh. Judging from evidence gathered about the murder of a merchant from Balkh who was killed by robbers in Kazan in 1638, traders from the region traveled widely in Muscovy and spent many years there. Considerable trade passed through the kingdom, including a steady traffic in Russian slaves that extended as far as India, as a Muscovite report noted in 1670. The Muscovites were interested in trade and the freeing of these captives. (Some of the Russians had even ended up serving in local military forces.) Besides relying on traders' accounts, the Kremlin gathered intelligence via its consuls in Iran. Information about the region reached Moscow more quickly than it did Europe, for example, when merchants brought news from Kandahar in 1649. In the late seventeenth century, Muscovite travelers followed the route through Bukhara, Karshi, Kelif, and Bukhara to Kabul. They rode on horseback from the Russian frontier at Iaitsk (Gur'ev) and could reach Khiva in two weeks. From there it was just a few more weeks to Balkh and then Kabul. Kandahar could be reached in about a month from Mashhad or Bukhara. Sailing from London to Calcutta, by contrast, required five to eight months until the early nineteenth century. In the 1750s, Kubek Bainazarov and Nadyr Iadgarov were among the merchants from Russia who dealt directly with traders in Balkh and Badakhshan. To the west, merchants from the region could be found as far as Moscow. Arriving with several thousand camels, they appeared frequently at the frontier town of Orenburg, a major entrepôt for Russia's eastern trade, and migrated on to the Makar'ev market, a vast fair where traders from throughout the Russian Empire and its southern and western borderlands brought goods from all corners of the globe. To accommodate merchants from Kabul and other trading centers, the authorities at Troitsk recorded taxes in rubles and rupees.[13]

To the south, these same mercantile networks fused with others that crossed the Arabian Sea and connected to ports throughout the

Persian Gulf. From the eighteenth century at the latest, these merchants traded directly with Masqat via the Indus River for African slaves and other commodities. Early nineteenth-century travel accounts identify traders and pilgrims from this region at various points along the maritime route to Mecca. Later that century, Muhammad Hayat Khan, a scholar in the employ of the British administration in India, sketched a romantic portrait of their peripatetic ways and supposedly boundless lust for profit: "These men, with no better means of transport than trains of camels, mules, ponies or oxen, but with an enterprise that nothing can daunt, make their way to far-distant markets, and the picturesque figure of the Farsiban [Persian-speaking] merchant, whom no toil will deter, when high profits allure him, with Afghan chogha [gown] and postin [sheepskin coat] and enormous turban, is familiar in the markets, not only of India, but of Russia, Iran and Turkistan, and even of Turkey, China and Tibet."[14]

Such commercial ties frequently deepened political contacts. Chinese envoys sent by the Ming dynasty visited Herat and Badakhshan. In turn, Timur (Tamerlane, r. 1370–1405) sent representatives to the court of the Chinese emperor. Timur's merchants sent horses to the Ming, and his spies gathered intelligence about their military. The Chinese interpreted these interactions as evidence of Timur's submission. But as the conqueror of much of Iran, Anatolia, Syria, Central Asia, and northern India, he denied he was a tributary of the emperor, confiscating the Chinese embassy's 800-camel caravan and insulting the emperor to underscore his independence. Under his son, Shahrukh (r. 1405–1447), relations between Herat and the Chinese improved, and trade and diplomatic contacts resumed. His envoys were present at the Chinese New Year ceremony of February 2, 1421, elevating Peking to the status of capital of the Ming empire. In the fifteenth and sixteenth centuries, China was also a destination for émigrés from the region. Merchants and emissaries settled there and entered state service. To the far north, the new state on the Moscow River was a growing political power with which the Timurids had to contend. In 1490 an embassy of the Timurid rulers of Herat (led by a man named "Urus," possibly the descendant of a Russian captive) arrived in Moscow seeking a treaty based "on love and friendship." In 1533, Babur, too, sent an envoy to Moscow with a proposal of "freedom and brotherhood." More than a century later, Tsar Alesksei Mikhailovich (r. 1645–1676) dispatched a Bukharan merchant, Muhammad Yusuf Kasimov, to make contact with the Mughal court in Delhi. In 1676, he managed to reach Kabul, a town Muscovites would describe, well into the eighteenth century, as "an Indian border town."[15]

The inhabitants of Kabul, Balkh, Herat, Kandahar, and other lo-cales traveled widely as traders, diplomats, and mercenaries, but, like the chronicler Nimatullah, they were also drawn to the holy places of Islam. The Prophet Muhammad had received God's revelations near Mecca in the western part of the Arabian Peninsula, the Hijaz. The teachings of Islam instructed Muslims who were able to embark on pilgrimage to Mecca to undertake this rite at least once in their lives. The hajj to this holy city became one of the five pillars of Islam. Travelers to the Hijaz also visited Medina, the site of the first mosque and home to the tomb of the Prophet, his daughter Fatima, and many other notables. Farther to the west, Jerusalem was another holy des-tination. The Prophet had been carried there from Mecca by the Buraq, a wondrous winged creature, in his famed "Night Journey." And it was from Jerusalem that he ascended into heaven with the angel Gabriel. Traces of pilgrims and merchants following these same routes can be found, for instance, in documents describing a lodge established in the fourteenth century for travelers from Balkh, May-mana, and Badakhshan, among other inhabitants of Central Asia, in Tarsus in Anatolia, not far from the Mediterranean coast.[16]

In Iraq, the shrine cities of Karbala and Najaf held the tombs of the sacred heroes of the Shia, the family of 'Ali, the cousin and son-in-law of the Prophet Muhammad and the first leader, or imam, of the Shia community. These sites attracted generations of pilgrims who came to revere the suffering of the martyred descendants of 'Ali. Najaf and Karbala ranked as the most important of these destinations, having become simultaneously centers of Shia scholarship and teaching. These shrine cities formed crucial nodes in Shia intellectual and patronage networks that ranged from the eastern Mediterranean to northern India, providing figures from Kandahar, Herat, Balkh, and other towns with an adaptive framework of study that guided students from locale to locale in search of expertise in particular areas of study, among them grammar, jurisprudence, philosophy, and ethics. Aspiring Afghan Shia scholars tended to begin their education at home or in a village or neighborhood school before joining these transregional circuits, starting with study in Mashhad, where pilgrims also visited the tomb of the eighth imam.

For Shiites as well as Sunnis, this Imam Reza shrine complex was another key focus of pilgrimage, despite its close political affiliation with the Iranian shahs who were its patrons. Due to proximity, trade, Shiism, and politics, Mashhad was closely linked to Herat, which was itself the site of numerous shrines with supraregional importance, including the Gazurgah, the burial site of the eleventh-century shaykh Abdullah Ansari. The author of an early nineteenth-century autobiography centered on Herat and its environs, Muhammad Riza Barnabadi (1750–1815), celebrates Mashhad as "the Holy Land." His native village of Barnabad, a majority Shia settlement sixty kilometers from Herat on the route to Mashhad, had its own shrine in the tomb of Wahid ad-Din Muhammad, a fifteenth-century figure whom the author's ancestor had followed from Mecca. His descendants, male and female, were buried around this tomb complex. Muhammad

Riza Barnabadi's world stretched from Barnabad and Herat to Turbat-i Jam and Mashhad, where later in his life he served as secretary and taught calligraphy to local notables. Alongside such career opportunities, business and intermarriage interlinked families in both places; the Imam Reza complex itself held considerable property in Herat as part of its endowment.[17] Circuits of pilgrimage endured, but they were not unchanging. Some sacred places declined in importance. Others emerged in their place.

According to many traditions, the first originating in an account of a traveler from Granada in Andalusia, 'Ali was buried in the region of Balkh. His shrine complex at Mazar-i Sharif became a major locus of pilgrimage for Muslim men and women of various religious orientations, especially during the new year of the Persian calendar, Nowruz. Yet pious Muslims also established satellite shrines such as the Langar-i Sakhi in Nimroz Province to commemorate 'Ali. A shrine in Sar-i Pul was devoted to his son Husayn, and another one to the west of Kabul honored the cloak of the Prophet (the *khirqah-yi mubarak*), which was said to travel from the Hijaz to Badakhshan and then on to Kabul and, finally, to a shrine complex built to preserve it at Kandahar.[18] The urban landscape was dotted with saints' tombs, including those of holy women, to whom locals and travelers would appeal, often for very specific remedies tailored to a particular saint thought to be efficacious in curing disease or infertility. Veneration stretched from neighborhood saints, often anonymous entities whose memory was marked only by a humble stone or tree, to those farther away. Mecca, Medina, Karbala, and Najaf entailed more logistical difficulties, but significant numbers of travelers from the region nonetheless made the trip for study and pilgrimage.

Intellectuals circulated among madrasas, princely courts, and literary circles from Samarkand to Istanbul. The most famous Balkhi, the Sufi poet Jamaluddin Rumi (d. 1273), found patrons in multiple

courts and capitals. Long after his passing, the circulation and performance of his poetry maintained connections among cosmopolitan
communities from the Balkans to western China. Robert McChesney
has shown how this "economy of poetry" crossed the Sunni-Shia
divide, linking reading (and listening) communities throughout
Central Asia, Iran, India, and beyond.[19]

A remarkable eclecticism sustained these networks, which provided a forum for conversations that bridged diverse genres. Astrology, poetry, ethics, law, and history were all among their pursuits. Another feature of this landscape was widespread membership
in Sufi confraternities, each with their own ritual and doctrinal profile, which brought together the devout under the direction of leaders
distinguished by charisma and closeness to God. Under the Timurids,
Naqshbandi shaykhs formed networks that connected Herat, Samarkand, Tashkent, Kashgar, Kabul, and Bukhara. The Naqshbandis
believed in active involvement in both the material and spiritual domains, becoming major property owners, merchants, and political
patrons and brokers. Under the leadership of Khoja 'Ubaydullah
Ahrar (1404–1490), his deputies took the confraternity in all directions. Disciples appeared on the frontiers of China, India, Iran, and
in the Ottoman lands. In the late sixteenth and early seventeenth centuries, the Naqshbandis joined the stream of migrants moving from
Central Asia to India. In later centuries, disciples of another branch
of this confraternity, inspired by Ahmad Sirhindi (1564–1624), would
retransmit his teachings from India to Central Asia, Russia, and the
Middle East via Kabul, Maymana, Bukhara, and other places. Other
Naqshbandi branches persisted alongside different Sufi confraternities. From the seventeenth century, the Qadiriya spread from India,
sinking deep roots by the nineteenth century in the Pashtun communities of the Indo–Afghan frontier. Many Afghans trace the
Chishtiya order to the town of Chist, northeast of Herat, but as with

the other confraternities, it appears to have expanded in India, where major shrines that emerged at Ajmer, Lahore, Delhi, and elsewhere became important pilgrimage destinations for Afghan Chishtis. In the case of the Chishtiya, too, the seventeenth century marked a turning point: Emperor Jahangir expelled a leading shaykh to Balkh. Other Chishtis migrated later from India to Kabul, becoming renowned as musicians.[20]

This is not to say that these heterogeneous Sufi projects were without controversy. Founded by Bayazid Ansari (ca. 1525–1585), a movement among Pashto speakers around Peshawar, later known as the Roshaniya, developed an eclectic body of teachings that may have espoused reincarnation, inspired perhaps by Hindu scholars, and incorporated Shia precepts. It met with opposition from more orthodox scholars, most notably Akhund Darwaze, who rejected the participation of women, music and dancing, and the belief among Ansari's followers that he was the Mahdi, the figure sent by God to restore justice before the end-time. The Mughals, too, were hostile to the Roshaniya. Despite its suppression, later intellectuals would seek inspiration in the writings of Ansari and his followers, reading in them the seeds of a Pashto-language literature and an anticolonial ideology. Other Sufi shrines, saints, and texts would continue to bind their members to devotees across the globe. Manuscripts recounting the miraculous deeds of Naqshbandi Sufis, for example, had their own afterlife: the journey of one such text, produced in mid-eighteenth-century Kabul, can be traced across the nineteenth and twentieth centuries to owners in Bukhara and perhaps Samarkand or Khiva and then to Kazan on the Volga River and Kuldja on the western frontier of China.[21]

Persian was a lingua franca that cut across political and ethnic lines. Intellectuals were multilingual, and many could compose in more than one language. Some writers produced translations of especially valuable texts. From the sixteenth to eighteenth centuries, translations from Arabic and Persian were particularly influential for the pioneers of Pashto literature in Peshawar, Multan, Lahore, Kohat, Bannu, and even Delhi and Calcutta.[22] While manuscripts circulated widely, scholars also convened in person. In Kandahar, for example, a seventeenth-century Safavid chronicle described a gathering of "Chaghatai notables, ulama and sayyids from Mawarannahr and India," highlighting the figure of "one of the great religious scholars of the day," Mawlana Husayn Qaini, "who spent forty years in the study of the religious sciences in holy Mashhad, in Bukhara and in India."[23] Qat'i Haravi was another peripatetic sixteenth-century scholar who moved among literary and scientific circles in Herat and Kandahar. In Kabul, he taught in the madrasa of Khwaja Khurd Mekka, a native of Herat who had spent considerable time in Mecca, before traveling on to Agra to serve the Mughal emperor Akbar (r. 1556–1605).

For all of their travel, men such as 'Abdur Rahim, a Pashto poet who lived in the second half of the seventeenth and first half of the eighteenth centuries, could voice nostalgia about their places of origin. Born into a Ghilzai family near Kandahar, 'Abdur Rahim spent much of his life in Iran, first on pilgrimage to the tomb of the late twelfth- and early thirteenth-century Persian poet 'Attar at Nishapur and then at study in Varamin (near Tehran). From there he went to study with a well-known Bukharan shaykh and Sufi poet, Muhammadi Imla', a devotee of the Qadiri, Naqshbandi, and Chishti Sufi confraternities. In addition to his translations from Persian and Arabic into Pashto, he composed his own verse, including poetry about his longing for the gardens and shrines of Kandahar and the Arghandab River.[24]

Mobility, whether for business or spiritual purposes, was not limited to the urban milieu. Inhabitants of small towns and villages traveled as well. Shia scholars illustrate this point. Outside of the major urban centers, they might follow a trajectory similar to scholars from the major cities. 'Ali Akbar Talaqani (1688–1747), from Talaqan, a hamlet in the northwest, was among many who set out on the road to study in Herat, Mashhad, and Najaf.[25]

Although these merchants, pilgrims, scholars, and Sufis pursued itinerant trajectories, their lives were still very much formed by the imperial settings in which they were embedded. Incorporation in one of these empires could mean displacement for some local elites, but for others it presented dazzling opportunities. The most striking examples may be found among notables of every sort who ascended the ladder into the imperial ruling class. "Besides Timurids and Afghans," notes Munis Faruqi, Babur prepared to descend on India from his base in Kabul gathering around himself allies that included "Uzbeks, Badakhshanis, Hazaras, Chaghatais, Mughals, sundry other Turko-Mongol groups, Tajiks, Baluch, Ghakkars, Janjuas, and even the occasional Hindu." Departing from their ancestral homes, Heratis, Uzbeks, Badakhshanis, and others circulated throughout the empire and entered into the service of subsequent Mughal emperors and princes as soldiers, artists, and Sufis. Mughal sovereigns granted Afghans land and dispatched them as colonists and military servitors to extend imperial authority against rivals, including other Afghans. Sufi ties were yet another bond that drew together a multiethnic elite.[26]

In northern India, the spread of Mughal authority from the 1550s dislodged earlier Afghan rulers. Afghan colonies had already emerged in the mid-fifteenth century at Agra, Sultan Sikandar Lodi's capital, and farther to the east, in Bihar. Settlements in Orissa and Bengal appeared in the sixteenth century. Feelings of resentment among former military and political leaders would linger, as would Mughal anxieties about the Afghans' loyalty. Akbar therefore blocked Afghans from joining the Mughal nobility. Yet his son, the future Emperor

Jahangir, resumed the practice of alliance making, and, in the alliance building that would enable Aurangzeb (r. 1658–1707) to ascend to the throne, Afghan soldiers fought under his banner as well.[27]

Under Mughal patronage, the Afghan diaspora in the subcontinent also came to inhabit a maritime world. They became trading seafarers in the east in Bengal and in the southeast in Karnatak Payanghat. In the early eighteenth century, "Pathans" traded from a Portuguese enclave, the port of São Tomé (Mylapore), where they mixed, and sometimes clashed, with European merchants, and where they set sail for destinations across the Bay of Bengal and around the Arabian Sea as well as to Southeast Asia. As servitors and mercenaries, Afghans from northern India and even émigrés from as far away as Badakhshan joined Mughal campaigns in the coastal southeast and settled in Karnatak Payanghat.[28]

The Mughals faced constant challenges in maintaining their diverse empire and labored constantly to shore up support. They faced rebellions from diverse groups, including, at times, from Afghans. In Bengal, Afghans rebelled in the early seventeenth century. Yet they did so in what had become classic Mughal fashion, with many of them joining forces with the dissident Mughal prince Khurram, who had turned on Emperor Jahangir. Later, they sided with Jahangir, aiding him in expanding his territory in the east and in expelling the Portuguese. From the 1630s, Afghans and Mughals cooperated more closely. Loyalist figures such as Khan Jahan Lodi kept up ties with Afghans throughout India, which stabilized Afghan communities and forestalled rebellions outside of Bengal. Similarly, when the population of Kabul refuted Mughal authority, it tended to be under the leadership of another Mughal notable, for instance, in the case of Prince Khusrau's revolt of 1606. Jahangir responded by crushing the rebellion and, to restore the loyalty of the Kabulis, showered them with food, gifts, entertainments, and tax amnesties. Here Mughal largesse touched the lives of the common folk. It secured trade routes and paid for a steady stream of soldiers.[29]

It is tempting to see the major towns of this period as places that would inevitably come together to constitute the Afghan nation-state. Yet this is anachronistic thinking. It bears emphasizing that for generations each was an imperial city, even if it changed hands between sovereigns on many occasions, with a strong political orientation toward other nodes of Safavid or Mughal power. Consider the example of Kabul. The emperor Babur's memoirs are effusive about his capital and its pleasures in the early sixteenth century. "Drink wine in Kabul citadel, send round the cup again and again," wrote Mullah Muhammad Talib Mu'amma'i in a piece of verse cited approvingly by Babur, who also pointed out "a secluded cozy spot" in the nearby orchards, "where much debauchery is indulged in."[30] Over a hundred years later, though now a more peripheral entity far from Delhi and Agra, its thoroughly Mughal character comes through vividly in Emperor Jahangir's description, which is worth quoting at some length.

Jahangir delighted in Kabul. In June 1608, he entered the town "scattering rupees, half-rupees, and quarter-rupees on both sides to the poor and needy, and entered the [Shahrara] garden," which he found "delightful and fresh." "Since it was Thursday," he recalled, "I held a drinking party with my intimates and cohorts." The emperor was so taken by the scene that he organized an impromptu game. "In the heat of the moment," he wrote, "I ordered those who were the same age as I to jump across a canal that ran down the middle of the garden, approximately four ells [eleven feet] broad. Most couldn't do it and fell at the edge of or in the middle of the stream. Although I jumped too, it wasn't the kind of leap I had made at age thirty in my exalted father's presence. These days, when I am in my forties, I cannot jump with such force and nimbleness." He

visited Kabul's "famous seven gardens," many of which were constructed by his grandmother and great-grandmother, and likened the
fruit of the cherry trees to "butterflies" and "chunks of round ruby
suspended from the branch." He continued his family tradition by
purchasing a plot of land adjacent to the Shahrara Garden for another,
which "would have no equal in all the world." He commissioned "a
slab of white stone," which he had inscribed with his name and those
of his ancestors. Across from one of Babur's monuments, where he
used to enjoy wine, he created a similar platform, to which he added
his name. He visited Babur's tomb and took special care, not only for
the poor, but to all of the "subjects and people" of Kabul who "were
given complete relief and [who] enjoyed total welfare" thanks to the
emperor's abolition of customs duties and excise taxes. At Babur's
throne platform he arranged "a wine party" and had "the basin carved
in the rock filled with wine. All the intimates and courtiers who were
present were given many goblets." "Few days have passed as pleas-
antly," he wistfully remembered.[31]

Herat has had an even longer association with Persianate dynasties and the broader cultural ecumene that they cultivated. For centuries, geographers identified it with a terrritory called Khorasan, a
designation that would retain meaning for its inhabitants as well as
for Iranian kings well into the nineteenth century. Its fame was inseparable from its literary heritage. Herati workshops were famous
for their artists who produced impeccable manuscript illustrations (a
skill that one eleventh-century governor put to use adorning his
palace with erotic images in imitation of the *Kamasutra*). They reproduced and circulated illustrated manuscripts such as Rashid al-
Din's fourteenth-century *Compendium of Chronicles* and the court historian Hafiz-i Abru's reworking of this daring world history in the
fifteenth century. These texts relayed knowledge about the ancient

1   "Chinese Emperor Standing in Pavilion," folio from a *Majma al-Tavarikh*
    (Compendium of Histories) of Hafiz-i Abru. The Metropolitan Museum
    of Art. www.metmuseum.org.

rulers of China, Arabia, Iran, India, and of the ancient Jewish prophets,
among other subjects.[32]

Herat became the epicenter of an artistic school that attracted
painters who had circulated between Tabriz and Baghdad. Under
Timurid patronage, it was renowned for its architecture, gardens,
painting, poetry, and the work of its artisans. The celebrated poet
Jami (d. 1492) lived in the city, as did Behzad (d. 1535), the most renowned Persian painter, alongside writers such as Mir 'Ali Shir Nava'i
(1441–1501) who composed in the Turkic literary language of Central

Asia, Chaghatai. It was fertile ground for female poets and mystics as well. Bija Monajjema, for example, was praised for her verse as well as for her mastery of knowledge in secular and religious domains, astrology and mathematics among them. In his memoirs, Babur comments on the competitive air of literary Herat by reproducing a conversation between two poets: " 'What a sad state this is,' Ali-Sher Beg said in jest, 'that in Herat one cannot stretch out a leg without poking a poet in the ass.' 'Yes,' Banna'i retorted, 'and if you pull your leg back in, you'll poke another.' "[33]

Radiating from such cosmopolitan urban centers, Safavid and Mughal realms offered windows onto a vast world beyond their immediate frontiers. Through trade, diplomacy, and warfare, they maintained frequent contact with other parts of the globe, including Europe and the Ottoman lands. Shah Abbas I (r. 1588–1626) opened up the Safavid realm to Christians, including missionaries, who also frequented the court of Akbar. Some of the Jesuits who visited him for proselytization and debate visited the western borderlands of the Mughal empire. Versed in the classical literature of the Greeks, they did not regard the region as the terra incognita that nineteenth- and twentieth-century travelers to Afghanistan would later portray. The Jesuits knew that parts of this territory had been known to their forebears as "Paropanisa," "Scythia," and "Gandara," among other place names. In their eyes, even the people seemed a bit familiar. When the Jesuit missionary Antoni de Montserrat encountered Afghans in the 1580s on his trek from India to Kabul, he engaged locals in debates about religion, describing their language as sounding "like Spanish," a language with which it shared "a number of words in common." In 1603, the Jesuit Bento de Goes (1562–1607) reached

Kabul from Lahore. One of his party, a merchant named Demetrius stayed on, while the priest traveled north by caravan to Badakhshan and then to Yarkand. Later in the century, the Uzbek ruler Subhan Quli Khan exchanged embassies with the Ottomans, Mughals, Crimea, and Kashgar.[34]

As these travelers learned, the political worlds of the Shibanids, Mughals, Safavids, and Badakhshanis were closely intertwined. They were rivals for territory and prestige and met often on the battlefield. At the same time, they exchanged embassies and gifts, including manuscripts that contributed to the circulation of knowledge among elites. Their sons and daughters sometimes intermarried. They also pitted their spies against each other, and, whenever possible, intervened in their neighbor's political struggles and offered patronage and refuge to dissidents. For example, in 1595 and again in 1638, the Safavid governor of Kandahar broke with the shah in his distant capital in Isfahan and defected to the Mughals, turning the town and its fortress over to them. Indeed this prized commercial hub along the caravan route between Iran and India passed back and forth between Mughal and Safavid control a dozen times.[35]

Kandahar long retained the reputation of a frontier town in the minds of those in the imperial centers. As the French traveler François Bernier described it, Kandahar was "situated equally on the frontiers of Persia, Hindustan and Usbec." Like the Mughals, Safavid elites engaged in a range of strategies to cultivate the loyalties of Kandaharis. As one Safavid source put it, the imperial authorities in Kandahar "attracted to our side Afghans and Hazaras and the individual Sistanis" there and "made study of the mores of the Turks and Tajiks and of their friendliness and enmity." Preexisting entities such as the khanate of Balkh presented similar logistical and political difficulties. Balkh extended from the river Murgab in the west to the Pamirs and from the Hindu Kush in the south to the Turkestan range in the north. In the seventeenth century, it included Bamiyan and Badakhshan as well as towns such as Balkh, Maymana, Sheberghan, Faryab, Kelif, and Akcha. Notables in Balkh frequently clamored for autonomy from the Shibanid seat of power in Bukhara. Badakhshan was another kingdom whose elites jealously guarded their autonomy and who periodically resisted subordination to their powerful neighbors on all sides. Matters could become particularly thorny when the larger political entities found common cause. For the Sunni Shibanids and Mughals, the anti-Shia cause was frequently a shared rally cry. The challenge was to mobilize it at the most opportune moment, a task taken up repeatedly by diplomats who shuttled between their courts.[36]

As in other dynastic settings, chroniclers constructed genealogies for their rulers and communities that celebrated their antiquity as well as their royal and martial valor. But negative characterizations were also weapons in the struggle for power. Less than flattering portrayals of Afghans and other groups inhabiting this region were usually more about their authors than they were about actual people. The tenth-century epic celebrating ancient Iranian kingship, the *Shahnameh* had referred to the king of Kabul, Mehrab, as an "idolatrous demon."[37] Disparaging remarks about Afghans appear in a text attributed to Timur and in subsequent works written by Persian historians.[38] Mughal texts such as the *Akbarnama* castigated the Afghan Sher Khan Suri, who wrested control over much Mughal territory from Humayun (r. 1530–1540, 1555–1556) for a time, referring to his challenger as a "trickster." It cast his supporters as "rascals and vagabonds" and as "black-hearted, unwashed Afghans."[39]

Such characterizations of Afghans in Mughal literature would find their way into translations by British colonial writers in the eighteenth and nineteenth centuries and thus lay a foundation for subsequent thinking about Afghanistan in the modern period. Already in the seventeenth century, though, news of Afghan rebellions reached distant capitals, shaping foreigners' perceptions of these populations. In 1677 a Russian envoy, Vasilii Daudov, reported to Tsar Feodor Alekseevich that the "Indian shah" had sent numerous forces into the mountains against the Afghans, but that they had submitted to no one. In the early eighteenth century, Russian travelers described Afghan rebellions against Safavid rule as well. Further reports of rebellious Afghan tribes resisting both Persian and Mughal rule continued to reach the Russians in later decades.[40] Largely overlooking the crucial role played by Afghan elites in imperial service, these accounts first presented Russians with images of groups we would now identify as Pashtuns as representatives of an unruly people with a fighting spirit.

Given the relatively patchy knowledge that foreigners had about the political history of the region, they would come to rely heavily on local chronicles in Persian and Pashto. Rhetorical flourishes that might appear in royal Mughal and Safavid texts disparaging reluctant taxpayers and ambivalent frontier subjects escaped their particular political contexts. On the one hand, many of them became generalized folk sayings, such as "it's easier to get water from a stone than money from an Afghan."[41] On the other, they generated collective labels that could inform how states ruled these populations and how, over time, they came to view themselves.

Consider the phenomenon of the "tribe." What many observers in the late twentieth and early twentieth-first centuries took to be timeless, traditional, and all-encompassing modes of political and social organization were in these early modern imperial settings instruments that rulers used to govern their peripheries. Particular communities, most notably the Pashtuns and the Baluch, touted their descent from a single ancestor. But this emphasis on a common genealogy did not inevitably translate into social or political cohesion. In practice, it was far more often the case that these genealogical claims did not paper over rivalries among such groups. A key factor in the antagonistic relations among these geneaological communities was the intervention of the imperial state. It was the sovereign's prerogative to shape their composition and appoint their leaders. He even determined where they lived and relocated whole populations, transplanting them to locales were they might prove more useful or less troublesome. The Safavid shah Abbas I resettled the Abdali Pashtuns in Herat, for example. When called upon, the tribes performed various tasks for the state. The Abdalis rose to prominence as the holders of land grants awarded by the Safavid shah in exchange for military service and the performance of administrative duties such as tax collecting in the Kandahar region. These social formations were, in many respects, creatures of imperial power. Of course, these groups frequently caused problems, and they sometimes enjoyed a preponderance of military might. Armed groups assigned to guard a frontier could turn their guns on their imperial patrons, compelling them to renegotiate the terms of imperial service. In short, tribes were never fixed in time and space. Nor did they inhabit their own insular worlds wholly removed from the context of empire.[42]

Given the interdependence of empires and tribes, dealing with the imperial center could be a highly competitive affair in which numerous subordinate groups jostled one another in a crowded field of actors seeking imperial patronage. This was precisely the context in which particular groups constructed genealogies for themselves. Indeed Nimatullah's *History of the Afghans* may have been intended as a response to an affront caused by the Safavid ambassador at the Mughal court. The diplomat had claimed that Afghans were the fruit of a scandalous sexual union between "a phantom" and a thousand virgins whose "unnatural offspring" an ancient Iranian king banished to the wilds.[43]

Rivalries among imperial elites intensified in the second half of the seventeenth century, when a series of contingent events radically shifted the balance of power on behalf of a few ambitious Afghan leaders who began to make their own claims to imperial power. Keeping centrifugal forces in check became more difficult. Throughout the wider region, from Ottoman Anatolia to the Indian subcontinent, elites on the periphery were on the rise. Some were able to leverage new commercial wealth and firearms against the imperial center.[44] Nationalist historians in Afghanistan, bolstered by foreign scholars sympathetic to their cause, would later point to this moment as the birth of an Afghan national state. They would feature the uprising of the Ghilzai and Abdali Pashtuns against the Safavids in the early eighteenth century as the spark fueling the seemingly inevitable realization of a political destiny culminating in a Pashtun-led nation-state.

What this perspective misses is the reality that, while heterogeneous forces had come together to weaken the coherence of the Safavid and Mughal states, empire remained a viable, indeed compelling, framework for organizing and ruling this region. What was at issue instead was who would seize the reins of imperial power. When Afghans around Kandahar launched a campaign to challenge the shah in Isfahan, their leaders would draw on far-flung connections to muster resources to embark on their own imperial project, one that capitalized on the cosmopolitan politics of the era. Their empire building would place the Afghans, albeit briefly, at the center of events that would attract a global audience in ways that would cement foreigners' views of them. This drama would then entangle Afghans even more deeply in a political space that stretched from China to the frontiers of Europe, itself home to several powers who would soon find themselves in dynamic contact with the heterogeneous populations straddling the Hindu Kush.

2 | FORGING AN AFGHAN EMPIRE

THE AFGHAN PATH to imperial power could scarcely have been more convoluted. The product of contingent events and opportunistic elites, its most striking feature was that it played out over a vast geographic space and with the participation of disparate parties far from its epicenter in Kandahar. In 1666, the decision of the Mughal emperor Aurangzeb (r. 1658–1707) to close the Indo-Iranian frontier and the subsequent stalling of the caravan trade may have fundamentally destabilized Kandahar, which had been under Safavid rule since 1649. Repeated droughts in 1652, 1666, and 1677 appear to have pushed nomadic raiding parties into settled populations by the end of the century.

Political developments elsewhere in the Safavid empire had an impact as well. At court, a weakened central government increasingly resorted to the persecution of non-Shia, and Shah Sultan Husayn (r. 1694–1722) grew more dependent upon administrators drawn from the Caucasus. In 1704 the shah appointed the former king of the Georgian kingdom of Kartli, Georgii XI, as governor of Kandahar. Taking the name Gurgin Khan, the Georgian governor relied on a policy of "divide and rule." He deported several thousand Abdali families to the area around Herat while cultivating Baluch elites and the ruler of Kabul. His policies favored the Ghilzais, and under his protection the wealthy Ghilzai merchant Mir Wais became essentially the mayor of Kandahar. Meanwhile, Gurgin Khan imposed sharp tax increases and resorted to exemplary punishments—including burying some Afghans alive and encasing others in the walls of the fortress—to quell unrest around Kandahar.[1]

In 1707, the Ghilzai notable Mir Wais made a journey of some forty days to Isfahan. Contemporary sources disagree about whether he went of his own free will. But they do suggest that once in the capital he complained about Gurgin Khan, whom some accused of losing himself in drink and women, and possibly of having designs on Mir Wais's daughter. Once in the Safavid capital, Mir Wais apparently confronted more anti-Sunni invective but nonetheless was permitted to depart on the hajj. In Mecca, after conferring with Sunni legal scholars, he secured a legal opinion (*fatwa*) justifying rebellion against the Shia governor of Kandahar. Returning to Isfahan in 1708, he persuaded the shah that he faced a grave danger from the Russian tsar, Peter the Great, who, he asserted, was conspiring to seize the Caucasus and then Iran with the connivance of Gurgin Khan and his Georgian followers. Concealing his Meccan conversations, Mir Wais was awarded a robe of honor and sent back to Kandahar as a counterweight to the now suspect Georgian. Upon his return to Kandahar, Mir Wais convinced a group of Ghilzais and Baluch to rebel, beginning with an attack on the Abdalis allied with Gurgin Khan in 1709.[2]

Their revolt and the murder of the Georgian governor have been frequently taken as the starting point for a determined nationalist campaign to establish an "Afghan" state. In reality, after Mir Wais's death in 1715, the actions of his successors reflect instead the inherited legacy of a cosmopolitan imperial politics. After a brief period of ambivalence in which Mir Wais's brother seems to have sought reconciliation with Isfahan, the Ghilzai invasion of Safavid Iran under Mir Wais's son Mahmud Khan is a telling illustration.

Dealing a final blow to the Safavid empire, their march from Kandahar on Isfahan, in which they used large swivel guns (*zamburaks*) mounted on camels to lethal effect, was seared into the collective memory of contemporaries. It produced apocalyptic scenes of wanton devastation, plunder, arson, murder, enslavement, forcible conversion, famine, panicked flight, the kidnapping of beautiful women and boys, and the charred heaps of human and animal bodies in its wake. Describing Kerman, one witness lamented that "the city has been so much destroyed that it has not happened in a millennium and will not happen in another millennium." Another judged that "the violence of the Afghans had been so excessive that our quills are incapable of describing it, we only say that during the existence of the world no city has ever been destroyed as Kerman has been, not even in the time of Nimrod."[3]

Merciless though they were on campaign, the Ghilzais under Mahmud showed notable flashes of the integrative politics of the imperial milieu that had produced them. At Kerman, Mahmud had coins struck in his name, an act asserting royal authority. Like his imperial predecessors in the region, he also recruited followers among different religious and ethnic communities. An Armenian chronicle identified Zoroastrians as enthusiastic supports of Mahmud, who allowed those who had been forcibly converted to Islam to return to their religion. He appointed two Zoroastrian captives as intermediaries and assigned other notables to oversee parts of the city. He recruited a multiethnic army, including numerous Zoroastrians, Hazaras, and Baluch and at least one African slave (who later defected to the Safavids) to serve alongside the Ghilzais. Turks and Multanis joined his forces, as did Armenian and Iranian musketeers and Georgians, although the same Armenian source claims that these last three categories were forcibly recruited. Similarly, during the siege of Isfahan in 1722, Mahmud pressed Armenians and Arabs into service.[4]

Adopting the title "shah," Mahmud Khan fashioned himself as a king. In imitation of the Safavid ruler, he wore a plume in his turban, though on the left-hand side (the shah wore his on the right). His attendants carried him in a palanquin. His retinue included thousands of camels to carry away loot from Iranian cities. Mahmud supposedly gave his troops orders to take only from the rich, and at Kerman he beheaded Muslims whom he suspected of disloyalty, but left Zoroastrians and Christians at peace.

In August 1722, several months into the battle for control of the Safavid capital, Mahmud is said to have proposed to withdraw if the shah would give him not only a large sum of money but one of his daughters in marriage, with Kerman and Mashhad as a dowry, and permit him to retain Kandahar as his own. However, two months later, Shah Sultan Husayn was forced to ride out of the city and place his crown on Mahmud's head and request that he accept rule of his lands.

Accompanied by drums and horns and with the dethroned shah mournfully in tow, the twenty-four-year-old Mahmud Shah entered the city in triumphant fashion and was greeted by the European traders who made up the staff of the Dutch East Indies Company and the East India Company. He next went about appointing (in many instances reappointing) Persians and a few Afghans to governorships and other offices. The Armenians of New Julfa managed to negotiate with the Ghilzais and were spared the fate of Isfahan. Having paid them seventy thousand tumans, the Armenians kept their churches as before, and a number of Armenians entered into Afghan service.[5] Mahmud Shah now presided over the core of a multi-religious and multi-ethnic imperial polity.

At the same time, the Ghilzais' siege of Isfahan in 1722 put the Afghans at the center of a drama that attracted global attention. This may sound hyperbolic for an early eighteenth-century event that was, though catastrophic in terms of human suffering, limited to a single city in central Iran. But the presence of so many Europeans, including representatives of the English and Dutch East India Companies, and the multifaceted geopolitical implications of the Safavid collapse guaranteed intense interest abroad. Moreover, given the conditions of the period, news of these developments circulated rapidly beyond Isfahan. Witnesses filed reports to the Ottoman and Russian capitals. There, correspondents quickly reworked these accounts for publication in European newspapers as the events unfolded.

The story of the rise of the Afghans and the downfall of the Safavids quickly became a sensation in print. In 1728, a Polish Jesuit and missionary named Judas Thaddaeus Krusínski published his firsthand account of the last years of the Safavid empire as *The History of the Revolution of Persia*. It was translated and rearranged by another Jesuit, Jean-Antoine du Certeau, and multiple Latin and English editions soon followed. In 1729, an Ottoman version was not only one of the first books printed by the new press established by Ibrahim Müteferrika in Istanbul; it also had the largest print run (1,200 copies) of any Ottoman Turkish title published in this era.[6]

Krusínski's text was pivotal in constructing an image of the Afghans that would endure in the imagination of imperial elites, the Ottomans among them. To Krusínski, the Afghans' victory at Isfahan announced their arrival on the world stage: "The Nation of the *AGHVANS*, hitherto unknown in *Europe*, and scarce known in *Asia*, where it lies in a Corner, has render'd it self so famous by the Conquest it has lately made of *Persia*, one of the greatest Kingdoms in the World, that there's no Body living, but will be very glad to have some Account of a People, who have begun to shew themselves to the World by so signal a Blow." The Ottoman adaptation of this work highlighted the stunning emergence of this people, reworking the original title as *A Chronicle of a Traveler on the Appearance of the Afghans [Zuhur-i Ağvaniyan] and the Reasons for the Decline of the State of the Safavid Shahs*. For decades to come, the Afghans would be defined almost wholly by their role in the Safavid collapse. As a geographical dictionary of 1760 put it, the term "Afghans" served "as the general denomination of a people in Persia, who . . . subverted the Persian monarchy." Such depictions, reinforced by images of the bellicose, uncivilized, and treacherous Afghans found in some Mughal texts, continued to appeal to scholars and observers of contemporary Afghan affairs. In 1840, in the midst of the Anglo-Afghan War (1838– 1842), it was hardly coincidental that another English translation of Krusínski's work, this time based on the Ottoman text, appeared in London.[7] These representations of the Afghans became canonical in Europe and persisted into the modern era.

Krusínski's influential portrayal of the Afghans was significant, too, in that it marked them as an "unmanageable People." Their "Love of Liberty and Independence" caused them to be "continually revolting." Although Krusínski was not without admiration for particular Afghan leaders, he saw them through the lens of a contemporary classificatory scheme that placed non-Europeans below Europeans on an evolutionary scale. By this logic, the Afghans lived in a state of nature beyond which Europeans had long ago progressed. Their primitive existence included living "for the most Part under Tents, like the *Tartars*, being inur'ed to Heat and Cold, and all the Inclemencies of the Seasons." Indeed the line between Afghan and animal was not altogether certain: "With them the Masters, Slaves, Horses, and Cattle lay confusedly under one and the same Tent; and this People is so accustomed to Ordure and Nastiness, that if a Horse drops down dead by their Side, there they let him die and rot, without being offended at the Stench, or taking any more Notice of it, than if they had not the Sense of Smelling." Worse still, it would seem for this Jesuit, they drank nothing but water, "there being scarce any Nation perhaps that is more averse to Wine."

If all of this were not enough to convince readers of the unsavory character of this people, the text added that their "Complexion is not altogether black, but swarthy, very brown, and inclining to black" and that they "are very ill shaped, but of a nervous and robust Constitution," and very skilled on horseback. He concluded his description of "the Character of this Nation" with one of the tropes that Europeans would find most attractive about the Afghans into the modern period: "there is not perhaps a People in the World that has so much Inclination to War, and that is better form'd and train'ed up to it, their whole Lives being spent almost in one continued Robbery, after the Manner of the *Tartars*, and in making Excursions among their Neighbours for Plunder."[8]

To the Europeans, this remarkable people was largely a distant wonder, but to the Ottomans, whose territories now lay within reach of Mahmud's forces, his growing fame posed a grave dilemma. From the sixteenth century, the Ottoman sultans had presented themselves to the world as the defenders of Sunni Islam. What did it mean to be caliph now that another Sunni ruler had vanquished their Shia rivals and now ruled land contiguous with the sultan's "well-protected domains"?

The 1724 treaty that partitioned Safavid territory between the Ottoman and Russian empires raised further questions. In pledging support for the Safavid heir to the throne—and recognizing Peter the Great's control over Muslim territories in the Caucasus—Ahmet III (r. 1703–1730) allied himself with Christian and Shia sovereigns against a Sunni leader who appeared more resolute than the sultan in his commitment to the faith. Meanwhile, Mahmud's reputation as a religious reformer who enjoyed his military successes thanks to God's favor alarmed the sultan's court. "The opinion of his [Mahmud's] sanctity," a British diplomat reported, "has spread so far that even in Constantinople he has a great many partisans, and the Pasha of Babylon writes that for the same reason he fears if he should come to an engagement with him, that most part of his army would go over to him, so that the ministers of the [Ottoman] Porte are now endeav-ouring to get him declared by the Mufti and the men of the law a rebel and usurper in order to put a stop to the high opinion the common people so greedily entertain of his merits."[9]

To the temporary relief of the Ottomans, Mahmud and his allies were unable to maintain their rule. The bloody struggle for succes-sion to the Safavid throne continued until an erstwhile ally of the Afghans, Nadir Qoli Beg, managed to gather sufficient forces to prop up a Safavid claimaint and finally, in 1736, to take the throne as shah. Nadir Shah (r. 1736–1747) waged campaigns from the northern Cau-casus to northern India, applying many of the imperial strategies of his predecessors. After capturing Kandahar in 1738, he forcibly shifted many Ghilzais (members of the Hotaki clan, in particular) to Khorasan and relocated numerous Abdalis to lands around Kandahar. Mean-while, as in earlier periods, Ghilzais and other local peoples joined his forces and traveled widely on campaign. For instance, Abdali cavalry fought under Nadir Shah's banner against the Ottomans at Baghdad and Kars in northeastern Anatolia.[10] The most important figure to enjoy Nadir's favor was Ahmad Khan Abdali, a fifteen-year-old who had been born in Multan. The shah found the boy in a dungeon in Kandahar, where he had been held as political prisoner by a rival family. Ahmad Khan grew close to Nadir, accompanying his military campaigns and becoming his treasury officer (*bank-bashi*).

When in 1747 Nadir Shah's guards turned against him, stran-gling Nadir in his tent, Ahmad Khan found himself in a remarkably fortuitous position. He managed to escape the royal tent with the seal from Nadir's finger and the famed Koh-i Nur diamond (which the British later claimed for the crown jewels). Armed with treasure from Kabul and India, Ahmad Khan turned to reviving Nadir's empire and had himself declared "shah," complete with the blessing of a shaykh of the Chishti Sufi confraternity. And, borrowing from the vocabulary of honorifics applied to Nadir, the twenty-five-year-old became the "pearl of pearls" (*durr-i durran*), and his Abdali tribe became "Durrani."

Ahmad Shah aspired to conquer a vast space, declaring himself ruler of India, Iran, and Transoxiana. He captured Ghazni, Kabul, and Peshawar before crossing the Indus River and seizing Shikarpur and Lahore in 1748. By 1752, despite temporary reversals, he took Kashmir and had wrested Multan and the Punjab from the Mughals. The lion's share of his revenues flowed into his treasury from northern India, where local communities also supplied slaves. In 1754, he captured Mashhad, and the local ruler became a vassal of Ahmad Shah. Elsewhere in Khorasan his forces took Shirvan, Kuchan, and Nishapur and then subjugated much of Sistan. In the early 1750s, Ahmad Shah's forces advanced to the north of the Hindu Kush. They defeated the Uzbek khanates of Balkh, Andkhoy, Sheberghan, and Maymana. By 1757, he had captured Baluchistan and Sind, and his name was read in sermons at the mosques in Delhi. When he faced a challenge from the Marathas in 1758, he formed an alliance with Muslim notables throughout northern India, among them the Rohilla Afghans and Baluch, against the "infidels." In 1761, Ahmad Shah's artillery and calvary ultimately defeated the Marathas at the Battle of Panipat north of Delhi.[11]

In the modern era, Afghan nationalists celebrated Ahmad Shah as "father" (*bābā*) of the nation and claimed his empire as the glorious founding moment of the Afghan nation-state. Although these ideas were central to the emergence of Afghan nationalist ideology, their proponents overlook a number of important facts. The Durrani empire was far from an Afghan nation-state, in the sense that all Afghans flocked to serve Ahmad Shah.[12] Indeed his state was hardly the only Afghan polity to emerge from Nadir Shah's empire after his assassination in 1747. A significant portion of Nadir's Afghan and

Uzbek forces did not fall in line with the Durrani leader. Instead they turned back to Iran and fought to establish their rule there.

Their most successful commander, Azad Khan, seized control of the western Iranian province of Azerbaijan. Drawing strength from Iranian, Kurdish, Georgian, and other allies, he campaigned widely, even contesting Erivan, though, for a time, he had to seek refuge with the Ottomans in Iraq and with his friend, the Georgian king Erekle. Throughout Iran, Afghan cavalry and soldiers banded together with other non-Afghan contenders for power, from the Georgians to the Qajars, Zands, and Afshars. Meanwhile, in the Indo-Afghan frontiers of Rohilkand, elites were cautious about severing ties with their Hindu patrons and supporting Ahmad Shah. Some who joined his forces sent letters of apology to the Marathas for waging war against them.[13]

The Durrani empire was less a nascent Afghan nation-state than a cosmopolitan polity that cobbled together heterogeneous and far-flung political traditions and resources, most notably ideas about sovereignty inherited from Nadir's reign. Ahmad Shah built his military forces on Nadir's model, recruiting Nadir's former troops, including his royal slave and Qizilbash core, as well as Abyssinians, Kalmuks, Kurds, and Tajiks. Armed with modern flintlock firearms, his cavalry deployed tactics that the Safavids and Ottomans had adapted from Europeans. They also used the camel-mounted swivel gun, inspiring others in India to imitate the practice. Jos Gommans has shown that the Durrani campaigns in India, where the empire derived most of its revenues, were not merely "chaotic tribal outbreaks" but were instead the thoughtful and strategic moves "planned by a strong coalition of Afghan leaders and Hindu bankers . . . designed to keep trade running and cash flowing."[14]

Ahmad Shah's royal court reflected his debt to Nadir Shah's conception of power. Staffed by officials bearing titles drawn from Nadir's time and regimented according to detailed norms of etiquette, the court was an opulent affair. Yet this was not opulence for its own sake. Ornamentation and display were means of projecting royal authority. The Durranis presented themselves to foreign envoys and travelers, and their own subjects, in the finest robes and gems. The famed Koh-i Nur diamond announced the grandeur of Durrani authority. From the Mughal Indian setting, they inherited the elephant as a symbol of power. They employed Indian merchants to organize their finances and cultivated scholars and poets. They relied on a multiethnic and multireligious elite. Durrani patronage announced to a wider world of Muslim letters, which spanned throughout the early modern period from the Balkans to northern India, that this dynasty was a refined master of religion, the sciences, literature, and the arts. This self-conscious projection of cosmopolitan refinement signaled to elites in Iran and India that the Durranis were a formidable force that stood poised to assume preeminence in all spheres of politics.[15]

Like imperial rulers elsewhere, the Durranis made urban space a privileged site for the display of their power. Nadir Shah had laid waste to Kandahar and attempted to found a new settlement nearby, which he named Nadirabad. Although it is reasonable to assume that Ahmad Shah would have known of recently constructed imperial centers such as St. Petersburg, his new capital appears to have been modeled on Herat, a city whose poets, saints, scholars, and rulers Afghans and Iranians would contest well into the modern period. Just as Kandahar would be reborn as "Ahmadshahi" in the image of the founder of the dynasty, the Durrani capital would now emerge as a destination for the literati, artists, mercenaries, and scholars who had long followed circuits of migration between Iran and India. When Ahmad Shah resolved to build this new capital following his return from his Indian campaign in 1761, artisans from throughout the region worked under the direction of an Indian architect, while thousands of Marathas, enslaved after defeat on the battlefield of Panipat, were resettled there to perform the heavy construction work.[16]

In addition to his imperial capital, Ahmad Shah arranged to have his memory preserved in the style of Nadir. He charged Muhammad Taki Khan Shirazi, one of Nadir's longtime Iranian servitors, to recruit a chronicler to compose a history like that celebrating Nadir, the *Tarikh-i Nadiri*. In Mashhad, Muhammad Taki Khan found a historian who had been acquainted with the author of the *Tarikh-i Nadiri* and who had even served Nadir as a secretary.[17] Portraiture may have been another device reflecting Ahmad Shah's emulation of Nadir. An anonymous portrait of Ahmad Shah Durrani looks very much like the image of Nadir in paintings of the period. It closely resembled Nadir, with his full but cropped beard, and his bejeweled, red headdress, and ceremonial weapon (though his ax, likely intended to symbolize a Sufi identity, differs from Nadir's dagger). Similarly, the Durranis minted coins, a traditional claim to sovereignty, to assert their parity with imperial rivals. Like the Safavids and Mughals, Ahmad Shah and his successors announced each reign with coins inscribed with Persian couplets praising the ruler and claiming divine favor.[18]

Ahmad Shah's vision of empire was territorially expansive, and he propagated an image of himself as the divinely inspired defender of Islam and Muslims in many lands. He minted coins from Khoi in Iranian Azerbaijan to Kashmir. Durrani coins struck in Kabul and Herat and even Kashmir (under his grandson Shah Zaman, r. 1793–1800) bore the inscription "capital." Durrani coins imitated Safavid and other Iranian coins in referring to Mashhad as "the Sacred." In 1753, Ahmad Shah invoked God's aid in bringing "the whole of Iran" under his control.[19] A year later, he cast himself in a long line of Sunni rulers of "Rum [the Ottoman lands] and Iran and Turan and Hindustan" who waged jihad against unbelief and criticized Shah Ismail

2 Anonymous. Ahmad Shah Durrani. © The British Library Board
29/09/2014, Add.Or.2685.

(r. 1501–1524) for pressuring Sunnis to adopt the Shia faith.[20] His propaganda fell on fertile ground in some quarters. Shah Waliullah (1703–1762), a learned theorist of jihad in India, wrote to Ahmad Shah asking him to combat polytheism in India and promising "incalculable booty" for those who would free the Muslims "from their bonds." As it turned out, Indian chroniclers of the subsequent Durrani sacking of Delhi in 1761 would remember it as a reign of terror: "wherever one looked one saw heads and limbs and torsos."[21]

From the late 1750s, Chinese expansion seemed to threaten Muslims in the region, and, according to indirect accounts, envoys from Badakhshan and Bukhara appealed to Ahmad Shah for protection. Amid the spread of prophecies that Manchu victory would inaugurate the end of the world, Ahmad Shah Durrani sought to rally the armies of the regional Muslim dynasties to block the Chinese. In 1762, he sent forces to block the Chinese path from Kokand to Tashkent and appealed to rulers and merchants to stop trading with the Chinese. He also ordered representatives to Peking to intercede on behalf of the deposed rulers of Kashgar.[22]

Following his victory at Panipat in 1761, Ahmad Shah sent a lengthy letter to the sultan in Istanbul, detailing in prose and verse the history of his conquests and lauding the bravery of his *ghazis* who fought for the faith.[23] He also sought to bolster his standing by encouraging the hajj. In 1762 he dispatched three diplomats to meet with Ottoman officials in Baghdad. They carried a letter requesting land for a mosque in Medina. Their petition apparently envisioned more than a refuge for Afghan pilgrims: the mosque would have simultaneously served as Ahmad Shah's outpost in the Hijaz. Keen on preserving control of the holy places, Sultan Mustafa III rebuffed the Afghans. By the end of the eighteenth century, however, Afghan hajjis had established a hostel for Afghan pilgrims who traveled over land or plied the maritime route from Sind to the Hijaz.[24]

Ahmad Shah died in 1773, leaving behind a sprawling, if loosely held, empire. For his successors, many of these heterogeneous territories and subjects would remain unwieldy and difficult to govern. The eastern and western fringes would soon slip out of their grasp. Nonetheless, Ahmad Shah had made his kingdom known to distant powers, the Chinese, the Ottomans, and the English—the latter, via the East India Company, whose steady rise in the subcontinent brought them into contact with the Durranis. The power of the Durranis would wane after his death, but the rulers who followed would stoke memories of their forefathers' territorial grandeur and aspirations to be recognized far and wide as a formidable Muslim kingdom. His reign had also begun to cement in the imagination of his political elite a sense of ownership of particular places. Yet there was not yet a rigid sense of territorial identities, a point demonstrated by Ahmad Shah's son Timur (r. 1773–1793), formerly governor of Herat, who chose Kabul as his new capital, away from challengers within his family in Kandahar.

After Ahmad Shah, the empire faced internal challenges in the form of intense elite competition, but the external ones proved more decisive. Throughout the wider region, the period of the late eighteenth and early nineteenth centuries was one in which intensive and dynamic state-building projects proliferated. To the east, the Sikhs grew powerful, to the west, the Zands in southern and the Qajars in northern Iran had gathered strength, while in the north, the Bukharans were also busy forging a more solid polity. The circulation of firearms, money, and new technologies was one underlying factor driving the formation of new states. Another was European expansion. Although their physical presence in the region remained modest, Europeans became a force to contend with insofar as their resources and expertise could tip the balance of power when rival political forces collided. The presence of Jews and Armenian Christians in

Kabul and other towns meant that Europeans might find familiar intermediaries in dealing with the Afghans. The European entry into factional struggles during this period shows again how disputes that might on the surface appear "tribal" or highly localized became instead much more complex affairs that drew together the local and the global.[25]

Timur thus found himself in a geopolitical environment that had radically shifted from that of his father. Many of the imperial strategies inherited from Ahmad Shah and, through him, his Iranian and Mughal predecessors were under stress. From Kabul, a strategically valuable location and home to a contingent of Qizilbash forces since the era of Nadir Shah, Timur attempted to strengthen centralized control of the realm. He relied on these Qizilbash, along with Hazaras, and others as his main base of military support, but territorial losses, especially in the Punjab, were a blow to his finances. In 1793, Shah Zaman succeeded Timur after overcoming resistance from his brothers and the factions that backed them.

Like his predecessors, Shah Zaman turned his attention to conquest in India. Although he was forced to withdraw his forces to address the Qajar challenge to Balkh and Herat, his incursions into India attracted growing European attention. The East India Company sounded the alarm about the Afghan threat to their growing power. Local notables, too, looked to form military alliances with the Afghans. In 1796 Tipu Sultan (r. 1782–1799), the ruler of perhaps the strongest of the independent kingdoms, sent an envoy from Mysore in south India to Shah Zaman to seek an agreement against the Marathas and the English, complementing his efforts to solicit support from Napoleonic France.[26] Two years later the advance of Afghan forces prompted an uprising at Awadh against the East India Company.

The British responded by convincing the Iranians to back a challenger to the Afghan throne. They supported Zaman's brother

Mahmud, who had been governor of Herat. But Mahmud's campaign against Kandahar failed. And he was forced to flee to Iran and then Bukhara and Khiva before launching another attack on Kandahar. His eventual capture of the town forced Zaman to return from India.[27] However, when some of Zaman's forces turned against him, he fled to Peshawar. Following Mahmud's capture (and blinding) of his brother Zaman, Mahmud assumed the throne in 1800, though the crisis sparked wider fighting, pitting Ghilzais against Durranis.[28] By 1803, another of Timur's sons, Shuja-ul-Mulk, had prevailed in his quest for the throne.

At this stage, the proliferation of claimants to royal authority and, equally significant, of potential sponsors, foreign and domestic, gave rise to a succession of political upheavals that would last nearly a century. Afghan and British politics became more entangled than ever, as European rivalries began to intrude throughout the Middle East and South Asia. There seemed no greater challenger to Great Britain's empire than France, which had invaded Egypt in 1798 and appeared poised to expand farther in the east. In 1809, a British mission led by Mountstuart Elphinstone met Shah Shuja at Peshawar, where they concluded a treaty of "friendship and union" and agreed to block any joint French and Iranian advance on the territory of the "King of Cabool" (the treaty also referred to him as the "King of the Dooranees") and British India. Each party pledged not to interfere in the affairs of the other, but Shah Shuja was additionally bound not to permit any Frenchman to enter his territory.[29]

For Shuja, though, a greater threat loomed closer to home. His brother Mahmud escaped from prison and deposed him in 1809, forcing Shuja to flee to the Sikh leader Ranjit Singh (r. 1801–1839) in Lahore and then to find refuge with the British in Ludhiana. By 1817, however, Mahmud's territory was limited to Herat. Ranjit Singh, in the meantime, took advantage of the fighting among Afghan elites to seize Peshawar. In building his state, he received aid from far away. Following the collapse of Napoleon's empire, a number of his European officers sought their fortunes beyond the continent, offering their services to the Ottomans, the Egyptians, and the Iranians. Setting out from Iran disguised as Georgians, two of them, Jean-François Allard and Jean-Baptiste Ventura, passed through Kabul, where they were said to have volunteered their expertise before taking command of a unit of Ranjit Singh's forces in 1822 in Lahore.[30]

From this crowded field of contenders, Afghan notables cast a wide net pursuing allies in the powerful states that were gradually encircling their kingdom. Another of Mahmud's brothers, Hajji Firuz al-Din, turned to the Qajar leader Fath 'Ali Shah (r. 1797–1834) in 1814 for aid against Mahmud. In 1825, Prince Kamran of Herat sent "presents befitting a king, the sight of which caused amazement, including a colossal elephant" to the khan of Khiva. Having taken the throne in Kabul in 1826, Dost Muhammad Khan, the representative of the Muhammadzai branch of the Durranis, explored ties to the British to recover Peshawar from the Sikhs. The British rebuffed him, however, and the Afghans looked to the Russians, pleading their case in person. A man claiming to be a prince, Shahzade Muhammad Mustafa, traveled to Astrakhan and Orenburg in 1828. In the early 1830s, Afghan emissaries claiming to have been sent by Dost Muhammad Khan arrived at Tbilisi, the seat of the Russian government in the Caucasus, to propose a union to block the advance of the Sikhs and the East India Company.

The two Afghans, Husayn Khan and Mirza Mahmud, were surprised to receive a cool reception from tsarist officials, who were quite suspicious. Russian diplomats suspected that Husaynn Khan was unreliable and that he harbored far-fetched illusions about Russia's willingness to deploy its forces on his patron's behalf. And judging by the dodgy looking seals on the documents that accompanied them, tsarist officials speculated that the pair had rewritten the letters at the advice of informants in Tehran who claimed that Russians would be more inclined to aid the Afghans if they claimed higher social status. The Russians were surprised that the Afghans seemed to think that they would rush to their defense. Upon learning about Russia's own troubles with rebels in the Caucasus, though, the Afghans grew disheartened. Nonetheless, the Russians recruited one of the Afghans to accompany a Russian official, Ivan Vitkevich, who carried instructions to reconcile the leaders of Kabul and Kandahar, to safeguard themselves "against foreign enemies and internal disturbances." The Russians wanted the Afghans to join forces with Iran against their common foes. Vitkevich was to explain that Russia was too far way to lend assistance directly, but that it would help with Iran, and that Afghan merchants would be welcomed and protected in Russia and enjoy the same rights as Iranian traders.[31]

Meanwhile, the exiled Shah Shuja signed a treaty with Ranjit Singh in preparation for challenging Dost Muhammad who, in turn, appealed to the Qajars, even though they had besieged Herat in 1817 and again in 1833. He wrote Muhammad Shah (r. 1834–1848) in 1837, reporting that the visit of a British envoy, Alexander Burnes, to Kabul had failed to convince him to leave "the Muslim lands of Peshawar and Afghanistan" to Ranjit Singh. Casting his foe as an enemy of the followers of the divine law (*shari'a*) and himself as *ghazi,* a warrior for the faith, Dost Muhammad explained that Vitkevich had offered Russian support and asked the Qajar shah to join their alliance.[32]

Dost Muhammad's search for foreign backing provoked a multifaceted crisis that played out in multiple locales, from Kabul, Herat, and Peshawar to London, Tehran, and St. Petersburg. One aspect involved Russo-Iranian relations. Following Qajar defeat in the

Russo-Iranian war of 1826–1828, tsarist authorities gained influence in Tehran. Having expelled the Iranians from the Caucasus, they encouraged Muhammad Shah to assert himself against Herat. They hoped the Afghans would become vassals of the Qajar shah who would keep the British from expanding deeper into a part of Asia that Russians increasingly considered their sphere of influence. In 1838, Qajar forces attacked Herat, which was under the rule of Prince Kamran and protected, in part, by a British military officer, Major Eldred Pottinger, who had come the previous year to support the defense of the city. Still, some Afghan elites had not given up on the idea of a pact with the Qajars. From Kandahar, Kohindal Khan volunteered to join forces with the shah; and some Heratis were prepared to turn on Kamran as well. The British responded aggressively to forestall what they feared to be the fall of Herat and Dost Muhammad's turn toward Russia. The British declared war against him in October 1838.

The British plan, improvised by the governor-general of India, Lord George Eden Auckland, was to restore Shah Shuja to the throne. When Ranjit Singh declined to lead the campaign on Kabul, some 39,000 troops composed of Shah Shuja's backers and the British Army of the Indus marched on Kabul. In April 1839, Shah Shuja triumphantly entered Kandahar. By August the invading army had returned him to power. Dost Muhammad was consigned to exile in India, and much of the British army returned as well.[33]

To the west, the British recognized Shah Kamran as the head of an independent Herat. In a treaty of August 1839, which proclaimed that the interests of the British government were "identical with those of the Afghan nation," Kamran agreed to prohibit kidnapping and slavery by his subjects, to inform the British representative of his court of any dealings with foreigners, to promote "the freedom of commerce," and to allow only British subjects into his service. In 1841,

Shah Kamran sought to strengthen his bond with his ally Queen Victoria (r. 1837–1901). Along with a manuscript copy of the *Shahnameh,* Kamran sent a letter addressed to Victoria from one of his wives in which the sultana praised the "alliance between the two mighty states (England and Herat)" and lauded British aid during the invasion from Iran, when "it was by the care and kindness of the ministers of your majesty's Government, that the inhabitants of this land preserved their lives and their honor."[34]

Meanwhile, in Kabul Shah Shuja's restoration had been relatively easy, but staying in power was another matter. Dost Muhammad, or the "amir," the commander of the faithful, as he was known for his exploits waging jihad against the Sikhs, continued to enjoy significant support. In his monumental history of the period, Fayz Muhammad Katib Hazarah tells the story of an episode from Dost Muhammad's exile. Traveling toward Calcutta with several hundred followers, the amir met "a delegation of Indian Muslims devoted to the cause of Islamic solidarity." One of them was Mulla 'Aziz Allah Qandahari "whom he [Dost Muhammad] recognized as an Afghan from both his bearing and his dress" and who "had come to this foreign land to learn the wonders of the sciences." A student of astrology, Mulla 'Aziz Allah predicted the amir's future: "After a year and ten months the knot of your affairs will be untied and you will be freed from your bondage."[35]

If Dost Muhammad had cause to be reassured by this prognostication, very different omens awaited his rival Shah Shuja. His grip shaky, Shah Shuja's dependence on British force of arms increasingly became a liability. Yet there was more to his crumbling legitimacy, as Fayz Muhammad's account suggests. In the spring of 1840, scandalous news about "adulterous women" consorting with British troops further eroded the ruler's standing in the eyes of influential circles. The shah's associates informed him that "indecent women have adorned themselves and are going to the English camp." Shuja complained to Sir William Hay Macnaghten, protesting that "the spread and continuation of this business will make it extremely difficult for the honor-worshipping Afghans to keep quiet" and warning that "this tree of wickedness is going to bear unwholesome fruit."[36] By autumn 1841, night letters appeared on the doors of Kabul houses, warning of exile at the hands of Shah Shuja: "O people, give thought to your situation for today or tomorrow you may be sent to India like prisoners."[37] In a stunning reversal, the British soon found themselves on the defensive. By the end of 1841, hostile crowds had stormed the British mission in Kabul. Macnaghten had been assassinated. And the British were compelled to negotiate their withdrawal.

The British defeat in 1842 had two principal legacies. The first flowed from the Afghan massacre of the retreating army, an event that further solidified in the writings of Europeans the image, first circulated widely by Krusínski in the eighteenth century, of the Afghans as savage and treacherous. The second was the intersection of the fates of Afghan exiles and European imperial power. Claimants to the Afghan throne had access to foreign patrons in nearly every direction; their challenge was to win them for their cause, to make their quest for power appear to advance the geopolitical interests of the British, Russians, or Iranians. Foreign fortunes rose or fell with Afghan contenders.

Dost Muhammad's second reign was devoted to resuming the imperial state building of the Durranis, but this time with foreign assistance. "Afghanistan" acquired more solid features, even though Dost Muhammad found the lands around Kabul in turmoil upon his return from Indian exile. Foreigners had begun to write with more consistency of a country called "Afghanistan" (often spelled *Affghanistan* in English). And there was greater certainty about the character of its people, thanks largely to Elphinstone, whose description of the

Afghans was taken up by others, including the French author of a geographical survey that asserted that what made the Afghans different from their neighbors was "a manly spirit of independence" and traits that were at once admirable and disgusting. Protestant missionaries were more optimistic, having established ties to Afghan exiles in India. They were exploring "what can be done to pour the Gospel day upon the darkness of their long and dismal night" and were heartened by the spread of missionary schools, for instance, at Ludhiana where they saw "so many heathen and Mussulman youths—some Hindus, some Sikhs, some from the Panjab, some from Kashmer, and some from Affghanistan—acquiring the knowledge of our language, and of our religion, in the same school." At midcentury, "Afghanistan" was widely in use, for instance by Karl Marx. But the term applied only very roughly to an area loosely circumscribing Kabul ("Cabool"), Herat, and Kandahar.[38]

Dost Muhammad had mixed success at his campaign to restore territories claimed by the Durrani empire. He accepted a Sikh request to fight the East India Company in 1848 but failed to expel the British or to achieve the reconquest of Peshawar. In the 1850s, however, he succeeded in capturing Kandahar and in wresting Turkestan from the Bukharans. Just before his death he claimed Herat in 1863. In expanding his kingdom, Dost Muhammad had the support, in the form of weapons and money, of the British, who saw him as a counterweight to a rapidly expanding Russia and to Iran, which had seized Herat in 1856. His alliance with the British guaranteed their recognition of his territorial gains. But it also limited the contacts he could have with Russia, effectively subordinating his foreign policy to London.[39]

His son Shir 'Ali inherited this geopolitical dilemma when he took the throne in 1863. Facing opposition from his brothers, he deployed state-building strategies that he had observed during his own Indian exile. Relying on a new technology, the amir printed texts

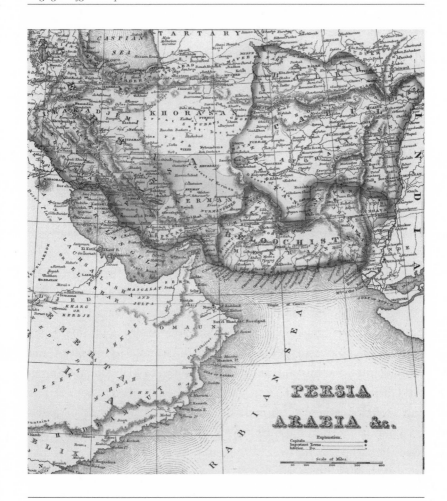

3 Persia Arabia & c. Published by J. H. Colton & Co., 1855. David Rumsey
Map Collection, www.davidrumsey.com.

to publicize his preeminence in a state that he called "Afghanistan,"
one that he was divinely appointed to rule, as extensive quotations
from the Quran demonstrated. Shir 'Ali had visited printing houses
in India and apparently purchased printing equipment in Peshawar
and arranged for Indian artisans to manage it at the citadel of Bala

Hissar. His lithographic printing house produced the first postal stamps, government forms, books, and a newspaper, the *Midday Sun of Kabul* (*Shams al-nahār-i Kābul*). A royal announcement described how the paper would "accurately describe events in Turkestan, Badakhshan, Herat, Kandahar, Russia and other countries," adding that "empty talk and bazaar news will not be included in this paper."[40]

Complementing the amir's opening of the first secular school and his decision to send Afghans to Europe for study, one of the chief goals of the paper was to acquaint Afghans with happenings in the rest of the world. It reprinted international news from Indian publications, which arrived via an Afghan press agent in Peshawar and which the amir read on a daily basis. (An Indian assistant translated the English papers for him.) The paper also claimed to have correspondents in places like Badakhshan. It reported official news alongside odes praising the amir and his family. The newspaper featured "useful" knowledge, invoking "progress" and the "spread of knowledge in the country." It also carried news from around the world: Afghans read about an epidemic afflicting pilgrims traveling to Mecca, railroad building in the United States, a gold theft in Prussia, as well as news about Russia and its diplomatic relations with China and Bukhara. Domestic news was another feature, often highlighting unusual events, like the freezing of the Kabul River in the bitter winter of 1874.[41]

Of all of these developments, the most noteworthy, from Kabul's point of view, was Russian expansion into Central Asia. The spread of tsarist authority toward the kingdom was more than a curious news item. The prospect of a friendly Russia opened up the possibility of reducing dependence on London. When the British rebuffed Shir 'Ali's request for security guarantees, the amir allowed a Russian envoy to visit Kabul in July 1878 to explore an alliance. The British responded by declaring war. Their forces occupied Kandahar and Kabul. Shir 'Ali then offered to aid the Russians should they invade

India, seeking in return military aid and, crucially, territorial compensation. The Afghan proposal demanded "Kashmir, the Punjab, Sind, and Baluchistan."[42]

The Second Anglo-Afghan War concluded in 1880 in another British withdrawal. On the one hand, it offered more fodder for the demonization of the Afghans in Europe. One typical British account described Afghan fighters who joined an anti-British uprising in Kabul as "a mob of scowling, dark-faced men, mad, and baying for their prey like bloodhounds that have tasted human flesh."[43] On the other hand, the war left London in control of Afghanistan's foreign affairs, while creating a space for a new amir to harness British resources and quasi-protectorate status to carve out a more powerful state in the zone lying between the British and Russian frontiers.

Shir 'Ali's death in 1879 paved the way for his nephew Abdur Rahman, who had fled Afghanistan after fighting for his father's claim on the throne, to return from his exile in Russian Central Asia. He spent most of his ten-year exile in Samarkand, which the tsarist army had seized in 1868, establishing a Russian colony in a new, planned city adjacent to the existing city. There he received a pension from the Russian government, who offered stipends to several Afghan émigrés who, they hoped, might prove useful in advancing Russian interests in the event of a crisis. Surrounded by a retinue of fellow Afghans and in frequent contact with local notables and Russian officials, Abdur Rahman busied himself with the study of tsarist military and state affairs, taking a special interest in experimenting with electricity. The future amir also mixed with elite society. He attended balls hosted by the Russian governor-general and, according to a description of one of these soirees, even danced the polonaise with "a young lady, attractive and with a low-cut neckline."[44]

These imperial experiences in Russian Turkestan—of exile, of European-style cities, technology, and science—inspired in Abdur

Rahman faith in the novel European concept of "progress," of the latest ideas about warfare and the modern infrastructure of statecraft, including the railroad, rifles, and artillery. All of these ideas figured into his ambitious scheme to forge a new kind of state, one that would stand on its own feet at a moment when European powers were redrawing the map of the world. Industry, electricity, and the printing press, together with a sophisticated intelligence network, would all be keys to establishing this order, one whose survival would hinge on Afghan elites' ability to embrace the idea of progress and change.

In remarks attributed to Abdur Rahman by the scribe who compiled his autobiography, the amir would contrast the condition of his country at his accession—when the people were "always engaged in rebellion and fighting against me"—with a later period, when they had become "the most peaceful, obedient, law-abiding, and civilised nation" and were busy "learning every kind of industry and manufacture, and making provision for the progress of their country generally and for their own happiness."[45] The amir's task, then, was to carry out the civilizing mission of empire, by force when necessary, within his own kingdom. The fruits of this imperial cosmopolitanism would be on display far beyond the borders that would soon demarcate his realm.

3 | BODIES IN MOTION

"WE DO NOT desire to be treated as 'social' equals of Europeans, but we claim we have as much right to fair and just treatment as any other nation," wrote Abdul Rahim Khan in February 1924. "An Afghan, no matter what his station in life," he continued, "is subject to disabilities which the most illiterate Russian, or other European is entirely free from." As a "race which prides itself on its honesty and business integrity" and "a peaceful people and law-abiding," Afghans deserved treatment "on the same footing" with Europeans.

Abdul Rahim's passionate appeal was not that of a decorated ambassador protesting the mistreatment of Afghans in the diplomatic arena. Rather, he was the secretary of a group of Afghans living and working far from their homeland, the Transvaal Afghan Association of Johannesburg, South Africa. On behalf of "some 100 members in the Transvaal, the majority of whom are Merchants," his petition criticized a proposal to create separate residential and commercial districts for Asians. To the Afghan petitioners, the proposed bill was an injustice that "borders on the barbarous." Rejecting the charge that the Asian merchant was "a menace to the white traders," they countered that their "years of industry and toil" had given rise to businesses that were beneficial to the country and to its white population. In Afghanistan, the petition explained, Europeans were treated "as all civilized people should be treated, with justice," adding that "we feel we are entitled to the same privileges as we give." Subject to a host of special restrictions, including separate trains and cabs, the Transvaal Afghans called for the repeal of all of these disabilities and for the granting of the right to vote and to own real estate. Although the petitioners identified themselves initially as "subjects of the Amir of Afghanistan" and then, somewhat ambiguously, as "citizens of the Union of South Africa," the Afghan ambassador to the United Kingdom intervened on their behalf to denounce the proposed legislation as an "open insult." In a letter to J. C. Smuts, the prime minister of the Union of South Africa, he asked that Afghans be exempted from such laws, so "that by respecting and revering the honour and self-respect of one another's citizens, as two independent nations are wont to do, an opportunity will be afforded for the satisfaction and gratification of your Afghan human brethren."[1]

This controversy over the status of Afghans in a dominion of the British Empire points to some of the most striking changes that Afghans had experienced in the half century since the reign of Amir Shir 'Ali. In 1880, the Second Anglo-Afghan War had concluded in a treaty that recognized a quasi-independent Afghan kingdom. However, its ruler, Abdur Rahman (r. 1880–1901), would continue to depend upon a British subsidy and was compelled to defer to London in conducting foreign affairs. It took nearly two decades to negotiate the country's borders with the British and Russians. Mistrust and equivocation would long hang over one particularly troublesome area, the Durand Line of 1893, which drew a line—on paper, at least—demarcating eastern Afghanistan and the North-West Frontier of British India.

Yet, by the end of the reign of Abdur Rahman's son Habibullah (r. 1901–1919), the Afghan political scene looked quite different. His son Amanullah (r. 1919–1929) sparked a third war with the British in 1919, announcing, "I have declared myself and my country entirely free, autonomous and independent both internally and externally." Afghanistan would "hereafter be as independent a state as the other states and powers of the world are."[2]

The Afghanistan that we know today is, then, a relatively recent phenomenon, its modern borders fixed only in the late nineteenth and early twentieth centuries. Yet the emergence of the Afghan state, far from being an anomalous or artificial development, was part of a global process. Afghan state formation coincided with the appearance of polities that we tend to take for granted as historically inevitable nation-states, including Italy, which was formed only in 1861, and Germany, established in 1871. Even these dates are deceptive, however, because the new states had not yet become part of the consciousness of the populations they aspired to rule and to integrate into these new nation-states. As the Italian nationalist Massimo d'Azeglio (1798–1866) observed, "We have made Italy, now we have to make Italians." Even in the case of France, the seemingly archetypal nation-state, the diverse regional cultures, languages, traditions, and habits of the people inhabiting the "hexagon" began to take on a more homogeneous and "French" coloring only in the decades just before and after 1900, when, as Eugen Weber has shown, schools, markets, roads, railways, military service, the press, and other national institutions knitted together the varied peoples and regions of the territory. Christopher Clark's description of Prussia could easily have been written about Afghanistan: "it was an assemblage of disparate territorial fragments lacking natural boundaries or a distinct national culture, dialect, or cuisine." "This predicament," he adds, "was amplified by the fact that Prussia's intermittent territorial expansion entailed the periodic incorporation of new populations whose loyalty to the Prussian state could be acquired, if at all, only through arduous processes of assimilation."[3] Afghan elites would face similar challenges in seeking to subjugate and integrate populations with similarly diverse linguistic, legal, social, and religious backgrounds, though they would pursue their project of constructing a nation-state under quite different geopolitical and environmental conditions.

Meanwhile, even as the Afghan nation-state was taking shape within its new boundaries, more and more subjects of the kingdom were traversing the globe. Afghans living abroad faced the challenge of adapting to very different social and legal milieus, from Russia, India, and China to Iran, the Ottoman Empire, and the British dominions in Africa and Australia. The Transvaal Afghans' engagement with colonial institutions was hardly a new or isolated phenomenon. Remembering his time working as an attorney in the South African courts between 1893 and 1914, Mohandas Gandhi pointed out that he had many Afghans as his clients, remarking favorably that "even bad ones among them fear God." Neither obsessively religious nor narrowly "tribal" in their logic, these Afghan petitioners defied conventional thinking about them. Drawing on the global circulation of contemporary political language, they deployed the idea that they belonged to an entity called humanity, an idea that had emerged out of the imperial politics of the nineteenth century as a justification for European colonialism and now, in the wake of the First World War, as a challenge to it.[4]

The case of the Afghans in South Africa reveals yet another global dimension to the story of the formation of the modern Afghan state. Negotiations over the borders of the kingdom were dominated by diplomats in London and St. Petersburg, where the balance of power between the European imperial powers in Asia was foremost in the minds of these actors. Their agents on the ground had to contend with Afghan authorities, but, in the main, the Europeans succeeded in dictating the terms of the territorial delimitation of the Afghan state. For Abdur Rahman and his successors, though, movement across these new borders was another matter. Controlling mobility became an essential means of demonstrating sovereignty.

The monarchy laid a fundamental claim to rule over Afghan bodies in motion. Nearly every aspect of building a novel kind of state centered on deploying the bodies of Afghans, seizing them for the army or the royal arms and munitions factory complex (*mashin khana*), dispatching them to colonize agricultural lands in the north, dragooning them into road-construction brigades, shipping them off to be reformed or treated in schools and hospitals, sending them to trade or study in foreign lands, and exiling them within the country or expelling them abroad. Vigilant in their scrutiny of potential opponents, royal authorities sought to make themselves the arbiters of contact with the wider world. The amir's intelligence network stretched beyond the borders of the kingdom, and Afghan spies infiltrated the diaspora. Similarly, his religious authorities, many of whom were recruited from India, carefully policed the circulation of religious ideas. The police were on the lookout for foreign preachers and texts whose influence royal printers countered by generating a body of religious scholarship that assigned the religious establishment a monopoly on the interpretation of Islam.

The monarchy wielded extraordinary violence in mobilizing Afghans for this state-building project. But nonelites and non-Afghans shaped the process in key ways. Some took up arms against the encroachment of the state or found other ways to resist the frequent resort of its officials to brutality. Many were forced to flee to neighboring lands. Others sought to channel the state for their own ends.

The diaspora played a crucial role in expanding the reach of the state. Leaving Afghan soil did not mean severing ties with the growing power of the Afghan authorities. In the Transvaal, by pointing to the "civilized" treatment of Europeans by the Afghan state, merchants mobilized the idea of diplomatic reciprocity. The Afghan ambassador treated their discriminatory treatment as an "insult" to all Afghans. He thereby invoked a sense of Afghan nationhood unifying the diaspora and other populations, while insisting on a universal humanity with "your Afghan human brethren." With the expansion of Afghan diplomatic representation and the growth in the early 1920s of a network of consulates abroad, the Afghan diaspora brought the state in tow when merchants and traders appealed, as Afghan subjects, for official intervention on their behalf.

The architects of the Afghan state faced numerous challenges, not least among them the fact that the would-be subjects of the kingdom, who were to be taxed, conscripted, and schooled to offer their loyalty to the Afghan nation–state and monarchy, were on the move like never before. Of the estimated five million inhabitants of the land, hundreds of thousands had historically been nomadic or otherwise seasonally migratory. Yet a number of factors account for the increased mobility of Afghans in the last quarter of the nineteenth century. Technology was among the most important. Ever heedful of the political threat of European penetration, Afghan rulers were suspicious of the railroad, which, as Abdur Rahman clearly understood, would establish an infrastructure that would yield rapid connections. But strategic vulnerabilities would follow. Watching the rail networks extend southward across the Russian Empire and steadily advance westward across India, he had ample reason to reject European plans to connect Afghan territory to a mode of transport that could quickly deliver foreign troops to Afghan soil. At the same time, the country lacked a navigable river system for steamship traffic. Still, these new modes of transportation and communication nonetheless had thoroughgoing effects on Afghans.[5]

By the end of the century, Afghan travelers and goods that reached the Russian or British frontiers gained access to a dense rail and steamship network. The Indian railway line began at Chaman and connected to Karachi and ports farther south. Steamers plied the

Indus. Completed in 1869, the Suez Canal dramatically accelerated the pace of travel by steamship between the subcontinent and the Middle East. Similarly, the Transcaspian Railroad, built in the 1880s and 1890s, created a continuous line from the northern Afghan border at Kushka to the Black Sea and, to the north, to the newly expanded European Russian railway system. Caravans of camels and other load-bearing animals continued to flow in large numbers into India and Iran. And Afghans would still take to dhows to sail to ports around the Arabian Sea and Persian Gulf. But rail and steamship travel now competed with these older modes of transport, accelerating and deepening Afghan contacts not just with far-flung markets but with traditional pilgrimage destinations, diaspora communities, and political and intellectual currents across the globe.

Among its most far-ranging effects, this transportation revolution intensified Afghan ties to the Hijaz, home to Mecca and the annual rite of the hajj. Shifting in greater numbers from the overland caravan route, by the mid-1860s the Afghan hajj had become an increasingly maritime affair. Arriving from all parts of Afghanistan, hajjis embarked on steamships in Karachi and Bombay that deposited them, after brief stops at ports along the way, at Jedda. Whether by land or sea, the journey was all the more noteworthy in that Afghans interacted with Muslims from other lands at every stage along the way. Arriving from the north and east, pilgrims from the Russian Empire and China were companions from nearly the start of their journey. Afghanistan lay along the hajj route for travelers from Central Asia, along which pilgrims passed via Bukhara and Samarkand through Afghanistan. In the early twentieth century, Russian authorities estimated that between four and seven thousand Central Asians opted for the route that took them to Mazar-i Sharif and then Kabul before connecting to the railroad in Peshawar, which took them on to Bombay and to the Hijaz by steamer. Entering into the cosmopolitan world of the Indian Ocean, Afghan pilgrims made contact with Indian and Arab trading partners in the ports.

The traffic also flowed in the opposite direction. From the north, Afghan pilgrims who found their way to Tashkent could connect to the Russian railroad and be in the Black Sea port of Odessa in just over eight days. In 1909, the British claimed that the Russians in Mashhad were recruiting Afghan pilgrims to take their railway to Mecca as an option that was cheaper than the Indian route.[6]

The available sources do not allow for a completely reliable estimate of the volume of the Afghan hajj traffic. An Iranian pilgrim who visited the Hijaz in the mid-1880s estimated that between 200 and 600 Afghans performed the hajj every year. By the late 1920s, though, British intelligence had established controls that yielded more comprehensive data, at least for the maritime hajjis. They recorded 1927 as a banner year for the hajj, the largest since the First World War: 3,858 Afghans arrived that year, making them the fourth largest group traveling by sea.[7]

Travel by steamship and rail made the hajj journey quicker, less strenuous, and more secure, even though cholera and other diseases that passed among pilgrims proved fatal on more than one occasion. It also seems to have expanded many Afghans' access to additional pilgrimage routes. In 1905, the authorities in Jerusalem counted nearly one hundred Afghans and Uzbeks residing in a hostel for pilgrims visiting the holy city. Around 1910, Austrian consular officials in the Mediterranean coastal town of Jaffa included 3,460 Afghans among a list of more than 35,000 pilgrims passing through their jurisdiction on the way to Jerusalem and other parts. In Iraq, a British official observed Sunni Muslims from Afghanistan and India venerating the shrine of Shaykh Abdul Qadir in Baghdad, which was also a transit point for pilgrims traveling from the Gulf. The mosque and tomb of this late eleventh- and early twelfth-century Sufi master and miracle worker attracted Sunnis from far and wide. When Mahmud Tarzi (1865–1933), an aristocratic figure sent into exile by Abdur Rahman and, later, an influential modernist thinker, traveled from Karachi to Baghdad in 1885, he spent considerable time at the shrine. There was a related shrine at Ajmer in India, "much venerated by Afghans and Pathans of the Indo-Afghan frontier from a belief that the individual buried there was a nephew of Shaikh 'Abdul Qadir, Gilani."[8]

This account from Baghdad points to another phenomen that accompanied the hajj: most Afghan pilgrims returned home, but an unknown number settled down and returned only much later, if at all. Indeed the British officer in Baghdad recommended to his superiors that they appoint personnel with knowledge of Pashto, "the surest road to the heart of the Afghans, of whom a number are met with here." In Istanbul, Afghans also had a long-standing presence. A Sufi lodge served Afghans who had migrated permanently as well as Afghan visitors who might stop in Üsküdar at a lodge near the Çinili mosque on their way to Istanbul. In the Hijaz itself, a British report on the assassination in 1880 of the "Grand Sheriff" of Mecca by a knife-wielding assailant later discovered to be an Afghan from a village near Kabul claimed that there were "many Afghans in Mecca." Later, in 1920, a British survey encountered "an overwhelming majority of foreign subjects living in Hedjaz towns, consisting of Indians, Afghans, Hadramis, Egyptians, Bukharis, Syrians, Persians, Javanese and Maghrabis." At Mecca, Afghans were clustered in the "Fuluk Mohalla." Most of these foreigners were engaged in trade, though with uncertain legal standing. In 1932, the Afghan state purchased a house for Afghan pilgrims in Mecca.[9]

The hajj was transformative, too, in that it brought significant numbers of Afghans of varied backgrounds into contact with Muslims from Asia, Africa, the Middle East, and Europe. Ikbal Ali

Shah, a contemporary Afghan traveler, saw the shared experience of diverse Muslims boarding a Hijaz-bound steamship as a moment of discovery: "In a fierce midday heat, enveloped in clouds of choking dust, sweating and with jaded faces, a heterogeneous mass of Moslim pilgrims plodded their way to Bombay harbor. Afghans, Persians, Javanese, Indians and Uzbegs, all staring at one another and endeavouring to understand the diverse languages they had never heard before." Each group admirably wrestled with seasickness and the harsh conditions of the sea, the Persians by making tea, the Bengalis by skinning fish, and the Pathans by making busy "with Palaws of excellent flavour." Yet these differences did not dissolve upon this initial contact, the author ruefully concluded. The passengers passed their afternoons onboard in discussions of religion and politics, but "both used to end where they began."[10]

Many other intellectuals, including the aforementioned exile and modernist Mahmud Tarzi, would view the hajj as an opportunity to forge unity among the faithful, an aspiration shared at the court of the Ottoman sultan, Abdülhamid II (r. 1876–1909), who presented himself as the legitimate leader not only of Mecca and Medina but of all the world's Muslims. In his appeal to Afghans to embrace the true meaning of their faith in order to strengthen the state and the nation, Tarzi attached special importance to these holy places. This was a challenge, he emphasized, that lay not just before Afghans but before Muslims everywhere, whom he enjoined to gather, at the holy shrines of Mecca and Medina and elsewhere, to unite "for the purpose of our own community's advancement, improvement, civilization, and cooperation."[11]

Closer to home, the Afghan presence in Iran reflected migratory patterns that were a mix of old and new. The shrines of Iran presented similar opportunities and were more accessible to many Afghans. The centuries-old Mashhad-Herat corridor, animated by pilgrims, students, religious scholars, pastoralists, itinerant scribes, and notables, thrived into the modern era. In the 1860s, Afghans were to be found in noticeable numbers in the Qajar capital, Tehran, where, together with Arabs, Indians, and other neighboring peoples, they made up, according to a Prussian traveler, "a not insignificant portion of the population of the city." Torbat-i Jam, just twenty-five miles west of the Afghan border, was home to a Sufi lodge that attracted Afghan, Iranian, and Indian adherents. West of Mashhad, Sabzevar was a cosmopolitan hub of Afghan commercial activity. In 1882, an Iranian official commented on its impressive vitality: "in reality it is a port where goods from Iraq and everywhere arrive and move on toward Afghanistan and others towns in Turkestan." A few years later a British consul general discovered that the local merchant community included a group of Russian Armenians trading in dried fruits, cotton, and wool and that the local deputy governor was an émigré from Herat who had fled with Qajar forces in 1857. From the 1880s, the expansion of the central Afghan government, combined with closer policing of the Russian side of the Russo-Afghan border, appears to have pushed greater numbers of Afghan pastoralists and others toward the Iranian province of Khorasan. Many settled near Sabzevar or migrated there with their herds during winter.[12]

Afghan subjects of various ethnic groups were also active in the Russian Empire. Merchants had long traveled throughout Central Asia and the eastern frontiers of the steppe. Some went on to trade in European Russia. They were among the million and a half visitors to the Nizhnii Novgorod summer fair in the Volga River region. There they attracted lasting attention only in 1890, when a barge of goods purchased by the Afghan merchants was destroyed in a fire. Under pressure from the local governor, who cited the desire to cultivate access to Afghan markets and to maintain tsarist prestige, Russian merchants raised 250,000 rubles to compensate the Afghan traders. They returned to the fair the following year and repaid their debt to the governor.[13]

Afghan traders were allowed to enter the governor-generalship of Turkestan as well the tsarist protectorate of Bukhara. Many Afghans migrated temporarily for trade or for study at Bukhara's famed madrasas. Others settled permanently in Bukhara, Turkestan, and Kashgar, and some engaged in agriculture or practiced various trades. Afghan emigration to Central Asia preceded the tsarist conquest of the region between the 1860s and 1880s. They served as mercenaries, first for Central Asian rulers, and later, for the Russians. Afghan Jews had also begun migrating to the region before the arrival of the Russians. They, along with Hazaras, Pashtuns, and other groups, moved in greater numbers after the establishment of Russian rule. Jews of Afghan origin turned to tsarist officials for protection against their Muslim neighbors or business partners, who, in turn, tried to mobilize the Russian authorities against them.[14]

Muslims from Afghanistan were frequently in court as well, and in some legal and political matters Muslim Afghans enjoyed a privileged status in the Russian Empire. In 1869, Abdur Rahman and his cousin Muhammad Ishaq Khan had found refuge there after struggles for the Afghan throne spilled into the region. When Ishaq's rebellion against his cousin failed to win Russian backing for an independent Afghan Turkestan in 1888, he fled to Russian territory a second time. Repeatedly in the late nineteenth century, a steady stream of notables turned up with their retinues on tsarist territory. Tsarist authorities often assigned such émigrés pensions, viewing them as potential assets to be deployed, under the right conditions, against British influence in the wider region. Russian authorities largely turned a blind eye to Afghan moneylending, and Afghans were exempt from laws forbidding foreigners from acquiring property. By 1897, however, the military governor of Samarkand and other officials had begun to criticize Afghan money-lenders, charging that their lending practices and acquisition of land had led to the exploitation of Russian subjects. As officials debated introducing restrictions on these activities, a number of Afghan notables opted to become tsarist subjects. Near Kokand, Afghans even founded a village known as Augani-kishlak. In 1897, over six hundred appeared in the Russian census, though the authorities acknowledged this figure was too low. Afghans with tsarist passports retained ties to communities and property in Afghanistan and traveled between the two states.

The poorer Afghan border communities were less fortunate. Migrations of extended kinship groups and whole villages followed the Afghan authorities' suppression of the revolt of 1888. Fleeing the Afghan state, Hazaras, Uzbeks, and other non-Pashtuns crossed the border in waves seeking permission to resettle there with access to pasture and water for their herds. Tsarist officials discouraged mass migrations. On occasion, though, they accepted smaller groups of migrants. Roughly nine thousand Jamshidis crossed the Amu in June 1908; about three thousand Hazara families followed in November 1910. The Russian authorities forcibly repatriated many, but not all, of the migrants who arrived in these two waves. By contrast, Afghan laborers were permitted to cross the border to work temporarily on Russian irrigation and other construction projects.[15]

Russian subjects, in turn, were permitted entry into Afghanistan. Muslim subjects of the tsar traded extensively and even acquired property there. Russian sources from the 1880s refer to at least two merchants who purchased homes and lived for extended periods in Mazar-i Sharif and Kabul, respectively. Both died there, and Afghan officials made arrangements with Muslim legal experts and the authorities in Turkestan to return their bodies and distribute their inheritance.[16]

As in earlier periods, India continued to be the land of opportunity for Afghans. A trading fair established in Karachi by the British in 1852 heightened its appeal. In the mid-1880s, the Iranian traveler Hajji Muhammad 'Ali Pirzadeh spotted laborers and traders from Afganistan, Baluchistan, and elsewhere at the port of Karachi. In the early twentieth century, nearly every tenth person in the province of Sind (to which Karachi belonged) was born elsewhere, among them tens of thousands from Afghanistan and Baluchistan.[17]

For all of the proximity of India and the antiquity of commercial and other ties, Afghan descriptions of travel are a reminder that this remained a hazardous undertaking. The frontier was "Yaghistan," an area where travelers frequently invoked the protection of a saint to guide them through treacherous territory. Hazrat Khalife Mir Jahan was one such saint to whom a merchant from Charikar, Ghulam Muhammad, appealed at the end of the nineteenth century to secure safe passage for him and his goods through the country of the Mohmand tribe. When a crowd of hundreds menacingly approached his column of camels and pack animals, his guide called out the saint's name. The would-be robbers wailed and dispersed, and the caravan made it back to "the sacred land of Afghanistan" (*khak-i muqadess-i Afghanistan*).[18]

Insecurity and violence prompted other kinds of movement. Perhaps the largest single group of permanent Afghan emigrants to India in the late nineteenth century was made up of the Hazaras, against whom Abdur Rahman's forces waged a bloody campaign. In the process, his religious scholars declared the Hazaras, most of whom were Shia, "infidels," leaving them subject to vicious retribution, and they lost many of their pastures and livestock. The conquest of the Hazarajat region had wider regional implications. In Iran, news of the mistreatment of the Shia heightened the Qajar dynasty's aspirations to serve as the protector of Shia everywhere. From the highland frontiers, now transformed into an interior of the kingdom, Hazaras migrated to Iran and India. Those who could manage it mostly fled to Quetta and the Punjab, where they found work on the railway or in other construction work. Some of this work was temporary, mostly taking place in winter. But a number of Hazaras left for India for good, some opting to join the Indian Army. British officers had begun recruiting Hazaras for military service in the First Anglo–Afghan War, and they enlisted later in the 124th and 126th Baluchistan Infantry and Guides Cavalry as well is in the 106th Hazara Pioneers established in 1904. They went on to serve in Iraq (Mesopotamia) and elsewhere during the First World War.[19]

Many more Afghans, mostly Ghilzai Pashtun migrant traders known as *kuchis* or *powindas*, traveled to India for seasonal commerce. Over the course of just a few months' time they carried on the bulk of Afghan trade. Traveling in caravans of several thousand horses and camels and other animals laden with dried fruits, nuts, wool, hides, and asafetida (used as a drug), hundreds of thousands of men, women, and children made their way each autumn from Kabul through the Khyber Pass to Peshawar. Some then went to other destinations in India to work as laborers. Moneylenders and petty merchants traveled on to Assam, Bengal, Burma, and Nepal, where they were renowned for their multilingualism. In preparation for their return to Afghanistan in the spring, they loaded their animals with kerosene, cloth, tea, salt, sugar, and other commodities and manufactured goods to be resold in Afghanistan, Central Asia, and Iran.[20] Typically bearing arms (until the British established a border depot to temporarily house their weapons) and moving from place to place in black tents, the powindas cut an imposing figure. A British military officer who encountered them at Peshawar in the early twentieth century snidely commented on the bearing of these cosmopolitan nomads: "It is the peculiarity of the Afghans that they are always thoroughly at home everywhere, and never seem to realize the necessity of dropping any of their swagger when in foreign lands."[21]

Beyond India, Afghans circulated throughout the British Empire. They were to be found in Sri Lanka (Ceylon), where they arrived in the late nineteenth century as "horse-dealers, traders and money-lenders." In Australia, they traded camels and led caravans that transported supplies to sparsely populated areas. They went as far west as South America: sometime in the nineteenth century, a small group of Afghan migrants, deportees from British India, ended up in Guyana and Suriname. In such cases, Afghans tended to come to the attention of colonial authorities only when they fell under suspicion of smuggling or other illicit activities. Much of what we know comes from colonial authorities' attempts to control their movement, for example, in the early 1880s when railway policemen in the train stations of the Punjab were directed to watch "the movements of Afghans proceeding to the Deccan in search of employment" and to warn them that "they will be turned back on arrival at Hyderabad." Colonial censuses often jumbled the identities of migrants who arrived via steamship from India. Further complicating matters, Muslim immigrants might claim Arab, Persian, or Afghan ancestry. More rarely do we encounter officials such as the South African police inspector who, in ranking the behavior of colonial subjects, placed "the Afghans recently imported" to South Africa behind the Arabs—but ahead of immigrants from Calcutta and Madras.[22]

Afghans confronted similar forms of racial categorization and discrimination in North America, where they had begun to find their way alongside other immigrants from South Asia by the early twentieth century. Americans had been exposed since the two Anglo-Afghan Wars to largely hostile portrayals of the Afghans in the British press. Many audiences knew the comic opera by the Irish-born Victor Herbert, *The Ameer* (first staged in 1899), in which the buffoonish ruler of Afghanistan (who doubles as a brigand) is bested by a British officer in his quest for the affections of an American girl. Afghans were also stock images in American advertising. Cigarette companies featured Afghans among the "Savage and Semi-Barbarous Chiefs and Rulers" of the world, alongside Native Americans, Africans, and other Asians. Direct contacts were few, except, for instance, a 1910 incident in Jerusalem, which the *Los Angeles Herald* presented under the headline "American Women Attacked by Fanatical Afghans," driving home the British view of the Afghans for an American audience.[23] An article in the *San Francisco Call* sounded the alarm about the immigration of Sikhs and Afghans, warning that the Afghans were "a race even more objectionable from an American point of view than the tall, helpless Sikhs." The Afghan, the article claimed, displayed "a treacherous cunning that makes him undesirable altogether apart from his color and previous condition of servitude." The article warned that there were about fifty Afghans in California "and more on the way."[24]

A 1913 immigration file recorded the landing at Angel Island in San Francisco of a twenty-nine-year-old carpenter from Afghanistan who gave his name as "Golab Deen." Arriving on the SS *Nile* with $170, he had been proceeded by one brother, "Feroz Deen," in Canada and another referred to in the document as "Russian Deen," who settled in Oakland seven years earlier. The latter was a carpenter, a member of the United Brotherhood of Carpenters union, who had recently married an American woman. When asked about his financial means, Russian Deen presented evidence of $500 in the bank, adding that he had loaned his other brother money to buy property in Washington State and that a man in Butte, Montana, owed him another $400. "I am a good mechanic," he told the immigration officials, "and make wagons the same way as they make in Chicago." He proposed "to start a big business" with his brother in anticipation of the upcoming 1915 San Francisco world's fair. And to vouch for his credibility, he brought along an F. Dubovsky, a hardware store owner who testified that he had allowed Deen to buy tools on credit. Despite the xenophobic tone of newspaper coverage of Afghan migrants, the immigration board approved his entry.[25]

At the turn of the twentieth century, legal restrictions on the movement of non-Europeans intensified discrimination against Afghans in other parts of the globe. In places like the Transvaal region of South Africa, white settlers launched an aggressive campaign against non-European immigration. Their agitation against the Indian settler community met with widespread resistance dating to the 1890s, when Gandhi had initiated the struggle against the unequal treatment of Indian immigrants. In 1924, Afghan petitioners demanded to be treated as equals and given the right to vote and acquire property. Observing that "the world is to-day crying for peace and for all nations to live in harmony," they protested that in South Africa they were "treated not as a civilized people, but as inferiors, who must be kept down." In 1927, Afghans protested to their government that British authorities prohibited their landing in Australia and South Africa. Complaints from Afghans in India reported being denied entry to Nepal as well.[26]

In fact, Afghans encountered a great variety of difficulties in India, where Afghans enjoyed a reputation among many Indians as rustics and brutes. In 1920, rumors of an Afghan invasion roiled Indian political circles. Indeed, one of Gandhi's interlocutors pointed to Henry Bellew's description of Afghan mistreatment of Hindus in Afghanistan, arguing that British rule was preferable to the Afghans: "The race to which this 'Satanic' [British] Government belongs never treated Indians so unfairly as the Muslim rulers of Afghanistan did the Hindus." Gandhi's retort to such accusations was that "the Afghans have no quarrel with India." Calling them "a godfearing people," he warned skeptics, with a degree of ambivalence, of "judging the Afghans by the few savage specimens we see in Bombay or Calcutta." British authorities also frequently complained of "outrages" committed by Afghan subjects. The authorities suspected them of importing their "blood feuds" to India. They commonly deported Afghans accused of this conduct and of other kinds of violence. Commercial and financial disputes were another source of conflict that directed hostile attention toward Afghans in India.[27]

In the early twentieth century, the Bengali writer Rabindranath Tagore addressed some of these stereotypes in *The Fruit-Seller of Kabul* (*Kabuliwala*). Set in Calcutta, the story featured an Afghan merchant who befriends a little Indian girl, sharing jokes along with his dried fruits and almonds, even while the girl's parents look upon him with suspicion. To the narrator, the sight of the Kabuliwala evokes images of "arid mountain peaks, with narrow little defiles twisting in and out amongst their towering heights" and "camels bearing the merchandise, and the company of turbanned merchants carrying some their queer old firearms, and some their spears, journeying downward towards the plains." This element of danger is heightened when the Afghan is jailed for his role in a violent assault. However, it is later revealed that he had left his own daughter back in Kabul, and the narrator, the Indian girl's father, gives the Afghan man money meant for his daughter's wedding festivities to return to "the barren mountains of Afghanistan" to reunite with his own daughter. Tagore's story ends in an act of generosity and empathy, one made possible by the Afghan's outsider status.[28]

With the establishment of Afghan consulates in India after a treaty agreement of 1922, Afghans turned to these state institutions to seek redress in disputes with Indians and with one another. One such case from 1932 involved Mohammad Yasin, an Afghan father from Paghman, whose son-in-law, Ghaus-ud-Din, had absconded to

India, where, according to his accuser, he found a job as "a Cook in some English School at Charsedda (Peshawar District)." Mohammad Yasin turned to the Afghan authorities to press Ghaus-ud-Din to send money back to the man's family. The Consulate General of Afghanistan then appealed to colonial authorities to force the cook to provide support for his family, but they refused, suggesting that they pursue the case in court.[29]

The British response aside, what is significant here is that Mohammad Yasin turned to the Afghan state to discipline his son-in-law in India and, equally noteworthy, that Afghan consular officials expected their writ to be advanced by the British colonial state. In the same year, a similar case began when a man named Ismail from the village of Saracha Ali Khan in the east of Afghanistan approached the Afghan authorities to complain that his daughter-in-law had refused to accompany his family when they moved back to Afghanistan from Peshawar. The woman, Begum Jan, had fled to a police station and sought refuge there, saying her husband was going to kill her. The Afghan consul general demanded that the British send her back to her husband. The subsequent British investigation revealed that there had been a long-running dispute between the husband and his father-in-law in the Mohalla Berizkiyan of Peshawar City, and that the city magistrate had intervened in September 1931, ordering them "to execute bonds to keep the peace for a period of one year." Although the outcome of this dispute is unclear, it suggests how the lives of Afghan expatriates became entangled with state authorities on both sides of the border and reveals the ways in which Afghans had come to view their own state as one that would reach across these boundaries to shore up patriarchal authority and enforce the claims of particular family members.[30]

In 1930, an Afghan consul went so far as to intervene in the case of an apparent love triangle in Bombay. The consul warned his British counterpart that the two rivals for the affections of the woman, Mohamed Baz and Nur Gul, might, together with their Afghan entourages, cause "an unexpected affray" and that lives might be lost. He requested that the authorities in Bombay take measures "as a matter of precaution, [that] the woman may be sent back to Kabul along with her brother and mother, simply to avoid any excitement, or they may be removed from Bombay to some other place in India so that there may occur no fight among them, and thus the peace and order may not be interrupted, and there be no trouble among the parties."[31] As each of these cases shows, leaving Afghanistan did not mean leaving the state behind. For many Afghans abroad, and, of course, for its officials, the Afghan state was a potential resource to resolve the most intimate of conflicts.

The scale of the Afghan presence in India is difficult to gauge. According to a mysterious figure who in 1939 issued proclamations in India under the name and seal of the Afghan government—an activity that Kabul strongly protested—there were "four million Afghans" there. They were to be found as moneylenders and traders in the major cities, but they tended to be mobile and often beyond the reach of the census taker or tax authorities.[32]

India had an almost magnetic appeal, but, it is crucial to understand, migration flows were not unidirectional. Afghanistan became a refuge for people escaping military service or criminal prosecution in the Russian and British empires. In the late nineteenth and early twentieth centuries, it was not uncommon for tsarist soldiers to flee across the Amu Darya to Afghan territory. Once in Afghanistan, the Russian soldiers sometimes offered to convert to Islam and sought permission to remain in the country. From the direction of India, Indian army deserters and Baluch migrants crossed from Baluchistan to Kandahar. After 1917, several waves of Central Asian migrants fled the Russian Revolution and the imposition of Soviet rule in Central Asia.

The Afghan government played a part in encouraging certain categories of immigrants. In the late nineteenth century, the amir Abdur Rahman justified this recruitment by explaining that God had created "the system of the world . . . in such a manner that every human being stands in need of the help of some other person." "A careful and attentive observer of modern life in various countries and kingdoms can easily judge for himself," the amir continued,

> whether it is the custom with all highly civilised and boastful powers to give the same rights, ranks, and appointments to all their servants and subjects without distinction as to nationality, colour, creed, or religion. . . .
>
> Insha'allah (God willing), if my sons and successors follow my example in employing able officials in their service without prejudice against nationality or religion, their country will always prosper.

Afghan authorities looked first to India for men suited to serving the modernizing state. There they recruited religious scholars, the Anglophone graduates of Aligarh University (founded as the "Mohammedan Anglo-Oriental College" by a leading modernist advocate), and gymnastics instructors. Intellectuals such as Maulvi Muhammad Hussain Punjabi arrived in Kabul fluent in English, Urdu, Arabic, and Pashto. They served as crucial intermediaries between the royal government and political and intellectual developments in other parts of the globe. These immigrants received positions in government offices and schools, advising the government and producing texts on geography, history, religion, law, literature, and other subjects to shore up the state and a sense of Afghan nationhood. Medical doctors arrived from India and the Ottoman Empire. A female doctor from England, Lillias Anna Hamilton, received an invitation from Abdur

Rahman to tutor women of his harem and to establish a hospital in 1894; the amir credited her with introducing the practice of vaccination to Afghans, which he called "a great blessing to the children, of whom large numbers used to die of small-pox, those who recovered being greatly disfigured by the pitting following this dreadful disease."[33]

Afghan officials hired printers, engineers, and other technical experts to staff government printing and manufacturing operations. Between 1885 and 1894, British engineers assisted with the construction of the royal workshops. To power them, the government hired an American engineer in 1910 to build a hydroelectric plant at Jabal-us-Siraj with British equipment imported on carts drawn by elephants. A. C. Jewett, whose previous projects included the first electric street railway in San Francisco and power plants in India and Brazil, was unsparing in his criticism of the foreigners who had come to work in Afghanistan. Portraying these Europeans as a collection of swindlers and frauds, Jewett singled out one agent of an automobile company sent to advise the amir who "first got drunk with the king's cook the night before he left, lost himself, and was found at three in the morning in the machine-shop gardens, lying on the ground fast asleep, his horse grazing nearby. He had been sick all over his room, which looked like a pig's. This 'gentleman' returned to India, and in a published interview for the Bombay *Times* told what dirty people the Afghans were." He characterized another Briton, who, he claimed, cheated the Afghan government by bringing a broken tractor, as "an unmitigated ass." He was "the most unprincipled man up here—and that is going some." Jewett complained that all of these dodgy Europeans called themselves "engineers"—"except the Amir's French cook." "Is it any wonder," Jewett asked, "Afghans believe that Europeans are all shaitans [devils]?"[34]

The American engineer identified a structural tension that informed so many subsequent interactions between Afghans and "experts" who arrived from Europe and the United States ostensibly to enlighten the Afghans. He called the Afghans' exposure to such charlatans "a brown man's burden." Yet Jewett himself typified another facet of this relationship, treating Afghans who labored on his project with disdain and subjecting them to verbal and physical abuse. "The average Afghan's mental development seems to have stopped at about the age of fourteen," he observed. In some ways they were "a lot like very bad children," Jewett concluded. He had an even dimmer view of the people of Kabul, "a lazy, lying, thieving, licentious lot." Because "the Afghan is way back in the time of Moses, as far as his customs and thoughts go," Jewett had offered his workers incentives but judged it was necessary in the end to resort to meting out harsh punishments. In trying "to educate them," Jewett "called them all the bad Persian names in my vocabulary. I have worked with them and tried to improve them, thrashed them, and put them in chains." He ended his condescending portrait by repeating another persistent Western canard asserting that the Afghan "knows nothing of geography or the world outside his own ring of mountains. . . . There is not one in a thousand that knows there is such a country as the United States."[35]

Other categories of foreigner had very different experiences. Of these, the most visible was Sayyid Hasan Gailani, the descendant of an elite religious family from Baghdad, where he was born around 1862. Afghans had long revered the Gailani (Gilani) dynasty, who traced their descent from Fatima, daugher of the Prophet Muhammad and her husband 'Ali, for their leadership role in the Qadiri Sufi confraternity. Afghan pilgrims congregated around the Gailani family shrine in Baghdad. When Sayyid Hasan had a falling out with his older brother, Afghan devotees persuaded him to emigrate to Afghanistan in 1905. With an allowance from Amir Habibullah, he established himself at Chaharbagh, not far from Jalalabad. He became an authoritative figure for the Afghan Qadiris and for Pashtuns in particular: through intermarriage with the royal family and the creative recasting of genealogies, the Gailanis came to be regarded as Pashtuns.[36]

Afghan Muslims traveled far and wide within the country and beyond its borders to seek religious guidance, but, as in earlier periods, commerce was the primary Afghan gateway to the world. From early in the nineteenth century, goods from distant ports of Europe and Russia were available in Afghan markets. The scale of the penetration of distant commodities is suggested by a British description of Kandahar in 1879 noting that besides kabobs, bread, and "some stamped silk handkerchiefs from Bokhara," nearly "everything else seemed to come from Bombay or Birmingham." The American Jewett described the caravans winding through the Khyber Pass in 1911 as "long strings of big Bokhara camels with their tawny beards and hairy legs" carrying loads of goods from around the globe: in addition to porcelain teacups, saucers, and pots arriving in blue and red patterns from Russia, they hauled tea and cotton goods and matches "made in Sweden" and kerosene labeled "Standard Oil Co., made in U.S.A." and other goods stamped "made in Germany and Austria" and "made in Japan." For Afghan elites, the import of luxury goods, including ladies' hats, dresses, and jewelry, reflected shifting tastes and the ongoing contest for distinction among notables near the amir's court. One of Amir Habibullah's Indian advisers remembered him as "an ardent lover of fashion." Besides his tailored European suits, he enjoyed looking at the illustrated papers from Europe and wanted to have something similar in Afghanistan, "whereby he would see himself seen and known by others in the full glory of his fashionable majesty in the midst of fashionable surroundings." Jewett was bemused by seeing wealthy Afghans in frock coats worn over cotton trousers. He noticed a healthy trade carried on by Jews in secondhand clothes from abroad. There was even strong demand for cast-off uniforms like the one his attendant wore with "Inspector no. 48" stamped on the collar. "It is not unusual," he added, "to see an Afghan strutting down the main street of Kabul in an admiral's uniform, cocked hat, gold braid and all."[37]

The sight of secondhand uniforms may have amused foreigners, but modern weapons were another matter. During the Second Anglo-Afghan War, evidence discovered by the British pointed to a vast but underground trade in arms and ammunition from Europe. By the end of the nineteenth century it had become clear that Afghans were enmeshed in arms smuggling networks that stretched from villages along the Indo-Afghan frontier to the arms factories of Birmingham, England. Their partners spanned every continent. Breech-loading rifles and ammunition were produced in Belgium, France, Germany, Britain, and other states. European firms, Indian merchants, Zanzibari commercial agents, Hindu bankers, and Armenian, Parsi, and Iranian intermediaries provided a conduit between manufacturers in Europe and markets along the Gulfs of Persia and Oman. Masqat became the most important entrepôt—and the destination of Afghans who arrived by dhow and steamer to arrange the purchase of hundreds (in some years, thousands) of rifles, revolvers, and packets of ammunition that would then be smuggled by caravan from the Persian Gulf to Afghanistan and beyond to the Indian frontier. In the early twentieth century, British authorities adopted more aggressive policies to interdict the traffic. They were particularly suspicious of Afghans traveling by steamer to Masqat, Bandar Abbas, and Bahrain who claimed to be on pilgrimage but who, the British suspected, were there to buy arms that would gain ten or twenty times in value by the time they reached consumers in Kabul or on the Indo-Afghan frontier. Arms stolen from Indian army garrisons were another source for Afghan markets, as were the artisans along the frontier and in Iran who perfected the art of counterfeiting European weapons, even down to the manufacturer's stamp.[38]

In comparison to this lucrative import and transit trade enterprise, prospects for Afghan exports were grim. Numerous obstacles to the expansion of trade persisted. The country lacked a network of rivers that might have made transport more economical. Snows blocked many of the vital mountain passes for several months of the year. There were also political impediments. Neither the Russians nor the British permitted the transit of goods to or from third countries.

Moreover, for the Afghan government and its neighbors alike, the country's borders were a perennial source of anxiety, serving as a potent symbol of their fragile control of mobile populations and a vast space. Abdur Rahman periodically issued bans on the entry of foreign merchants and regarded his own with suspicion. Besides confiscating goods and money from merchants to supplement his treasury, he was cautious in permitting Afghans to travel abroad; his passport system forced the relatives of traders to pay a bond during their time abroad. In 1899, he permitted only six Herati merchants to travel to the trading fair at Nizhnii Novgorod.[39] For their part, tsarist authorities were frustrated by the Afghans and expressed disappointment at not having more direct ties to the trading hub of Herat. The head of the Transcaspian regional administration complained about the "conservatism" of Afghan traders who insisted on buying their goods in Iran on annual trips during which they would visit the shrine in Mashhad. Moreover, there was only one customs post, in the settlement of Takhta Bazaar, where direct Russo-Afghan exchange was possible.[40] And the amir had only approved trade through the Kelif crossing. From the perspective of Afghan traders, the multiple duties and currency exchanges that came with having to deal in Afghan, Russian, and Bukharan money were a constant drain on their finances.

Despite these obstacles, Afghan trade steadily increased. Precise figures are hard to come by, however. Deals between merchants tended to be based on oral agreements. Merchants hoped to avoid customs duties, often finding officials willing to collude in the practice. State record-keeping practices changed as well. And, of course, smuggling—always difficult to trace in official records—was the economic lifeblood of frontier communities who adapted to state efforts to police borders and monitor the movement of people and goods. Still, broad patterns are discernible thanks to the work of Soviet and other scholars of Afghan trade. Enabled by the extension of colonial railway and road networks to the Afghan border, the volume of external Afghan trade nearly tripled across the British frontier and more than quadrupled across the Russian frontier between 1896 and 1915. Although trade with British India remained predominant, Russia received nearly a third of all Afghan exports, and Russian exports made up roughly a third of Afghan imports.[41]

Imperial encroachment altered not just the size of trade but the composition of those who engaged in it. Partly as a result of the transactions with Russian trading firms and state authorities, the position of Indian, Jewish, and Persian traders and moneylenders appears to have deteriorated little by little in favor of Muslim Afghan subjects. The most striking example was the amir himself, who became the wealthiest merchant in the kingdom. With extensive commercial and financial connections in India and beyond, Abdur Rahman established a monopoly on certain goods and even maintained his own stalls in the bazaar. He used his commercial empire to benefit the royal family and its servitors, who also entered into the business of trade and moneylending. Trade with British commercial agents, by contrast, continued to rely more on the mediation of Indian subjects. Besides direct trade through Russian territory, commerce with Russia followed indirect routes through Bukhara and Iran. Russian traders brought sugar, textiles, crockery, kerosene, matches, and candles to the bazaars of Mashhad. Following the Russian annexation of territories east of the Caspian Sea in the 1880s, the Transcaspian Railway shipped more and more of these Russian commodities to the Iranian frontier. After 1917, connections with Soviet traders and officials proved especially advantageous for merchants based in Herat.[42]

For all the financial benefits that commerce might bring his treasury, Abdur Rahman was determined to establish a new kind of state with the capacity to monitor and discipline his subjects, whose unauthorized movement he associated with disorder and sedition. His official biography recounts how, upon taking the throne, he placed his foot "in the stirrup of progress and administration." In the major towns he appointed governors, judges, and heads of the Caravan and Police Departments. The last of these, the police, oversaw the "Rahdari Department," which issued passports necessary for travel between towns. Each passport authorizing travel within the country bore the seal of the passport officer, the head of police, and the governor. A passport for foreign travel required the additional signature and seal of "the Amir's own son, in the name of the Amir." To combat those "exhibiting a rebellious spirit," the amir assigned "private detectives and spies to report to me [the amir] all that went on among the people, thus finding out with abundant proofs those who were loyal and friendly."[43] The amir's surveillance regime was imperfect, however. Officials took bribes, and travelers evaded controls. At the same time, straying from the main thoroughfares that led from the gate of one town to the next was a dangerous proposition, making surveillance an easier task than it might seem to a modern observer.

The amir aspired to make his state the regulator of all cross-border flows. By the early twentieth century, Afghans and foreigners in state service had to apply to Prince Inayatullah to seek permission to leave the country, even for the hajj; foreigners had to do the same to return home on vacation or other business. Inayatullah received petitions from all walks of life, ranging from soldiers who had deserted to Peshawar and now wanted to return home and Indian printers seeking vacation leave, to a Muslim legal expert (*mufti*) from Farah asking to take his sick wife to Peshawar. Petitions involving travel sometimes overlapped with the intimate, mundane, and everyday concerns of hundreds of other men and women who appealed to the prince to solve commercial and land disputes, religious controversies, divorce cases, property crimes, and abductions. In one such case, a worker from the royal workshops, Muhammad Afzal, petitioned in 1914 complaining that he had not had "close relations" with his wife in their six years of marriage due to his impotence. The prince approved his request to be given a leave from work and be allowed to travel to India to seek a cure for his affliction.[44]

Populations on the border were subject to special scrutiny. In 1909, Amir Habibullah sent two riders with an order for the people of the Wakhan corridor not to cross the border or to engage in any kind of relations, whether commercial or marital, with the populations of neighboring states, threatening them with removal to the interior of the country. Local Tajiks were compelled to sign pledges to obey. Russian spies who penetrated the north found locals generally hesitant to engage in conversation. But they did report that Tajik populations were inclined to try their luck emigrating to the Russian Empire to escape their degradation by the local Pashtun elite. They were only held back by uncertainty about whether tsarist border units would force their return and leave them vulnerable to severe punishment by Afghan authorities. The Russians were equally convinced that the Afghans were responding in kind, sending dozens of spies into neighboring states with the intention of gathering information about how military and civilian administrative affairs were organized there.[45]

In July 1910, to the surprise and embarrassment of tsarist authorities, these "agitators" managed to convince more than a dozen low-ranking local officials to abandon their posts and flee to Afghanistan. The Russians heard they were promised better pay, uniforms, and even wives and were to be offered the opportunity to become Afghan officers. Their success produced mixed reactions, though. Were some of the deserters actually double agents? Their flight surprised all parties involved. And there were more wonders to come. Although the tsarist government employed numerous local officials who were Muslims, these deserters were overwhelmingly non-Muslim. Their subsequent conversion to Islam and swearing of loyalty oaths to the amir on the Quran seems to have deepened anxieties in some quarters on both sides of the border.[46] The amir's envoys also persuaded some of his former subjects to return from the Russian Empire and resettle in Afghanistan, offering them monthly stipends of sixty rupees or more and other benefits. Across the border in Iran, a man named Fazl Khan claimed he had a decree from the Afghan amir inviting the border tribes to settle in Afghanistan, where he would provide them with land and water. Despite this competition over loyalties and bodies on the border, Russian and Afghan authorities exchanged notes agreeing to tackle the opium trade in the Pamir region, which had steadily increased from the first half of the nineteenth century in response to growing Chinese demand.[47]

Thus it was not mobility in and of itself that the new Afghan state sought to combat. Between the 1880s and 1930s, Afghan surveillance was part of an international system tightly linked to wider processes of state building. The British spied on the Afghans, Russians, and Iranians. And each party, in turn, spied on all of the others. At the heart of this system lay an anxiety about people freed from territorialized control. In a variation on an older European state practice, these states imagined themselves to be competing for the loyalties of dissidents across the border. Each of these regimes, to varying degrees, encouraged the flight of exiles who might prove politically useful. Afghan exiles deemed to be of value received pensions in Turkestan as well as in India. Abdur Rahman, too, noted that he had "tried by every possible means to increase the number of the rulers and chiefs of the neighbouring states of Afghanistan about my [his] Court, as well as to gather together there the most influential followers of my [his] rivals, either from India or Russia." He advised his sons to do the same, offering "a home to all men of any importance from neighbouring countries who seek protection in their dominions. Such people will always be of use in supporting them, as well as in opposing their enemies."[48]

Consider the Afghan exile Iskander Khan. The son of the late Sultan Muhammad Khan of Herat, he fled to Russian territory when his father lost the city. Together with his 286 Afghan soldiers, he joined forces with the Russians as they advanced on Samarkand in 1868. For his bravery in service to the tsar, the Russian authorities made Iskander a lieutenant colonel and awarded him a gold medal and the Order of Stanislav. He went on to receive officers' training and studied Russian as well as French. He eventually retired from the tsarist army and sought to return to Afghanistan, but Shir 'Ali refused to permit his return. Iskander later claimed to have spent six years in London and another three in Paris before ending up in the service of the shah of Iran. From Mashhad, he was suspected in 1881 of inciting people in Herat to revolt against Abdur Rahman.[49]

The northeastern Iranian city of Mashhad became the epicenter of intrigue between Russian and British operatives carving out spheres of influence at the expense of a weakening Qajar dynasty. At the turn of the century, the British and Russians competed to act as patrons of Afghan traders there. It was a mark of imperial prestige to receive an application from an Afghan for a British or Russian passport or for legal representation by one of the European consular officials who guarded the extraterritorial legal rights of foreigners on Iranian soil. However, the Iranian government challenged this practice. In the case of a group of moneylenders originally from Herat, for example, the Iranian authorities convinced them to end their association with the British consulate in Mashhad, where they had sought protection. In September 1903, a British intelligence report accused an Iranian official of having "openly thrown in his lot with the Russians" and of "endeavouring to induce Afghan traders to take their cases direct to him, and not to the British Consul-General." For their part, the Iranians accused the British of recruiting Berberis or Hazaras to serve at Quetta for the government of India.

Meanwhile, Afghan attentions were focused on the supposed political machinations of an exile named Abdul Majid, a descendant of the last independent ruler of Herat, who had enjoyed the protection of first the Iranian and then the Russian authorities. Later, Mashhad was at the center of another kind of international controversy: a dissident from Herat, Muhammad Yusuf Khan, who styled himself a "commander of the Herati émigrés," led a movement in Khorasan to restore the Qajar monarch Muhammad 'Ali Shah (r. 1907–1909). He ultimately took refuge in the Imam Reza shrine, an act that led to political crisis and the infamous Russian bombing of the complex in April 1912.[50]

★   ★   ★

In seeking to safeguard the loyalties of his subjects, the Afghan amir was concerned not only with their physical movement but also with the circulation of news and ideas that might weaken his hold on the country. From Kabul, the royal government could exert relatively close control through the passport system over Afghans' access to the world. But it was a different story with communications. Even for those who did not physically range beyond the borders of the country, the world came to them. Commercial flows, molded by shifting trade patterns, were one crucial channel to the global economy. Politics was yet another arena through which Afghans engaged with the international scene, closely following news about events throughout the country and across the globe. A remarkable body of contemporary sources allows us to eavesdrop on conversations among commoners and elites alike in bazaars, teahouses, weddings and other social gatherings, as well as at *darbars,* the public court assemblies held by Afghan rulers.

Take the case of a most perceptive listener in Kandahar. In June 1885, Mir Hashim composed a letter recounting the news of the day. North of the town, communities on the border of the Hazarajat in central Afghanistan were in rebellion and fighting among themselves. In Kandahar itself, a regional trading center of some thirty thousand inhabitants, the governor had recently insulted elders of the Tokhi, a subgroup of the Pashtun Ghilzai tribes at his darbar. A traveler had arrived from Kabul, reporting that the people there were "hard-pressed" and all "hoping to hear of some thing happening somewhere, so that they may also act in opposition." This traveler also reported that he had heard Ghilzai people grumbling about how they would turn on Amir Abdur Rahman and support his rivals if pressed into military service. But the amir's own people, the Durranis, were no more content, Mir Hashim wrote, since "several of them are passing their days in disgrace, and are in want of daily bread; and some of them are in prison or under surveillance at Kabul." He expected that the amir would, in the event of confrontation with a foreign power, "have to defend himself both against the enemy and his own people."

Mir Hashim relayed information about subversion from other parts of Afghanistan as well. From the western town of Herat, people said that the Russians could settle "the Herat question," referring to competition among the Iranians, Russians, and Afghans for control of the town, merely by giving "a hint to their Turkoman subjects." When the Russians had challenged the Afghans at Panjdeh on the Russo-Afghan border earlier in the year, "the shops were shut, and the gates of the town were closed," leaving the "leading men of the day" to conclude that it was only British support that kept the amir in power. At the same time, Mir Hashim observed, the people of Kandahar were "much pleased" to learn of the rumor that the amir might replace their governor, whom "all the people hate," with the late governor of Herat, who was said to have "treated the people there with justice."

Mir Hashim also had seemingly prosaic news to report. "The people say in confidence among themselves," he wrote, "that the Amir has a boil on his foot, others say that some one fired a pistol at him at night and wounded his foot." The letter writer expressed doubt about the veracity of these accounts but pointed out that such talk was nonetheless significant: "rumors like these tend to show that the people are dissatisfied with His Highness's Government." Finally, he recounted rumors circulating in Kandahar about fighting half a world away, in Sudan. According to one version of events, the British had largely ceded authority to the Khedive. Another asserted that this figure regarded himself as a deputy of the Mahdi, the mythical deliverer of the faithful, who had "fought and killed all the British troops that were in Egypt," causing the British to send reinforcements.[51]

Mir Hashim's letter offers a window onto the communication of social knowledge, the circulation of news, and the practice of political surveillance that linked major commercial towns extending from the Indus River north to the Caspian and Aral Seas. His work was, of course, political. He and a handful of men like him were employed by the British government to serve as "newswriters" in towns in the kingdom of Afghanistan. The newswriters were a crucial link between Afghan society and the government of India, though they were not necessarily British subjects. Some were local Kandaharis, Kabulis, and Heratis. Their presence was known to Afghan authorities, and they regularly participated in public darbars and communicated with governors and the amir. At the same time, the newswriters kept up ties to local society, and their family relations also seem to have resided in the town. (One noted an interruption in his work for his son's marriage in a ceremony that the local governor attended.) They mixed relatively freely with town notables and frequented the bazaar to learn of the disposition of the lower orders as well. At moments when political tensions were more pronounced, the governor might increase surveillance of the newswriter or discourage locals from mixing with him or visiting him at his home. Otherwise they conducted much of their work in the open and filled their letters with the contents of conversations held in public. Afghan authorities looked to these newswriters to convey information to British officials. They relayed official statements communicated at the darbars to which they often received special invitations. Their newsletters reproduced the contents (and sometimes exact copies) of letters distributed among Afghan officials throughout the country.

Newswriters found ample material for their weekly letters. Foreign news, disease, rebellion, the coming and going of caravans and travelers, the fate of the seasonal harvest, the price of commodities, the movement of troops, the actions of provincial governors, and the latest actions of the amir and the intrigues of his supporters and rivals kept them busy. Only rarely did they have to report that "nothing of interest has happened." Newswriters sent their messages across the border to officials in Baluchistan who, in turn, passed on the reports, often in summary form, to superiors in the Foreign Office. Naturally this was knowledge intended to sustain British imperial hegemony. But the newsletters differ from European ethnographic descriptions and travelers' accounts in that they did not explicitly seek to legitimate colonial rule. Expressions of what might be identified as political opinion or policy recommendations were extremely infrequent, except for the occasional mention of suspicious figures passing into British territory who might merit surveillance upon arrival. At times they may have exaggerated opposition to Abdur Rahman, for example, as at least one British official who received the Kandahar newsletter suggested. Yet we know from numerous other sources, including those describing the dozens of rebellions that marked his reign, that resistance to the brutal rule of the "iron amir" was indeed widespread. Much of the content of the newsletters can be corroborated with reference to different kinds of materials, including the songs and poetry reliably documenting historical events that Afghans memorized and circulated (and which, in turn, can be compared to European accounts).[52] Newswriters sitting in Kandahar or Herat—or traveling with the amir and reporting from Mazar-i Sharif—recorded with extraordinary accuracy events taking place in other parts of the country and the region. Much of this reportage started out as "rumor" whose veracity the newswriters rarely took for granted. Some stories overheard in the bazaar or picked up from a merchant traveling from Russia or India were clearly worth conveying, because—as in the case of the amir's suspected boil—they

captured popular political sentiment, while others might be flagged
because they were believed only by the lower classes or because they
struck the newswriter as improbable. The newswriters thus passed
on "news" and "rumor" as useful intelligence.

British newswriters formed a critical part of what C. A. Bayly
has called an "information order." For the towns lying between the
Caspian and the Indus, this order was shaped by the circulation of
knowledge by diverse social actors and an emergent apparatus of state
surveillance directed by the courts of St. Petersburg, London, Tehran,
Kabul, Bukhara, and their local deputies.[53] Figures such as Mir
Hashim were hardly alone, then. Merchants, pilgrims, fugitives, exiles, refugees, and other travelers had long spread word of recent developments from town to town. Warfare and insecurity along the
major thoroughfares periodically disrupted this traffic in the eighteenth and nineteenth centuries. With Russian and British territorial and commercial expansion, however, the volume of trade
increased again, flowing through and connecting Bukhara, Balkh,
Mashhad, Herat, Kandahar, Kabul, Peshawar, Multan, and Shikarpur.
Townspeople passed on news that would be useful for travelers about
the security of roads, epidemics, and prices. Or they might corre-
spond about business arrangements. Oral communication predomi-
nated, but official and private letter writing was also common among
the many literate townspeople.

Throughout the region governments had their own postal system
of couriers and special envoys to deliver communications. They also
employed newswriters and spies. Abdur Rahman had his own network of such informants, according to one report, "in Peshawar,
Rawalpindi, Lahore, Karachi, and other places."[54] He also appointed
secret newswriters to towns within the kingdom to monitor his administration and the local populace. Intelligence gathering was not
a British monopoly.

Afghan agents pursued the many elites that the amir had dispersed beyond his borders. In September 1889, Sayyid Diwan Muhammad, the British newswriter at Kabul reported:

> An Afghan, who went to Kashmir during Amir Sher Ali's reign as a shawl-merchant, will shortly go there again in order to find out the condition in which the Maharaja and the Rajas of Jammu, as well as Sardar Muhammad Ayub Khan are, and the visits paid to Kashmir by, and the movements of, the Kabuli fugitives, and their intercourse with the Kashmir merchants. He will possibly go to Turkistan via Gilgit. . . . All letters which pass through the Kabul Post Office are now opened, read and then despatched.[55]

The amir's own newswriters informed on corrupt officials, including Islamic authorities who "were in the habit of taking bribes and of deciding cases contrary to the Muhammadan law."[56] In addition to these agents, the amir's government solicited denunciations, and, in at least one case recounted by a newswriter, a group of Kandaharis attempted to frame an opponent by sending seditious letters in his name.[57]

The amir practiced surveillance but also circulated and indeed dramatized news. His government distributed accounts of his constant military campaigns to vanquish challengers and to consolidate control over territory he claimed for Afghanistan. Broadsheets appeared in town centers. Announcements were celebrated at darbars. Prayer ceremonies marked holidays and victories in battle. The amir used the British newswriter to pass on to the government of India descriptions of military victories at Balkh and Tashkurgan in 1888.[58] While the amir was on campaign or in Kabul, townspeople throughout his kingdom were meant to share in his victories. He ordered the towns to be illuminated for several days to commemorate major events like the defeat of his enemies and the birth of his sons.[59] In Kandahar, the British newswriter reported that "the city was gay with decorations for three successive days, and for three nights illuminations were kept up. The Governor and other officials elaborately decorated their residences, and each made displays suited to their rank and dignity. As my house is situated in the centre of the bazaar, I felt myself constrained to do something toward the general illumination."[60] Upon learning of the amir's military victories in Afghan Turkestan, the governor and military commander (Sipah Salar) of Herat fired one hundred guns in salute and had the city "illuminated for three nights." Commanders such as Naib Salar Ghulam Haidar Khan marked his entry into Mazar-i Sharif in October 1888 with a salute of sixty-one guns in honor of the Shah-i Mardan Shrine. The governor and commander of Herat also organized a darbar in the Chaharbagh, which was "crowded with people throughout the whole day." The maliks and chiefs brought cows as an offering to the authorities, and the Sipah Salar arranged a fireworks display and a parade of troops carrying lanterns. Both the governor and the commander viewed the illuminations after entertaining the officers of the garrison with the aim, the Herat newswriter concluded, "to show that they take an interest in the doings of the inhabitants, and thereby to conciliate them."[61]

Despite such efforts, the British newswriters recorded dissent. When news arrived in Kandahar with a group of travelers, they learned that one of the amir's foes, Muhammad Ishaq Khan, was "still in Turkistan and has not as yet been utterly and entirely defeated." "The people of Kandahar are inclined to treat the statements contained in this [the amir's] proclamation somewhat sceptically," the newswriter reported. "In truth, they think that the main object of the proclamation is to delude the people of Afghanistan as to the real state of affairs, and that the Governor of Kandahar was actuated by the same motive when he ordered the illumination of the city to be carried out. Moreover, it is rumoured in Kandahar that the Russians have supplied Muhammad Ishak Khan with ten thousand breechloading rifles and are covertly assisting the rebellious Sardar to the full extent of their power." As evidence for these claims, talk at the bazaar countered that "His Highness would undoubtedly have ordered illumination in Kabul as well as in other cities of Afghanistan, and that the force under Sipah Salar Ghulam Haidar Khan, Charkhi, would not have been recalled to Kabul without having completed the coercion of the Shinwari tribe."[62] Another newsletter noted that "the people of Kandahar have in no way welcomed the news of His Highness the Amir's recent successes. They imagine that His Highness will now restrain himself within no bounds and are hopeless of mild or even considerate treatment at his hands."[63] In this and other cases, the newswriters asserted that "the people of Kandahar form their own opinions in these matters."[64]

In addition to the evidence provided by newswriters, travelers' accounts registered surprise at the extent to which Afghans were connected to happenings in places far away. In 1893, the British lieutenant colonel C. E. Yate visited Kandahar, where he was struck by "the curious ignorance of all the Afghan officials" about British rule and the "ways and customs across the frontier." Yate pointed out, however, that it was only the official class that was "tied down in this respect." He contrasted their outlook with that of the "lower classes, fruitsellers and traders generally, [who] visit India in large numbers every year, and some even extend their travels beyond it." He recalled meeting a man in Baluchistan who "accosted" him "in English in the airy manner of a colonial workman" and another who had traveled to Australia to trade camels—and had returned with an Australian wife and her two daughters.[65] On the Russo-Afghan border in northwest Afghanistan, Yate found Afghans who had been in the Punjab, Quetta, and elsewhere working on the railway and roads or serving in the army. "All the intercourse of Afghans and all their interests seem to lie with India," Yate concluded. This constant traffic, he argued, "tends to turn the minds of the Afghan people to India." The Russian border seemed quiet by contrast. With the exception of some Afghans who may have gone to work on the Murghab Railway, he judged that there was "comparatively little trade, no enlistment, and little work."[66]

Yate likely underestimated the traffic on the Russo-Afghan frontier, but it was impossible to miss the role that Russia played when talk turned to war. Turkmen migrants and merchants who circulated between Herat and Mashhad brought reports of troop movements and political and economic activity in the Transcaspian region. Rumors of the arrival of a new group of spies spread from Badakhshan to Kandahar and Herat. News of dodgy travelers, blue-eyed or suspiciously dark-skinned (meaning a tsarist Muslim subject), fed anxieties about yet another effort on the part of the Russians to seize the north. Meanwhile, merchants bringing goods to Kandahar followed the advance of the British toward the nearby frontier. Townspeople constantly guessed at what particular official announcements meant about prospects for war with one of their more powerful neighbors. War talk frequently discouraged trade or inflated grain prices. The "Great Game" between Russia and Britain had numerous effects on everyday life.[67]

In 1893 Yate heard Afghan informants speak of an imminent battle between the British and Russians on the Dasht-i Bakwa between Kandahar and Herat. Yate had first heard this story in 1886 in Afghan Turkestan and then elsewhere. He noted that this "prophecy" invariably concluded with the image of "12,000 riderless horses [who] would be found wandering over the plain" at the conclusion of this fierce battle. Yate claimed to have found the "author" of this tale at Mashhad. Through a local informant, who was speaking to a cleric from Herat, he learned that a man named Shah Neamatollah had been responsible: "a native of Kuchan, who travelled a good deal in Iran, Turan, and Arabia, lived in Yezd for a time, then went to Shiraz where he was the friend of Hafiz, and afterwards to Herat at the invitation of Shah Rukh Mirza" in the early fifteenth century.[68] In 1903, rumors of conflict between the Russians and Afghans along the Herat frontier continued to punctuate conversations in Mashhad. Reports reached British authorities from Herat, Merv, and Karej that there was "considerable excitement" about a Russo-Afghan confrontation. Prices rose for "supplies of all sorts," and villages stopped paying taxes.[69] Even rumors of war between a more distant power, the Ottomans, and the neighboring Qajars in 1889 had consequences for the towns along these networks of commerce and pilgrimage. "Some Heratis," the British newswriter observed, "who intended to proceed to Karbala and Najaf via Persia, have now, owing to the Shah's prohibition [on pilgrimages to these sites], changed their mind and intend to go via Kandahar and Karachi, and thence by sea to Arabia."[70]

To Abdur Rahman, the circulation of such talk was how conspiracies against his fragile legitimacy spread. Neighboring states were also interested in acquiring knowledge about affairs within the country that might affect their commercial or security interests. Besides Quetta, Mashhad was a primary nodal point for British operations, while the Russians sent agents from Tashkent, Samarkand, Bukhara, and from the early twentieth century, Bombay. Afghan officials, in turn, vigilantly policed their towns. They placed sentries at the gates and on the roads entering each town and punished guards who let unauthorized travelers pass. Locals turned in suspicious people who spoke English or who "looked Russian." The amir gave orders against talking and rumormongering. Gossips had their mouths sewn shut.

Russian authorities, too, suspected that the Afghan spy network had succeeded in corrupting the minds of their Muslim subjects in Turkestan and the tsarist protectorate of Bukhara. The tsarist police imagined that Afghanistan was, alongside the Ottoman Empire, at the vanguard of a global Pan-Islamic movement. A Russian police report of 1910 warned that the Afghans were making more headway than the Turks in Bukhara. Sharing close religious, linguistic, and commercial ties with their Bukharan neighbors, Afghan agents took advantage of a poorly secured border to infiltrate the emirate. They smuggled arms, including revolvers, to Bukharan towns and villages. The Russian police identified Old Bukhara as the link between Bukhara and Kabul and a band of men from the Afghan capital— Ahmed Jan, Sayyid Muhammad Khan, and Mamed Kerim Khan— as the chief Afghan agents. They also singled out Muhammad Ghauss Khan, an Afghan subject who had settled in Old Bukhara as a merchant and commercial agent and who, the police claimed, carried on "far-reaching political and military espionage." They suspected that the amir's brother Nasrullah Khan oversaw the spy network and had arranged for a delegation of Bukharan clerics to visit Kabul and then to receive hundreds of young Afghans in Bukhara. The local Russian police also claimed to have intercepted a petition from fifty-six notable Bukharans addressed to Kabul and Istanbul complaining about conditions for Muslims in Bukhara and Turkestan and agitating for Afghan backing of the overthrow of the Russian-supported emir of Bukhara.

Other sources confirm cross-border links between Afghans and Bukharans. In February 1912, a party of pilgrims visited the shrine of Hazrat-i Karkh in Herat. However, in this instance, too, Afghan authorities were exceedingly cautious. They were wary of lending weight to Russian fears of provocation or of permitting unfettered contact between Afghans and foreign subjects. An escort provided by the governor of Herat limited the movement of the pilgrims to the shrine itself.[71]

In seeking to manage this flow of people, commodities, news, and ideas across its newly demarcated borders and in asserting protections for subjects in the diaspora, the Afghan state asserted its authority as a full-fledged member of an international community of nations. And, as the story of the Afghans in Bukhara reveals, the diaspora presented more than an opportunity to demonstrate Afghan sovereignty. Afghans abroad were simultaneously potential resources through which the monarchy could project its power into neighboring states, to discipline exiles and political opponents and to probe the vulnerabilities of its more powerful neighbors. Foreign dissidents who sought refuge in the kingdom could prove useful as well. Thus the Afghan approach in the early twentieth century was not exclusively about defensive isolation. Particularly after 1919, the elites of newly independent Afghanistan imagined a far more expansive role for themselves in the world.

4 | THE STAR OF ASIA

As one of the few remaining Muslim powers that survived in the early twentieth century, an era when European colonial powers were aggressively carving up the globe, Afghanistan lay at the center of various schemes to transform Asia and the Muslim world. Afghan state elites faced intense pressure from a host of actors domestic and foreign who wanted Afghanistan to assume an ambitious leadership role. More than a refuge for exiles, revolutionaries, deserters, and adventurers from neighboring countries, the kingdom became a beacon for diverse actors seeking to unleash the revolutionary potential of Muslims, alongside other Asians, to challenge the global British Empire. In these utopian scenarios, change would begin within Afghanistan and then radiate throughout the world.

If Afghan elites were fearful of unregulated contact with neighboring populations, more distant lands were another matter. Under Habibullah (r. 1901–1919), the government made discussions of the fate of the Ottoman Empire a vehicle for demonstrating its fidelity to the Muslim cause globally. Afghan defense of the Ottomans was a testament to the Pan-Islamic credentials of the state and a means to consolidate public support for the ideology of the monarchy.

On the pages of the *Lamp of the News* (*Sirāj al-akhbār*), its publisher, the former exile Mahmud Tarzi, and his allies at Habibullah's court infused Afghan patriotism with calls for Islamic solidarity. The Italian invasion of Ottoman Libya in 1911 rallied public sentiment in Afghan towns. The public responded to official calls for donations to relieve the suffering of the people of Tripoli. From Herat and Kandahar, Hindus and Muslims alike gave money intended for Libyan orphans and widows. In January 1912, some two thousand people attended a gathering where the governor of Kandahar called for donations, and "great excitement prevailed." Despite Afghan officials' attempts to discourage Afghans from joining the fray, some Afghans who were already abroad when the war broke out tried to do more. At Jaffa in Palestine, British authorities noticed that roughly one hundred Afghans had turned up at a local Ottoman barracks and wanted to volunteer to fight in the war. "It is, of course, impossible to foresee absolutely what may happen in a place like Jaffa, where," the British official remarked, "in addition to the usual disorderly and turbulent element to be found in a sea-port, there are also a number of doubtful characters, Algerians, Afghans, and the like, employed as watchmen in the orange-gardens, and where the non-Moslem population, which includes many Jews, is nervous and timid." Closer to home, the amir contributed to the cause of Islamic solidarity by cultivating mullahs along the Indo-Afghan frontier who were not Afghan subjects in the eyes of the government of India but who nonetheless traveled to Kabul to receive cash allowances.[1]

Growing exposure to global political currents proved to be a double-edged sword for the monarchy. Through the Persian-language press and contact with cosmopolitan urban centers in India, Iran, Russia, and the Ottoman Empire, Afghans gained exposure to movements demanding that the people gain a political voice and limit the authority of autocrats everywhere. Aristocrats and courtiers, among them a number of Indian expatriates clustered around Dr. Abdul Ghani, founder of the first secular high school, Habibia College, established in 1903 in Kabul, were drawn to the new thinking about constitutions, parliaments, and civil rights.[2]

In 1905, with news of Russia's military defeat at the hands of a rising Asian power in the Russo-Japanese war and with revolutions under way in Russia and Iran, Afghans formed a group called

"Constitution" (*Mashruta*) and began to agitate for a new political order. One of the leaders, Mir Said Qasim Laghmani, developed a program calling for a constitutional monarchy and a parliament *(majles)*. Demanding the spread of "contemporary civilization," Laghmani envisioned a state that would cultivate the development of culture and science. It would educate the people, respect their rights, and gain their independence as a nation. After the amir's agents discovered their conspiratorial plans in 1909, they suffered repression. But a younger wave of critics offered a broader challenge to the monarchy: teachers and students at the Habibia and a military school founded in 1909 and led by Turkish officers, the Harbiya, many of whom drew inspiration from the Young Turk movement in the Ottoman Empire, added to the movement.[3]

These "Young Afghans" pushed Habibullah to lead Muslim activists across the globe and to unite them under the banner of Islam in a common struggle against European domination. The publisher and writer Mahmud Tarzi was a direct link to the Ottoman intellectual world, having learned Turkish (so well that Turks supposedly took him for a native of Anatolia) as well as Arabic and some French during his exile. In his eighteen years in Damascus and in short trips to Istanbul and Egypt, he saw firsthand the massive transformations sweeping through the Ottoman Empire. He married the daughter of a local shaykh, read French novels (in Turkish) and other translated works, and purchased a phonograph in the local bazaar. One of his first articles explored the changes under way in Japan, a source of intense fascination for Turkish and Egyptian reformers who admired the Japanese state's introduction of mass schooling, industrialization, and law codes from abroad. In 1896, he met the Pan-Islamic activist Sayyid Jamal ad-Din Afghani (1838/39–1897) and in the following year read the American scientist and philosopher John William Draper's *History of the Conflict between Religion and Science* (1875).[4] When

Habibullah allowed him to return to Afghanistan, Tarzi wielded the pen in the service of enlightening his countrymen. It was, he declared "an age of progress" and an "era of renewal and modernity" in which "love of the homeland (*vatan*) is the foundation of faith and religion." What patriotic Afghans needed was the proper view of Islam, which encouraged science, industry, exploration and the development of the material world.[5]

In 1912, Tarzi sketched out a vision for restoring the Afghan nation to greatness in an essay entitled "What Is to Be Done?" Tarzi lamented that in the nineteenth century "Baluchistan, Shalkut, the Diras, Peshawar, and other territories were lost." He blamed not only "the practice of marrying a multitude of wives" but also the Afghans' lack of knowledge about "news from the outside world" and "lack of education." These flaws had come to the fore during the Second Anglo-Afghan War (1878–1880), when "treacherous people, because of ignorance, lack of education, and ignorance of patriotism and religiosity, sold out their faith in religion for the vile carcass of worldly gains and committed all sorts of contemptible indecencies." Under Abdur Rahman (r. 1880–1901), however, the country had reemerged as "a mighty and powerful state, with all the aptitude and potential to establish and build a great Islamic state in Asia." And under Abdur Rahman's son Habibullah, Tarzi likened his kingdom to "the beam of the scale of justice and equality in Asia." Tarzi called on Afghans to return to their neglected Quran and, with its teachings, to apply science and knowledge in this world: "If we dominate our mountains, mines, oceans, and rivers, we have done nothing more than obey the commands of our Quran." This was a challenge, he emphasized, that lay not just before Afghans but before all Muslims.[6]

Tarzi and his allies identified Afghanistan's subordination to British colonialism as another source of the Afghans' "backwardness." Colonialism stood in the way of the "progress" of the nation, which

was to be liberated by asserting its independence and by adopting reforms that would effect a systematic restructuring of the polity: a
constitution would limit the authority of the monarch, a cabinet and
national council would express the views of the enlightened, and
education and culture would spread throughout the land. They ran
afoul of the royal court on occasion, but the boundaries that separated Habibullah and his closest associates from aristocratic, tribal,
military, and religious elites were porous, and the new debates tended
to connect these various circles. Indeed, Habibullah's son and heir,
Prince Amanullah, would embrace much of Tarzi's program, and figures such as Dr. Ghani would be released from prison and head his
Ministry of Education. In the meantime, the reformers' voice was
amplified by the founding in 1911 of two printing presses in the capital, which published the writings of Tarzi, translations by Tarzi and
others, and a great variety of literature, religious and secular, including
textbooks for the new schools. The *Lamp of the News* served not only
as a mouthpiece for reformers but also a forum for debate between
them and their more conservative rivals clustered around the amir's
brother Nasrullah Khan, who rejected most of their calls for change,
although they sympathized with the Young Afghans' Pan-Islamic
aspirations.

Sharing some elements of Tarzi's vision and opposing others,
Habibullah was a paradoxical cosmopolitan. On the one hand, many
European diplomats eyed him warily as the fulcrum of a Pan-Islamic
movement with global pretensions. On the other, observers praised
him for touring India in 1907 and for taking an interest in modern
technology such as cameras and phonographs. They marveled, too,
at his mania for golf, which he took up in 1912, when he sought out
a British coach to refine his game. The author of a *Popular Mechanics*
article from 1914 was amazed that the ruler of the "hermit kingdom"
had fifty-eight motor cars, which he purchased for import into his

"forbidden land" from foreign catalogs; in addition to these automobiles in his royal garage, he also maintained four carriages sent as gifts from Queen Victoria and a herd of some fifty elephants.[7]

The amir's curiosity set in motion a series of transformations that would spread beyond the royal court. Road construction mobilized workers, and to sustain his automotive passion, the amir sent dozens of students to learn to drive and repair his fleet of automobiles at the Bombay Motor Works.[8] Among Afghans, wonder, gossip, admiration, and consternation were not limited to the court. European observers tended to underscore any sign of hostility against such "Western" pursuits.

However, insisting upon strict typologies separating "Islamic" and "European" or "East" and "West" obscures a more complicated past. Afghans had, of course, long appropriated multiple cultural repertoires and technologies. Golf, polo, cricket, the camera, and the motor car were only the latest. Grumbling about the amir's hobbies is difficult to interpret. Among the placards that occasionally appeared overnight on the walls of Kabul mosques, one posted to the central mosque in January 1912 described how the amir spent his time "shooting, cooking, driving" and so on.[9] Did this critic fault Habibullah for engaging in frivolous conduct unbecoming an Afghan monarch or for being distracted from adopting domestic and foreign policies more befitting a dynamic "modern" statesman confronting a perilous geopolitical environment?

New educational institutions and methods were another feature of this emergent modernist landscape. For Mahmud Tarzi, a key step toward realizing his vision was the establishment of a school system that would share the fruits of science with young children. Another imperative was a conscript army. Tarzi argued that those who neglected the duty to protect the nation and "its statehood" would "surely be punished in this world and the next." Beyond the Habibia and Harbiya colleges, science, arithmetic, and other secular topics were introduced into several Islamic schools in the capital. Mirroring developments in schools across the world, the schools reflected some of the latest pedagogies of progress and nationhood. Initially focusing on the sons of the elite, in 1921 the state opened the first schools for girls.[10]

The Ministry of Education oversaw the production of textbooks designed to inculcate new sensibilities for an era attuned to the future. Islam was no less essential for the modernist age. Its core precepts, as distilled by scholars employed by the state, were pillars of patriotism and loyalty. Betraying the new pedagogy and perhaps reflecting the influence of Christian missionary texts printed at Peshawar and other towns in India, one such text on Islam followed the question-and-answer format of a Christian catechism. It posed questions such as "Who is a Muslim?" and "Who is God?" and "Can God be seen or not?" A third-grade text related the history of the prophets from Adam to Muhammad. Through print, the children of the elite were to enter a universe of geometry, botany, and chemistry. Students were introduced to the geography of Afghanistan and its place on the globe, learning, as one illustrated text demonstrated, how to orient one's body to the north, south, east, and west. The formal rules of the Persian language were a priority, though the official curriculum also included the study of Arabic grammar and, to a lesser extent, Pashto. Afghan children gained exposure to a universal language of enlightenment and reason, doing so at a moment when the politics of schooling everywhere were stamped by the imperative to cultivate a sense of national belonging.

Yet a "modern" curriculum did not simply look forward. History told the story of the nation, folding its readers into its collective past and future. Combining all of these disciplines, the new schools taught students what it meant to be Afghan.[11] For Afghans in the diaspora, too, print media, letters, and less formal, oral networks of communication maintained connections to these intellectual developments. A letter to Tarzi's newspaper from Afghans in Australia provided assurances that the community there was charting a similar path of progressive piety, even if they were far from Afghan soil.[12]

While Afghan elites were preoccupied with the pursuit of the modern, the European powers continued to think about the Afghans as primitive but formidable warriors. And, as war clouds gathered in Europe, the Germans and Russians looked to Kabul as a weapon against the British Empire. In 1903 Kaiser Wilhelm II had written to Nicholas II, singling out the Indo-Afghan frontier as "the only place on the planet" where the cannons of the British fleet could not reach. In the same year, an anonymous letter that came across the desk of the Russian consul in Bombay promised the Russians a warm reception throughout India, urging them to focus on the Afghans (meaning Pashtuns here), who "hate the English and respect the Russians." The Pashtuns would act as the tip of the Russian spear, destabilizing the vast tribal zone between the Hindu Kush and the Indus River and sparking a wider revolt throughout India of Muslims, who looked to Russia as their liberator. "I'll prove myself, when the Russians arrive," the letter quoted a native Muslim officer boasting, "I'll stand at the head of two hundred thousand men. The English treat us badly, and we await the arrival of Russia."[13]

When the war erupted in August 1914, the German General Staff was confident that Habibullah would unleash revolution by invading India. But the amir announced that Afghanistan would remain neutral. Nonetheless, the Ottoman sultan declared jihad and joined the war in October, a move that sparked enthusiasm among a number of Afghan notables who were keen to back the Ottoman cause.

In 1915, the Germans dispatched a mission to Afghanistan to convince the amir in person to join the war on their side. The mission was a motley collection of critics of British rule. Besides Germans and Turks, it included two Afghans from the United States. Its leader was Mahendra Pratap, who hailed from a princely Indian family, and who was an itinerant anticolonial activist who had been crisscrossing the globe seeking support for a resistance movement to liberate India. He was joined by Muhammad Barakatullah, who had also been active in anticolonial circles, meeting with members of the Indian and Irish diaspora in the United States and traveling to Japan to promote his subversive ideas.

He was only the latest of a series of Muslims who had looked to Afghan rulers to lead the holy struggle against the British. The Pan-Islamic agitator Sayyid Jamal ad-Din Afghani had traveled from Iran to Afghanistan in 1866 and became an adviser first to the Afghan leaders Azam Khan and then to Shir 'Ali, pressing them both to adopt a more hostile line with the British and possibly to look to Russia as an ally. During the Second Anglo-Afghan War, he published an Arabic-language *History of Afghanistan* in Cairo in which he presented Afghan resistance to the British as a model for Muslim rulers everywhere. In the 1880s, Afghani advocated an anti-British coalition made up of Russia, France, the Ottoman Empire, and Afghanistan. In a new variation on this scheme, on the eve of the war Muhammad Barakatullah had touted the promise of a German-Afghan alliance to liberate India. "All that is required," he argued, "is a leader, and that leader will arise in Central Asia, probably in Afghanistan. The firing of an Afghan gun will give the signal for the rising of all Islam as soon as she is ready and willing to open her gates for believers to fight under the green banner of the prophet, or under her own."[14]

These foreign agitators urged Habibullah to invade India. In exchange, Mahendra Pratap promised him a "Great Afghanistan," with borders extending to Bukhara in the north and Baluchistan and part of India to the south. The amir rebuffed the overture, despite pressure from some circles at court who were eager to take up the fight. To make sure the visitors did not cause more trouble, he had them put under house arrest.[15]

Despite the failure of this plan to have the Afghans join the German-led "jihad," Afghanistan became a magnet during the war for Asians seeking to challenge the global British empire, turning Kabul into a hotbed of anti-British agitation. This assortment of characters seeking the amir's attention included, in addition to the Turko-German mission, Indian émigrés and Muslim activists, among them members of the Ghadr Party, which was founded by Indian immigrant mill workers in the U.S. state of Oregon and which waged from its headquarters in San Francisco a global campaign calling for the end of British rule in India. Herat, too, became for a time the focus of Ottoman and other activists who circulated anti-Russian propaganda. Unrest in the North-West Frontier of India also spilled into Afghanistan. Dissidents from the area, including a group that the British castigated as the "Hindustani Fanatics" as well as students who left colleges in India were determined to enter Afghanistan and then travel on to the Ottoman Empire to join the war.

In August 1916, British authorities apprehended a courier in Multan carrying yellow silk handkerchiefs bearing secret messages in Urdu. Dubbing the discovery "the Silk letters conspiracy," the government of India concluded that the plot originated with these renegades in Kabul, "with tentacles in India and Hedjaz, which though fantastic in detail might if unchecked have serious developments." One official saw it as an effort to mobilize "the only living bodies among the dry bones of militant Islam in India" and draw on "the practical machinery of the Wahabi movement, the Islamic fervour of the Maulvi class and the political enegy and bitterness of the pan-Islamists."[16]

In 1916, Indian nationalists approached the Russians for support. Admitting that they had initially placed their hopes with the Germans and the Turks, they looked now to Russia, especially since Afghanistan seemed poised to join the Indians in their liberation. In fact, these activists had declared themselves subjects of Afghanistan and had been supplied with Afghan passports.[17] Muhammad Barakatullah appealed to the tsarist government during the war as head of an expatriate "Provisional Government of India" established in Kabul in 1915; and after the Bolsheviks took power in Petrograd in November 1917, many of these activists in Kabul drew inspiration from the Bolsheviks' anticolonial ideology.

In April 1919 Muhammad Barakatullah wrote to Vladimir Lenin, the head of the Bolshevik party and recently established Soviet state, proposing an alliance against "the common enemy of Bolshevism and Islam—England." Requesting money and arms, Barakatullah also sought printing presses (with English and Persian type) and paper for pamphlets of a "religious and political character" that would win the Pashtuns over. He had already worked out this vision in 1913 in an article published in Tokyo that he forwarded to Moscow along with his requests. Lauding the martial qualities of the Pashtuns, he argued that they had enough "strength and bravery . . . to conquer the world. . . . Just as the Prophet sent preachers to the Arab tribes, so should we send preachers to all the border tribes." For the Soviet commissar of war Leon Trotsky, this was enough to convince him, in the context of 1919, that "the path to Paris and London lies through the towns of Afghanistan, Punjab, and Bengal." For his part, Nikolai Bravin, the first Soviet diplomat in Kabul, sought a million gold rubles, machine guns, and airplanes—as well as the opening of consulates in Jalalabad, Kandahar, Ghazni, and Kaniguram—to incite a massive anti-British rebellion among the tribes.[18]

Following Habibullah's assassination in February 1919 at the hands of nationalist opponents at court, his son Amanullah took the throne and in April proclaimed Afghanistan's independence from Britain. The amir backed up his claim by launching a brief war, fought between May and June. The Afghan victory was a triumph for the more aggressive nationalist and reformist circles who had been somewhat marginalized under Habibullah. The amir appointed Mahmud Tarzi to the post of foreign minister. All of this was a signal to Muslims in surrounding lands that a new leader, one who might even become caliph, had arrived on the stage to take up the defense of Islam.

This posture resonated first in India. At the end of the First World War, Muslim activists and nationalists had anxiously followed the fate of the defeated Ottoman Empire. Their criticism of the British treatment of the Ottomans gained force from Muslim clerics who had begun to revisit Islamic legal arguments to the effect that Muslims should depart India because it was under infidel rule. They launched a movement to migrate—on the model of the Prophet Muhammad—from India to Afghanistan. There they eventually hoped to assemble forces to retake India and expel the British.

Working from a hub in Peshawar, Indian Muslim activists orchestrated a mass migration in 1920, despite their inability to gain significant clerical support. The government of Amanullah initially encouraged this anticolonial gesture as a boost to his legitimacy and a rebuke to the British. By the end of the year, some sixty thousand immigrants had entered Afghanistan. There they exceeded the Afghan government's capacity to deal with them. Hungry and desperate, most returned or traveled on to Russia or Turkey.[19]

Still, the Afghans continued to provoke deep anxieties among British officials, who feared that, beyond the bonds of solidarity that might link communities across the Indo-Afghan frontier, the Afghan diaspora might form a vast network of espionage and intrigue. Indeed, they had reason to fear the sophisticated means the Afghan government had for gathering and circulating intelligence. The British suspected, in particular, that the Afghan "postmaster" office in Peshawar was at the heart of Afghan espionage in India. In the 1920s, places like Abbottabad were home to several important Afghan political refugees, which both Afghan and British authorities watched with care.[20]

Meanwhile, to the east, Amanullah attracted the attention of Muslims in China as well. Afghans had long interacted with Chinese merchants at Kashgar and Yarkand. Before 1922, Afghans in China enjoyed the status of protected British subjects. They had access to special courts and protection, even when British consular authorities suspected them of being gunrunners and opium smugglers. However, in the 1920s the Afghan state sought to expand its influence there.

In 1922, a mission led by an Afghan general sought the appointment of a consul and Chinese recognition of extraterritorial rights for Afghans. The Afghans requested permission to import opium into Xinjiang, a practice that was at least a century old, but which the Chinese had banned in 1912. The British representative at Kashgar filed an anxious report about the Afghan visitors:

> The reception given by the Mussalman population to the General, who is a devout and highly respected member of the Muhammadzai family, was most striking. Such was the press of the people in the streets prostrating themselves before him and trying to kiss his hand, that he had to walk through the

bazars to his residence. Great crowds flock to the Jama Masjid [mosque] whenever he goes there. These popular demonstrations are reported to be most distasteful to the Chinese, who are said to have instructed their Begs to prevent the people going in great numbers to the Jama Masjid. The General is stated to have remonstrated with Mr. Chu on this account.

Although the Chinese rebuffed these requests, the head of the Afghan mission offered protection to local Muslims who had petitioned Amanullah about their mistreatment at the hands of the Chinese.[21]

In the north, the Bolshevik takeover in the towns of tsarist Turkestan sent refugees across the border into Afghanistan, Persia, and China. The insurgent groups who challenged Soviet power, known collectively by their opponents as the "Basmachi," used Afghan territory as a safe haven and launched cross-border raids well into the 1920s. As before 1917, nomadic communities continued to follow their pastures and herds across the Afghan-Persian-Russian frontiers east of the Caspian. Some followed the ecological cycles of the grasslands, others fled state authorities who sought to expropriate their flocks or disarm them.

The new Soviet rulers initially saw themselves as the liberators of India's suffering masses—and looked hopefully to the tribal areas of the Indo-Afghan frontier for the spark that might fuel a wider colonial revolt. Moscow rushed to recognize Afghan independence in 1919. But when uprisings failed to materialize along the frontier despite the work of Soviet agitators, Moscow cooled toward Amanullah. In the early 1920s, Soviet authorities found themselves in a tense relationship with the Afghan state. In December 1924 the Soviet foreign ministry representative in Central Asia reported to Moscow that a text recovered from Herat revealed an Afghan plan to attract inhabitants of neighboring states to migrate to Afghanistan. This *Law on*

Emigrants was said to promise land and exemption from military service and taxation. There was steady traffic across the Amu and Panj Rivers, a Soviet official charged, by small boats now in the hands of Afghans, who used them to move people and property from Bukhara to Afghanistan, forming the backbone of a lively smuggling operation.[22]

As under tsarist rule, though, migrants moved in both directions. In 1925, for instance, some eight thousand men, women, and children crossed the Amu River from Afghanistan into Badakhshan in Tajikistan. Spokesmen for the group asked to be recognized as "full-fledged citizens of the [Soviet] Union." They explained that they had led a rebellion against the representatives of the Afghan state, who had stolen their land and had forced them into military service. Soviet authorities were not certain what to do. Who had provoked this uprising? Searching for conspiratorial motives, they focused on the British—and then on the Aga Khan, the spiritual head of the Ismaili Shia worldwide, and thus the leader of this group of Ismaili migrants.

When Soviet officials investigated more thoroughly, they discovered correspondence between these rebels and local communist officials in Khorog in Soviet Badakhshan. Many of the participants in this conspiracy, which included local Tajik communists and Afghan subjects, the Soviets concluded, had been relatives. The event remained murky. Yet it seems clear that the Tajik communists provoked the uprising, promising Soviet support. Thus in this case, Soviet power and kinship ties cut across the border in the same direction, promising to lay the foundation for a wider solidarity. In the end, this unauthorized bid failed, and higher-ranking Soviet authorities took care to patch things up with their colleagues on the Afghan side. A degree of order was restored on the border. Underground traffic nonetheless continued in secret, and the subject of cross-border ties remained a focus in Soviet police work in the region, which included surveillance of the Afghan and Iranian diasporas there.[23]

The migration of these Afghans pointed to some of the limits of Amanullah's Pan-Islamic appeal among his own subjects. A rebellion in Khost in 1924, led in part by an exile who recently returned from India, was yet another challenge to Amanullah's reform program, which consisted chiefly of an expansive legislative agenda that promulgated a constitution and introduced family reforms that discouraged polygamy and banned child marriages. Declaring jihad against the rebels, Amanullah repressed the revolt, though the campaign dragged on for over a year.

Meanwhile, Afghan persecution of the minority Ahmadi community may have shored up his standing in some clerical circles, but these cases came to the attention of influential foreigners who rallied international opinion against the Afghans. In 1925, Afghan authorities stoned two shopkeepers who belonged to the Ahmadi community in Kabul (estimated by Ahmadis in the diaspora to number eighty thousand or more), and a number of others charged with apostasy. News also trickled out of the country that a major Ahmadi figure had been murdered during the Khost rebellion the year before. Outrage flashed through the Ahmadi community, from India to Ceylon to London, where the news prompted a wider outcry. Signed by English academics and writers, among them H. G. Wells and Sir Arthur Conan Doyle (whose character Dr. John Watson was cast as a veteran of the Second Anglo-Afghan War in his Sherlock Holmes stories), a letter to the British foreign secretary condemned the Afghan government and expressed hope that it would never again follow "a course of conduct so repugnant to the notions of the civilised world."[24]

Such rebukes must have come as a sting to Amanullah, who had tried to put into practice so much of Mahmud Tarzi's reformist vision and who imagined himself as the leader who would make Afghans modern. Assuming the title *king* in 1926, Amanullah demonstrated his care for the enlightenment, health, and well-being of the nation. He established private property in land, reduced land taxes, and introduced other measures to encourage settled agriculture and colonization.

More important, the king founded schools in which Afghans learned foreign languages, science, literature, and a closely controlled and self-consciously progressive Islamic curriculum. Afghans learned to play soccer and tennis. His "Afghan Sports Club" competed with the British Legation, whose members were pleased to learn that the king had taken a special interest in squash. Afghan teams would soon compete internationally, demonstrating the physical prowess of the Afghan nation. Amanullah also founded hospitals, and his officials encouraged Afghans to shed their "lazy" ways and take up physical exercise just like other nations. Celebrating news that four Afghan subjects had been cured of tuberculosis in a newly built facility, loanwords such as *sanatoryum* and *estatistik* entered Dari, the Afghan variant of the Persian language, which adapted to take in an ever-expanding international vocabulary of scientific management of health, hygiene, and the body.[25]

Amanullah also sent the sons and daughters of the elite to Europe and Turkey in growing numbers. Before his reign, relatively few had seen Europe firsthand. They had read about it through Mahmud Tarzi's translations, and some may have heard about Prince Nasrullah's travels to Europe at the end of the nineteenth century. Now young Afghans spent extended periods of time there and became fluent in European languages. Tarzi, for instance, sent his sons to study in France and Great Britain. Born around the turn of the century, Abdul Tawab Khan studied at the École Spéciale Militaire de Saint-Cyr, the elite French cavalry school, and Abdul Wahab was educated at Exeter College, Oxford. Afghan elites even sent their relatives, including female members of their families, to Europe for medical treatment.[26]

Others traveled to Europe in pursuit of commerce. Amanullah's state was desperately in need of arms. Afghan agents and intermediaries inquired about supplies from Germany, Italy, France, and the United Kingdom. However, Afghan diplomats had to request permission from the British for the import of arms shipments from European and American dealers at Bombay.[27]

In 1924, Abdul Wahid established the Durrani Syndicate in Europe. Originally from Kunar, he had migrated to Australia as a child. Abdul Wahid made his fortune there and married an Australian woman before returning to Afghanistan, where he acquired the rights to mine for gold in the Kandahar area. In Europe his firm assembled a group of engineers to prospect in Kandahar, though their venture failed to turn up gold deposits. Similarly, Sher Ahmad Khan was sent to purchase arms for the state. Elites who had traveled to Europe returned to Afghanistan to take up official positions or were sent back to the continent as envoys for the king.

Still others worked in Afghanistan for foreign enterprises. In 1920, Allah Nawaz fled Lahore and found refuge in Afghanistan. After working as an editor and superintendent of schools in Jalalabad and in Tashkent and Kabul as a representative of the Indian Revolutionary Party, he began work as an interpreter for a German–Afghan firm. The German school in Kabul was yet another window onto Europe.[28]

A European assignment for an Afghan official was often a sign of rehabilitation after a period of disfavor or exile or the result of a shift in the balance of political factions at court. Ata-ul-Haq, for instance, had lived in India until the age of sixteen. In 1907, he accompanied Habibullah on his tour of India and then was sent for two years to Moscow to oversee Afghans studying there in the 1920s. When a rebellion swept Amanullah from power following his own European tour in 1929, Ata-ul-Haq became foreign minister for his successor, Habibullah Kalakani. He was one of several such elite figures who apparently threw his lot in with Habibullah II, or the Bachcha-i Saqqa ("water carrier's son"), as his opponents labeled him.

Following Habibullah's downfall, the next foreign minister, Fayz Muhammad Khan, had extensive international experience. Throughout the 1920s he had served as an adviser on Afghan missions to the United States, England, France, Italy, and the Soviet Union. For contemporary observers of Afghan politics, though, this cosmopolitan background was almost unremarkable. British intelligence judged him to be "well-educated and intelligent," even as they criticized him for his penchant for drugs—"the use of which renders him incapable of sustained mental effort"—and for becoming "tiresome when he feels obliged to live up to his reputation as a humorist."[29]

Nearly all of the highest placed Afghan leaders would subsequently be educated abroad. Muhammad Daoud Khan spent nine years in France, returning in 1930 and becoming major general in 1932. Muhammad Ihsan Khan studied flying in Italy for three years and later assumed leadership of the Afghan Air Force. Muhammad Nadir, who became "shah" in 1929, spent more than four years in France, first as an envoy and then in exile. In addition to being fluent in Urdu, he knew French and some English. His son, the future Muhammad Zahir Shah (r. 1933–1973), also received a French education while traveling with his father. Muhammad Umar Khan, chief of the general staff in 1932, spoke Russian and German. He had studied Soviet military operations in Moscow, served as military attaché in Berlin, and observed military maneuvers in Delhi.[30]

Outside of these rather rarefied circles, it was not entirely un-common for Afghans from other regions to study outside the country, even without official sponsorship. While many Pashtuns looked to the religious institutions of the North-West Frontier of India, some Shia followed the path of the twentieth-century luminary Sayyid Ismail Balkhi. In the 1920s he left his native village in Balkh to travel with his father and brothers to Mashhad, where he received extensive clerical training and advanced through the ranks fast enough to play a role in leading opposition to the unveiling campaign of Reza Shah (r. 1921–1941). Balkhi then seems to have fled to Herat, where he took up a teaching position. He then went on pilgrimage to Karbala and Najaf before returning to a political and religious career that bridged Iran and Afghanistan.[31]

To many observers, though, the most dramatic reflection of Amanullah's modernist aspirations was Kabul, which took on a new appearance when the royal family pursued a building boom that employed international designs. Inspired by Nasrullah Khan's Italian Renaissance-style mansion that he had admired while visiting London in 1895, grand palaces and villas with their eclectic architectural styles marked a clear departure from the past. At Paghman, the summer capital, the king laid the foundations of a European-style resort. There Amanullah also ordered the construction of a victory arch to commemorate his triumph of 1919. It was here in 1928 that Queen Soraya appeared beside the king in a skirt and tailored jacket—a scene that shocked opponents of the king's reforms. Other photos of the era capture members of the court wearing bobbed hair and "flapper" fashions.[32]

One of Amanullah's propagandists, Ikbal Ali Shah, confidently proclaimed that the king's urbanism was evidence that "the future political and moral evolution of Central Asia is going to begin and end in Afghanistan." Continuing his praise, he explained that "Kabul is, indeed, on the verge of a complete and thorough-going reconstruction. A French architect of distinction has been retained to plan and design Dar-ul-Aman, the new city, which is to be laid out on Western lines, with spacious boulevards, parks and lofty buildings, the change of site being in a measure necessitated by the frequent flooding of Kabul, which is almost annually visited by inundations of the most distressing kind, causing great loss and materially impeding business." The king's subjects on display in Kabul were further proof. He highlighted the "new Afghan soldier, with shaven chin, black astrakhan cap, decked in a greenish uniform, [who] walks smartly; with him a would-be soldier cousin, wearing a brownish suit, trailing along on a bicycle." All of this showed that "the political drama of the rising, revolting East will be enacted in and around the Kingdom of Kabul," where, Ikbal Ali Shah proclaimed, the "young King's one and great desire is to see his nation amongst the foremost peoples of the modern world."[33]

Indeed it was the kingdom's very entanglement with this "modern world" that placed Amanullah in peril in 1929, a fateful year throughout the region. In the Soviet Union, Josef Stalin's drive to collectivize rural communities decimated pastoralists in Central Asia. The violence sent many in border zones fleeing, often with their livestock, across the Soviet borders into neighboring states. South of the Amu River, civil war erupted when tribal militias challenged the reformist agenda of King Amanullah and deposed him in early 1929. Inflamed by military confrontations, food shortages, and ecological and humanitarian crises, social upheaval from the Hindu Kush to deep within Soviet territory uprooted tens of thousands of cultivators, pastoralists, and townspeople. Meanwhile, Moscow, Kabul, and Tehran shared a common suspicion of the British Empire, while competing for leadership of a Muslim progressivism. In the late 1920s Soviet suspicions were heightened both by wide-scale emigration (which, beginning with the Basmachis, Moscow feared the Afghans had encouraged) and anxiety about Amanullah's designs on Soviet territory and on the loyalties of Soviet Muslims.[34]

In Afghanistan, the rebellion against Amanullah had multiple international dimensions. The supporters of Habibullah II circulated leaflets in the south and east in March 1929, addressing the "Afghan Nation and Muslim World at Large," accusing his opponents of having migrated from Afghanistan to an "infidel land," meaning France, where they consumed "ham and bacon which has permeated their blood vessels and blackened all their fibre and veins."[35] Moreover, in December 1928, the Soviet leadership had concluded that the opposition movement was part of a British plot whose targets were Amanullah and the USSR. In Amanullah, they saw "the sole progressive current" in Afghanistan and the kingdom's only hope for independence. Facing mounting opposition, the Afghan king looked, in turn, to Moscow for support. The Soviets fretted about the spillover of instability from the Afghan north but retained a cautious distance, denying the Afghan government's request for shells loaded with chemical weapons—because the Soviets had none to offer. They proposed instead to form troops from Afghan groups in the north, equipped with Soviet arms and advisers.[36]

Another of Amanullah's backers in the USSR, Ghulam Nabi Khan, Kabul's ambassador to Moscow, launched an effort from Soviet territory to defend him. In January 1929, he assembled a group of Afghans who had trained in Soviet military schools. Other notable families, namely the Charkhis and Gailanis, mobilized forces that included a group of roughly eighty Afghan students in Turkey (and a few from Europe) to approach the Afghan north via the Soviet Union.[37] The Afghan ambassador was impatient to secure arms and raised the specter, so unpalatable to the Soviets, that Britain would gain the upper hand in Afghanistan, or that the Afghans would turn to the Germans for weapons. In February 1929, the Politburo declined his request, fearing that weapons would be used against Amanullah and frustrated by not knowing the deposed king's plans. A request from Jamshidis to cross over to Soviet territory for weapons was also declined. Still, Ghulam Nabi forged ahead. He recruited eight officers studying in the Soviet Union and tried to gather volunteers at Termez from Afghan émigrés. A notable of the Gailani religious dynasty also gathered a group of Hazaras at Merv. By the end of March, the Politburo had taken up a plan to send in an Afghan force made up of roughly one thousand Hazaras and equipped by the Soviets to take Herat. A joint Afghan-Soviet operation was then to lead to the creation of a contingent of five to six thousand in Mazar-i Sharif, which would then march on Kabul. In April, Soviet and Afghan forces took Mazar-i Sharif, but they continued to face resistance, even with Soviet reinforcements and air support. In May, the movement to restore the king dissolved when Amanullah fled the country, and Soviet forces retreated across the border.[38]

Despite his flight, Amanullah continued to exert a hold on the imagination of admirers who retained faith in Afghanistan as a land with a uniquely pivotal role to play in the modern world. Mahendra Pratap, the Indian revolutionary, was undeterred. Under Amanullah, Afghanistan was "worthy of respect and attention equally to hoary Asia and young Europe and America." Having failed to convince Habibullah to join the war while on the German expedition, Pratap returned to Afghanistan under Amanullah, who appointed him to diplomatic missions to China, Japan, Siam, Tibet, Europe and the United States. In Afghanistan, he took pleasure in seeing "the country of my adoption making fast progress" with schools, factories, and an

administration "remodelled on modern lines." He regretted Amanullah's downfall—accusing the British of circulating photos of Queen
Soraya in immodest clothes—but offered his services to the new king,
Muhammad Nadir Shah, after his victory over Habibullah II in
1929, pledging to travel the globe to solicit foreign capital "to develop the country." His travels took him from San Francisco to Japan
and China on behalf of the Afghans. Pratap also called on Nadir to
"make common cause with Nationalist India, Persia, Turkey and
Arabia to save Asia from the fate of Africa."

The country was, moreover, rich in natural resources, and, he
argued, well suited for "industrial culture." "Electric tram cars, electric rope lines and electrically worked factories can be spread over
most of the country," he concluded. Noting that the Germans and
French had begun to consider investing there, he added that the
Americans remained aloof. Pratap chastised this reticence, claiming
that "the Islamic conception of society which is ruling Afghanistan
makes it a safe place of investment." "Capitalists of Europe and America can," he insisted, "find here much more genial ground for their
economic activity than in their own native lands." "I want to enlist
the sympathy of [the] proletariat as well as the bourgeoisie to accel-
erate the modernization of Afghanistan," Pratap explained, as part
of his wider goal to forge a new polity, "the District of Ancient
Aryan" out of Afghanistan, Persia, and India.[39]

In the views of such admirers, then, Afghanistan had a wholly unique
role to play in the world as a shining example of anticolonialism, capitalism, and modernist development. Under Nadir Shah, the monarchy embraced and expanded on this obligation. Official declarations cast the Afghan state as the guardian of the frontier tribes against

British oppression and, more than that, of universal humanity. The Disarmament Conference, an international forum launched in 1932 for the discussion of international affairs in Geneva, presented an occasion for Nadir, amplified by the Afghan press, to bring the Afghans' global cause to a wider audience. The newspaper *Reform* (*Islah*) reported that the Afghans at the conference had protested the British aerial bombardment of the frontier communities, "which belong to the same religion, speak the same language and descend from [the] same ancestors." Expressing outrage at British hypocrisy, the Afghan position contended:

> In the world of Humanity this issue blots very much the honour of the Afghans when aerial bombardment may be prohibited for all nations of the world and may be regarded as "lawful" for Afghans only. If in Europe aerial bombardment is regarded against humanity, it is also against humanity in the case of the Afghans. The question that beautiful buildings should be given right of protection from the aerial bombardment and the humble cottages of the Afghans only be the targets of aerial bombardment, is not based on Justice and Equity.[40]

By this logic, the Afghan state forged by the monarchy had established itself as the equal of any other in the world. The language of humanity—once used as a cudgel against the supposedly barbaric Afghans—had become a staple of Afghan political rhetoric and an essential claim to equality in the world. However, the assertion masked more than a little bravado. Mahendra Pratap's campaign to solicit foreign investors by touting Afghans' propensity for capitalist development was rooted in insecurity about the solidity of the modernist venture initiated by Nadir Shah's predecessors. British bombers might not confine themselves to the frontier in the future. To fully realize Afghans' place in the avant-garde of the defense of global humanity, their elite would have to tend to their own "humble cottages." They would have to bring an important piece of the world to Afghanistan.

5 | SEDUCED BY CAPITAL

IN THE YEARS immediately following the Great Depression of 1929, Afghans achieved a stunning breakthrough in the arena of global capitalism. Finally realizing visions of an industrial and capitalist Afghanistan outlined by Mahendra Pratap and other proponents of Amanullah's modernist politics, their channel was finance, their instrument an adaptation of the modern bank and joint-stock company, the National Bank (Bank-i Milli). By 1940, its operations extended from Afghanistan to branches in Peshawar, Karachi, Berlin, London, and New York. In Manhattan, the Bank was established as the Afghan American Trading Company on West Thirtieth Street, where it moved in 1947 into a former textile school building, as the *New York Times* described it, with a "modern facade of cast limestones with unbroken bays of special steel sash, six ground-floor stores with sloped fronts to eliminate street reflections" and "a penthouse dining room."[1]

The New York financial scene was a world apart from that of most Afghans. But not for the Bank's founder, Abdul Majid Zabuli. Born into a merchant family at the turn of the century, Abdul Majid spent his early years in Herat, then a window onto the markets of Iran and Russia. Abdul Majid followed his father to Tashkent, in Russian Turkestan, where he studied at the Islamic College during the First World War. Despite, or perhaps because of, the turmoil caused by the Bolshevik revolution and the civil war that followed, the family business prospered. Having taken over from his father, Abdul Majid shifted the firm's headquarters to Moscow, an ideal location for exporting and importing goods (some detractors would call it "smuggling," thanks to ties to Afghan and Soviet customs agents) and for running a textile mill. Business flourished, insofar as Soviet authorities permitted pockets of capitalism under their New Economic Policy. When they soured on this Afghan capitalist in 1929, he transferred his international trade and investment firm, now apparently shorn of some assets expropriated by the Bolsheviks, to Berlin. In Kabul, the authorities were closely following the exploits of this Afghan expatriate, as they did with nearly all émigrés, and in 1931, Prime Minister Hashim Khan urged Abdul Majid to return to Afghanistan to build a vast industrial, commercial, and banking empire. He reluctantly agreed, leaving his business and German wife in Berlin. In 1932 he arrived in Afghanistan on what he hoped would be just a short trip to advise the government.

Photographed in official publications with slick black hair, neat mustache, and in a European suit and tie, Abdul Majid brought with him a technocratic sensibility influenced by the crisis of capitalism in Europe. Afghanistan, he proposed, needed an economic policy defined by rationalism and planning. The state would join hands with private capital, and together they would direct investment into infrastructure and industry. The primary vehicle for this linking of the private and public sectors would be the Ashami Company, a holding company that would pay a dividend in lieu of interest payments, which were prohibited by Islamic law. Partly owned by the government, it became in 1934 the foundation of the country's nascent banking system, the National Bank. In addition to printing currency and managing imports and government purchases, it pumped money into industrial development.[2] Afghan elites became enthralled by the promise of industry. Framed in glass and steel, the factory served as a measure of Afghan progress, a symbol of the country's break from a backward past and arrival in a modernist age. Official publications celebrated the dawning of this new era with emblems of modernity, for instance, telling the story of the motorcyle, illustrated with a collage image of a dirigible, train, factory with smokestacks, ship, and airplane.[3]

The National Bank was the engine of Afghan industrialization. Its capital, accumulated through monopolies on a lengthy list of commodities from sugar to automobiles, laid the industrial foundations of the country. In the late 1930s and early 1940s, the Bank recruited entrepreneurs and formed industrial organizations (*shirkats*) in Kunduz, Baghlan, and Kabul that built the first factories to treat cotton and sugar and to weave textiles. This flurry of industrial activity was concentrated in the north, where cotton production facilities appeared in Mazar-i Sharif, Balkh, Daulatabad and Akcha. By the mid-1930s, the Afghan "ring road" had incorporated the region, opening up its resources to exploitation by the National Bank and its partners.

The National Bank stood at the center of an ambitious vision to wield the transformative power of global capital. Abdul Majid saw this financial network, one that would directly connect the herdsmen who raised karakul sheep to markets across the globe, as the essential basis of national wealth. Armed with this capital, newly rationalized trading companies would supply international markets with Afghan products. Afghan consumers, in turn, would enjoy an unprecedented standard of living. Backed by foreign investment and guided by the state, infrastructure and industry would follow, in accordance with a highly rationalist and planned scheme.

In Abdul Majid's view, global capital was crucial for the consolidation of the nation. For Afghan elites of his generation, questions about who belonged to this nation and what it meant to be a loyal subject of the kingdom remained in flux. Yet Abdul Majid's answer was clear. His scheme was to create a "national" trading class; and it was the responsibility of the National Bank, supported by the state, to see that these traders dislodged the historically prominent foreigners and those they took to be marginal to the nation—namely, Indians and Jews—from their leading positions and claimed their rightful place in the economy.[4]

The National Bank's bold entry into global finance established novel connections to a world beset by numerous overlapping crises. The global depression was only one factor for a country still recovering from the civil war of 1929. The ascendant Indian national movement was another source of anxiety for Kabul. The British were a perennial threat to Afghan sovereignty. But Afghan elites wondered, what might British decline and Indian "home rule" mean for Afghanistan and its frontiers? Empire looked more and more vulnerable in this part of Asia for another reason beyond the immediate region: the rise of Nazi Germany and Imperial Japan promised an intensified struggle for global domination. Meanwhile, Stalin's first Five-Year Plan, a frenetic and bloody campaign of forced collectivization to fuel an industrial surge, brought expanded trade opportunities, especially for Afghans in the west and the north. Yet it also marked the return of a more powerful neighbor whose geopolitical interests spanned Europe, the Middle East, and Asia. Similarly, in Iran Kabul faced a dynamic rival under Reza Shah whose authoritarian state-building program had inaugurated far-reaching changes in Iranian society, challenging conventional views on gender, religion, nationhood, and other matters.

Against this backdrop of geopolitical rivalry and ideological ferment, Afghanistan's own political future was unsettled. Amanullah and his network of supporters were dispersed but still alive. They gave life to a key chapter in the long story of Afghan diaspora politics and their great power entanglements.

The National Bank project inaugurated an era of deepening Afghan engagement with the competing intellectual currents of the day. In the 1930s, more and more Afghans had direct contact with foreign political movements and actors. They debated, on a global scale and through a comparative lens, the merits of capitalism and socialism, liberalism and fascism, anticolonialism and nationalist mobilization, to name just the main trends. The Afghan diplomatic corps was one important point of contact with global intellectual flows. The first wave of students sent abroad by the state was another. Many of them, including influential members of the royal family, returned to Afghanistan in the 1930s. The expanded presence of foreign embassy personnel and foreign experts in various technical fields gave rise to still other links with Afghan elite circles. The Musahiban dynasty continued to be preoccupied with security and devoted most of its budget to maintaining control of the Afghan population; however, the 1930s also witnessed the development of schemes such as Abdul Majid Zabuli's banking and trade operations that called for the application of expert knowledge to improve and transform Afghan society. What the architects of this project could not yet foresee was how this quest for capital would ultimately subject Afghanistan to particularly destabilizing global forces that would unleash shockwaves throughout Afghan society in the decades to come.

The dual crises of 1929, the Afghan civil war and the global economic crisis, wracked Afghanistan. International demand for Afghan commodities dipped. Merchants and capital fled the country. The value of the afghani fell sharply, and Afghan trading institutions fell into disarray. Muhammad Nadir Shah sought to restore stability to the kingdom, but he did not enjoy the luxury of turning his back on the international scene. Amanullah remained alive, and he clearly retained aspirations of a return to power, but with a refurbished image. Having embarked on the hajj, the now ostentatiously pious Amanullah made the Hijaz a bridge to his former subjects in Afghanistan. Nadir Shah remained paranoid about the former king. He arrested and executed several notables whom he suspected of plotting with Amanullah and arrested dozens of others, including students who had recently returned from Germany and who may have had contact with the former king's entourage in Europe.[5]

Nonetheless, Nadir himself looked to Germany and to Turkey to recruit experts to transform key state institutions. German and Turkish officers trained the sons of Afghan notables in new officer academies founded early in his reign and took up positions as advisers to the general staff. At the same time, he sent Afghans to study in military schools in Germany, Turkey, Italy, France, British India, Japan, and the Soviet Union. The government also began developing a police force under the Ministry of the Interior and with German direction. British and Italian aviation specialists prepared Afghan pilots, many of whom trained in India. Translations of foreign instructional material became the foundation of Afghan military education. With foreign aid, the armed forces grew to 80,000 by 1936 and 90,000 by the outbreak of the Second World War. Absorbing at least half of the state budget, the army served as a crucial pillar of the new order, drawing on Pashtun tribal and clerical elite families.[6]

To pay for these expanded security forces—and to pursue Nadir's vision of development—the government turned to the resourceful Abdul Majid Zabuli. Amanullah's government had made halting steps toward industrial development, aided in 1928 by a credit of five million marks from Germany. The National Bank went much further. It developed a monopoly on hard currency operations and foreign trade. It concluded deals with a major Soviet foreign trade enterprise (Sovafgantorg), among many international trade arrangements. The right to own shares in its industrial organizations, or *shirkats*, was limited to Afghan subjects. With its growing capital reserves, the National Bank had by mid-decade squeezed out more and more non-Afghan merchants and creditors, most of whom abandoned the country by the end of the 1930s. Meanwhile, the value of Afghan exports had grown from around $7 million in the period from 1911 to 1915 to nearly $12 million in 1938–1939. By this time, the National Bank and its shareholders had spawned affiliates that established a cotton processing factory at Qataghan, a textile facility at Pul-i Khumri, and a sugar factory in Baghlan.[7]

The National Bank had strong ties to Europe. To strengthen investment in Afghan industry, the state guaranteed credits the Bank received from European firms. The Bank's representative in Germany had spent nearly a decade of his life there by the time of his appointment to the Berlin branch in 1933. Born in 1911, Abdul Rauf Haidar began his studies in Germany at the age of thirteen and received a PhD in economics in 1935. He represented Afghanistan in commercial negotiations and then served as the director of the Bank-i Milli and Afghan commercial attaché throughout the war. Haidar was later posted in New York for the Ministry of National Economy and carried on talks with the United States for support of development projects.[8]

Afghan connections to Europe took on new significance on November 8, 1933, when a student of the German high school raised a gun at the king, killing him with a single shot during a midafternoon awards ceremony at the school. This assassination followed the killing in June of Prince Muhammad Aziz by a pro-Amanullah activist in Berlin. Sensing an opening from his exile in Italy, Amanullah dispatched an address to Afghanistan in which he called on the people of Kabul, Mazar-i Sharif, and Maymana to "be true to [the] salt which you have eaten from my father, grandfather and myself. Now when God has emancipated [the] country from Nadir Khan, do not obey the family who sell their country. If you send for me I am ready to serve religion and country."[9]

With the accession of Nadir Shah's son, Muhammad Zahir Shah, the Afghan government remained wary of Amanullah, fearing a European patron might intervene to back him. At the same time, though, officials around Zahir Shah continued to explore contacts with Europe in hopes of pursuing their development agenda and shoring up their domestic political base. Working hand in hand with the Bank-i Milli, the state asserted further control over the main channels of international commerce, squeezing out private merchants and middlemen. In July 1933 the Ministry of Commerce established rules strictly regulating how foreigners could exhibit their goods in Afghanistan. Such exhibitions would be confined to Kabul, and any foreign goods purchased would be exchanged for Afghan exports, not cash. The British diplomat who reported on this development added that he and an Italian colleague found this arrangement peculiar, and similar only to Soviet economic policy: "whereas in all other countries except Russia, every inducement is offered to foreign merchants to send their goods for exhibition, here conditions are made as unattractive as they can possibly be." Whereas such policy might benefit Soviet trade officials, who would participate for political purposes, private traders, they concluded, "if any were misguided enough to sell their goods at an exhibition of this kind, would eventually find themselves recrossing the Indian frontier with a lorry-load of moth-eaten 'Persian lamb' or unsaleable lapis lazuli, for which they had been obliged to pay exorbitant prices."[10]

Soviet trade organizations were more comfortable with such arrangements, however. One of their trade exhibitions put into circulation cigarettes, perfumes, and candy. The Soviets also brought trucks resembling the British-made Bedford. But its poor performance—the water in its cooling system boiled when a French archaeologist tried to ascend a mountain road—stoked suspicions about the quality of Soviet goods. In this case, the owner returned it to the Soviet embassy, supposedly protesting that he needed "a lorry not a samovar."[11]

Despite such state-imposed constraints, international trade and finance were not the sole arenas where the pace of transformation was accelerating. Although change did not touch every corner of the country with the same speed and intensity, remarkable developments were especially visible along major veins of transport and communication and in urban centers. Automobiles and trucks passed through transit corridors teeming with animal traffic. Several hundred thousand nomadic traders and laborers continued to make the annual spring migration to India, but they now had to contend with more aggressive British controls. Camels were still used to transport Soviet petrol to places like Kandahar, and they could be counted on to pull lorries that had become stuck in impassable roads. But motorized transportation was gaining the upper hand.[12]

The urban landscape took on a radically different appearance, too. In 1933, a film projector, brought to Kandahar for independence day celebrations, was to be made a more permanent feature of the city as a cinema hall. The government demolished houses to clear a path for new construction. Telegraph poles dotted major thoroughfares. A Swiss architect reflecting on the architectural styles of the 1930s observed that buildings constructed under the amirs Abdur Rahman and Habibullah had employed an Indian colonial style, but that more recently foreign architects had introduced an eclectic array of designs so that "one can identify the Russian, Italian, and German influences in the architecture." At Pul-i Khumri, in particular, he was struck by a "strange" sensation to see the work of a German engineer and its "taut but pleasant style." In Herat, another German engineer was at work from 1935 laying out a new city adjacent to the existing one. Designed in the style of European colonial urbanism, this modern construction was intended, a Swiss visitor concluded, to meet "the representational needs of the central government and its desire not to fall behind neighboring states." Domestic interiors were changing in tune with their exteriors, especially among elite families who could afford to import European furnishings. A patriotic British commentator found it all too "German," remarking that "Siemens opened an agency in Kabul, and houses and furniture of hideous German design were increasingly in evidence."[13]

Thanks in large measure to the trading arm of the National Bank, the Ashami Company, the country began to import cars, trucks, and other machinery manufactured by the likes of Chevrolet, Caterpillar, and Ford. Abdul Majid recounted to the American scholar and diplomat Leon Poullada how he had to engage in subterfuge—hiring a German expatriate to create a front operation in Kashgar—to bypass an Indian middleman in order to import General Motors trucks directly. The monarchy incorporated the motorcar into its demonstrations of power; the annual independence celebrations featured royal tours by automobile of the capital. More than the motorcar, though, it was the truck that began to revolutionize Afghan society. Afghan lorries plied the route from Peshawar to Kabul and from Chaman to Kandahar. Afghan drivers displaced Indian owner-operators who faced new restrictions on their movement beyond Kandahar; some Indian drivers abandoned the route altogether for Iran.[14]

For all of these changes, foreign visitors tended to see what they wanted to see and frequently downplayed the scale of change to preserve received ideas about the country. In the central mountainous region of the Hazarajat, Ernest F. Fox, an American who traveled in the country to explore oil and minerals in 1937, confidently proclaimed that "Panjao is typical of the present Afghanistan, where the old prevails, the new intrudes, and the people remain unchanged."

Others were crestfallen to observe any change at all. Kandahar's neatly planned streets and orderly bazaar quarter disappointed more than one European observer seeking a more exotic experience of the Orient. The market area was "no longer interesting," quipped Kurt Ziemke, the German envoy who visited the town in 1934. "One seeks delicacies, the so-called treasures of the Orient, in vain here," he complained, echoing the nineteenth-century refrain that "cheap consumer goods from India and Europe make up the staple commodities." The only locally made goods that Ziemke could identify were "bowls, cups, writing implements, toys, prayer beads and sometimes kitsch" crafted out of turpentine stone. The gold disks and thread that embroidered the colorful caps and coats of Kandahari men came from Germany. Still, Kandahar was far from the highly internationalized Kabul. With fewer foreigners resident there, Kandahar's merchants did not sell coffee, jam, potatoes, or other European vegetables that the German diplomat had found in the capital. Over time, though, a small German colony did take shape in Kandahar. Engineers and factory managers arrived, together with their wives, to oversee factories for processing wool. A Siemens electrical station powered these new industrial enterprises.[15]

In the north, a less visible but more far-reaching transformation was quietly under way as the sprawling Soviet frontier pushed Afghanistan's commercial relations with the world in new directions. When anti-Soviet rebels finally gave up their struggle against the Red Army in the early 1920s and fled Soviet territory, many arrived in Afghanistan with vast flocks of karakul sheep. This migration of people and animals transformed not just the politics but also the physical environment of the northern and western regions of the country. The sheep were bred with local varieties, and their numbers grew rapidly.

Raw karakul hides became Afghanistan's number one export, supplying demand for luxury clothing items, primarily in Europe and the United States. A trade publication in New York, *Fur Trade Review*, dramatized its role in the forging of this connection: "From the foothills of the far off Himalayas an Indian firm got in touch with a famous American house, and as a result rare Persian and Afghanistan fur skins found their way direct to the great New York market."[16]

A particular aesthetic conjuncture linked the Afghan north to middle- and upper-class consumers in the United States, where furs were at the height of fashion. Marketing Afghan karakul primarily as "Persian lambskin," designers integrated animal skins into men and women's clothing in dozens of ways in ready-to-wear and haute couture fashion. At a "$1,000,000 Fur Show" in June 1939, New York furriers displayed "such diverse modes as those inspired by the papal influence, elaborate Byzantine effects, and prim princess and dignified mid-Victorian trends." A reporter at a fashion luncheon at the Waldorf-Astoria admired Saks Fifth Avenue furs used "to soften necklines, to tie at waistlines, to face lapels, for bags, hats and peplums." An advertisement by the fur retailer John Wanamaker, featuring an elegant woman in a "Persian Lambskin" coat, described a "Shining bodice V'd into a Victorian waist" with a "Cascade of skirt" and "Regal bell sleeve." It informed consumers that this fur came from Russia or Afghanistan and "was the easiest fur to remodel and repair, and should last for many years." It came dyed black, with the finest ones marked by a "smaller, tighter curl."[17] Afghan karakul producers faced competition from an emergent fur industry in southwest Africa, and American regulatory agencies and furriers wrangled over labels attached to "Persian lambskin." But in spite of these difficulties, the near collapse of domestic fur production in the United States during the Second World War proved a boon to Afghan exporters—and to the many communities in the Afghan north whose livelihoods depended on the karakul trade.

Closer to home, however, the politics of the Afghan north and Soviet frontier remained unsettled. During the civil war of 1929 Herati merchants had not only fled to their traditional refuge in Mashhad but also relocated to Soviet territory. Pastoralists and farmers poured into Soviet territory for different reasons. Facing abuse from provincial authorities and growing competition for land and water from Pashtun migrants whom the government had settled in these provinces, Jamshidis, Hazaras, and Baluch migrated with their extended kin and herds, as their ancestors had periodically done from the late nineteenth century, across the border to the north. Once on the Soviet side of the border, many received a warm welcome from officials who saw them as potential allies in an effort to gain the sympathies of "class-friendly elements" in the borderlands. The Soviets promised land and attempted to integrate them into Bolshevik party units organized along "national" lines.

Among the Afghan émigrés were those who considered themselves political refugees who left with the fall of Amanullah. Their case reveals the strained political and material circumstances in which so many Afghan émigrés found themselves. When a dozen or so of them requested assistance in 1933 in founding a political organization in Tashkent, housed in a facility with a dormitory and a club, Soviet authorities declined. They also ignored émigré complaints about expensive prices and the "absence of products in the markets."[18]

Émigré communities and families were torn by disagreements about whether or not to turn back to Afghanistan. Their situation worsened in 1930 and 1931, the height of the Bolsheviks' violent campaign to collectivize agriculture and "liquidate" class enemies. Of more than six thousand Baluch households in the Turkmen republic, roughly one hundred crossed into Afghanistan or Iran in 1930. Adding to the chaos on the frontier, a number of Soviet Turkmen pastoralists rebelled in spring 1931 and fled to Afghanistan.[19]

The Soviet secret police acknowledged the economic grievances of the migrants. At the same time, they contended that some Afghan tribal leaders who had emigrated to the Soviet Union were engaged in a conspiracy headed by the governor of Herat, Abdul Rahim Khan. They suspected that the plot involved the Afghan consulates in Merv and Tashkent and a network of Afghan elders, accusing them of inciting flight and threatening to harm the relatives of any émigrés who adopted Soviet citizenship. This controversy reached a climax in October 1930, when a Baluch leader, Kerim Khan, guided one hundred Baluch households and their livestock into Afghanistan, all while fighting running gun battles with Soviet forces and aircraft in pursuit. In November he met with the Soviet consul in Herat and explained that the Baluch had not been cared for by Soviet authorities. Kerim Khan added that the Baluch also objected to the introduction of schooling for women and the closing of mosques.

Still, some Afghan émigrés who had returned to Afghanistan were prepared to try life among the Soviets a second time. Led by an émigré who had become the chairman of a "Hazara Revolutionary Committee" in the Kushka district, a group of Hazaras who left the USSR in 1931 wrote to Soviet officials in 1933 complaining about Afghan officials and offering to bring hundreds of households and thousands of heads of livestock in exchange for land.[20]

Despite hardships—and an apparent campaign by the Afghan consulate to discredit Soviet rule among the Afghan émigrés—Soviet officials claimed that more than 5,500 Baluch households had accepted Soviet citizenship. For many, however, this distinction appears to have mattered little during Stalin's purges in the late 1930s, when dozens of Afghans, some with Afghan, others with Soviet, passports, were swept up in police repression and sent to the Gulag. Their number reached a high point of about two hundred in 1940.[21]

The frontier provoked anxieties on the Soviet side as well. The Afghan Soviet border remained quite porous. Soviet authorities complained about smugglers, including women, who brought opium into the Tajik Soviet Socialist Republic and especially Soviet Badakhshan, where opium use was endemic and local populations had imported opium from Afghan Badakhshan from at least the nineteenth century.[22] From the early 1930s, the Soviets worried that northern Afghanistan, with its more than 2,000-kilometer-long border and potentially transnational ethnic groups, was being prepared as "a bridgehead for military aggression against the USSR." Afghan soil in the north was, at the same time, a constant refuge for Soviet citizens escaping the USSR. By 1932, party officials in the Tajik Republic estimated that roughly thirty thousand households, mostly Uzbeks and Turkmen, had left for Afghanistan at various moments since the revolution. Reflecting the chaos of the frontier, though, Soviet authorities calculated that seven or eight thousand of these households returned between 1926 and 1928.[23]

Afghan communities in the north had long tried to accommodate these migrants, on the condition that they were not involved in espionage and that they did not settle near the border, but in 1932 the Afghan position hardened. By agreement with Moscow, newly established border commissars guarded the border with instructions to return the migrants or deport them to Xinjiang. By 1933, a policy of differential treatment for Muslims and non-Muslims had taken shape, with the Afghan state offering asylum to the former and detention and deportation for most of the latter.

When word of this policy toward Christians and Jews reached British authorities, they tried to mediate on their behalf. Bukharan Jews in London and Palestine also appealed to the British government to intervene to seek safe passage for some two thousand Soviet Jews whom Afghan authorities had interned in Kabul and Herat. "We are worse off than the Jews in Germany," complained one Bukharan Jew in a letter sent to London (apparently smuggled via India) describing the desperate conditions for the men, women, and children under Afghan detention. The British followed the plight of the Jews but were wary of allowing passage to India of refugees whom they feared might be Bolshevik agents. A September 1933 decree banned all Jews in Afghanistan, indigenous and immigrant alike, from residing within thirty miles of the border. Jews in Mazar, Maymana, and Andkhoy were forced to return to their towns of birth, usually Herat or Kabul, disrupting their business activities and pushing them out of the northern karakul trade.[24]

One key figure at the heart of the controversy over the status of the Jews in Afghanistan was Shmuel Shabtai Dadas, a Herati Jew who went to the Soviet Union as a student in 1924 and who managed to stay on as an inspector of Soviet schools in the Pamir Mountains. Apparently he worked out an arrangement with the Afghan ambassador to Moscow, Muhammad Aziz Khan, who helped him secure travel papers for Jews seeking to emigrate in the early 1930s. Afghan authorities arrested him when he returned to the country in 1934. They then used his case, alongside others involving Afghan-passport-holding Jews in England, to cast doubt on the citizenship of Jews with Afghan passports more generally. Afghan consulates in India, Jerusalem, Berlin, Paris, and London revoked or refused renewal of the passports of Jews in the diaspora. The British took particular notice of this policy when Afghans refused to repatriate Afghan Jews accused of committing crimes in India. In August 1934, an Afghan official insisted to a French paper that such Jews were in fact inhabitants of Bukhara and Daghestan and that they had acquired passports "irregularly." Meanwhile in summer 1935 in Herat, townspeople reacted to a fight between a Jewish boy and a Muslim child by rioting and attacking Jews, many of whom were forced to flee to Kabul or to emigrate to Jewish communities in Mashhad or Karachi. A letter sent to a newspaper in Jerusalem reported that the Jewish community had been subject to "blood libels" and other forms of abuse.[25]

The scapegoating of Jews in Germany and elsewhere in Europe may have provided some inspiration for these policies. However, the treatment of Afghan and Central Asian Jews was just one aspect of a more general campaign, of which Abdul Majid Zabuli's National Bank project was also a key part, to answer the nationalist challenge of the day. Constructing a national economy, army, and other institutions was inseparable from the project of creating a national ideology. For Afghan officials and intellectuals, the benchmarks of modernity were Europe and "progressive" Muslim nations. At a moment when a wave of intense nationalism swept across the European continent and throughout the globe, Afghans faced the test of demonstrating their right to belong in this world of nation-states by articulating a national language, culture, and past. Playwrights, poets, novelists, historians, artists, filmmakers, and musicians were the sculptors of the national spirit. Other experts worked to forge the ideal physical form, making the human body an object of nationalist imagination. From physicians to criminologists and sports trainers, various specialists claiming medical expertise proposed new ways to reshape populations in the service of the nation. In Afghanistan, too, commemorations of the nation, such as the annual independence day ceremonies, celebrated the cult of the body, as in the disciplined and daring Afghan national gymnastics team.

In many countries, this obsession drew on, or gave rise to, racial categorization. Such thinkers reimagined the family, and mothers in

4 Gymnasts at the Afghanistan Independence Day Celebrations. *Da Kabul kalanay* (Kabul 1319/1940–41).

particular, as the guardians of the "healthy" bodies that the nation demanded. A generation of Afghan university students had encountered European nationalist ideologies firsthand. Closer to home, nationalist movements in neighboring states presented more proximate models of nation formation while presenting a multiplicity of challenges to possible Afghan national narratives. The leadership of the Soviet Union had proclaimed the existence of Uzbek, Tajik, and Turkmen nations. Each of these peoples, Moscow certified, now had a national language and national cultural institutions. Their republics had national borders, national flags, and national communist parties. National elites occupied visible administrative positions in the party and state apparatus in a system that offered a kind of quota system for those formerly oppressed by the Russians. In India, too, nationalist organizations projected a future free from British rule, though elites hotly contested what it would mean for the territories and communities that shared political, cultural, commercial, and kinship ties with the Afghans. Along the Indo-Afghan frontier, a group calling itself the "Servants of God" (Khudai Khidmatgars) under Abdul Ghaffar Khan mobilized a nonviolent campaign for the political rights of the Pashtuns. Meanwhile, in Iran, intellectuals were revisiting the Iranian past, seeking models for a progressive future, often appealing to historical events, people, and places that clashed with Afghan claims, for example, of primary descent from the mythical "Aryans" and of a special connection to their putative territory in ancient times.

Given this competitive environment, the search for a national identity overlapped with attempts to define a distinctively Afghan path of development. The official Afghan press posed these questions to the country's small, but influential reading public. In February 1932, a contributor to the official paper *Anis* predicted that the mining of Afghanistan's natural resources, among them, iron, coal, copper, gold, silver, and oil, would play an increasingly important role in "the world of today and tomorrow," particularly given the "world's future economic revolutions." Situated "in the heart of the East," Afghanistan was poised to serve as a crucial corridor for its four neighbors. Thus the progress and strength of the "fatherland" (*vatan*) would be built upon "transport" (Dari had by this time assimilated the term *trānspūrt*). Afghanistan's economic vigor, the writer stressed, would solidify peace and stability in the region, serving as a bulwark in the East against "imperialists" (literally, "the world conquerers" [*jahāngīrān-i dunyā*]). To realize this hopeful future, it was essential that Islam unify Afghans, because economic matters were interlinked with the social; society depended upon a spirit of unity and agreement. Citing the French thinker Gustave Le Bon, the article went on to argue that society must transform the economy from a state of "inactivity" to one of movement and a shift away from all that is "the irrational." The author also invoked the leader of the nation, Muhammad Nadir Shah, who had called for struggle for and devotion to the *vatan*. Afghanistan had faced war, revolution, and crises, but attention to the study of "developed nations" that had achieved progress over time showed the way. In Germany, for instance, intellectuals understood that railways could form the "arteries" of a nation. Committing themselves to the philosophy of reform and discovery, Afghans could learn, in particular, from the experience of the Americans and the Japanese.[26]

In this contentious atmosphere of competing nationalisms, a thirty-year-old professor of history at Habibia College and the scion of the Afghan diaspora in India, Mohammed Ali (ca. 1908–1972), presented an authoritative handbook to reintroduce the Afghan nation to the world. Published in an English edition in Kabul in 1938, Ali's *Guide to Afghanistan* reworked some of the existing, mostly negative, tropes about Afghans and reformulated them as the positive attributes of a formidably nationalist yet uniquely progressive and cosmopolitan nation. His book first surveyed the geography and history of the country, arguing that each had left an indelible imprint on the national character in the past and would guide Afghanistan's promising course in the future. Fitting the racially inflected language of the day, Ali boasted that "as a race the Afghan is tall and athletic, with handsome features. He is bold and warlike, fond of freedom and resolute in maintaining it." A "born soldier" with a "warlike and martial spirit," the Afghan had "furnished a long list of generals who succeeded in founding vast and powerful empires not only in Afghanistan, but in the neighbouring countries as well." Responsible for bringing Islam to the subcontinent, Afghans could count among their number luminaries from Avicenna to Sultan Mahmud Ghaznavi and from Sayyid Jamal ad-Din Afghani to King Muhammad Nadir Shah, all of whom had a remarkable place in the history of Asia.

Ali's account failed, however, to clarify a vexing question that haunted Afghan nationalist thinkers: were the Afghans one nation or many? In the late nineteenth century the amir Abdur Rahman had some concept of a multiethnic state, for instance, in an officially sponsored text that mentioned Durranis and Ghilzais, as well as Farsiban, Hazaras, and Turks as belonging to Afghanistan.[27] Yet the policies of the royal government frequently offered advantages, when it came to allocating resources and distributing positions of authority, to members of the Pashtun tribes, whose designation as "Afghan" deepened uncertainty about which groups formed the "nation." Thus in Ali's book, too, his characterization of Afghan racial identity reflected considerable ambiguity, noting that the Afghans were mostly "of the original Indo-European stock, but like the people of other countries, they, too, are a strange mixture of races and languages." Avoiding use of *Pashtun* or any other ethnonym, he appears to have used *Afghan* in its heretofore customary mode as the term for "Pashtun." The "national language" was Pashto, which was experiencing a "revival" after a long period of neglect and would soon be the official language as well. He acknowledged that Persian was an important language in the towns. But he left the other languages of the country, which he termed mere "dialects," unnamed. In a section devoted to Afghan law, Ali again invoked the diversity of the country's population when he noted that there was more than one religion (asserting there was "freedom of faith" for all) and that there were other forms of diversity as well: "All the people of the country, without regard to race, religion or tribe, are considered brethren and equal in sight of law." While acknowledging the country's multiethnic and multireligious character, Ali stridently insisted that "despite the medley of races and tongues, the Afghans form one nation, and are united to live and die in defence of their Fatherland." "Love of country and love of freedom," he continued, "form the bond of union among the peoples." Their identity was marked by "simplicity, courtesy, hospitality, love of nature, and a high sense of honour and patriotism," and they were all "extremely religious." Lovers of "sports and physical culture," their "national sport" was the game of *buzkashi* (a kind of polo match played on horseback with an animal carcass), a unique endeavor that, like so much else, set Afghans apart from others.

The Afghan notion of progress was different, too, in that it "seems to consist in a proper balance of material advancement and spiritual renovation." The Afghan nation was capable of assimilating "the substance of the main cultures of the world, without impairing its national individuality." In this connection, Europe had a special role to play, Ali suggested, but the Afghans had something to teach the Europeans as well. Afghans were intent on keeping up "a spiritual

civilisation on an even keel with material progress, realising that the
European civilisation, with all its great achievements in science and
art and other departments of knowledge, is wanting in this respect."

Afghanistan had been held back by its neighbors but was now
committed to progress and the restoration of its past splendor. The
country had suffered at the hands of "hordes of invaders," which,
along with "the intrigues of the neighbouring powers . . . greatly
hampered its material progress and crippled its moral and intellectual development." Yet Ali was optimistic because Afghanistan was
determined to "regain its lost commercial status" at the heart of Asia
before the development of seaborne trade. Ali sketched out a vision
whereby Afghanistan would assume center stage along a rail line that
would pass from London, via Calais, Moscow, Baku, Krasnovodsk,
and then to Herat, Kandahar, and New Chaman on to India. The
new route through Afghanistan would reduce the journey by a week,
while the "horrors of the Red Sea and the monsoons would dwindle
into dreams for the Indian tourists." "Afghanistan has once more
begun a progressive career as a modern nation," he concluded, "and
by pursuing the peaceful course of educational and industrial reconstruction and developing its natural resources, is rapidly advancing
to retrieve its lost status of a world power."[28]

Other historical discoveries provided further fodder for such
claims. Work by French archaeologists, who had arrived in the early
1920s, sparked Afghan intellectuals' interests in the ancient and pre-
Islamic past of the country. French cooperation led to the founding
of the Kabul Museum, which housed treasures unearthed at Bagram,
Kunduz, and elsewhere. The journal *Kabul* celebrated the discovery
of Afghanistan's Aryan origins. Some of these writers also pioneered
the search for a deeper past for Pashto literary culture, an interest that
found favor with a government bent on crafting a national culture
that would not be overshadowed by Iran or the Soviet Union and

might solidify a hierarchy of ethnic groups. Founded in 1943, *Aryana* became a platform for the celebration of the antiquity of the nation and the unearthing of evidence of literary and other ties joining the Pashtuns to the ancient Aryans.[29]

For such nationalist thinkers, the outbreak of the Second World War presented an unusual opportunity—and challenge. Although the European and Pacific theaters were far away, Afghanistan was no oasis. In August 1940, the king declared Afghan neutrality. Nonetheless, the great powers worked hard to draw Afghans to one side or another, and Afghans themselves were divided about which policies to pursue in a war that had brought about an alliance between the British and the Soviets, the two traditional foes of the Afghans. Carefully monitoring news from the battlefronts for signs of Allied or Axis advantage, Afghans debated their impact on Afghanistan's relations with the great powers. Tensions mounted when British shipping to and from India shifted to a wartime footing, and the transport of war materiel displaced goods bound for Karachi and the corridor to Afghan markets. Amid critical shortages in consumer and other goods, the mood in Kabul and key urban centers darkened further when news surfaced that Afghanistan was once more at the center of great power intrigues.

The wartime crisis created a space for various actors to reinvigorate older political projects. Kabul society watched nervously as German, British, Italian, French, Turkish, and Japanese diplomats sought to instrumentalize Afghans and Afghan territory for the war effort. At the same time, the conflict made possible the entry of a new actor who would utilize the opportunity to lay foundations for the reshaping of Afghanistan beyond the war: in July 1942, Muhammad Zahir Shah received Cornelius Van H. Engert, the minister of the new American legation, an institution whose influence would be strengthened by the war.

At the start of the conflict, though, the Axis powers already had extensive ties to numerous Afghan contacts and a clear vision of Afghanistan's utility. Foreign observers marveled at the inroads representatives of the Nazi regime had made. In the 1930s, Berlin had offered credit, technology, and specialists—doctors, teachers, engineers, agronomists, surveyors, and urban planners. German spies eyed the north, where Soviet émigrés might be mobilized against the Bolsheviks. Like the Russians and Soviets before them, they simultaneously cast a hopeful gaze on the tumultuous politics of the Indo-Afghan frontier. Meanwhile, the Nazis of the German colony in Kabul agitated for their cause among Afghan officials. On the eve of the war, the British worried that the Berlin Olympic Games of 1936 had allowed "young Afghan athletes to see something of German organisation and efficiency, and the tales they brought back of their experiences in Germany as compared with the hospitality they met with elsewhere in Europe lost nothing in the telling." Moreover, a new airplane flight—"of only forty hours' duration"—between Kabul and Berlin was having "an effect on the young *intelligentsia* of Afghanistan, among whom admiration and respect for the rising power of Germany is widespread."[30]

Rumors swirled about senior Afghan officials' sympathies for Berlin. Critics pointed to the ministers of health and public works, a high-ranking official of the National Bank, and others. Abdul Majid Zabuli's name arose again and again, with more than one commentator drawing attention to his ethnic German wife. According to other German accounts, the prime minister, Hashim Khan, pledged Afghan backing in the event that German forces pushed deep into Soviet territory. Meanwhile, by 1938, the Germans had become the largest of the European expatriate communities in Kabul, with some 270 men, women, and children. Some, but not all, had ties to the Nazi Party. However, from the vantage point of Nazi activists such as Siegfried Rohmeder, the influence of the German colony was ubiquitous in Afghan life, serving "the German state as well as Germany's interests." Writing for a Nazi journal that celebrated Germans around the globe, Rohmeder claimed an impressive list of successes. The German-run Nejat school had been reopened in November 1929 and counted over nine hundred students by 1938. He praised it as the top school in the country and a pipeline to German universities, pointing to one of its first graduates, who had just received marks of "very good" on all of his finals in Germany. Another school, this one associated with the Nazi Party, offered instruction to German expatriates alongside Afghans and Iranians; most were girls. Other German institutions specialized in technical education. German physicians, engineers, officers, architects, flying instructors, mining, post, and banking experts, wool traders, and insurance specialists were also active. Siemens had projects throughout the land, and Lufthansa was planning to make Kabul a hub on its sprawling Berlin to Shanghai line. Little was beyond the reach of the Germans: "The building of the Afghan sports system lays in the hands of a German sports instructor." Rohmeder emphasized that this was challenging terrain for "difficult cultural work" (*Kulturarbeit*).[31]

The Allies had further cause for anxiety about the political leanings of Afghan elites because of developments in another part of the globe. In 1939, a department of the Afghan Council of Nobles held a discussion in which some members criticized British policy in Palestine. Others disagreed and wondered how Germany or Italy would have acted in its place. According to British intelligence, the Italian government had also seized on the issue. Reaching out to mullahs throughout the country, the Italians circulated claims that Britain intended to create a Jewish state in Palestine and thus was no "friend" of the Muslim world. Like the Italians, the Germans were said to be engaging in propaganda playing up the themes of Palestine and Waziristan, the restive region in the North-West Frontier of India.[32]

In June 1941, Adolf Hitler expressed confidence that Afghanistan, together with "other small peoples," would actively cooperate with the Nazis, if only out of fear of Russia. However, Afghan authorities faced pressure from the British and Soviets to arrest or expel Axis agents, who by October 1941 had established themselves throughout the country. The Afghans risked compromising their neutrality agreement with the Soviets and feared that a successful German campaign of subversion might embolden Uzbek and Turkic émigrés to wrest Afghan Turkestan from Kabul's control. The Germans complained that Afghan surveillance paralyzed these émigré activists, preventing them from carrying out activities across the border. After the Allies invaded Iran in September, the Afghan government, eager to avoid a similar fate, gave in to the Allies' request to expel the Axis personnel. Now limited to embassy staff but buoyed by the Japanese joining the war in December 1941 and Hitler's push toward the Caucasus—as he put it, to "get hold of oil and Iran and Iraq"—German officials wanted to seize the moment to stoke unrest along the Indo-Afghan frontier.[33]

In the second half of 1942 Axis officials revived discussion, first raised in 1939–1940, of backing Amanullah's return to Afghanistan. In January 1943, one of Amanullah's Afghan followers, who had also served a year as an officer in the Reichswehr, proposed a joint operation to return the exiled king to power. He was certain that four thousand German soldiers and four hundred officers could take Kabul and depose the current government. The campaign would, by his reckoning, take about eight hours, forty-eight at the most. But developments on a distant battlefield caused yet another shift. By the end of the year, news of the German reversal at Stalingrad cooled enthusiasm among the Afghan Germanophiles and calmed Allied anxieties. At the same time, the Afghan police intensified their campaign against Axis agents and their Afghan contacts. Yakub Khan, who had traveled to Berlin for the Olympics and who was in the employ of the Abwehr, was among them. In March 1943, they arrested Bukharans, including the Bukharan amir's son-in-law. Still, German officials in Kabul reassured their bosses at home that they retained "ties to Iran, Baluchistan, Northern Afghanistan and to Afghan circles."[34]

Axis diplomats in Kabul saw the country as a staging ground for frontier uprisings against the British in India. Together with the Italian embassy, the Germans cultivated the Fakir of Ipi, also known as Mirza Ali Khan, a Qadiri Sufi leader who had led a revolt on the British side of the frontier in 1936–1937, sending him hundreds of thousands of deutschmarks to agitate against the British. Afghanistan also remained a focal point of the German campaign against the Soviet Union. Its lengthy border with the USSR appeared vulnerable, and thousands of disaffected former Soviet citizens who emigrated in the 1920s and 1930s were still in the country. The German embassy boasted that, in addition to the former amir of Bukhara and the followers of the recently deceased khan of Khiva, more than ten thousand Turkmen stood at the ready to take up arms against the Soviets. And the Soviets suspected the Germans of recruiting a Turkmen religious leader, Ishan Khalifa Kyzyl-Aiiak, as well as the brother of a leader of the anti-Soviet Basmachis.[35] Despite such claims, mobilizing the Central Asian émigrés proved challenging. Some harbored political ambitions that clashed with those of the Germans, who were wary of talk of a Turkic state on the territory of a defeated USSR. Berlin ordered its diplomats to keep their Turkish counterparts at arms length, lest they hijack the German conspiracy to serve a Pan-Turkish project.[36]

From Kabul, the Japanese launched their own spies and saboteurs against India. The Afghan government permitted Japanese engineers at Kandahar but rejected Tokyo's political overtures. Anti-Japanese agitators from China also entered the fray. In October 1942, Osman Wu, a representative of the Chinese Islamic Salvation Federation, showed up in Kabul and made the rounds to raise the alarm about Japanese mistreatment of the Chinese and to collect donations for Chinese Muslims.[37]

Afghan elites now faced intense lobbying from the Germans, Italians, and Japanese, as well as from the British, the Soviets, and the Americans. However, the Axis powers were not the only ones jockeying among themselves for domination of an India liberated from British rule as well as for control of Soviet Central Asia. Afghans, too, had their own claims on Indian and Soviet territory. A number of Afghan leaders looked to the Axis powers to return the territories lost in the nineteenth century.[38]

Following the defeat of Italy and the collapse of the Axis alliance, however, Allied victory appeared more certain. Afghan officials looked more and more to the Americans in anticipation of the need to counterbalance the growing power of the Soviets. From his arrival in 1942, the American envoy Engert had worked to convince the Afghans of the inevitability of an Allied victory. He and Muhammad Zahir Shah conversed in French, which the king spoke fluently. Engert found Prime Minister Muhammad Hashim Khan "extremely intelligent" and "capable of an objective and impartial point of view which is quite unoriental" and was much impressed by his "fairly" fluent English. The Afghans, in turn, sought a way out of the economic impasse caused by the war: Afghan goods were stuck in Karachi, and American shipping was the Afghans' lifeline to the world.[39]

The United States had become the only market open to Afghan karakul. In August 1942, the Ministry of Foreign Affairs appealed for space on American ships returning to the United States for "approximately 900 bales of karakul, 100 bales [of] furs, 250 tons of wool and 40 tons [of] pistachio nuts, all of which are now lying at Karachi." To counter the despondency that Engert found in August 1942 he wrote to Washington with "a practical suggestion to raise [the] morale of Afghan Government: Arrival of a few American bomber squadrons even if only for purely temporary duty in North and Northeastern Persia would make profound impression in Afghanistan." "It would immediately create belief here," Engert suggested, that the "United States will help stop [the] German advance into Turkestan which may have important bearing on Afghanistan Government decisions in near future."[40]

Engert was already looking beyond the war in anticipation of a greater role for the Americans in Afghanistan. In December 1942 he proposed to "build up Anglo-Saxon cultural influences" as a foundation for closer ties in the postwar period, and in January 1943 Engert proposed to assist with shipping Afghan products, so that "the Government would hail us as a true friend who had helped to free the country from the economic domination of the Axis."[41] Meanwhile, in August 1943, the Afghan ambassador in Washington, Muhammad Ayub Aziz, had complained to a State Department official that the British were strangling Afghan trade by denying access to their ships. He charged that this formed part of a longer pattern of hostility to Afghans, one demonstrated by the fact that they kept "thousands of Afghans under alien domination" along the North-West Frontier of British India. He went on to tell the American official that the Afghans would one day "take back unto itself the Afghans in question and their lands" and would do the same with Afghans under Soviet rule.

Engert was not the only American interested in an expanded role in Afghanistan. In 1942, the Board of Foreign Missions of the Presbyterian Church had sent an inquiry to the State Department about sending missionaries to Afghanistan. Engert wrote a memo to Washington saying that he thought that after the war the U.S. government should raise the issue of establishing Christian missions in Afghanistan, which he proposed to present "in a perfectly detached manner and as part of the spiritual reconstruction of the world in harmony with the ideals for which we are fighting." "Liberty of conscience and of worship," Engert argued, "is undoubtedly among the freedoms which the civilized world cherishes and which we hope to see adopted by as many countries as possible, not so much on purely religious grounds as for ethical reasons, general enlightenment, and international good will."[42]

Missionary work could not be done "in the narrow technical sense," he explained, because the Afghan government had "to deal with an extremely backward population which is very much under the domination of fanatical mullahs." Instead, he suggested that the "presence in Afghanistan of carefully selected American teachers and doctors would in itself constitute 'missionary' work of the highest order. It is the kind of work which has made itself felt, slowly but surely, throughout the world by the example set by unselfish Christians whose personal integrity, clean lives, and intellectual honesty have 'converted' thousands of men to the western (i.e. Christian) concept of life without outwardly changing their religion." In March he wrote Washington requesting irrigation engineers to replace Japanese experts working with the Afghan Ministry of Public Works in Kandahar. In March 1943 the Ministry of Foreign Affairs turned to the Americans seeking seven American teachers for physics, mathematics, and English language and literature. Engert appealed to Washington to honor the request for teachers citing a rare opportunity not only of access to a new nation in the making but of helping and guiding it in connection with the intimate problems of mental and moral adjustment which the pressure of modern forces have created. If the presence of tactful and intelligent teachers can add to the merely superficial modernization of the country a sincere effort to adapt the old Islamic creed and tradition to a new way of living we shall not only render a great service to Afghanistan but we shall make American idealism and justice and vision a positive and constructive force in the whole of Central Asia.[43]

In April, Engert confidently reported that the prime minister "was quite willing to entrust to us most of the technical development of the country as well as the education of its youth." (He noted that this was "a complete break" from the formerly pro-German minister of public works.) Engert thus emphasized the need to select candidates carefully: "Apart from professional qualifications they must have tact, patience and adaptability in primitive surroundings." Finding such personnel proved more difficult, though. An American engineer finally arrived for a week in April 1944. He was John L. Savage, of the U.S. Bureau of Reclamation, who had worked on projects that had included the Boulder and Imperial dams in the United States and other projects in Puerto Rico and the Soviet Union.[44]

In August 1944, Engert pushed for more assistance to Afghan trade, a concession that he envisioned as central to American strategy across much of the globe. He maintained that a curb in Afghan trade could lead to social unrest, and the "resulting difficulties might rouse the turbulent Afghans to widespread disturbances directed against the existing Government" and affect "the tribal areas abutting on India." "Moreover," he emphasized, "trouble in Afghanistan might have repercussions throughout the Middle East and Near Eastern area, from Iran to Saudi Arabia." Engert saw American assistance as "a small premium to insure against an annoying distraction while the war is still in progress, and a focus of Moslem disaffection in the post-war period."[45]

Thus what had begun in the early 1930s as an effort to attract global capital to fuel industrial development in Afghanistan had evolved, in a series of contingent events, to an unanticipated dependence by the end of the war on the United States, both as a market for Afghan karakul and for development assistance. American capital and know-how came to Afghanistan, as Engert's comments show, as a kind of insurance policy against the elemental dangers that supposedly lurked in Afghanistan's mountainous redoubts and that threatened to radiate into neighboring Muslim lands. The stage was then set for drawing Afghans into the heart of the nascent Cold War, a contest whose outcomes contemporaries could scarcely predict but which would ripple throughout all layers of Afghan society.

6 | THE ATOMIC AGE

THE YEAR 1946 proved to be pivotal in the history of Afghan globalism. On January 1, the official daily *Anis* printed an article that informed readers that, in the wake of Hiroshima and Nagasaki, Afghans, too, had entered the "Atomic age." Later in the year, an American engineering firm based in Idaho, Morrison-Knudsen, known worldwide for its work on the Golden Gate Bridge in San Francisco and other monumental projects, took over a canal construction project begun in 1939 by Japanese engineers in Helmand Province. The company signed a contract with the Afghan government to build irrigation works and roads in the south as part of a more ambitious scheme masterminded by Abdul Majid Zabuli, then minister of economy, to develop industry, power generation, mining, health care, and infrastructure to the tune of $450 million. Nearly a quarter of this amount would come from foreign pledges of assistance. Afghan development quickly took on a pace and international scale that Afghan elites had scarcely ever imagined.[1]

The Americans led the way. And not just in Helmand. By January 1947, the number of Morrison-Knudsen employees in Afghanistan exceeded seventy people. An American urban planner also arrived in Kabul to begin a contract for work in Kabul. In the same year the government began distributing American flour; rents had begun to rise steeply in Kabul after American engineers and French doctors and nurses flooded the city. Wages in the south also climbed sharply as Morrison-Knudsen began to recruit laborers at far above the customary rates. By 1949, the Germans were back.

Afghans dusted off the original German plans for the Sarobi hydroelectric project and hired three German engineers to resume the work.[2]

The Americans were making an impression with their promises
of technical and material progress. They put all of this on display in
the capital, with American domestic goods like the Pyrex teapot and
a Transworld Airways flight circling overhead. But their ascendant
rival, the Soviet Union, was not prepared to cede the country to
Washington's sphere of influence. The Soviet embassy staff busied
themselves with Persian and Pashto, warily eyeing the expansion
of U.S. involvement, and the Soviet Trade Agency pushed household
goods, kerosene, bicycles, cigarettes, and other items.

A British report of 1947 highlighted the growing reliance of the
Afghan government on the Americans for aid. It conceded, a bit re-
gretfully, that it was "perhaps inevitable that the Americans should
more and more occupy the position formerly held in Afghanistan by
ourselves." But the report added an important qualification: "American performance has not been impressive and has lagged very far
behind American promise." Elaborating on this skeptical note, it
continued:

> It is the Americans who, through the Morrison-Knudsen
> Company, are undertaking the improvement of the country's
> roads and the main irrigation projects; though a whole year
> has passed and there is nothing to show for all the company's
> activities except an ever-increasing number of camps and
> buildings for the housing of their employees. Work on the road
> from Chaman to Kandahar has indeed begun at last, and that
> on the Torkham to Jalalabad section should begin shortly as
> most of the machinery is believed now to have arrived; but
> the grand project for a cement or asphalt road between Kabul
> and India appears to have been abandoned, presumably owing

to Afghan lack of dollars. A number of American teachers have also been promised for the Habibia and Teachers' Training Colleges, though so far none of them has arrived.[3]

Such sniping about the Americans' capacity to work in Afghanistan began as a whisper in diplomatic circles. But it would soon gain momentum, as questions would mount about the efficacy of the partnership between the Americans and the Afghan government, a dynamic that would not have surprised the American engineer A. C. Jewett, who had offered such a devastating critique of foreign specialists fleecing the country at the beginning of the century under Habibullah.

In time, the role of Morrison-Knudsen and other foreign operations would invite growing criticism of Abdul Majid Zabuli's foray into capitalist development. In the 1930s, his scheme targeted "non-Afghans" and aimed at their exclusion from the economy while marginalizing small traders, who resented the monopolistic authority of the National Bank and its discriminatory lending practices. Rumors about suspect loans to members of the royal family and their clients swirled around the bank. Abdul Majid Zabuli's pursuit of American capital during and after the war raised further questions. The Americans were far away and untainted by a history of colonial aggression toward Afghanistan. But, as the Afghans discovered, the Americans arrived with their own agenda. They did not agree to fund everything the Afghans requested. When work on the Morrison-Knudsen project began after lengthy negotiations and multiple interruptions, it became apparent that its high costs were far more problematic than expected. There were numerous signs that the irrigation works were not having the effect that overly optimistic planners had projected. Salination was a recurrent problem, which repeatedly forced improvisation, which, in turn drove up costs. In 1950 the firm began work on the Kajaki dam, a project financed by a \$21 million credit from the American Export–Import Bank. Meanwhile, Afghans noticed that the foreign staff of Morrison-Knudsen, with their own swimming pool, medical facilities, and special housing, appeared to be enjoying lavish lifestyles. They even enjoyed bootleg alcohol bought from a Czech secretary who worked for Skoda (and who also supplied French, Russian, and Afghan drinkers). An American journalist elaborated on the tension during a visit in 1960. He observed that the inhabitants of the Kandahar suburb known as "Little America"— experts with aid agencies and American companies—excluded Afghans from their modern homes and parties and were not overly self-conscious about tooling around the town in their Plymouths, Chevys, Fords, and at least one Cadillac. He claimed that Afghans accused "the Americans of clannishness, of baseless fear of experimenting with local food and mingling with the masses on local transport, of unwillingness to let their children play with Afghans." Soviet expatriates, by contrast, mixed with the locals, living and shopping among them.[4]

The presence of the Americans drained the Afghan budget with astonishing speed but accomplished little that the royal government could celebrate as evidence of the state's paternal care for the betterment of the kingdom. The Afghans faulted the Americans, and the Americans reciprocated, pointing to a severe scarcity of competent Afghan officials who could meet their responsibilities in the Helmand Valley. Nevertheless, both parties chose to ignore or downplay mounting evidence of the infeasibility of the original project. Political face-saving tightened their wary embrace. To the Americans, Afghan authorities cited pressure to match Soviet development. In a 1952 conversation with a U.S. diplomat, an Afghan official explained that Afghans could no longer be left in the "stone age," when their neighbors across the Amu River experienced the Soviet industrial age.[5]

Contrary to the glowing accounts presented by American and Afghan authorities, the Helmand Valley project was from the outset a lightning rod for critics who smelled something rotten. In parliament, deputies demanded details about the Morrison-Knudsen deal. They panned the Americans for what they took to be the unfavorable terms dictated by the Export-Import Bank and the demands for luxury conditions for Morrison-Knudsen staff. Their hostility toward the scheme was inseparable from their reproach of Abdul Majid Zabuli for the state of the economy. Detractors condemned state cooperatives and the predatory practices of the Bank-i Milli. Well beyond the halls of parliament, Afghans of all classes grumbled about the lack of consumer goods such as sugar and soap. A chorus of critics howled about corruption. Beyond the walls of "Little America" and the royal palace, the troubles in Helmand prompted anxieties in intellectual circles about the political implications of the government's dealings with the United States. In the late 1950s, Eric Newby, a British traveler, found that locals attached "much vague ill" to the project, though in Girishk an elderly man was more explicit, complaining that the Americans had left him without electricity and that the land below the American dam turned to salt: "They did not trouble to find out, but now the people will eat *namak* (salt) for ever and ever."[6]

While Afghan elites increasingly tied their developmentalist visions to their Cold War patrons, they counterbalanced this strategy by adopting a stridently anticolonial posture. They directed this critique first toward Pakistan, condemning the new state that emerged in August 1947 as an instrument of British imperialism. The Pakistani project was fragile as it was, with considerable resistance from frontier elites. Thus it is hardly surprising that Pakistanis were not amused by the Afghan challenge to the identity of the new state. Rumors of Indian support for subversive activities intended to draw Pakistani forces away from the Kashmir theater heightened their anxiety.[7]

But the Pakistanis had inherited forceful leverage from the empire: a stranglehold on Afghan access to crucial transportation infrastructure linking Afghanistan to the world. Pakistani authorities wielded this weapon by canceling transit concessions established by the British on goods traveling by rail from Karachi to Afghanistan. In late 1949, they banned the entry of Afghan petrol trucks into Pakistan. Afghan nomads confronted new challenges on the border as well. Pakistan now insisted on the issuing of passes for the herders, traders, laborers, and moneylenders who sought to cross into Pakistani and Indian territory. Some managed to acquire passes, while others evaded the border controls. For their part, the Afghans also suspected the Pakistanis of backing Afghan exiles, including Amanullah and his relatives, and criticized the aerial strafing of Afghans by a Pakistani air force plane at Moghalgai, an outpost on the Afghan side of the border, an event that both sides later agreed to treat as an accident.[8]

In the Afghan press, the demand for autonomy for Pashtunistan, a new, autonomous entity to be carved out of Pakistan for Pashtuns, was a noble cause for Afghans, who were called on to resist the expansionist designs of their neighbor and to defend their Pashtun brethren.[9] Toward this end, Kabul dispatched agents to the frontier to recruit for the Pashtunistan campaign, and the Afghan press boasted of fervent enthusiasm among the Safis, Shiwnaris, Mohmands, and other tribal communites for the red flag of Pashtunistan.

In reality, local responses were far more mixed. Some groups sent deputies to Kabul; others pledged fealty to Pakistan. The Pakistani press reciprocated by accusing Afghanistan of being manipulated by a third party in its anti-Pakistan campaign. In September 1949, the Pakistani newspaper *Dawn* published articles that highlighted popular resentment of the government in Kabul. They pointed to opposition to the government monopoly on trade and claimed that Uzbeks and Turkmen were emigrating to the Soviet Union.[10]

The Pashtunistan issue evoked varied responses from Afghans as well. On the one hand, it was a strategy to weaken the new state of Pakistan, a rival whose universalist claim to be a homeland for Muslims everywhere was a challenge to the Afghan state. On the other, pressing the Pakistanis was a vehicle for particular elites to realize their hazy and sentimental vision of a greater Afghanistan, a campaign to recover the "lost" lands of a grand imperial past. To the Afghan regime, mobilizing intellectuals and youth for the Pashtunistan cause furnished a ready-made outlet for political participation and venting, all while beefing up the populist credentials of the dynasty. For Pashtun ethnonationalists, though, the proposition of ultimately drawing all Pashtuns into a single state was the primary attraction. Pragmatically, the Pashtunistan cause offered leverage over a space that contained Afghanistan's commercial corridor to the port of Karachi and global shipping networks. Finally, there was the weight of history, emotion, and memory of Afghanistan's contested Durand Line and its colonial origins.

It was this theme that King Zahir Shah underscored, with great fervor, in a conversation with an American official in 1961. He insisted that "an artificial border" could not erase historical ties and cited the example of tribesmen from the frontier district of Bajaur who had traveled during winter across the border to suppress the revolt of 1929. The American official's account paraphrased the king's comments: "What was he now to say to people of Bajaur when they ask for Afghanistan help, and what was he to say to his own bodyguard which contained many sons of tribesmen who had once fought shoulder to shoulder with Afghanistanis?"[11]

For many elites in Kabul, the Pashtunistan issue lay at the heart of U.S.-Afghan relations. In a meeting with U.S. officials in January 1954, Ambassador Muhammad Ludin had complained that American military aid for Pakistan unsettled the Afghans and might jeopardize prospects for resolving the Pashtunistan problem. The Afghan diplomat warned that American aid to his country's neighbors might undermine the legitimacy of the rulers in Kabul: "The relatively slower rate of economic development in Afghanistan would be difficult for the Government to explain to the Afghan people, who aspire, as do the Pakistanis and Iranians, to a better way of life."[12] Ludin expounded on the geopolitical significance of the region, sounding the leitmotifs of midcentury Afghan nationalist ideology:

> We appreciate more than anyone else that the passes which cut through [the] Hindu Kush and Sulaimen range of mountains, to wit: Khawak, Shiber-Shikari, Salung, Bamyan, Khayber, Gomal and Bolan, are critical sections of the important land routes that debouch into the Indian Subcontinent. The routes traversing these passes have been, throughout historic periods and in prehistoric times, the main highways of migration, invasion, and commerce, as well as the passageways for the traffic of ideas and thoughts. This area will inevitably be the keystone of the arch of any future scheme of defense for the free world in the Middle East. The area between [the] Oxus and Indus, and beyond that to the Arabian Sea, is one defensive unit. It has been so throughout history. The mountain

citadel in this area has always been the abode of freedom loving peoples. The strengthening, economically and militarily, of the people inhabiting this area to preserve their freedom is an obvious necessity of the defense of this part of the world.

Ambassador Ludin pledged Afghanistan's cooperation but noted that a prerequisite remained "the solution of the problem of our kinfolks, the inhabitants of Pashtoonistan."

The strengthening of Pakistan and Iran at the expense of Afghanistan risked creating a dire scenario—"a political and ideological vacuum"—and historical events linking Afghanistan and the subcontinent might come to pass again. From "their first abodes in the Hindu Kush" the "Aryan migrants" had brought "the very germs of Hinduism" to India. Afghans played a central role in a later phase of history as well: "Afghanistan was the instrument or the agency that The Almighty chose to send forth the religion of Islam into India." "Conversely," he added, it had also acted as a "bulwark" against "physical or ideological invasion of the subcontinent." "If Afghanistan should succumb to an economic and political collapse," Ludin warned, "and an ideology foreign to its history and tradition should overtake it, partly because of the cataclysmic events over which we have no control, and partly because of the lack of interest in its fate by the free world and its leaders, that will indeed be a dark day in the history of Asia. It will be a great blow to the free world and to humanity as well." The ambassador concluded by returning to an explanation of Kabul's commitment to the Muslims beyond its borders: "God was pleased to choose our people as His instrument to propagate the light of Islam in the subcontinent and to hold in common with one hundred million people the same faith and beliefs. They are our natural friends and sympathizers. We wish to strengthen this mutual friendship by preserving our identity and independence and by respecting the natural desires of others to cherish the same privileges." The Pashtunistan campaign reached a crisis point on March 30, 1955, when a group of agitators, mainly young people in student uniforms, attacked the Pakistani embassy and ambassador's residence to protest the merger of the North-West Frontier and other territories into the West Pakistan Province in a centralizing policy that the Pakistani authorities called the "One Unit Scheme." The night before, Prime Minister Muhammad Daoud had called for protests. After arriving on buses apparently arranged by the government, protesters sacked and looted the Pakistani diplomatic installations and tore down the Pakistani flag. The police did not intervene, providing foreign observers with further evidence of government complicity. Afghan crowds assaulted the Pakistani consulates in Kandahar and Jalalabad the following day.

Across the border, Pakistanis countered by attacking the Afghan consulate in Peshawar; however, the Pakistani police intervened, and the government blamed Afghan republican dissidents. The escalation in hostilities brought offers of mediation from the Americans, British, Egyptians, Iraqis, Turks, and Saudis. For their part, the Afghans were particularly inclined toward a leading role for Saudi Arabia.[13]

Visiting the Foreign Office in London in September, the Afghan ambassador explained that "Afghanistan pleads the right of self-determination of Pakhtoons who are racially a distinct entity and quite different from the rest of Pakistanis." "They are Afghans as any other Afghan inside Afghanistan," Ambassador Ludin continued, adding that these territories had been separated in the nineteenth century but never incorporated by the British. The problem, he stressed, was that "the so-called Durand Line was not in reality an order line like the other international frontiers." This bond of "race and kinship" had created unique difficulties for the Afghan state. The presence of "armed and uncontrolled tribesmen" was keeping Kabul from disarming its tribes and applying "modernisation schemes inside Afghanistan." In the end, the rulers of Afghanistan were in a delicate position: if the government did not show "moral support to the cause of the Pakhtoons they were considered anti-national and unpatriotic by the people of Afghanistan and in most cases they were overthrown, and if they followed the popular feelings, they were considered hostile by the British authorities." He claimed that it was a great injustice that the Pashtuns had been denied their right to self-determination and were forced to join Pakistan or India. The latest administrative change (the "one unit" arrangement) was "a mortal blow" to "the national existence" of the Pashtuns, one that was "as unjust and unfair as Hitler's scheme of annihilating Czechoslovakia and perhaps more." Afghanistan faced a "complete blockade" by Pakistan, in violation of all international laws, but the ambassador warned that the "Afghan nation as a whole resisted for their freedom and honour all through their history and they will do it now by all means."[14]

Afghan anticolonial agitation was not limited to mobilization against Pakistan. Afghans expressed solidarity with nationalist movements that opposed European hegemony around the globe. In 1948, fighting in Palestine was a daily front-page story in the Afghan press. During the same year, Afghan media lashed out at Dutch interference in newly independent Indonesia. In 1955, Afghanistan joined the Non-Aligned Nations movement at the Afro-Asian Conference in Bandung, Indonesia. Afghan delegates encountered activists from around the globe, among them African-American intellectuals, who would spark the curiosity of their Afghan counterparts in the decades to come. Paul Robeson and W. E. B. Du Bois sent telegrams to the conference (their passports had been revoked by the United

States), while Adam Clayton Powell, Richard Wright, and Malcom X attended in person. Richard Wright later wrote about his identification with "the despised, the insulted, the hurt, the dispossessed—in short, the underdogs of the human race who were meeting." At a speech in Detroit in 1963, Malcolm X counted Afghans among the victims of the racial injustice of colonialism. He invoked Bandung as the moment when Asians and Africans began to "recognize who their enemy was." It was the white man who was the "same one in the Congo [who] was colonizing our people in South Africa, and in Southern Rhodesia, and in Burma, and in India, and in Afghanistan, and in Pakistan. They realized all over the world where the dark man was being oppressed, he was being oppressed by the white man." The Afghan prime minister Muhammad Daoud called the conference "an historical event, worthy of the attention of the whole world, in as much as it represents the overwhelming majority of the population of the planet and is the representative of the aspirations of this population in social, economic, and other spheres."[15]

In 1956, the Suez Crisis, precipitated by the Egyptian leader Gamal Abdel Nasser's nationalization of the Anglo-French Suez Canal Company in July, prompted strong reactions from Afghan official and intellectual circles. In an address aired on Radio Kabul on August 24, Prime Minister Daoud proclaimed the familiar refrain about Pashtunistan and signaled a broader commitment to "the preservation and restoration of human rights" everywhere, though Afghan elites were especially exercised about developments in Muslim countries. They followed the Algerian struggle for independence against France and were troubled by developments in Palestine. Indeed, the Afghan representative to the recently formed United Nations had voted against the partition of Palestine on November 29, 1947, making Afghanistan just one of thirteen states to reject the UN plan for the creation of the state of Israel. Afghan media kept Palestine and, later South Africa, alive in the minds of Afghan elites and nonelites alike, and popular consumption of news in social settings such as the bazaar could connect Afghans of all social strata to these global political movements.[16]

Anti-Zionism would persist as a major trend in Afghan political life, a position that Prime Minister Daoud's Radio Kabul speech reinforced. "In accordance with this unselfish policy," Daoud continued, the government "has expressed its sympathy with and full support for the Algerian issue and the rights of the Arabs of Palestine." Addressing the controversy over the Suez, he noted that "the Government of Afghanistan expresses sympathy with Egypt and supports the right of the freedom of that country to carry out the national aspirations of the people of Egypt."[17]

Afghan outrage intensified after Israeli, French, and British forces conducted military operations against the Egyptians. In November, the British embassy in Kabul described how two days earlier, "when the news first began to spread of our bombardment of Egyptian aerodromes, a fairly large crowd of students and riffraff assembled in the town with a view to marching on this Embassy and wrecking it."[18] The ambassador, Sir Daniel Lascelles, was certain that Afghan officials had connived in the protests but that they were not keen on letting them get out of hand in a repeat of the Pakistani embassy storming in 1955. The ambassador was more alarmed, however, about "very reliable information" that the Egyptian embassy had managed to raise "from Indian merchants in the town the large sum of two million afghanis," which, Lascelles feared, would be used to orchestrate more anti-British disturbances and even a mullah-led "jihad." More broadly, the ambassador saw the events in Egypt as a grave setback for British-Afghan relations: "You will not need to be told that the

5   Afghan merchant reading paper at stand in Kabul market. 1953.
    Harrison Forman Collection at the American Geographical Society
    Library, University of Wisconsin-Milwaukee Libraries.

local effect of our 'police action' in Egypt has been deplorable.
Nothing that I can say will ever make the Afghan authorities believe
that we did not put the Israelis up to it."[19]

As in earlier periods, though, foreigners frequently overlooked
the ideological dimensions of Afghan globalism and saw what they
wanted to see, often sustaining contradictory views. In 1957, the U.S.
State Department was still referring to the country as "isolated and
primitive." In their own policy analysis, though, the Americans saw
Afghanistan through a Cold War lens. The Pashtunistan issue, one
report concluded, had meant that "relations with Pakistan are chroni-
cally embittered and Afghanistan's political and geographic isolation
from the rest of the free world has been made more complete." From

Washington, Afghanistan seemed more vulnerable than ever to the Soviet threat: "This dispute, combined with Afghanistan's desire for rapid economic development, has made its leaders receptive to offers of Communist bloc economic, technical and military assistance." The Americans remained cautiously optimistic, though, since they counted on "traditional Afghan suspicions of the USSR" and reckoned that the "Afghans are willing to accept Western assistance and technical advice and hope to have the best of both worlds." They held out hope that continued American involvement in the Helmand Valley, "both financially and in terms of American prestige," could, together with efforts to improve Afghan-Pakistani relations, prevent the Afghans from becoming dependent upon the Soviets.[20]

The foremost American priority was to court the monarchy, particularly after 1955, when the Soviet leaders Nikolai Bulganin and Nikita Khrushchev visited Kabul. American overtures led to a visit in 1963 by the Afghan king, Muhammad Zahir Shah, to the United States. He received a ticker-tape parade on Broadway in New York City and saw Cape Canaveral, Florida, and Fort Bragg, North Carolina. At the University of Wyoming, he drove a tractor and inspected cows and horses. Stylishly sporting an ensemble consisting of a hat, suit, and gloves, his wife, Queen Humaira, toured the Golden Gate Bridge and visited a supermarket in San Francisco. The royal couple also saw Los Angeles and were photographed smiling with Mickey Mouse.[21]

Viewing Afghan development almost exclusively as an arena of superpower competition, Washington and Moscow pushed flashy public works projects, even as they tended to overlook more subtle social changes initiated by the Afghan state's development efforts. When the Afghan government launched a "Five-Year Plan" (1956–1961), drawn in part from Soviet economic planning principles, a chief goal was to bring electricity to the Afghan population. Beginning in 1918, electricity produced at Jabal-us-Siraj had powered the military workshops and royal court. From 1941, a power plant at Chak-i Wardak supplied Kabul. Another followed in 1957. Diesel generators filled the gaps in the capital and in provincial centers throughout the country, even as Soviet and German aid allowed for the spread of more hydroelectric plants in the 1960s and 1970s. Two-thirds of the power infrastructure was around Kabul. Although the northern areas of Pul-i Khumri, Baghlan, and Kunduz and along the Surkhab River in Qataghan as well as Mazar-i Sharif were connected to this expanding power grid, there were fewer resources in the west and south. Kandahar finally received power from the Kajaki dam in 1977, while Herat lagged behind the rest, remaining dependent on diesel and with limited availability. Other towns had only temporary electricity.[22]

Road building was another priority of the First Five-Year Plan and, together with the construction of airports, roads were the type of high-profile infrastructure project that the superpowers favored. In 1964, the Soviets completed a 2.7-kilometer-long tunnel that cut through the Hindu Kush at the Salang Pass, radically shortening the distance to the north. American engineers had recently finished an airport at Kandahar, and in Kabul Soviet builders constructed another one. While these were for civilian use, three further airfields, all contributed by the USSR, were at military bases at Bagram, Shindand, and Dehdadi.[23]

Of all of these, the hypermodernist Kandahar airport, designed by the American firm Pacific Architects and Engineers as a series of nine arched domes arrayed in a curved line, never realized its futuristic promise. From the beginning, skeptics derided it as a white elephant. Just two weeks after President Dwight D. Eisenhower made a brief stop in Kabul where he landed at the Soviet built airfield in December 1959, protesters in Kandahar attacked a theater and a girl's school to protest the unveiling campaign recently initiated by Muhammad Zahir Shah. They also turned on the offices of two American institutions involved in the airport project, the International Cooperation Administration (ICA), a precursor to the United States Agency for International Development (USAID), and the Federal Aviation Administration (FAA). The rioters tried to storm the home of the main FAA engineer, C. Morgan Holmes, destroying his car and killing his dog. Now facing only Mrs. Holmes and her automatic rifle, the crowd nearly gained entry. Another American woman, who happened to be a former policewoman and was carrying a revolver, appeared on the scene, almost simultaneously followed by a Soviet tank driven by Afghan forces. Another ICA staff member was not as lucky: a crowd beat him in another part of the city. Between the rioting and the police repression, eyewitnesses estimated that dozens of people, perhaps as many as seven hundred, had been killed.[24]

Despite this dramatic incident, schooling was another area of intervention that quietly had important follow-on effects throughout society. At the start of the 1960s, there were some 180,000 children in school, doubling the total of 1945. The number would climb steadily to almost one million by 1978. Girls were attending in greater numbers than before, but their schooling varied by region and never reached more than about 16 percent of the total. Kabul was exceptional in this respect, too: girls made up 38 percent of the school population. At the prompting of the U.S.-based Asia Society, the Ministry of Education established local branches of the Boy Scouts and Girl Scouts, sending troop leaders abroad for further training.[25]

University education also expanded from the 1930s, when the state founded a handful of separate faculties to train Afghans in medicine and other fields with mostly European assistance. The government brought these different specialized branches of higher education under the control of Kabul University in 1947, and in 1964, USAID funded the construction by a West German firm of a campus to house the university. In 1967, the Soviets backed the addition of a Polytechnic Institute.[26]

Following the partial emancipation of women in 1959, a wave of urban women entered the workforce, taking up key positions in the expanding network of schools. Here, too, foreigners eagerly backed schemes to offer women business courses, handicrafts training, and birth control. In 1961, the Asia Society proudly touted a cooperative project with the Afghan Women's Welfare Society to establish "typing classes and a typing pool at the Society where various government officials could obtain much-needed secretarial services." The number of women working in Kabul rose from some 1,210 in March 1960 to 3,000 in September 1963, nearly all of them in the public service sector. By 1965, this figure rose to 5,680, with over half still in public service. Within two years, the government calculated that roughly a half million women were working throughout the country. A few of them were also participating in international meetings of feminist organizations in Europe and China.[27]

Families were also adapting to the times. Established in 1968 and affiliated with the International Planned Parenthood Federation, the Afghan Family Guidance Association received international assistance to disseminate information about family planning as well as to provide birth control services throughout the country. The number of Afghans who visited its clinics for contraceptives rose from 7,670 in 1969 to 78,390 in 1976.[28]

Such changes were not confined to Afghan cities. Tense relations with Pakistan had far-reaching effects beyond Afghan nationalist circles who agitated for Pashtunistan. When Pakistani authorities countered these activities by closing the border in 1961, it blocked the seasonal migration pattern of one hundred thousand or more Afghan nomads. The closure forced these traders and laborers to winter within Afghanistan and, together with other Afghan policies, hastened the decline of nomadic communities in Afghanistan. Following years of frustration with Pakistani leverage over Afghan trade and migration, the Afghans concluded a transport agreement in 1961 with the Soviets, which deepened commercial and other ties between the two countries. Increasing contact had a sizable impact on the infrastructure of the north. In 1965, the Soviet press noted the transformation of the port of Termez. "Instead of the miserable wharf of eight years ago," a Soviet journalist noted, "Termez now boasts a berthing quay more than a kilometre long, a railway network, and a forest of cranes."[29]

Aviation played a growing role as well. In 1955, Peter Baldwin, an American businessman, collaborated with Afghan investors to launch an airline company that flew domestic and regional domestic flights, and in 1956 the United States provided $14 million to expand civil aviation in Afghanistan. In 1957, Pan American Airways bought his share of the company, which was renamed Ariana Afghan Airlines. Routes to Europe, India, Iran, and the USSR followed, supplemented by Aeroflot and regional airlines. In addition to bringing an unprecedented number of foreigners to Afghanistan, this new technology had a profound effect on the sacred pilgrimage to Mecca. The *Kabul Times* reported that in March 1970, more than 3,300 pilgrims were returning from the hajj on Ariana Airlines in the next two weeks. In the immediate years that followed, some 6,000 to 8,000 went on the hajj annually.[30]

The integration of Afghanistan into these aviation networks fundamentally reshaped how audiences at home and abroad thought about the country. If in 1929, international news coverage concentrated on the panicked evacuation of hundreds of foreigners by air to escape the civil war, some forty years later Afghanistan had become a place of enchantment and exoticism in the minds of most foreigners. By the late 1960s, Kabul beckoned newlyweds from Pakistan and tourists from Europe and North America. Afghanistan became a destination for adventurers and tourists from the West. Its poppies and hashish bewitched a younger generation who crossed the globe to escape the strictures of American and European societies and to lose themselves in intoxication in the hotel rooms, or "freak hangouts" of Herat and Kabul.

For the more entrepreneurially inclined, there proved to be numerous opportunities to bring some of this experience back home, and with a fine profit. Global crime syndicates soon gained access to the country in a perfect storm enabled by an increase in air travel, a U.S.-led crackdown on opium and marijuana cultivation in other parts of the world, and a seemingly insatiable hunger among Western youth for psychotropic pleasures. Western authorities increasingly saw Afghan drugs as a threat to the world. In Iran, Muhammad Reza Shah Pahlavi pointed to opium smuggled from his eastern neighbor as one of the sources of his society's endemic drug crises and of its addict population of several hundred thousand. The shah saw another danger in Afghanistan, one also tied to Afghan youth's exposure to global currents: from Tehran, the monarchy in Kabul looked vulnerable to the penetration of communism. In reality, the youth politics that roiled Afghanistan in the 1970s were linked to the global Islamist movement as well as the global left.

This increasing connectivity inspired Prita Shalizi, the author of an English-language book meant to boost foreign interest in Afghanistan, to predict in 1966 that "as air travel comes within the reach of more people the growing cities of Afghanistan may once again participate more prominently in world trade and history, not because they still stand on that celebrated mercantile route of yore, but because they may have blossomed into important commercial centres and tourist stops on the shortest air-routes between the cities of the West and East." For the "true adventurer," travel to this "Asian Switzerland" promised a "most exciting, unforgettable and rewarding experience." Shalizi pointed out that this land from which the Aryans came was taking on a "modern look" in its cities. Women were visible like never before and "ready to face the world." The Afghan woman, Shalizi observed, "is unhesitatingly taking her place in school and hospital, in factory or office, and even in the air. Indeed, where there is work to be done, she is eager to try her hand at it, if thereby she can help her country and her people on their road to progress."

Women were even to be seen shopping at "a splendid department store," which "stands stocked to the brim with modern goods, gadgets and gee-gaws in bewildering variety, garnered from all parts of the world" catering to "fashion-conscious feminine demands that are setting a much higher standard for supply than before." "New ideas are fast infiltrating this interesting capital, nestled among the mighty crags," Shalizi added, and the country is "once again aware of the rest of the world as Kabul, the capital, reveals." Indeed, Kabul's bazaars were "crowded with merchandise that reflect this awareness—in the unbreakable glassware from France, in the handsome wools from Holland, in shoes from Italy and Beirut, in cut glass from Czechoslovakia, in piece goods from India and Japan, in electrical equipment and sanitary fitments from Germany, in watches and pumps from Russia, in stationery from Poland and the like." Shalizi presented the capital as an international city par excellence, with twenty embassies and numerous international organizations and experts, concluding that one could find here the "fascinating situation of a Britisher conversing with a Russian in stilted Persian, or an Yugoslavian jabbering animatedly in French to an Indian who reciprocates with lively gestures and English! This, then is Kabul, our capital emerging from history to catch up with the 20th Century."[31]

Indeed the physical infrastructure of Kabul and other cities had taken on a fundamentally new appearance, as new urban areas took shape according to the architectural plans of foreign architects and of Afghan architects trained abroad. In the 1930s, a district known as the "New City" (*Shahr-i nau*), had stretched out along a grid pattern to the northwest of the old royal palace, attracting foreign embassies and expatriates as well as wealthier and more Europeanized Afghans who constructed bungalows and green spaces. Muhammad Nadir Shah had even allowed a small Christian chapel to be built there in the garden of the Italian legation. The district would later be home to Western-style department stores, hotels, and restaurants. Several more planned quarters followed. In the 1960s, prefabricated apartment units modeled on Soviet housing projects emerged to the northeast of the center, an area that became known, following the Russian, as the "Mikrorayon." By 1965, Kabul was home to some 435,000 inhabitants.[32]

Against the backdrop of expanding educational, employment, and travel opportunities for men and women of means, Afghan material, consumer, and literary cultures were rapidly changing as well. From the 1940s, Radio Afghanistan was an important conduit of foreign news and music. In 1958, the Soviets began broadcasts in Pashto. Neighboring countries joined the BBC in offering similar services. Afghans discovered Elvis Presley and the female Iranian singing superstar Delkash, as well as other Pakistani, Indian, and Arab singers.

These broadcasts were entertainment, but some of them also struck Afghan political imaginations in ways that had important local effects. Afghans learned, for instance, about the Arab-Israeli War of 1967 from the BBC. Shabnam, then a girl in Herat, recalled how the news made her a partisan of the Arab cause. Word soon spread in the town that Jews were abducting Muslim children (and Shabnam herself thought she nearly escaped being grabbed on the street by a mysterious woman). Local Jews apparently fled the tense atmosphere in Herat as a result.[33]

Radio also introduced new commodities. British records were on sale at a shop across from the Kabul Cinema. By the end of the decade, foreign embassies were distributing records as well. Libraries and cinemas (among them at least one that catered just to women) were among the other new venues that connected Afghans to contemporary cultural happenings elsewhere. In the late 1950s, the Khyber Restaurant and the Hotel Kabul offered European-style dining. Upper-class Afghans discreetly sipped imported alcohol on picnics to Paghman. At the same time, Afghans also adopted new clothing styles. Harrison Forman, an American who visited Kabul in the early 1950s, spotted numerous men in Kabul wearing surplus U.S. army jackets. On outdoor racks in the street he found Western dresses for sale. Consumer goods from all over the world were available in Kabul's market stalls. The Cold War superpowers put their material achievements on display: in August 1960, 332,691 Afghans visited a U.S. Trade Exhibit in Kabul within a week of its opening. Even the languages that Afghans spoke reflected this cosmopolitan sensibility. The vocabulary of Pashto expanded in ways that reflected the growing intensity of contact with Russian and English-language technical literature. Meanwhile, more and more Afghans began using first, middle, and last names.[34]

Afghan reading habits were being transformed by a wave of foreign literature. Persian was the most important conduit to global writers. It formed a bridge to the expansive and diverse Iranian book market. Mohammad Asef Soltanzadeh remembered how he surreptitiously read American detective stories in translation while sitting at his desk at school. He later discovered Raymond Carver, who

6   Afghan merchant displaying American automobile products at Kabul
    market. 1953. Harrison Forman Collection at the American
    Geographical Society Library, University of Wisconsin-Milwaukee
    Libraries.

would inform Soltanzadeh's own short stories, which he would further develop as a successful writer in Denmark. Via his father's book-
store in Mazar-i Sharif, Aziz Arianfar encountered Iranian writers
who debated the pros and cons of socialism. Leftist tracts printed by
the Iranian Tudeh Party also circulated widely. On his path to becoming a socialist, Sultan 'Ali Kishtmand read Jack London's *The Iron
Heel* (1908) and Maxim Gorky's *Mother* (1906) as well as works by Ernest
Hemingway, Victor Hugo, and the Iranian writer Sadeq Hedayat,
who had a large following among Afghan readers. Besides this
eclectic collection of works, Kishtmand also studied the literature of
the Tudeh Party. For Soraya Baha', reading the life stories of female

Algerian revolutionaries such as Djamila Boupacha, alongside nineteenth-century French novels that opened her eyes to the injustices of Afghan society, was at the core of her intellectual formation and her commitment to revolutionary ideology. Abdul Zuhur Razmjo, another figure who would become a leading figure on the left, read a similarly diverse body of literature, ranging from Boupacha's story to Nikolai Chernyshevsky's nineteenth-century Russian revolutionary classic, *What Is to Be Done?* (1863).[35]

A generation of Afghan writers began to assimilate many of the themes that they encountered in these texts to craft an Afghan literature that would speak to the politics of their day. The socialist realism of the Soviet bloc had a special appeal for a number of men and women working in Pashto and Dari who responded to Soviet authors such as Gorky by crafting their own stories about the struggles of the Afghan countryside, about the difficulties of Afghan family life, and about the travails of migrants whose poverty and misery forced them to move in search of a more decent life.[36]

For many urban Afghans it was the cinema that brought the world to Afghanistan. It was a conduit of fashion and music and a guide to the rapidly changing mores of global society. New films tended to arrive from the United States, Europe, the USSR, Iran, and, above all, India, a few years after their premieres. All-male traveling theater troupes had crisscrossed the country in the 1930s, and in 1947 the Kabul municipality established a permanent theater, staging Afghan works devoted to patriotic and historical themes by the Afghan writers Rashid Latifi, Abdulgafur Breshna, Abdurrahman Pazhwak, Abdurrauf Benava, and others—alongside Shakespeare, Gogol, Chekhov, and Molière, while the Women's Charitable Society maintained its own theatrical group. However, in the 1950s film became king. By the late 1950s, movie theaters had sprung up in towns throughout the country. Afghan authorities annually imported some three hundred films, nearly three-quarters of which came from the Indian film industry and were usually not dubbed into local languages. Some Soviet films were accompanied by subtitles or were produced in (or dubbed into) Tajik (generally comprehensible to Dari speakers) and Uzbek, a language spoken in much of the north. In the early 1960s, Kabul had four movie theaters. The Women's Charitable Society also sponsored separate screenings for women, and the Behzad theater scheduled women-only shows. The Goethe Institute and American Center also organized special film screenings that were available for free to the general public. Perhaps reflecting a preference for subject matter that was prominent in popular Soviet cinema, a Soviet commentator claimed Afghan audiences were particularly drawn to films about battles, sports, the circus, and ballet. Yet in 1962, Elvis Presley's *Love Me Tender* arrived, and Elvis songs became a staple of youth performances. In December 1963 the Kabul, Behzad, and Zaineb cinemas played Russian films with translation into Persian, while the Park cinema featured the Disney Western *Ten Who Dared*. Afghan viewers were treated to seeing the American actor Dean Martin "speaking in flawless Dari," as one bemused foreigner put it, in *How to Save a Marriage and Ruin Your Life* in a Kabul theater.[37]

Many of these changes were concentrated in the capital, but the state's infrastructural projects, coupled with migration, affected other vital regions and a much wider population as well. In the east, the Afghan government founded a new city, Khost, in Paktia Province as part of a wider effort to reorient the local population away from neighboring Pakistan. A German technical-assistance team advanced this same goal by launching several projects aimed at modernizing agriculture and irrigation infrastructure and at managing the region's forests. Mark Slobin, an American ethnomusicologist who did fieldwork in the north in the late 1960s and early 1970s, saw Kunduz as "a kind of Afghan California, where people have drifted in from all parts of the country for jobs and new land, and have developed a generalized dialect and way of life, while keeping roots in the old homeland and maintaining some local traditions." Pul-i Khumri was "the most important truckstop in the country." Slobin viewed it as "a forward-looking community." It was "a town created by Afghan-Russian city planning, with a textile plant, a large hydroelectric station, a cement factory (built with Czech aid), and a huge silo for grain storage." In the mid-1970s, German researchers identified traders as the most mobile group in Afghan urban society who served as intermediaries between the cities and the countryside. Most of the traders they questioned in Kabul had visited several provinces on business or religious pilgrimage, and almost a third had been abroad, mostly to Saudi Arabia, Iran, Syria, Iraq, Kuwait, Pakistan, and India. A few had been to Europe as well.[38]

Herat, too, was being remade by labor migration. The surge in oil revenues in neighboring Iran drew as many as a half million Afghan laborers across the border. In 1976, a British visitor found Herat "noticeably deserted," adding that crops had been left in the field, and that women had taken up many jobs formerly done by men. In order to construct a slaughterhouse, a local builder had to resort to prison labor. However, remittances from Afghan workers in Iran were substantial, perhaps as much as $200 million a year. Indeed the Iranian embassy in Kabul thought that Afghans sent $200,000 home on a daily basis.[39]

All of this development infrastructure and industrial energy—what many Afghan elites took to be the dawning of an era of industrial modernity—prompted some intellectuals to imagine a very different political order that would reflect this spirit. Amid the relatively permissive political atmosphere of the immediate postwar years and the

return of some political prisoners from prison and other figures
from exile, writers, scholars, and landed notables gathered to discuss
how to launch a political struggle on behalf of the people against
the monarchy, which they regarded as a corrupt and despotic pillar
of a profoundly unjust society. Calling themselves "Awakening
Youth" (*Wish Zalmayan*), they formed a political circle in Kandahar
in 1947.

One of its leading thinkers was the writer Nur Muhammad
Taraki, who was born into a poor shepherd's family in Ghazni Province in 1917. As a young man, he encountered firsthand the workings
of Afghanistan's most dynamic transnational capitalist network. In
Kandahar he went to work for a fruit processing factory run by the
Pashtun Trading Company owned by the capitalist magnate and,
later, minister of national economy Abdul Majid Zabuli (whom we
met in Chapter 5). In 1935, his fruit company sent the young Taraki
to India to serve as a clerk for the firm. In Bombay, Taraki confronted
a colonial city in the throes of economic depression and civic agitation. While taking night classes, he apparently became interested in
socialist and anticolonial thought. He may have also been exposed
in Bombay to the Khudai Khidmatgars, or "Servants of God," the
pacifist movement that mobilized the Pashtuns of the North-West
Frontier in an alliance with Mahatma Gandhi in the struggle for independence from the British. Somewhere along the way Taraki
discovered the Soviet writer Maxim Gorky, whose work he would
emulate in his own stories of poor Afghans who found dignity in labor
and suffering.

Taraki and his fellow writers and activists pledged to work for
the progress of the nation and the enlightenment of the masses,
joining the relatively open parliamentary elections of 1949 and em-
bracing new press freedoms introduced in 1951. They established a

paper, *Angar*, named after a minor official of the National Bank, in which Taraki demanded food, clothing, work, and political liberties on behalf of the people. Other contributors wrote essays identifying progressive intellectuals with the will of the people or called for a constitutional system with political parties and proper elections, while others sketched out a vision for a more enlightened, but still powerful, monarchy. Critiquing how the state had pursued development thus far, a number of the essays in *Angar* focused on the plight of workers and the toiling masses.[40]

As in imperial Russia, several of these intellectuals internalized the Marxist expectation that workers would be at the heart of the political struggle even before there were substantial numbers of workers to speak of. An event to the north of Kabul in 1963 seemed to spark this revolutionary process at last. The Gulbahar textile factory was an emblem of Afghan industrial development. Built with German assistance on the Panjshir River, a town grew up around the complex in 1960. Its manager was a German-educated protégé of Abdul Majid Zabuli, who sent him around the world to visit textile operations in North Carolina and elsewhere. In 1963, workers' demonstrations broke out at the Gulbahar factory. The Persian-language service of the BBC broadcast news about the workers' plight, and it became a national event.[41]

Financed largely by foreign capital and export revenues, the appearance of sites such as Gulbahar and the presence of a modest, but symbolically powerful, contingent of industrial workers seemed, at least to university students and their allies in literary and clerical milieus, to be leading to a world that mirrored the scenarios laid out by theorists and critics in countries that had already experienced similar transformations. Industrial society was on the march, and to the young radicals who formed the People's Democratic Party of

Afghanistan (PDPA) in 1965, the class struggle outlined by Marx had begun.

To intellectuals and students who drew inspiration from leftist critiques of the status quo, this was a portent of an emancipatory struggle for democracy. For students and army officers studying abroad, time in the Soviet Union and even in the United States strengthened their commitment to a leftist future in Afghanistan. Hafizullah Amin, the revolutionary who would ultimately come to power in 1979, would later claim that he had been drawn to socialist student groups while taking political science and economics classes at the University of Wisconsin in the summer of 1958. As a graduate student, his political activities at Columbia University Teachers College earned him the scrutiny of the American authorities, who apparently convinced him to return to Kabul before completing his degree, a disappointment that may have lingered as a source of resentment for Amin. Afghan student organizations in places like the University of California–Berkeley also attracted the attention of the American Friends of the Middle East, widely thought to be a front organization for American security organs (and the Central Intelligence Agency, in particular), which tried to recruit Afghan students from the early 1960s, offering them scholarships and cash. One Afghan student in California, Abdul Latif Hotaki, accused Zia Noorzay, a former president of an Afghan student group at Berkeley, of being on the CIA payroll, along with many others who went back to assume key positions in the Afghan government. Hotaki's charge was, of course, that such characters did the bidding of Washington. But exposure to American life could have the opposite effect. One young army officer, Nur ul-Haq Ulumi, who received training at Fort Knox and other American facilities, alongside his Soviet training, would command troops on behalf of the socialist government in the south of the country in the 1980s. Decades later, when interviewed in

Kabul in 2013, he would remember his Soviet counterparts fondly and draw a stark contrast with the post-2001 American approach to Afghanistan.[42]

Afghans studying in the United States or Soviet Union were not the only ones paying attention to the left and the broader geopolitical context, however. Afghan students returning from Cairo and cities in Iran had a different reading of the situation. Having been exposed to the writings of Hassan al-Banna and Sayyid Qutb, among others who believed that Islam offered a comprehensive political program that answered every question of modern politics, they were convinced that Islam offered a path of development that was superior both to the imperialism of the capitalist and materialist West and to the atheist socialism of the East.

Pakistan was another conduit of this critique. In 1960, Pakistan had retaliated against Kabul's Pashtunistan campaign by deploying its own Pashto-language print media and radio campaign. The Pakistanis charged that it was, in fact, the state of Afghanistan, not Pakistan, that oppressed the Pashtuns. Afghans were miserable under the autocratic rule of the royal family, they charged, and would be better off under an Islamic republic. Worse still, they were under the spell of the godless communists and were taking orders from Moscow. To this rising tide of Islamists, these events foretold the terrible onslaught of godless materialism and a betrayal of righteous virtues and traditions. Both sides took up the struggle in print and in the hallways and dormitories of Kabul University and other public spaces in the capital and, after a new constitution opened up political space for debate in the parliament and the press in 1964, these debates intensified.[43]

The next major shock to the Afghan political system came in 1968, when student protests radiated from the Sorbonne and Paris to the rest of Europe and on to Mexico, the United States, and elsewhere. Afghanistan did not escape this global wave of protest. Students at the teachers' colleges (Higher Teachers' College and the Academy for Teacher Educators) staged "sit-ins," and student activists tried to forge ties with factory workers. In May and June, students and workers staged demonstrations in Kabul. In June, another strike broke out at the Gulbahar textile mill. The Parcham (meaning "Banner") branch of the PDPA claimed that fifteen to twenty thousand people had joined in demonstrations at the factory. Demonstrators ultimately won concessions from the factory management following the involvement of the governor of Parwan Province and a visit by members of parliament. They received a new boss and a 20 percent raise. Later in the month, workers at the Jangalak factory in Kabul staged demonstrations, though the police intervened and arrested some ninety people, among them writers and editors of a Maoist paper, *Eternal Flame (Shola-yi jawid)*. The arrests targeted several members of the Mahmudi family, relatives of Dr. Abdul Rahman Mahmudi, who had been imprisoned for his liberal activism in 1952, where he remained until his death in 1961. The government then banned the paper. Roughly a week later, strikes spread farther to the north. In Kunduz, workers at the Spinzar ("White Gold") cottonseed-oil factory called a general strike. British managers at the factory retreated to Kabul during the standoff with police and military forces.[44]

A leading Marxist intellectual named Babrak Karmal interpreted the events of 1968 as confirmation of what he understood to be "the scientific insight of revolutionary theory." The working class, led by its avant-garde, the PDPA, would be Afghanistan's savior. In an essay of 1969 entitled "On the Strategy and Tactics of the People's Democratic Party of Afghanistan," Karmal emphasized that the "strategic goal" of the party in the historical epoch in which Afghanistan found itself was "the transfer of ruling power from the reactionary forces

of the feudal large landowners, from the large comprador bourgeoisie who are dependent upon imperialism, feudal and bourgeois
bureaucrats and the senior officials into the hands of the national and
democratic forces like the workers, peasants, and urban and rural
laborers, the great majority of the intelligentsia, the administrators of
state and private institutions, the lower middle class, the middle class
and the so-called 'national bourgeoisie.'" The second phase was to be
the creation of a "socialist system in our land," but according to "scientific" criteria, the country was still in the first epoch of "national
democratic revolution." "Revolutionary theory teaches us that under
the conditions of the reign of imperialism, the national democratic
revolution is directed not only against feudalism, but also against
foreign and domestic monopoly capital." The "working class" was
the most progressive force, with the leading role to play. Those who
doubted this committed "treason against the cause of democracy,
progress and the interests of the Afghan people." Karmal suggested
that the transition between the two epochs might be hastened. The
goal of any government to emerge from a national democratic revolution would be to be put an end to "the remaining imperialist
influences, destruction of the feudal system, introduction of land
reform, establishment of national industry and the industrialization
of the land, the following of a non-capitalist development path, and
an independent, progressive, and peace-loving foreign policy." And
it was the duty of the avant-garde of the working class to secure the
position of the working class in the revolutionary democratic order.

Karmal stressed that revolution, as the "locomotive" of society,
was natural and inevitable. However, he added, a revolution was not
to be confused with "pseudorevolution," that is, a conspiracy or the
will of some extraordinary individual. Revolution was the fruit of
"concrete historical circumstances." The role of the avant-garde then
was to understand when the timing was right for the appropriate

measures. It could not be rushed. Toward this end, victory of the national democratic movement depended on the "creation of a front with the participation of all democratic, national, patriotic and progressive forces" with the goal of fighting "reaction and imperialism" and of forging unity between workers and peasants.[45]

Karmal's program found the deepest resonance among Afghan urban youth, which remained the most dynamic force in the country, but they also explored political agendas and interests that went far beyond PDPA dogma. Of all Afghan social groups, young people maintained the most active ties to a wider world. By the mid-1970s, various experts estimated that, out of a total population of roughly thirteen to fifteen million, there were about one hundred thousand who might be counted as newly educated and "middle-class," and that this number included about ten thousand who belonged to the "intelligentsia."[46]

The sons and daughters of these urban and educated Afghans and more established aristocratic circles studied foreign languages in the prestigious high schools and at university, giving them access to an array of international radio and print media. They enjoyed expanded opportunities to study abroad. Many of their teachers had returned from study at European, Soviet, or American institutions such as the Columbia University Teachers College, where Afghans had trained since the early 1950s with USAID funding. Some had direct access to foreign instructors, including the likes of Herman Hudson, an African American professor from Detroit who taught through the Columbia program. Many young Afghans consumed the countercultural music, dress, and politicized language that circulated globally, not least among the thousands of young people from the United States and Europe who visited Kabul from the late 1960s on the "hippie trail." Perhaps as many as five thousand or so of these young foreigners stayed on in the capital, mixing with young Afghans, who sported their own "mod hair styles and bell-bottom pants" at places like the Khyber restaurant.[47]

Concern with the American war in Vietnam was another point of connection with the hippies and political youth around the globe, but the Afghan context differed. Afghans were exposed to foreign media coverage of the antiwar movement in Europe, the Soviet Union, the United States, Iran, and elsewhere. However, disapproval of U.S. policy in Southeast Asia was long an official Afghan position, one first established by its participation in a 1964 document signed by seventeen nonaligned countries, and never confined to Maoist or pro-Soviet circles. Coverage of the war was a staple of the official Afghan press and a key issue upon which Afghan rulers could establish their Third Worldist bona fides. Yet expression of concern about the war was more than a pretext for official posturing or propaganda, though it served these purposes too. When Prime Minister Muhammad Hashim Maiwandwal visited the White House in March 1967, discussion of Vietnam was a top priority in his meeting with President Lyndon Johnson. The American president defended the U.S. position on negotiations with the Vietnamese and criticized Hanoi's rejection of the latest UN proposal. For his part, Prime Minister Maiwandwal confirmed Afghanistan's commitment to the principles of the 1964 declaration and explained that the issue "attracted a good deal of attention and now that there is democracy in the country it was sometimes used by the politicians for their own purposes." He went on to express "his concern over the problem describing it as an explosive situation which he feared might escalate into a bigger danger."[48]

Just as Maiwandwal feared, antiwar agitation escaped government management and became a major cause among the Afghan left. Even the young U.S. Peace Corps volunteers, who were supposed to be putting a positive face on American power in Kabul, included vocal opponents of the war. Antiwar protests rocked Kabul in January 1970, when U.S. vice president Spiro Agnew arrived for talks with the prime minister and a visit with the king. Journalists estimated that some three hundred to four hundred protesters marched through the streets with banners that read "Agnew go home" and "Stop killing Vietnamese." One reporter described many of the demonstrators as "wearing Western-style clothes," pointing to the seeming incongruity of political agitation in "this hippie mecca of cheap and legal marijuana." They also reportedly threw bricks and destroyed an American flag but were kept at a distance from Agnew's motorcade, which passed along Kabul streets with U.S. and Afghan flags and cheering onlookers. Among the protesters who were arrested for throwing eggs was a figure named Najibullah, a burly twenty-three-year-old medical student and member of the Parcham faction of the PDPA who had already made a name for himself as a wrestler and strongman and who would play a pivotal role in the following decade.[49]

Afghan responses to Americans were not entirely negative, however. Later in 1970 several thousand on-lookers gathered at an outdoor arena to watch the Afghan national basketball team defeat a visiting Chinese squad. The Afghan players employed a defensive scheme adapted by their American coach, a former Peace Corps volunteer, from the playbook of the famed UCLA basketball coach John Wooden.[50]

The mobilization of young people and the explosion of global youth culture had many other consequences for Afghanistan. In the large cities, and Kabul in particular, young men and women became consumers of international trends in music, literature, and film and adopted the latest hairstyles and clothing. Erika Knabe, a German scholar studying Afghan women in the late 1960s and early 1970s, estimated that new fashion trends appeared in Kabul only six months after they hit elsewhere, though sometimes the lag might be a year. "Mini, midi, and maxi [skirts] compete in the Kabul streets," she reported, and in summer 1972, Afghan women began wearing sleeveless dresses, "a shocking spectacle for many Afghans." New and used articles imported from the United States were available at a vast secondhand-clothing bazaar. In Herat, the used clothing market was known as the "American Bazaar." From the early 1960s, the international distribution by Western charities of used clothing had created a vast global traffic in tens of thousands of tons of clothing; Afghanistan's markets were among the top recipients.[51]

Clothing styles and appearance symbolized class differences and more. An American visitor to Herat explained that the shops in the American Bazaar did "a thriving business for Afghans in Herat and elsewhere [who] seem convinced that Western clothing, no matter how ragged, is a symbol of status and that native costume is a symbol of ignorance and low position in the Afghan social hierarchy." Some Afghans, male and female alike, resented the ostentatiousness of those who tried to appear fashionable by turning their back on all things Afghan. Class resentment came through in letters that women sent to the editors of a family radio program complaining about makeup and young people trying to look like the Beatles and decrying the fact that so many educated Afghan women were marrying foreigners. To conservatives, these new styles of youth dress and sociability were an affront to piety and morality. Student radicals from the faculty of Islamic law and theology at Kabul University joined their teachers and clerical allies in reading these developments as proof of a most diabolical intrusion of Western materialism and Soviet atheism. Adapting their political programs to counter what they saw as a kind of disease, they also lashed out on occasion at women in public. In confronting women on the street, they were not alone. Harassment of women seems to have been most frequent along the fringes of the most cosmopolitan spaces of the capital around Shahr-i Nau, where the most modern restaurants, hotels, and department stores catered to well-heeled and foreign consumers.[52]

Within these enclaves, though, more traditional social conventions were suspended, and more fashionable international norms prevailed. Whereas elite Afghan families had hosted private parties in secluded compounds (and continued to do so), these sites were public, offering opportunities for the mixing of the sexes and conspicuous consumption. Popular gathering places for young people included the Charikar kabob shop in Shahr-i Nau, which attracted teenagers and middle-aged people as well, especially on Friday evenings. The "modern" department-style shopping experience, with imported goods and fixed prices, could be found at Qari Aman and Hamidi, while some venues blended local and global commodities, for example, where street vendors sold salted nuts and potatoes along with Coca-Cola and Fanta.[53] Music was another attraction. Some cafés had jukeboxes, and there were even a few nightclubs, where the legendary singing star Ahmad Zahir got his start. The Intercontinental Hotel hosted dances. Mári Saeed writes in her memoirs that being a teenager at the Intercontinental was like being in Europe, "as we knew it from television and magazines." Besides the opulent surroundings, she noticed Iranians and Pakistanis enjoying themselves there as well.

In 1976, the hotel staged a beauty contest, organized by a Pakistani, to find "Miss Kabul," a title Saeed's sister Rana won one evening. By this period, middle- and upper-class Afghans had absorbed standards of beauty found in the West; lighter skin had became an ideal. Mixing with foreigners—and with the opposite sex—also happened in the darkened cinema of the American Center (most other theaters held segregated screenings). As with women's dress, such sites became the targets of critics on the right, but they also attracted the ire of leftists like the protesters who singled out the Marco Polo and Gulzar Restaurants as well as the 25 Hour and Rotary Clubs as "places of revelry and corrupt morals." At the same time, the spread of telephone lines afforded young people a more private means to socialize without such scrutiny, as several accounts attest, to flirt or play pranks on their friends and enemies.[54]

Young elite women also traveled extensively. A 1977 graduate of the Malalay school, Shahla (Popal) Wadud visited Kandahar, Herat, Mazar-i Sharif, Sheberghan, Ghazni, Laghman, and Jalalabad. Before leaving Afghanistan in 1982, first for India and then California, she had visited Germany, Austria, Czechoslovakia, Yugoslavia, Turkey, and Iran. Upper-class Herati women traveled a lot as well, especially to neighboring Iran. Sometimes the destination was related to the performance of ritual duties; but sometimes the purpose was a visit to one of the Iranian banks where wealthier families deposited much of their assets. Marriage was another factor in women's mobility. In the north and east, in particular, women often married men from other locales. Mores were also changing in domestic spaces. An American researcher in the early 1970s observed that Heratis, like other Afghan women, were "devoted card-plays" ("card sharks whom you must keep your eye on") who "were very interested in Western card games and took readily to 'stud-poker,'" all while passing a water pipe filled with tobacco and a "pinch of hashish which tends to create a happy euphoria among the group."[55]

Illustrated print media were another way of connecting to global culture. The Afghan press reported widely on foreign artists, musicians, and film and commented on recent dance crazes. Afghan writers tried to contextualize all of these phenomena, an effort that often led them to explore the topic of race in American life and, in the case of the guitarist Larry Coryell, to speculate about the lines between "black" and "white" music. Postcards and illustrated magazines about Indian film actors and actresses and Indian and Iranian singers circulated as well.[56]

Urban demand for popular entertainment prompted local artists to answer the flood of foreign music and film and the accompanying cult of celebrity with adaptations of traditional Afghan genres and themes for mass consumption. Nationalist intellectuals and state officials in the Ministry for Information and Culture pushed amateurs and the hereditary class of professional musicians alike to develop an authentically Afghan voice. Gramophone technology and records had circulated from the early 1930s, but radio presented a major impetus for domestic musical production on a grander scale. Radio Kabul, subsequently renamed Radio Afghanistan, housed in a modern architectural complex built with Soviet aid in a Kabul suburb, was the epicenter of musical transformation, beaming live performances and, eventually, recordings throughout the country. The descendants of Indian musicians who had performed at the royal court played a central role in organizing ensembles to perform on the radio. American and Soviet advisers were also involved, though Afghan artists were apparently more resistant to Western advice. The *rubab,* a short-necked lute, remained the preferred instrument, and Hindustani styles were predominant. However, the Radio Afghanistan orchestras steadily incorporated saxophone, piano, clarinet, electric organ and guitar, and drum kits alongside more traditional Afghan and Indian drums, lutes, and harmonium, though some of these, too, underwent modifications for the radio and the spread of popular radio songs. The station broadcast a variety of musical styles, including local styles from Afghanistan's diverse regions, and Uzbek, Turkmen, Baluch, and Pashai programs were started in 1972, leading many to turn off Soviet broadcasts in those languages to hear what was coming from Kabul.[57]

Indian and Pakistani film was another resource, and Afghan artists copied or reworked the film songs, occasionally with Persian lyrics, or drew on favorites that entered western Afghanistan from the prolific Iranian recording industry.[58] An amateur hour showcased high school and university students from Kabul performing "in a style combining elements of Afghan, Iranian and Western pop music."[59] During research in Herat in the mid-1970s, the ethnomusicologist John Baily found that musicians spoke of demand for constantly revitalized songs and used the term *mod*, from the French *mode,* to characterize "fashionable tunes" and "fashionable songs." Children, Baily discovered, were a key barometer of the constantly changing music scene, singing and dancing to their parents' repertoire of recent popular songs. Listeners recorded their favorite songs via the increasingly ubiquitous audiocassette recorders, some of them brought from Iran by migrant laborers, and a lively trade in cassette tapes ensued. Observers like Baily saw the spread of music by way of radio and cassettes as a sign of the weakening of the religious establishment, and in some instances of a shift in some mullahs' views, which had long been critical of music.[60]

Radio Afghanistan polled its listeners to weigh in on their favorite performers and songs. In 1969, the official newspaper *Anis* sponsored a poll to determine the country's favorite singers and actors. The top vote-getter in the singing category was a figure whose songs in Dari, Pashto, and Hindi circulated by audiocassette for some fifteen years but wanted to remain anonymous, apparently due to concern about his family's disdain for the dubious reputation of the singer in the eyes of more traditionally minded Afghans. He thus became known as "Nashenas" (Sadiq Fitrat Nashenas)—"the Unknown"—and garnered 1,170 votes, more than three times that of his closest competitor. In the female category, Mrs. Zhila edged out Mrs. Rokhshana. Rafiq Sadiq topped the "best actor" poll, and Aman Ashkrez won out as the best radio performer. The future superstar Ahmad Zahir, the son of Dr. Abdul Zahir, emerged from the amateur student milieu and went on to play in nightclubs and mixed parties in Kabul, accompanied by electric organ and drums. Shahla (Popal) Wadud remembered Ahmad Zahir being at the peak of his popularity when she graduated from Malalay Lycée in 1977: "everyone was seduced by his pleasant voice." (His strong resemblance to Elvis Presley may have played a role as well.) Once ostracized in some circles because many Afghans associated singers with barbers—a social category thought to be shifty and untrustworthy—radio singers became stars, receiving fanmail, adulation in the newspapers, and more. "I was able to marry the girl I wanted," boasted one of them, "and if I wanted another wife a thousand women would write and ask for my hand."[61]

Beneath this cheery, entertainment-filled veneer, Afghan dependence on foreign capital and a deepening divide about the course of development sharpened political tensions in the kingdom. In shoring up the Afghan monarchy, one strategy on the part of the Americans and a like-minded faction in Afghan officialdom was to expand the private sector. "Afghanistan is experiencing a tentative and limited but nevertheless important swing toward capitalism," wrote the American scholar Louis Dupree in 1970. Previously, Dupree remarked, private investment had been a marginal phenomenon. As recently as 1967, it was the work of "minority groups"—"the Hindus, Sikhs, Uzbeks, and Qizilbash" who engaged in "export-import business." The only fully private enterprises were the Omeed Textile Factory, the Herat Cotton Company, the Leather and Shoe Company, and the Afghan Woolen Industry.

From the 1950s, foreign advisers had pushed greater private investment. Their advice met with a cool response, though. Dupree singled out Muhammad Daoud's premiership from 1953 to 1963. Daoud had "put the brakes" on the National Bank and other would-be investors, foreign and domestic. A meddling bureaucracy and burdensome taxes stifled private enterprise, even as foreign debts became due for the grand infrastructural projects of the 1950s. Dupree credited a 1967 Afghan law with "a great leap forward in private investments," inspite of Daoud's mistrust of businessmen. Afghans involved in the foreign development projects parlayed their newly learned skills into their own enterprises, while Afghan students returning from abroad did much the same. Some of these businesses imported "radios, cameras, watches, electrical appliances, and other gadgets," which they then sold to Indian and Pakistani consumers who traveled there for the express purpose of making such purchases. According to Dupree, the new law was the handiwork of William McCullogh, an American attorney whom the Asia Foundation sent to Kabul to advise the government. Housed in the Ministry of Commerce, an American advisory team, Thomas H. Miner and Associates, played a role in its implementation.

The law, Dupree claimed, had the effect of opening up the investment market to new actors who applied for licenses that permitted new commercial activities, including duty-free imports from around the globe. This development angered established merchants like the one who complained to Dupree: "In the past, barbers were pariahs. Now they invest money with the best of us. And Royal Family women do not hesitate to open beauty salons and shops. And *mullahs* now charge even higher interest on loans. The vermin are coming out of the barbershops, the bazaars, and the palace to take advantage of the new laws. But we with legitimate interests have our hands tied." Within roughly three years, Afghans had opened some thirty-eight firms, drawing on about $3.5 million in domestic capital and $6.3 million from numerous European and regional investors. Against this rosy picture, Dupree also noted that Afghan factory labor was unstable and that the country lacked a stable food supply as well as an adequate network of lending institutions, even though the Afghan Commercial Bank (Pashtany Tejarati) had recently lowered its rates. After exploring options with the World Bank, the government then turned to Chase Manhattan Bank, and Afghan merchants apparently offered to pool $2.5 million to facilitate the creation of an "Industrial Development Bank."[62]

But this foreign aid, perceptive critics noted, backed members of the ruling class, giving them leverage against rival contenders and freezing the contest for political power. Numerous observers found fault with the "glamour" projects backed by the great powers. Writing in 1969, an American expert, Richard S. Newell, cautioned that, despite the stunning changes in Afghanistan's infrastructure, "Afghan development to date has been dominated, if not overrun, by foreign money and foreign ideas." "One can hardly resist drawing a lesson from the cooperation achieved between groups of Russian, East European, American, West German and UN advisors in the conference rooms of the Afghan ministries," he continued, crediting the Afghans with playing "an impeccable role as an honest broker of political goods." However, Newell's aim was to point out the "obvious drawbacks to multisided aid." Rivalries among donors was one problem. Kabul University hosted advisory teams from four countries, while the Ministry of Planning had representatives from three countries plus the United Nations. He worried that donors' priorities would overwhelm the objectives of the government and the Afghan people. As examples he cited redundant and incomplete projects and a general pattern of "delay, duplication and confusion."

Bidding wars led to shortcuts. Some foreign private companies resorted to bribes to secure government contracts. Afghan officialdom, already a small community, was stretched to the limits by having to devote so much time and energy to meeting with and managing the aid missions. Newell claimed that many Afghans had come to see the foreign donors as being chiefly responsible for development, adding that this "dependence has taken its moral toll and corruption may not be its most important symptom."

The training of Afghans abroad brought its own set of problems. They returned home, Newell claimed, "with imperfectly digested ambitions, prejudices and professional or technical standards garnered from their foreign experience." Thus these specialists reflected the conflicting orientations of the donor countries, a dynamic absent only in the military, which was squarely the bailiwick of the Soviets. He warned that without an authentically Afghan approach to development the country risked instability and "civil commotion abetted by foreign meddling, a prospect far more destructive to contemporary Afghan society than were the dynastic wars of the nineteenth century."[63]

Even Abdul Majid Zabuli, the architect behind Afghanistan's global search for capital to propel development and political stability, had by 1970 expressed regret. Warning of "anarchy" and faulting incompetent officials and parliamentarians, he argued that, above all, the mistake Afghans had made was to accept more and more loans from abroad without developing their own administrative talents to manage Afghanistan's resources. The foreigners were following "their own plans and goals." They had injected the "morphium of their loans" and Afghans had been left "strangled and delirious," facing a deep crisis.[64]

Abdul Majid probably did not choose his metaphors lightly. Away from the ministries, banks, and prestige project construction sites,

contact with foreigners had begun to transform the Afghan countryside in staggering fashion—and for decades to come. Western
youth instigated far-reaching changes. New fashion trends among
hippies in the United States and Europe made Afghan brightly colored hides and skins *(pustins)* all the rage. Foreign entrepreneurs descended on Kabul and exported some $2 million of them in 1967–
1968. Louis Dupree remarked on the swift Afghan response: "Some
twenty shops, employing many women, sprang into being in Kabul
to meet the demand shaped by articles in *Life* and *Look* and featured
on the Twiggy-like models on the covers of fashion magazines." But
foreign consumers were capricious. By the second half of 1969, pustin
sales dropped precipitously, and many Afghans who had increased
their investments and hired more workers faced losses, and most of
the new pustin factories went under.[65]

Hippies and other young Westerners had a taste for two additional commodities from Afghanistan—cannabis and opium—that
proved far more consequential for Afghanistan's place in the world.
From Hamburg cafés to the surfer bars of Laguna Beach, California,
word spread like wildfire about the exotic, intoxicating pleasures to
be found in the Hindu Kush. Young adventurers arrived by plane
and car, typically passing from a starting point in Europe and then
through the Balkans, Turkey, Iran, and then Afghanistan before traveling on to India or perhaps Kathmandu. The route, and its illicit
treats, became more routine when a network of buses and low-cost
hotels sprouted up along the way. Travelers could also turn to a staple
of information aimed at this audience and its tastes.

In 1973, Tony Wheeler's *Across Asia on the Cheap* (the inaugural
volume of the Lonely Planet travel series) informed readers that the
"big seller in Afghanistan" was "weed" and advised them, "so long
as you only buy in small amounts you're extremely unlikely to run
afoul of the law. Have your last drag before you get to the Iranian

border." In its Pashto vocabulary section, alongside the words for "bread," "tea," "water," "yes," and "no," the guide helpfully explained how to say "hashish," "marijuana," and "How much?"[66]

In the early 1970s, several thousand hippies flooded Kabul in midsummer. Of the ten thousand visitors who arrived annually from Great Britain, a small number joined American, German, and French youths at cheap hotels where hashish was inexpensive and plentiful, and other drugs could be purchased over the counter in nearby pharmacies. Smuggling was another temptation. Hashish costing ten pounds a kilo in Kabul could fetch four hundred pounds in Europe. Tourists smuggled small amounts in their luggage, while major operators shipped large quantities by airfreight or car or sent them in rail containers via the Soviet Union. When the Afghan authorities did catch smugglers, the professionals among the foreigners managed to bribe their way to freedom; opportunistic young tourists often faced more serious trouble: the British embassy conceded that "we have our share of British subjects in medieval Afghan gaols." But once in prison, foreigners still had access to drugs. Prison guards sold enough hash, British authorities feared, to keep the would-be smugglers "permanently stoned."[67] Worse still, the report pointed out, the British embassy had "buried twenty British subjects in the last two years" in the cemetery established after the Second Anglo-Afghan War.[68]

In 1971, Peter Willey, a British scholar who visited Afghanistan on behalf of the Anti-Slavery Society, sounded the alarm about "two evils, slavery and narcotics, which, acting together, are destroying not only the lives of the Afghans but tens of thousands of young men and women all over Western Europe and North America." Willey claimed that foreign addicts, lying in "sun drenched squares that reek of death and decay or in sordid, tawdry lodging houses," had become so ravaged by hashish that Afghans kept them as pets: "I have seen young Englishmen begging like dogs for scraps of bread and hash."[69]

In February 1971, law enforcement authorities announced the largest seizure of hashish to date in the United States. With a street value of about $1.5 million, the shipment of 170 pounds of hashish had originated in Afghanistan and was concealed in a specially outfitted Ford truck, which smugglers had shipped from Holland to New York. Counternarcotics officials identified William F. Wilson, a twenty-five-year-old surfboard maker from Honolulu, as the driver of the truck who traveled to Afghanistan to buy the hashish. The accused "ringleader" was a filmmaker and their accomplices were New York college students.[70]

Another smuggling gang, the Brotherhood of Eternal Love, formed a network that stretched from Laguna Beach across the border into Mexico. It reached to the East Coast of the United States and eventually spanned the route that took hippies and drug enthusiasts from Western Europe to Afghanistan and beyond. Inspired by Timothy Leary's celebration of LSD, its distribution chain supplied countercultural luminaries from Jimi Hendrix to Charles Manson. Leary himself ended his flight from the law in Afghanistan.[71]

Illicit drugs brought Afghanistan into a global web of trafficking and regulation. Afghan poppies had fed the enormous demand of Iranians, especially after the shah decreed a ban on opium in 1955 in Iran (followed by partial legalization in 1969), but now Afghan opium and hashish drew criminal organizations from every continent. The great powers and transnational institutions like the United Nations and World Health Organization followed. For the United States in the late 1960s and early 1970s, the focus on drugs fed on anxieties about the youth counterculture and challenges to American foreign policy and the war in Vietnam. American law enforcement fought Richard Nixon's "War on Drugs" around the globe. "The men and women who operate the global heroin trade are a menace not to Americans alone, but to all mankind," Nixon proclaimed. He condemned them as "the slave traders of our time" and "traffickers in living death" who "must be hunted to the end of the earth" and "left no base in any nation for their operation."[72]

The United States made aid contingent upon cooperation with American-led drug control. By the early 1970s, Afghanistan was squarely in its sights. Turkey had recently agreed to end opium production. The Afghan state had first banned opium production in 1946, and the Afghans had signed on to international agreements to control narcotics production and established two cabinet-level committees on the issue. Still, various international observers recognized that farmers continued to harvest significant amounts of opium. Poppies grew in at least four provinces, often within view of major roads. Afghan opium and hashish were already in the pipes and syringes of consumers in Europe and North America—and had likely reached these markets in smaller amounts for a decade or more—but drug control experts did not yet know the scale of Afghan integration into global trafficking networks. Meanwhile, a growing stream of American and European travelers flowed toward the Hindu Kush.

In search of escape and intoxication in an exotic locale, thousands of young tourists—castigated as "freaks" and "hippies" in official British documents—backpacked and hitchhiked to Afghanistan. At the Iran-Afghanistan border, many were ferried across the frontier by a German who ran a special commuter service for Western travelers. David Zurick, who made the voyage in 1975, recalled making the seven-mile trip in "a battered Mercedes bus, painted in psychedelic hues faded from the sun" that was also home to the German driver. Others flew directly to Kabul, where hotels had begun to cater to guests with a vast appetite for hashish and opiates. Already in 1972, British authorities claimed these small hotels numbered one hundred in Kabul alone. Much of the smuggled opium ended up in Europe, especially Germany, and the British thought the

Frankfurt and Amsterdam routes of Ariana Airlines had been thoroughly compromised by smugglers. "Canadian junkies," they concluded, were among the main culprits in carrying on the European trade.

To the Western powers, Afghan criminal law and procedures seemed hopelessly outmatched. When caught, those in possession of narcotics might pay a fine. From the beginning of 1971 to August 1972, one British report noted, Afghan authorities had arrested thirty-three foreigners on drug charges (twelve Britons, nine Canadians, and two Australians). To date, only one person sat in jail for drug possession: an American citizen. The expatriates were turning to harder drugs, including cocaine and heroin, and international drug syndicates appeared to be entering the scene, all at a moment when the Afghan state lacked an antidrug and antismuggling infrastructure. Already in 1965, the director of USAID in Afganistan, Delmas H. Nucker, had singled out the need to reform tax collection and combat smuggling and corruption as the key to improving Afghan finances. Indeed, smuggling of all manner of commodities—from timber, karakul, yarn, and tires to watches and millions of heads of livestock—likely exceeded the value of legal trade, especially in the southeast, but also along the Soviet and Iranian frontiers. High tariffs on imports made smuggling attractive, as did the tariffs levied by the Iranian and Pakistani governments.[73]

To answer this challenge, American, German, and British law enforcement offered the Afghan police training and advice but found their efforts stifled. These advisers complained, for instance, that Afghan authorities arrested a key trafficker—a merchant named Sufizadah—only to release him within an hour, after members of parliament and other influential figures intervened on his behalf. According to the foreign drug enforcement officials, one of the most audacious traffickers was the nephew of the minister of the interior.

They suspected Ahmadullah Rahmati Mansuri of organizing in 1971 a $3 million shipment of hashish that had been intended for Denver, Colorado, but had been intercepted in Edmonton, Canada. Terence Burke, the head of the Bureau of Narcotics and Dangerous Drugs, concluded that drug traffickers had set up labs to process heroin and morphine in Herat and Kandahar. According to a British colleague, Burke was certain that the Afghan drug traders had learned about his investigations; and he feared that his life would be in danger if he traveled to Kandahar, where more and more of the processing took place. Behind the scenes, British and American advisers counseled the Afghan authorities, warning them of the immense dangers they confronted and proposing crop substitution and other measures to gain control over the situation.[74]

In 1973, Afghan farmers answered this demand by turning to poppy cultivation like never before. The U.S. embassy in Kabul warned Washington that the "poppy problem is countrywide." However, it heatedly refuted charges that poppy growing was rife in the U.S.-backed Helmand River Valley area. A recent inspection visit by foreign experts had resulted in accusations that USAID technicians and a Peace Corps volunteer had been assisting an Afghan farmer who happened to be photographed in his lush poppy field. Noting that the USAID director cut off aid to opium growers in May, the embassy insisted that USAID support was actually a deterrent. Embassy estimates suggested that poppy cultivation was just 1–2 percent of total cultivation in USAID areas but as high as 10–15 percent in others.[75] The embassy reasoned that the rise in poppy cultivation was a reasonable response to demand created by U.S. eradication efforts in Turkey, Thailand, and Mexico. Life was always precarious in Afghanistan, but two years of drought had made farmers even more desperate. The embassy cautioned against withdrawing aid, including expertise, seeds, and technology from farmers at a critical time when "the Palace and the Prime Ministry have expressed determination to take definitive steps, country-wide, with help from the international community, to eliminate the cultivation of the poppy in Afghanistan."[76]

After Muhammad Daoud overthrew his cousin Muhammad Zahir Shah in a coup of 1973, the republican government stepped up measures against the drug trade—and the hippies that sustained it. Long-haired youths found it harder to get visas. Hotels became more strict. The American writer Paul Theroux saw a major change as well. Afghanistan had been "cheap and barbarous," a place where visitors could "spend weeks in the filthy hotels of Herat and Kabul, staying high." Since Daoud's seizure of power, things had changed. It had, the misanthropic Theroux grumbled, become "expensive but just as barbarous as before." "Even the hippies have begun to find it intolerable," he complained, adding, "the food smells of cholera, travel there is always uncomfortable and sometimes dangerous, and the Afghans are lazy, idle, and violent."[77]

Foreign donors ratcheted up the pressure. The Nixon administration threatened to end aid for states that did not go along with the American drug control program. Discussions about a U.S.-backed proposal for a road construction project between Kunduz and Fayzabad stalled, especially given the disappointing news coming from the Helmand River Valley, where the Americans had invested twenty years and some $80 million. In a 1974 conversation with U.S. officials, Muhammad Naim, Daoud's brother, referred to the Helmand Valley project as "an unfinished symphony" and requested more support. The reputation of both governments was on the line. By this stage, the Asian Development Bank and the Iranians were involved in parts of the Helmand development scheme. The Afghans continued to look to the Americans for further aid, though. And the U.S. Embassy remained disappointed in the Afghan response: "Nobody can be as interested in the development of the Valley as the Afghans themselves. Yet the Government of the Republic of Afghanistan has not yet demonstrated that it is sufficiently interested in the Valley to make the administrative decisions and to assign the competent personnel there that are required for a successful development effort." The embassy thus recommended that the United States not "reinsert its presence on an overall basis in the Valley" because it would allow the Afghan government "to postpone its assuming the responsibilities in the Valley it should and can assume." It proposed to signal a generic willingness to help the government "improve the lives of its rural population in whatever area of the country appears appropriate, including the Helmand–Arghandab region." The British Embassy in Kabul summed up the mood: "The Americans were very embarrassed to find that local farmers had been making use of the irrigation and fertiliser provided through the project to grow opium poppies."[78]

Afghanistan was both a producer of opium and a transit point for drugs moving from Pakistan to Iran by car, truck, camel caravan, and even boat. The Americans cited "the government's limited police enforcement capability and the rugged terrain" as the chief factors making the country so vulnerable to drug trafficking but let the UN Fund for Drug Abuse Control take the initiative with Daoud, who had agreed to strengthen the government's drug control measures.[79] In negotiations with the UN and American drug control authorities and citing success in eliminating opium in Helmand, the government agreed in summer 1974 to use UN funding to survey cultivating areas including Paktia, Badakhshan, and Nangarhar followed by an eradication program. Indian experts were to survey areas of cultivation, and a new Soviet-built road would open up the remote area to closer scrutiny by international agencies.[80] Moreover, Kabul established an antismuggling unit staffed by twenty officers, and a

UN narcotics adviser from West Germany was in place to consult with Afghan authorities, pushing them to join Interpol. At this stage, the United States remained unhappy about what it took to be a very weak commitment on the part of Afghan officials to the issue and was hopeful that the U.S. Drug Enforcement Agency (DEA) could play a greater role.[81]

In December 1974, the Americans found cannabis cultivation to be even more extensive than opium production. They estimated that Afghan farmers produced some four hundred tons annually, nearly one third of total global production in 1970. The harvest was then refined as hashish for export and dispatched along the same trafficking routes as opium in small consignments. Foreigners were thought to be involved in the production of hashish oil, a skill that Afghans had recently developed as well. Daoud's coup had disrupted some smuggling networks by stepping up policing in Kabul and by intensifying surveillance at Kabul International Airport, but the traffic in hashish persisted, with deliveries made in the countryside and the product moved by car and truck.[82] By 1975, there were two DEA agents working out of the U.S. embassy. The government acknowledged that drug addiction had become a problem in opium cultivating regions but maintained that in the cities it was limited to the foreigners. There was evidence of some heroin production: in one instance an Iranian chemist was identified. Raids during the first part of 1975 found a cornucopia of drugs, raw and manufactured: "3.5 tons opium; 2.5 kg heroin; 21,450 dosage units pharmaceutical morphine; 50 grams pharmaceutical morphine powder; 14 kg hashish oil; 1.5 tons hashish; 150 dosage units LSD; 4,500 dosage units pharmaceutical amphetamine; and 1.5 kg manicured cannabis." Seventy-three Afghans and thirty-one foreigners were arrested.[83]

Cannabis fields were ubiquitous in some areas. A UN official claimed in Turghundi (near the USSR border) that "nearly every field

I saw was a hashish field." But in autumn 1976 the government went on the offensive, burning cannabis crops in Kandahar, where the crop was interspersed with peanuts and melons, as well as fields near Mazar-i Sharif. The most aggressive effort was near Kushka in Herat Province, where the security forces reportedly destroyed 25,000 acres of cannabis plants, according to the UN. However, by the spring of 1977, the U.S. State Department was in consultation with the British about cutting off aid to rural areas if the Afghans did not do more to eradicate poppies.[84] Meanwhile, the British proposed to make Badakhshan a showcase of treatment for addicts.

On April 5, 1978, in testimony before Congress, Mathea Falco, director of the narcotics control program of the State Department, requested $500,000 for a crop substitution project designed by UN and U.S. experts in Upper Helmand. Additional funds were to come from other international donors. In the same testimony, the American official acknowledged that the United States had been advising the Afghans not to permit development funds being diverted to promote opium cultivation. As a sign of progress, she cited news that in January the government had destroyed seventy hectares of opium poppies that were being grown in a USAID project area.[85] Despite this rather optimistic assessment, it was clear to all parties that Afghan farmers had adapted these American development projects to their own ends. A Cold War infrastructure project now anchored an illicit commodity chain that stretched across the globe. The Afghan countryside would be mired in these dense webs for decades to come.

Capitalizing on seemingly limitless demand and generous foreign aid, Afghan exports had found a lucrative market generating vast financial resources, but not at all as Abdul Majid Zabuli had anticipated when he dreamed in the 1930s of constructing a progressive, industrial order in Afghanistan. Afghanistan was awash with technocrats from East and West and with aid programs that supported everything from birth control clinics and business classes for women to basketball and foreign languages. These were precisely the secular missionaries the American envoy Cornelius Van H. Engert had in mind during the Second World War.

Per capita, Afghans enjoyed some of the highest rates of foreign assistance anywhere. On a tour of the Middle East and Eastern Europe in 1974 alone, Afghan diplomats received offers from Kuwait, Czechoslovakia, Bulgaria, Iraq, and Libya. Even remote villages were seamlessly integrated into the global economy, if only through an aid project, the cultivation of drugs, seasonal labor migration to Iran or Pakistan, or the smuggling trade with their neighbors. By the end of the 1970s, then, Afghans inhabited a modernity shaped by kaleidoscopic forces, fusing the local and global, that enmeshed Afghans in relationships that increasingly placed them in a perilous position within a world order whose norms were dictated by the Cold War superpowers. Drugs had drawn Afghans more deeply into the global economy through illicit channels. Similarly, foreign aid projects had targeted Afghans as pawns in an ideological contest between the great powers.

However, Afghans were far from powerless. The commitment to the Pashtunistan cause in elite circles—punctuated in 1974 by Afghans and Pakistanis trading charges of terrorism—had trapped Afghans in a nationalist project that challenged the territorial integrity and identity of their neighbor and thus guaranteed regional instability. To break free from these entanglements—and to engage the world on their own terms—would lie at the heart of new kinds of globalism that would captivate the next generation of Afghans.[86]

7 | REVOLUTIONARY DREAMS

WHEN THE AMERICAN miniseries *Roots* appeared on Pakistani television in the early 1990s, it inspired an Afghan writer based in Peshawar to reflect on the state of the world. He was one of seven million Afghans who had fled the country following a coup against Muhammad Daoud by a leftist revolutionary party in April 1978 and the Soviet military intervention that began in December 1979. Writing in 1991 for *Blood-Pact (Mīṣāq-i khūn)*, an organ of the Afghan jihadist political party Jamiat-i Islami-yi Afghanistan, the anonymous author detailed some of the most dramatic scenes of Alex Haley's 1976 novel and film of the following year. The capture of the African Kunta Kinte by white-skinned Europeans, followed by his vicious bondage in chains and arduous journey to a life of slavery in America, offered a poignant lesson. To flesh out its meaning, the author focused on a glaring discrepancy between Haley's book and the film. Unlike the novel, the television adaptation ignored the fact that the noble Kunta Kinte was a refined Muslim who had been forcibly converted to Christianity.

The film, then, was tangible evidence of a long-running campaign, a war, in fact, to discredit Islam. Referring to the recent withdrawal of Soviet forces from Afghanistan following a nearly ten-year occupation in 1989, he noted that the victorious Afghans had since fallen into disfavor in the eyes of the West. The just cause of the Kashmiris and Palestinians, the author added, had similarly been ignored. Meanwhile, Christians were exploiting differences among Muslims everywhere. Recently, though, Muslim nations were beginning to awaken. In the United States, Islam had also been enjoying a revival, the author claimed, despite poor leadership under Elijah Muhammad, the leader of the Nation of Islam, who "lacked sufficient knowledge" and who gave Islam "a bad name," hinting that he may have been a saboteur put in place by white elites. Under Malcolm X, and particularly after his hajj journey and meeting with scholars in Saudi Arabia, where he adopted the name Malik Shabazz, black Muslims in America had entered the main currents of the Muslim revival by forging extensive contacts with Muslims around the world. To counter the rise of Islam in the United States, the American filmmakers had deprived Kunta Kinte of his true religious identity, one of sophistication and nobility, as part of a broader Christian strategy to weaken and ultimately destroy Islam.[1]

A similar pathos and sense of betrayal marked other Afghan thinkers' reflections on the world at the conclusion of the anticommunist jihad. At a 1993 speech in Mazar-i Sharif, Abdul 'Ali Mazari, whose charismatic leadership a majority of the Hazaras came to accept in the 1980s, stressed that no one but the Afghans who waged jihad—the *mujahidin*—had sacrificed so much to bring about such sweeping transformations. In Mazari's account, Afghans stood at the center of the world's attention. Indeed, his speech featured echoes of the visual imagery that some mujahidin employed to portray the planet as a living witness to the struggle between the mujahid and the communist. "The world witnessed how two empires met with defeat in this valiant land," he argued. "The world was amazed," he continued, by the story of the Afghan defeat of the British, resulting in the independence of India and the creation of Pakistan. Because of the Afghans, the British were compelled to "withdraw from the world and return to Europe." Despite enjoying a high level of development and possessing nuclear weapons, the Russians met with a similar fate, even as the world had written off Afghanistan and devoted its energies instead to saving Pakistan and the Persian Gulf from the

Soviet menace. It was the blood of the mujahidin that had changed the course of history for all of humanity.[2]

These two illustrations of Afghan globalism reveal how militants of various stripes, while mired in the early 1990s in a bloody struggle pitting faction against faction for control within the country, brought an extraordinarily diverse and cosmopolitan repertoire of ideas and conceptual frameworks to bear in interpreting the anti-Soviet jihad. Foreign commentators tended to emphasize the increasing resort of the mujahidin groups to ethnic recruitment and the general ethnicization of Afghan politics during this period.[3] However, these illustrations demonstrate the continued appeal of key themes of twentieth-century Afghan thought. Amid the breakdown of the Afghan state, and the strategic use of ethnic categories to frame political mobilization, Afghans continued to express curiosity about African Americans and the politics of race in the United States, to seek unity in anticolonial nationalist sentiment, to search for religious authenticity and global solidarity, and to think comparatively about development, among other concerns.

What unified these different elites, together with their enemies on the left, was the conviction that something truly momentous and universal was under way in Afghanistan from the late 1970s. "Revolution" was the key word that seemed to capture the political moment. From left to right, these thinkers resembled so many others in the twentieth century who saw themselves as participants, to borrow the language of Ernst Jünger, himself a veteran of the First World War, in an entangled drama of war and revolution that was "of cosmic significance."[4]

And for each, the project of transforming Afghanistan had a performative aspect. Leading figures who shaped the conflict positioned themselves as actors on a global stage. Whether waging a struggle against capitalist imperialism or godless socialism, they told their followers and themselves that "the world" *(dunyā)* had focused its collective attention on the drama unfolding in Afghanistan. Either as audience or field of action, the *dunyā* had become an indispensable part of the struggle.

In fact, the period from 1978 to the present has been one in which Afghan political struggles escaped the country's borders completely, becoming entangled with myriad regional and global forces. Nearly half of all Afghans were displaced or became refugees. They improvised new lives in camps in Pakistan or struggled to survive in less than hospitable conditions in Iran. Others made their way to Europe, the United States, or Australia, but new hardships awaited them wherever they turned. Soon after the April coup in 1978, Moscow and Washington both began seeking ways to direct political developments in the country. The Soviets sent advisers and finally troops, while the Americans formed a coalition of European, Saudi, Egyptian, and other allies to supply weapons and fighters. Foreigners of all political orientations made the Afghan cause their own, arguing that this was the pivotal struggle of our time. Dozens of foreign aid organizations, not to mention as many criminal networks who built on their experiences in the 1970s to expand the drug trade, swarmed the refugee camps and parts of the country.

The revolutionaries who seized power in Kabul in April 1978 saw themselves as agents of universal progress and enlightenment. Declaring the foundation of the "Democratic Republic of Afghanistan" (DRA), they set out to remake their country. And quickly, too. They were determined to put an end to all "feudal relations" in Afghanistan, to spread literacy, spur industrialization, emancipate women, and end discrimination against ethnic minorities. They clearly looked to the Soviet Union for inspiration. But, as staunch nationalists, they resisted the accusation that they were merely Trojan horses for the USSR. Indeed the People's Democratic Party of Afghanistan (PDPA) would remain highly factionalized, and its members, though numbering just a few thousand, would harbor diverse agendas. Their sympathizers, mostly young and educated, would bring a similarly eclectic enthusiasm to some, but not all, elements of the revolution.

In an interview with a Swiss journalist in June 1978, the sixty-one-year-old writer turned revolutionary Nur Muhammad Taraki denied that the PDPA merited the label "communist" at all. "We are Afghans and represent the class of the working people," he explained. The general-secretary was equally coy about calling the party "Marxist." "We regard ourselves as radical reformers and progressive democrats," Taraki insisted. The new rulers wanted to improve the welfare of the people. They respected Islam and other customs and accepted private property. They were, he continued, committed to an impartial foreign policy and were open to foreign assistance from any quarter.

A revealing bit of tragicomedy followed. Taraki urged his interviewer to read the party program for himself. The journalist, Andreas Kohlschütter, replied that no foreign journalists, or indeed any of the foreign embassy staff, had managed to find a copy of this text to see what the new regime was all about. An apologetic Taraki admitted that he had left his at home. Kohlschütter's description of Taraki's desk, featuring a Dutch preserves jar repurposed as a flower vase, suggests the image of a quixotic figure hurtling the country toward some unknown abyss. Later accounts by journalists and historians have generally been less perceptive and even more invested in the idea that it was the Soviets who imposed this project and necessarily provoked mass resistance—and, insofar as scholars have paid attention to Afghan actors, that the Afghan left was doomed to fail in such an ostensibly conservative and religious society.[5]

With the passing of time and the cooling of some of the passions of the Cold War, however, the story of Afghan socialism and its relationship to global communist movements appears more complicated. The Soviet KGB recruited Taraki in 1951 and paid him an allowance to provide intelligence and occasionally mount a protest against the Chinese embassy or engage in some other vaguely subversive activity. But Afghan socialists were not necessarily interested in towing Moscow's line. For intellectuals such as Dastagir Panjshiri, a PDPA activist, watching the American defeat at the hands of the Vietnamese, a nation of peasants who had achieved socialist revolution and anticolonial victory without a working class or the other preconditions of more orthodox Marxist theorizing, was a profound inspiration. Moreover, there is more to Taraki's quibbling about political labels than subterfuge.[6]

As a group of intellectuals, the PDPA leadership was small and unrepresentative of the society as a whole, but they connected with a broader stratum of educated Afghans who identified with the left, progressivism and anticolonialism. Most came from urban backgrounds, but others had been raised in rural settings, where they witnessed firsthand the brutal exploitation of peasants and where, they later claimed, they developed a critical attitude toward Afghan political and social realities. Dialectical thinking and Marxian categories were staples of the Afghan intelligentsia, for whom "objective conditions" pointed to a brighter future. From the mid-1950s, the Soviets had assumed the leading role in training and equipping the Afghan military. They offered stipends for civilians to study in the Soviet Union as well. Officers who returned from the Soviet bloc added to the ranks of military personnel who had become dissatisfied with the monarchy.[7]

For many Afghans who were sent abroad for study, though, their placement did not completely determine their political orientation, or at least not in an easily predictable way. Perhaps as many as half of the top rung of PDPA leaders had gone to university in the United States. They included Hafizullah Amin, who had studied at the University of Wisconsin and Columbia University Teachers College (and went on to become president in September 1979). In similar fashion, in 1972, the Soviets managed to recruit Azhar Abdullah Samad, who had received police training in the United States and Egypt and who once ran the Kabul airport, to work for the KGB.[8]

When questioned about their experiences as students in Moscow and Leningrad, Afghan men recalled warm friendships. Livened by drink and female students, dormitory life was international, multi-ethnic, and social. General Abdul Qadir, the son of a shepherd who led the military coup that brought the PDPA to power, was regularly invited to the home of the Soviet trainer who prepared Afghan pilots and shared meals with him and his wife. By the early to mid-1980s, however, Soviet citizens were not the true believers of a bygone day. The Afghans discovered that Soviet reality did not live up to Soviet propaganda. Especially after Mikhail Gorbachev launched perestroika, student debates were lively, and the presence of Jews and other non-Russians added to the skeptical environment that many Afghan students found on Soviet soil.[9]

Given this range of ideological perspectives and some ambiguity about what the new government stood for in 1978, rival Afghan political groups took great care from the outset to manage how they were represented. Significantly, they deployed labels derived from a universalist conception of history and attached them to events that they imagined as the dawning of a new political order. Bitterly divided by questions of ideology, Afghan elites and counter-elites nonetheless arrived at a kind of consensus: the Afghan nation would be remade in this moment of world-historical import. For the communists, the events of 1978 constituted a "revolution." Like the Bolsheviks and other revolutionary movements before them, they branded their opponents "counterrevolutionaries" and "reactionaries." And like so many of their radical forefathers, the Afghan socialists' reading of this master revolutionary script alerted them to the dangers of internal enemies. Conspiracy haunted the Saur Revolution (*Saur* was the Afghan month in which it occurred) at every turn. The bitter history of antagonism behind the Parcham ("Banner") and Khalq ("Masses") factions provided a ready-made fault line that seemed to present the party, and the Khalqis in particular, with a clear guide to identifying internal conspiracies that had stalked revolutionary movements everywhere.

The Khalqis imagined their foes not merely as conspirators and traitors, but as villains aligned with a global movement to stamp out progress wherever it might advance. Nur Muhammad Taraki labeled his Parchamist rival Babrak Karmal and his cronies "lackeys of foreign reaction." Having seen Muslim religious leaders mobilize against Muhammad Daoud's unveiling campaign and the spread of education for girls and having battled them at Kabul University and elsewhere, the leftist revolutionaries expected a backlash from religious circles as well. They charged that their religious opponents in the mosque were under the control of the Muslim Brothers, the mostly underground international network of Muslim activists who agitated against socialism and Western capitalism and imperialism in Egypt, Syria, Jordan, and elsewhere in the Arab Middle East.

The Khalqis branded their Muslim opponents "Ikhwanis," castigating them as "enslaved servants of the international reaction and colonialism." Articles in the *Kabul Times* challenged their claims about Islam, countering that it was "a religion in the interest of humanity and progress and advancement" and "a means of hapiness [*sic*] in this world and the other." One article cited the work of a professor from al-Azhar, the prestigious Islamic school and mosque in

Cairo, and condemned the Muslim Brothers' campaign to undermine the Egyptian government and its modern infrastructure of dams, industry, trains, hospitals, power plants, and clean water. At the same time, the Democratic Republic worked to bolster its Islamic credentials. Officials publicized their participation at a meeting in Benghazi, Libya, of the Islamic Red Crescent Society. They also hailed the doubling of the number of pilgrims to Mecca. At a ceremony at Kabul International Airport in October 1978, the head of the state-backed clerical body sent the pilgrims—who would number six thousand that year—on their way with the reminder that "with the establishment of the Democratic Republic of Afghanistan we Afghans have gained high status in the international society and therefore our behavior should be in such a way to represent real Afghans and Muslims."[10]

For the Afghan communists, expressions of solidarity from socialist movements in other countries were further proof of their inevitable victory over the "dark" forces arrayed against them. In October 1978, the Kabul Times covered a visit by a trade representative from the Socialist Republic of Vietnam to the Nangarhar Valley Development Project. The Afghans greeted their guest with verses from the Quran and speeches celebrating the revolution and condemning the "corrupt intrigue of the reactionary elements" such as Babrak Karmal and his allies. Reminding the Afghans that the Vietnamese had struggled for thirty years "against colonialism and imperialism," the Vietnamese official had arrived, the article claimed, to congratulate the Afghan people on the Saur Revolution, which was not just a "victory" for Afghans but a "victory for all progressive people." Similarly, in New Delhi, a representative of the new Afghan government joined an international conference pledging solidarity with the antiapartheid struggle in South Africa and with anti-Zionism in the Middle East. In Kabul, Afghan and Indian officials marked the

109th birthday of Gandhi by highlighting their "common bond" in fighting against "world colonialism."[11]

By the one-year anniversary of the coup, though, the Afghan socialists' relationship with their most important ally, the USSR, had grown tense. Evidence mounted that their revolutionary project was faltering and that the revolutionaries had embarked on a dangerous path that the Soviets might not be able to correct. Caught unaware by the plans of the coup plotters, Soviet advisers scrambled to get a grip on what this government was doing in the name of international socialism. Leonid Bogdanov worked as an adviser in Afghanistan from 1978 to 1980 as the top KGB official and has left a revealing account of the strained relations between Soviet and Afghan officials. Like many other Soviet memoirs from Afghanistan, his work betrays an inclination to disassociate himself from brutal and disastrous policies and to cast blame on the Afghans. Still, one can corroborate much of his narrative by comparing it with documents produced at the time.

Like many other Soviets performing their "internationalist duty" in Afghanistan, Bogdanov was shocked at both the brutality and radicalism of key Afghan figures. KGB officials could not be accused of being particularly squeamish about the use of force against perceived enemies, but Soviet politics had changed in significant ways since Stalin's death in 1953 and the subsequent disavowal of mass terror under Nikita Khrushchev beginning in 1956. Bogdanov singled out Hafizullah Amin and Asadullah Sarwari, defense and security officials respectively, as figures whose ideological zeal—and penchant for executing large numbers of people—posed grave dangers to the state. The Afghan revolutionaries struck him as being oddly detached from reality. He claimed that Amin twice boasted that the Soviet Union had taken sixty years to build socialism, but that the Afghans would do it in six. "You'll see," Taraki assured him, "in a year nobody here will even go to the mosque."

Bogdanov found Afghan pronouncements about the territorial ambitions of the DRA disconcerting as well. The minister of internal affairs told him that Afghan borders should extend to the Indus River, while Hafizullah Amin predicted that the Afghans would be swimming in the Indian Ocean at Karachi. Bogdanov described another chilling impression of the security chief Asadullah Sarwari: after the KGB adviser lost his wristwatch while on a fishing trip, Sarwari dispatched a force of some 120 soldiers to find it, threatening to shoot them if the watch was not found by morning. Bogdanov also expressed dismay when he learned that a military official (and future head of the general staff) personally shot 150 people implicated in a mutiny at Jalalabad in summer 1979. In all such cases, Bogdanov asserted, he and other Soviet advisers, whose numbers grew to about five thousand by autumn 1978, cautioned against mass reprisals and the arrest of party members. The Soviets would not shy away from violence when they found it necessary, of course, but their advisers did not want the reputation of the USSR to be tainted by violence they could not themselves fully control. Moreover, as in their criticism of the ways Afghans had introduced land reforms and targeted Muslim clerics, the Soviets cautioned that the Afghan revolutionaries were alienating the masses and not doing enough to build a social base for the revolution. The Afghans rarely asked for advice, according to Bogdanov. When they did seek Soviet input, the Afghans rarely listened. Bodganov cited the example of Hafizullah Amin's determination to eliminate the Mujaddidis, the politically influential family that led many Naqshbandi Sufis. The KGB adviser warned against it, but Amin arrested and executed them anyway.[12]

Meanwhile, opposition to the rule of Nur Muhammad Taraki grew within party and government circles and across Afghan society. Afghans poured across the border into Pakistan. Regional developments compounded the challenges facing the Democratic Republic.

In 1977, General Zia ul-Haq had come to power in Pakistan in a military coup. A committed anticommunist, he launched a multifaceted program to make Islam and Islamic law the guiding principles of Pakistani politics and public life. Muslim religious activists with revolutionary ambitions were on the march in Iran as well. In January 1979, a figure scarcely known outside of Iran, Ayatollah Ruhollah Khomeini, rode a massive wave of protest against Shah Muhammad Reza Pahlavi and returned to Tehran from exile to spearhead the creation of a revolutionary "Islamic Republic."

By March 1979, these tensions came to a head in the western Afghan city of Herat. Rebels launched attacks on government and Soviet positions, killing a number of the Soviet staff and the family members who had accompanied them. Soviet military advisers then recommended firing on unarmed crowds of protesters. The fighting claimed some 3,500 civilian lives.

A transcript of a March 1979 telephone conversation illustrates the rocky nature of the Afghan-Soviet relationship at this pivotal moment of crisis. Speaking with the Soviet premier Aleksei Kosygin, the Afghan revolutionary Taraki claimed that Iranian forces in civilian clothes had crossed the border and seized Herat. He conceded that the new regime had little support from the population because, he asserted, they were in the grip of "Shi'i slogans." When Kosygin asked about finding workers to shore up the government, Taraki admitted that, of Herat's population of 200,000 to 250,000, there were only 1,000 to 2,000 workers. The Afghan leader warned that the city would fall to the enemy soon and requested "practical and technical support in the form of people and arms." He feared the enemy would lead "half of Iran into Afghanistan" and march on Kandahar and then Kabul. Warning Kosygin that the Iranians and Pakistanis were turning Afghan refugees against the revolution, he suggested that a Soviet-led attack on Herat might "save the revolution."[13]

To Kosygin's reply that he would engage in consultations with the leadership in Moscow, Taraki replied sharply, "While you are consulting Herat will fall and there will be even greater difficulties both for the Soviet Union and for Afghanistan." Kosygin in turn advised Taraki to convince the Iranians that their greatest foe at the moment was the United States. When the discussion turned to Pakistan's role, Taraki predicted that, like Tehran, Islamabad would send troops in plainclothes. He pressed on with his demands, suggesting that the Soviets "put Afghan markings on your [their] tanks and helicopters, and nobody will know anything." He proposed that they advance from Kushka and Kabul and assured him that Soviet forces would be taken for Afghan units based in the Afghan capital.

Kosygin was by this stage growing frustrated. "I don't want to upset you," the premier responded, "but concealing this would be impossible." He punctured Taraki's grand ruse by stating flatly that "it would be clear to the whole world in two hours. Everyone is starting to cry that the Soviet Union is beginning to intervene in Afghanistan. Tell me, Taraki, if we deliver arms to you by airplane in Kabul, including tanks, can you find tank drivers or not?" When Taraki admitted that very few would be available, Kosygin grew more exasperated, inquiring about the "hundreds of Afghan officers" trained in the USSR: "Where have they been sent?" Taraki answered curtly, "Most of them are Muslim reactionaries, Ikhwanis, or as they're also called, 'Muslim Brothers.' We cannot rely on or trust them." When Kosygin asked about the population and military resources of Kabul, Taraki expressed confidence that he could rely on youth, principally from the university and the eleventh and twelfth grades of the lycées. Kosygin again asked about workers. Taraki confessed, "There is not much of a working class in Afghanistan." Kosygin asked about recruiting "the poorest among the peasantry." But Taraki replied that the government could really only rely on "lycée students of the oldest grades, students, and a few workers." With all alternatives seemingly exhausted, Kosygin reported that the Soviets had decided to send military equipment immediately and to repair airplanes and helicopters, adding, "all of this is free." He promised 100,000 tons of grain and offered to pay $37.82 per cubic meter for natural gas (raising the price from $21).

"That's good," Taraki countered, "but let's talk about Herat." He deflected Kosygin's suggestion that Taraki assemble several divisions from "progressive people" and urged the Soviet leader to follow the lead of the Iranians and Pakistanis who, he insisted, had sent in their military personnel in Afghan clothing. "Why can't the Soviet Union," Taraki persisted, "send Uzbeks, Tajiks, [and] Turkmen in civilian dress? Nobody will find out." It would be "an easy task" to send representatives of these peoples—all of whom "are to be found in Afghanistan"—to drive tanks. This annoyed Kosygin. "Of course, you simplify the question," he retorted, adding that they faced "a complicated, political, [and] international question." He pushed Taraki to identify Afghan forces "who will risk their lives to defend you and will fight for you." Taraki returned to the subject of military equipment, this time asking for armored infantry carriers. Kosygin reminded him about the problem of drivers and wondered whether they had reliable people who would not transfer this equipment to the enemy. Taraki again called for "vehicles together with drivers who know our language, Tajiks, Uzbeks." Kosygin finally ended the phone call by promising to call him back with a decision, but not before signaling some disappointment with him. Perhaps not wanting to be harsh on a leader whose fragility and naïveté seemed to grow daily, Kosygin affirmed that they were "comrades" and that they shared "a common struggle."[14]

Soviet advisers on the ground became more and more discouraged about the quality of the Afghan leadership. Facing growing opposition, Taraki continued to underscore the international character of the struggle. "Our revolution," he announced to a visiting delegation of Soviet generals in summer 1979, "is a revolution for all progressive humanity, the socialist camp, a part of the world revolution. This is why its enemies fight."[15]

The new leaders were embattled abroad and in the provinces, but in Kabul they were determined to revolutionize the city, where over nine hundred thousand Afghans now lived. For all of the conspiratorial obsessions of the new regime and its secretive repression of its opponents real and imagined, the leaders of the Democratic Republic were devoted to public displays of power. Through collective rituals and symbolism, they sought to demonstrate that the Saur events were the inevitable culmination of a global wave of revolutionary Marxism. In adopting symbols to represent the new Afghanistan, they appropriated stock images of Marxist internationalism. The Afghan flag became a banner of red. Its only unique features were a sprig of wheat and a mechanical gear to portray the alliance of Afghan peasants and workers that ostensibly lay at the foundation of the revolutionary government.[16]

Taraki was soon forced, though, to resort to a more established Afghan political tactic. Facing resistance from Muslim clerics who called on the faithful to wage jihad against the Democratic Republic, Taraki declared his own jihad in support of the revolution. In moving to consolidate his leadership of the revolution and the new order, Taraki simultaneously made his status as the "great leader" a central component of the iconography of the revolution. Some of this appears to have been a product of his personality. Throughout his adult life he had nursed a sense of resentment at not having been given his due as the writer and leader that he held himself to be. What is even more likely is that he also reasoned that a loyal party organization was not enough. From China and Vietnam to Cuba

and Hungary, strong men had emerged at the head of socialist parties. Afghanistan needed a bold and charismatic figure, a Lenin, or
even better, a Stalin, whose imposing presence would shepherd the
people to progress and whose ubiquitous photograph might look out
over the masses, serving as an inspiration and a warning.[17]

Kabul became a theater of revolution. In emulation of the pa-
rades that paid tribute to the Soviet elite arrayed on Lenin's tomb on
Red Square in Moscow, closely choreographed rows of Afghan
marchers passed before Afghan officials, their wives, and foreign dig-
nitaries. They carried party and national flags and marched under
red banners emblazoned with the faces of Lenin, Marx, and Engels.[18]
Tanks, cannons, rocket launchers, motorcycles with sidecars, and
other military hardware rolled down Kabul's central thoroughfares.
Schoolchildren appeared in uniforms modeled on the young Soviet
Pioneers, complete with cap and scarf. Posters showing bearded and
mustachioed Afghans in turbans, hardhats, and military caps shaking
the hands of their clean-shaven Soviet counterparts in "friendship"
were symbols of fidelity.[19] Others portrayed national unity under the
ruling party in Soviet iconographic fashion. They featured workers
and peasants, but also soldiers, clerics, intellectuals, and, in the folk-
loric style that the Soviets had crafted, a patchwork of figures don-
ning headdresses, turbans, and flowing robes and tunics that Afghans
would recognize as representing tribal communities and minority na-
tionalities. To many Afghans and foreigners alike, the most striking
change in the revolutionary capital was the mobilization of women.
The first thing a European anthropologist noticed upon arrival in
Kabul in 1979 was "the large number of unveiled women in the streets
and the overall presence of red banners bearing the emblem of the
khalqi government."[20]

Women were central to this visual narrative of emancipation and
progress. Artists, sculptors, photographers, and writers assigned them

key roles. As in modernist visual propaganda elsewhere in the twentieth century, women stood in for rural society. A statue in Kabul, crafted in an international socialist realist style, portrayed a strapping male worker and a peasant woman raising a banner to the new socialist order. The image of the liberated working woman who was active on the industrial front was another feature of the story that the elites of the Democratic Republic wanted to tell about themselves. For instance, a Soviet-produced photo album featured a smiling Afghan female crane operator at the Kabul House-Building Enterprise.[21] By the late 1980s, photographs of marching female militia members wielding Kalashnikov rifles on behalf of the revolutionary regime had entered the repertoire of official images of the emancipated Afghan woman.

That the DRA mobilized women in a propagandistic way is beyond question, but among some educated women, especially in the capital and among those who had studied abroad, there was legitimate enthusiasm for the revolutionary project. Soon after the coup—and particularly before rival groups within the party escalated repression—women who had no direct ties to the party might join in pro-revolutionary marches or offer their support in other ways because they saw the new government as a progressive force for women and girls. For women tied to the party, trips to Moscow, including a pilgrimage to Red Square and Lenin's Tomb, as well as journeys to other countries in the East Bloc were an additional perk.[22]

The presence of a prominent woman, Anahita Ratebzad, in the revolutionary government was another factor. In 1978, she became minister of social welfare and then ambassador to Bulgaria, the latter position being a form of political exile due to her association with the Parcham faction of the party. In the meantime, Hafizullah Amin overthrew Nur Muhammad Taraki in September 1979, a development that further unsettled Moscow, where fears grew that Hafizullah

Amin may have been turned by the CIA during his student days in New York. This was a key factor in the Kremlin's decision to invade Afghanistan and remove Amin in December 1979. Ratebzad then returned to Afghanistan and took on an iconic role as the official face of Afghan feminism, becoming a member of the Politburo, the Revolutionary Council and head of the Democratic Organization of Afghan Women, among other titles.

Anahita Ratebzad was born into a politically active Tajik family in 1931. Her father, a provincial subgovernor, had backed King Amanullah after his fall and was arrested while she was still very little. She never saw her father again. Having read his letters and heard, as she later recounted, "how he loved his country and his people," the young Anahita resolved to follow in his path, even though her mother was illiterate and poor. She thus married young. She followed her physician husband to the United States. Nursing interested her, but, having studied French in Kabul, she first had to enroll in English courses at the University of Michigan, where she eventually studied nursing for three years. Upon returning to Kabul, Ratebzad became director of a woman's hospital and nursing instructor. She then began studying medicine at the University of Kabul. Her children were sent abroad for university. Her daughter studied international law at Moscow State University, while one son became an architecture student in Bulgaria, and another did electrical engineering in Paris. In 1965, she won election to parliament representing Kabul. Recalling her campaign many years later, she explained that "when we first made electoral speeches we spoke about the people, their living conditions, their problems and said perhaps we can do something for you, because for a long time in history men could not do anything. Men could not really reject this argument, except for the reactionaries among them, and so I got in."[23]

Ratebzad was adamant in her defense of the Democratic Republic and its commitment to improving the lot of Afghan men, women, and children. In January 1980, the *Times of India* described her as a "short, slim, dark-haired and sad-eyed woman" who "looks, at first sight, remarkably like *La Passionara* [sic] of the Spanish Civil War" (referring to the communist leader Dolores Ibárruri) and who "speaks with great emotion, in a language which is close to picturesque." She emphasized the transformative power of the government's literacy campaign, insisting that it would allow women to enter into all kinds of professions and make them better mothers, so that Afghan children "will be brought up broad-minded," and the country as a whole would benefit. "We would like to reach a stage," she explained to an Indian journalist, "when even a woman cook can be prime minister and there are no privileges." Fulfilling the aspirations of all Afghans who since 1919 had desired true independence, this was "the revolution of the people."[24]

However, the entry of Soviet troops to depose Hafizullah Amin in December 1979 further undermined such arguments in favor of the revolution. Ratebzad and her ilk had to explain their dependence on their powerful neighbor. In her case, in addition to patriotic objections to Soviet forces and the broader backlash against the education of women and girls, she faced gossip to the effect that she had been engaged for many years in a love affair with Babrak Karmal. In spring 1980, on the eve of the second-year anniversary of the coup, shopkeepers and students protested the Soviet presence as well as the introduction of a new flag—this one displaying the colors of the pre-revolutionary flag, red, black, and green, and with an image of the Quran. According to accounts that leaked out to the Western press, in April hundreds of protesters from the Malalay girls school singled out Ratebzad, calling her a "prostitute puppet of Babrak

Karmal." Demonstrations spread to other high schools and the university.[25]

But Ratebzad held fast. In comments in the *Kabul New Times* of March 1981, Ratebzad cast the Soviet-Afghan relationship as a bond that strengthened Afghanistan's historic struggle for liberation and benefited humanity as a whole. She called the Twenty-Sixth Party Congress of the USSR "a great event in the life of humanity under the circumstances where imperialism, headed by the U.S., Peking chauvinism and Zionism continue stubbornly with its conspiracy to bring misery and destruction of the peoples of the world." Citing the sixty-year anniversary of the Soviet-Afghan friendship treaty of 1921 and exchanges between Lenin and Amanullah, she praised Moscow's "brotherly assistance" and railed against its conspiratorial enemies. In a poem that she composed for the occasion, she blended universalism, patriotism, and feminism:

> Forward towards struggle for peace, prosperity and happiness
>   of humanity today and the future generations.
> Long live our revolutionary homeland, the beautiful land of
>   our martyred and heroic mothers, fathers and sons.
> The final victory is with the industrious and suffering people
>   of Afghanistan.[26]

The regime further highlighted her stature as a feminist and internationalist that same month when it publicized her role in defusing an international incident. After a group of hijackers led by Murtaza Bhutto, the son of the recently deposed prime minister of Pakistan, hijacked a Pakistani International Airlines flight and diverted it to Kabul, Ratebzad made an appeal to the hijackers from the flight control tower of the airport. She called on them to release the women on board so that they could celebrate International Women's Day,

. when "all the toiling women all over the world rally their ranks in struggle for social justice, [and] equal rights with men in all spheres of activities for their rightful place in society." The *Kabul New Times* published a photograph of her in headphones in the tower speaking to the hijackers and another showing her talking to two American women whom the hijackers then released (three Pakistani women remained on the plane). At ceremonies to mark the holiday the following day, Ratebzad's speeches included a greeting to the Women's International Democratic Federation, the organization founded in 1945 that she characterized as

> the righteous vanguard of the women's struggle, the combatant women, the world progressive forces and the heroic women of Africa, Asia, and Latin America who relentlessly and fearlessly fight against the most savage and beastlike enemy of freedom, independence, peace and democracy, against war and against atomic weapons which threaten human beings, and those who are waiting for the dawn of prosperity and mothers whose hearts are filled with love for freedom and beat for releasing the women from the family and social restrictions.

In Ratebzad, then, the regime sought out a bridge to a progressive world beyond the Soviet bloc.[27]

Such appeals to feminism and internationalism mobilized women beyond the elite. On March 8, 1983, some eight thousand women celebrated International Women's Day in Kabul at the Polytechnic Institute, the Soviet-backed engineering school established in 1967. Iurii Krushinskii, a Soviet adviser who was present, recalled that these were mostly young women, some veiled, others in European clothing. Also in tow were children—a phenomenon that many Soviet commentators mentioned as a sign of their acceptance, especially when the kids greeted them with smiles, handshakes, and cries of "Comrade!" More troubling for Krushinskii was an official gathering in Mazar-i Sharif at which the communist anthem "The Internationale" was played, but without the Afghan participants knowing the words. Still, he was encouraged by meeting Afghan military and civilian officials who had been to numerous countries and spoke several languages, including excellent Russian.

Krushinskii and men like him were unsettled about their role. Few fully trusted their Afghan partners, though there were exceptions. Service in Afghanistan was dangerous for Soviet men and women, but access to consumer goods unavailable in the USSR was a perk. They bought blue jeans, electronic watches, cassette players, women's underwear, and many other items that could be resold on the black market at home. Red Army soldiers even sold fuel and weapons to Afghans who, they must have known, were going to use them against the Soviets. The story of tobacco reveals another aspect of this illicit traffic. The tobacco multinationals continued to supply the trade entrepôt of Kandahar, where the commodity fed into new commercial networks. As the internal memo of one San Francisco–based supplier explained, some of the cigarettes imported at Kandahar were consumed locally. Many more appear to have been destined for reexport by Afghan traders from Kandahar to the Indian and Pakistani markets.[28] But much of the supply ended up in the hands of Soviet forces who sent them on to Leningrad and elsewhere in the USSR. Smuggling networks among soldiers and veterans became significant enterprises and survived after the Soviet withdrawal to capitalize on Moscow's shift to "markets" under Gorbachev and Boris Yeltsin.

Nevertheless, the gap between the Soviet and Afghan "brothers" remained wide: in one especially poignant section of Krushinskii's memoirs, he described being confined to his room in the Ariana

Hotel because everyone expected the rebels to attack the city at the end of Ramadan in July 1983. Not being able to afford the hotel restaurant, he passed the time in front of his television—a Japanese model that was larger and with brighter colors than anything he had seen at home—but was demoralized by the programs, which were a mixture of Ramadan festivities showing state leaders at prayer, interspersed with Indian films, all of which gave him the impression that the Afghan socialists were only at a developmental stage through which the Soviets had advanced in the 1920s.[29]

Interactions with Soviet advisers were only one type of contact that Afghans developed with the world beyond their borders under the DRA. Its leaders injected the universal vocabulary and symbols of socialist ideology into national politics; and party activists brought them to far-flung locales throughout the country. Their resort to violence to implement compulsory literacy classes and land reform and other revolutionary measures, in turn, prompted resistance and protests from below. The revolutionary process unleashed a vicious civil war.

Within months of the PDPA takeover, hundreds of thousands of Afghans responded with a mass exodus to Pakistan and Iran. This stream would soon swell to as many as seven million men, women, and children who would attempt to wait out the war, or start new lives altogether by moving on to the Gulf states, Europe, the United States, or Australia. Many migrants moved back and forth between these states and returned periodically to Afghanistan. Thus this movement did not sever ties between these migrants and their communities of origin within Afghanistan. Indeed many families traced familiar paths. Varied populations had long moved back and forth across these borders, smugglers, pilgrims, dissidents, rebels, students, and traders among them. Many held (or would acquire) Afghan and Pakistani passports and established residencies in multiple locales, frequently distributing family members among these different sites. Some went to live with kinfolk who already lived across the border. Visits, letters, telephone calls, cash, and various kinds of mutual assistance kept relatives in contact. Sometimes new commercial opportunities grew out of these networks. International organizations registered a great number of these migrants as "refugees," but not all Afghans accepted this categorization. Flight to neighboring Iran or Pakistan was, for many, a strategy to establish a base from which the new government could be challenged.[30]

What the People's Democratic Party identified as "the counter-revolution" could take many forms. Cries of opposition to the new order came from an ideological spectrum ranging from monarchists and Maoists to liberal secularists and ethnic nationalists. In the many provincial settings where Afghans took up arms against state authority and formed fighting "fronts," one can also identify more localized voices that may have seized upon the breakdown of central authority to press for local autonomy or to settle local scores with state officials or neighbors.[31]

To their adversaries, the leaders of the DRA had achieved nothing more than an illegal and illegitimate coup. Numerous opposition groups, increasingly organized as modern political parties, countered government propaganda by promising their own "revolution." They could be confident in such utopian dreaming because they were buoyed by what appeared to be a wave of Islamic resurgence washing through the region. In Pakistan, a generation of Afghans, from exiles and migrants to students and religious scholars, had seen firsthand how the charismatic leader Sayyid Abu al-A'la Mawdudi (1903–1979) had engineered a political party that married a rigidly hierarchical Leninist organizational structure and the promise of forging a more thoroughly Islamic society. In Iran, Afghans living there, mostly as migrant laborers and religious students, found themselves caught up in the revolution that deposed the shah. They watched how Khomeini's supporters outmaneuvered their rivals and consolidated their authority in the new revolutionary order. The events that led to the foundation of the Islamic Republic electrified Afghan circles in the seminaries of Iraq and gave inspiration to Shia and Sunni alike within Afghanistan and throughout the diaspora.[32]

If communists and anticommunists alike conceived of their projects within the same global framework of transformations like the French or Russian revolutions, they simultaneously mobilized slogans that drew on an Islamic vocabulary. The Taraki government answered critics by declaring a "jihad" against the "Satanic Brotherhood," a label that collapsed opposition groups with the Muslim Brotherhood organization centered in Egypt. Meanwhile, the Soviets condemned the regime's enemies as "terrorists."[33]

The scale of the conflict can only be appreciated by extending our view beyond Afghanistan's borders. One key feature of the wider context was the global nature of the Cold War between the Americans and Soviets. Security officials under President Jimmy Carter have since revealed covert operations against the Soviets from Grenada to Jamaica to Nicaragua, El Salvador, and Yemen. They were watching events in Afghanistan closely. The abduction and murder of the American ambassador Adolph Dubs by a shadowy group in February 1979 further drew Washington into events unfolding in Kabul. Already in March, besides boycotting the Olympic Games in Moscow, American officials were discussing behind closed doors the prospect, as one Department of Defense insider put it, of "sucking the Soviets into a Vietnamese quagmire." The idea of an alliance with Muslim radicals against communists was nothing new. Already in 1972, an Afghan student activist had approached the U.S. Embassy in Kabul, wearing a coat and tie and armed with an automatic pistol, to propose American financial support for printing the anticommunist publications of his Muslim youth organization.[34] But it was apparently only after the coup of 1978 that American interest in such figures matured. Covert support in the amount of half a million dollars began in July 1979.

Some six months in advance of the Soviet invasion, American security officials had begun to coordinate support for the rebels with Pakistan and Saudi Arabia. Recalling how "the first elements of an extraordinary logistics pipeline from suppliers around the world were assembled," Robert Gates later remarked with satisfaction that "the stage was set for the vast future expansion of outside help, all run by CIA." Following the entry of Soviet troops in December 1979, U.S. aid ballooned by summer 1980, Gates tells us, to "tens of millions [of dollars], and most assuredly included the provision of weapons." Under Ronald Reagan, Afghanistan became a theater for covert CIA action alongside operations in a dozen or more countries in Africa, Asia, and Latin America.[35]

In giving refuge to Afghan migrants and political parties, Iran and Pakistan had innumerable advantages in determining which actors would figure as legitimate and viable challengers to the revolutionary project. Pakistan was the logistical base and transit territory for foreign fighters. The Central Intelligence Agency managed the logistical and financial support and worked closely with their Pakistani counterparts, the ISI. The Americans and their European partners, including the West Germans and French, funded the Pakistani security forces' favorites, though they also lobbied for their own preferences on occasion.[36] The Pakistani leadership also shaped how the Americans viewed the Afghan fighters. Convinced that Islam might play a role similar to Catholicism in Poland in rolling back the Soviet Union, Reagan's CIA chief William Casey gradually expanded American assistance to the opposition. During a conversation with the Pakistani leader, Casey was apparently impressed by General Zia's interpretation of how the British had ostensibly stopped Russian expansionism in the nineteenth century. According to Robert Gates, at the end of the lesson Zia punctuated his remarks by insisting on more powerful ground-to-air weapons, remarking, "The Pathans [Pashtuns] are great fighters, but shit-scared when it comes to air power."[37]

The CIA had to import thousands of mules from China to transport the surge of weaponry sent to the Afghan fighters in 1985. This deluge of deadly hardware, manufactured in a dozen countries—the United States, the USSR, Great Britain, China, Pakistan, Israel, Germany, Switzerland, France, and elsewhere—is but one illustration of the global arms networks that the superpowers unleashed with such lethal effects in Afghanistan. To take just one category of weapon, the landmines deployed by the millions in the country, and a source of hundreds of thousands of civilian and animal casualties that persist into the present, were produced in Italy, Great Britain, the USSR, and the United States. To the frustration of the DRA and Soviet security forces, these weapons moved in large caravans interspersed with commercial goods and people from Pakistan and along inaccessible smuggling routes that only locals knew. The Pakistani port city of Karachi served as the key point of entry for arms on the way to Afghanistan. It was also a central transit point for the export of a highly valuable and transportable commodity moving in the other direction: opium, which Afghan farmers had begun to cultivate more intensively and which, following processing in Pakistani laboratories, accounted for nearly half of all heroin consumed in Europe and the United States. Drugs and weapons leaked out along the supply chain, fueling addiction and gun violence in Pakistan.[38]

There was nothing inevitable, however, about the identification of the antigovernment struggle as "jihad." Agitators who circulated the label could point to the venerable history of Afghan struggle against British colonialism, of course, but by 1978 Afghans had long been exposed to use of the term in a great variety of contexts and with conflicting associations. Afghans were likely to encounter *jihad* most frequently as part of official state discourse. It was a staple of Afghan military education, in particular. Soldiers learned that their service was a sacred duty, a jihad, for the Afghan nation. When opponents of the Afghan leader Muhammad Daoud called for jihad against the government they were challenging the state's claim to monopolize the concept. In the wake of the Saur Revolution, though, this was not the only oppositional language available to Afghan actors. Many decades of liberal, constitutionalist thought remained alive in literary and academic circles, even though some fell victim to the new regime and others had to flee abroad.

On the international scene, though, protests against the Soviet intervention inevitably cited international law—and the hoary myths about the Russians' inexorable compulsion to seize warm-water ports. Predictably, Jimmy Carter mentioned these factors, along with the supposed threat the Soviets posed to the energy resources of the Persian Gulf region in his radio address of January 1980. At the same time, though, he included a striking claim that gave credence to the view that Islam was the target. In a concession of sorts that he clearly intended to address to Muslim activists at a moment when the American confrontation with Iranian revolutionaries had reached a critical impasse with the November 1979 seizure of the U.S. embassy in Tehran, Carter labeled the Soviet invasion "a deliberate effort of a powerful atheistic government to subjugate an independent Islamic people."[39]

The U.S. position went beyond rhetorical support. Beginning in 1984, the U.S. Agency for International Development (USAID) paid the University of Nebraska Omaha $50 million to produce textbooks for Afghan schools. Printed in Dari and Pashto, the books taught basic literacy and numeracy through words and images that glorified the killing of Soviets in the name of jihad. Children learned arithmetic by adding and subtracting guns, tanks, and bullets. The letter "jim" was for *jihad*, and "mim" was for *mujahidin,* who "fight the infidels." Similarly, many U.S. officials were drawn to shifting arms and cash to fighters who developed a reputation for being particularly zealous in religion and combat because, the Americans assumed, they would inflict the most damage on the Soviet enemy.[40]

On the ground, though, there was a broad disjuncture between the political outlook of the U.S.-supplied parties that called themselves *mujahidin* and the refugee communities in Pakistan who were compelled to live in camps whose management Pakistani authorities had largely consigned to these parties. In spite of their dependence on the jihadist parties, Afghans in these camps constantly contested their leadership. In one of the rare surveys of Afghans displaced in Pakistan, over 70 percent of men and 50 percent of women proposed the exiled king, Muhammad Zahir Shah (who was then living in Rome), as the ideal national leader. The party heads, by contrast, polled in the single digits. Fewer than 2 percent of the men expressed a preference for one of the commanders; among female respondents, 5 percent named Burhanuddin Rabbani, followed by Ishaq Gailani (just under 4 percent) and Gulbuddin Hekmatyar (just over 2.5 percent).[41]

Relations with fighters at the various fronts within the country could be similarly contentious. They looked to the parties in Peshawar or Tehran for arms and money. But questions of ideology were more complex. Party affiliations meant different things to different fighters. The reminiscence left by a Shia fighter from Gardez in eastern Afghanistan is revealing in this respect. For him, the everyday experience of the war was about extreme hunger and thirst. It was, at the same time, a glorious age for religion. The locale was connected to Iran and Muslims elsewhere in a meaningful way in 1989, when news of Ayatollah Khomeini's death arrived, and Shia and Sunnis in Gardez commemorated the Imam by joining in the seven-day mourning cycle. One of these gatherings was targeted by a Scud *(askud)* rocket fired by the government forces, who announced that the missile had destroyed the mourners. Thanks to the wondrous powers *(karamat)* of Khomeini, however, no harm came to them.[42]

To many Muslims, though, the struggle being waged in Afghanistan knew no boundaries. The two Afghans who were initially best situated to appeal to Pan-Islamic sentiments were Abd (Rabb) al-Rasul Sayyaf, who had studied in Saudi Arabia, and Jamaluddin Haqqani, who had established extensive ties to Persian Gulf patrons. At this stage, however, foreign Muslims began to imagine the significance of the jihad in a radically new light, writing Afghans into yet another revolutionary script.

Jamaluddin Haqqani's envoys toured the Gulf seeking funds and recruits, but few answered the call until a charismatic Palestinian, Muslim Brother, and graduate of al-Azhar University in Cairo, Abdullah Azzam, began issuing calls for Arabs to turn their attention to the struggle in Afghanistan. Writing from Islamabad, where he had moved in 1981 at the age of forty, Azzam invited Muslims around the globe to "join the caravan." His treatise on the Afghan jihad, *The Defense of Muslim Territories Is the First Individual Duty*, was a radical intervention in scholarship on Islamic jurisprudence.

For Muslim scholars, one of the key questions about the legal standing of jihad turned on the question of whether participation was an individual or collective duty. Azzam argued that jihad was an individual duty for all Muslims. His interpretation was revolutionary, even among Muslims who enthusiastically championed the Afghan

jihad. It challenged the status quo in the Saudi kingdom, not to mention other states throughout the Middle East. A number of Saudi
clerics recoiled at Azzam's reworking of defensive jihad as an individual duty, and the most important one at that, for all Muslims.
Shaykh Salman al-'Awda countered that "donating the price of an
airline ticket is better than going there." Opening up another avenue
of criticism, skeptics like Shaykh Safar al-Hawali worried that this
cause did little more than advance American interests. In addition to
authoring *Signs of the Merciful in the Afghan Jihad*, a highly influential
recruitment plea that highlighted the miraculous in the stories of
martyrs in the jihad, Azzam founded in 1984 his Bureau of Services.
Through it, he produced media appeals and carried on recruitment
with funds from the scion of a wealthy Saudi family, Osama bin
Laden, who founded his own camp to recruit and train fighters, the
"Den of the Companions."

Despite Azzam's rhetoric, these training camps reflected a vast
gap separating the foreigners' experience of the war from that of the
Afghans. To be sure, Pan-Islamic activists blended humanitarian and
militant activities, and so they would have interacted with Afghans
seeking medical care from the Saudi Red Crescent in Peshawar, for
instance. But the Arabs tended to bring their own agenda to the fight.
To bin Laden and like-minded radicals, this battle was the precursor
to the greater one to be launched against Arab regimes at home.
Moreover, in a telling development, the creation by Arab volunteers
of separate camps for Arabs was intended to "protect" them from
what they took to be a dubious Afghan religious environment.[43] And,
unlike Afghan fighters and civilians, relatively few of these volunteers
saw any combat. But media campaigns launched by the Organization
of the Islamic Conference and Muslim World League and through
it, the Muslim Brotherhood, aimed at smoothing over these internal
tensions.

Simultaneously, the Afghan jihad was the centerpiece of Saudi efforts to present the kingdom as the leader of the world's Muslims from the mid-1980s and to solidify the monarchy's iron grip at home. From 1987 to 1989 alone, the Saudis contributed at least $1.8 billion. Their preferred client was Abd (Rabb) al-Rasul Sayyaf, whose sermons in front of the king were broadcast by Saudi television. But they also aided Arab fighters, maintaining contact with bin Laden and Azzam, among others. Saudi airlines gave discounted rates for flights to Peshawar, and Saudi television broadcast fund-raising telethons. The mid to late 1980s was the period when most volunteers traveled from the kingdom for the Afghan theater. By the late 1980s, moreover, the Saudi religious establishment had come to prefer a fighter in Kunar Province, Jamil al-Rahman, an Afghan Salafi who had studied in Pakistan and who was known for his campaign against "innovations." He also received financial backing from Kuwaiti and Saudi businessmen.[44] Still, other Saudi Islamists repeatedly expressed skepticism about the purity of the Afghan cause and, in particular, of its American entanglements. Nevertheless, from the late 1980s until the DRA government collapsed in 1992 a few thousand Saudis and others from neighboring states made the trek and committed themselves to a cause that they would later take to places such as Tajikistan, Bosnia, and Chechnya.

If the Arab and Muslim foreign fighters were primarily invested in molding the Afghan jihad to serve their own ambitions, the same can be said of the Western powers. They were equally attentive to the language of Afghan politics, above all, to refute the "terrorist" label for their allies and to make the mujahidin palatable in the West as part of a broader anticommunist cause. Managing media representations of the war lay at the center of this strategy. Indiscriminate attacks by the mujahidin on Kabul and the civilian casualties resulting from a campaign of bombings and assassinations had to be given new labels. As early as mid-1980, NATO officials agreed to discourage news outlets from using the term "rebels," as the BBC frequently did, or from referring to them as "insurgents." An internal Foreign and Commonwealth Office memo of June 1980 clarified the British stance: "We would suggest that 'nationalists' and 'the resistance'—qualified on occasion by 'Muslim'—serve us best. They do, indeed, indulge in 'guerrilla' (but never 'terrorist') activities but to describe them as 'guerrillas' may irk some of our readers, both official and unofficial, who are used to this term in a Marxist context. 'National Liberation Movement' and 'freedom fighters' might fit some circumstances, while 'patriots' is always a possibility." Western officials were also careful not to mention (or attempt to prosecute) Afghan and Pakistani allies who were simultaneously complicit in the opium trafficking boom of the 1980s.[45]

In Washington, Ronald Reagan's White House settled on "freedom fighters." Declaring March 21, 1983, "Afghanistan Day," Reagan proclaimed that "the resistance of the Afghan freedom fighters is an example to all the world of the invincibility of the ideals we in this country hold most dear, the ideals of freedom and independence."[46] Two years later, Reagan called support for the mujahidin "a compelling, moral responsibility of all free people." The convergence of the president's language with that of the mujahidin and indeed of their Afghan foes in the DRA came to the fore in a radio address to the American public in December 1985, when Reagan explained how backing this cause was an exemplary way to serve humanity and was, in the end, fundamentally American:

> What takes place in that far-off land is of vital importance to our country and the world. Certainly the struggle in Afghanistan is

of great strategic military importance. Yet the most important battle involves not guns, but the human spirit—the longing to be free and the duty to help the oppressed. If the free world were to turn its back on Afghanistan, then, in a sense, the free world would become less free and less humane. But when we support the Afghan people, we become caught up in and ennobled by their struggle for freedom. Isn't that what America is always—what it has always stood for and what we should stand for in 1986 and beyond?[47]

Media outlets took up Reagan's call with alacrity. American domestic support for the Afghan opposition was enthusiastic and had grown even stronger by the mid-1980s.

By 1988, much of the American public was primed to revel in Sylvester Stallone's *Rambo III*. Grossing $189 million worldwide, the film told the story of an American Vietnam War veteran who traveled to Afghanistan to rescue a buddy whom the Soviets took prisoner for aiding the mujahidin. Although the American played the dominant role in confounding his exploding cast of enemies, the film showed how he came to see the Afghan cause as a noble one and how the Afghans, in turn, accepted him.

A few critics thought some American media were too eager, in fact, to run with the White House narrative and to suppress criticism from Afghan feminist organizations such as the Revolutionary Association of the Women of Afghanistan (RAWA) and other Afghan political groups who warned that the mujahidin parties were guilty of atrocities against other Afghans and that their vision for the future was an unattractive one for many Afghans. In 1987, the American network CBS faced accusations of staging rebel raids and of faking images of Soviet bombings of Afghan villages and of bombs made to look like toys. Questions emerged in the same year about

Joachim Maitre, who was director of the Afghan Media Project (and dean of the College of Communication) at Boston University. Having fled East Germany in 1953, Maitre became an authority in the United States on communism and the recipient of funding from numerous agencies to train Afghan journalists in Peshawar, for a time, with the Hearst Corporation. Critics pointed to his ties to Oliver North, then under scrutiny for being at the center of the Iran–Contra scandal and with whom he shared a strong antipathy toward the Latin American left. Skeptics wondered whether he was funneling funds to produce favorable reporting on a war that was notoriously challenging to cover.[48] The Soviets, by contrast, floundered in using media to their advantage internationally even though Gorbachev was very keen to negotiate a departure from Afghanistan to improve their standing in the eyes of international opinion.

Meanwhile, with American assistance, the mujahidin parties developed a very sophisticated media infrastructure. Their most remarkable achievement was to craft an image of a single commander, Ahmad Shah Massoud, as a global icon of the Afghan resistance. Affiliated with the Jamiat-i Islami party and based in the relatively remote Panjshir Valley, Massoud was, in fact, an unlikely candidate to grab the world's attention in a way that allowed observers to see what they wanted in the struggle of the Afghan mujahidin.

This was, after all, a crowded field. In the 1970s, the communists' first challengers had formed rival intellectual circles around the Department of Islamic Law at Kabul University under Burhanuddin Rabbani, who launched the Muslim Youth organization upon his return from Egypt. Gulbuddin Hekmatyar also built on his charismatic leadership of radical circles at the university and emerged as a major figure among the exiles who took up arms. Western intelligence agencies identified him as the figure to whom many Afghans pointed when naming the leader of the resistance. A British report observed that crowds chanted his name during antigovernment demonstrations in Kabul in February 1980 and in later protests.

Long-established religious families were positioned to broaden their influence as well. The Mujaddidis had a long history of pious opposition to the state, and the Gailanis stood atop a broad network of Sufi devotees. Yet both dynasties were hobbled at the outset of the jihad, partly because of state repression and partly because key players had shifted their activities abroad years earlier. In March 1979, the communist government arrested Ibrahim Jan Mujaddidi, the "Hazrat Sahib of Shor Bazaar," whom many Afghans regarded as the most respected Muslim scholar in the country. His cousin Sibghatullah Mujaddidi had spent most of the 1970s in Copenhagen, Denmark, as the head of a school and mosque. He later founded the Afghan National Liberation Front in Peshawar, though his family retained ties to its new base in Europe. The Gailanis followed a similar trajectory. The son of the Pir, Sayyid Ahmed Gailani, had moved his family to an apartment in London. From there, as well as from Peshawar, where he established the United Islamic Front of Afghanistan, he lobbied Western governments, even though the British suspected he exaggerated his influence and were perhaps made more cautious by a line that they included in his Foreign and Commonwealth Office file: "it is rumoured that his wife was once the ex-King's mistress."[49]

In the case of Abd (Rabb) al-Rasul Sayyaf, his association with the Saudi regime was a double-edged sword. He had a ready supply of cash. But everything about him—from his Arabized name to his religious views—was suspect in the eyes of many in the resistance and the diaspora more generally. Together with Hekmatyar, Sayyaf was the object of much sarcasm. His claim to be a sayyid, a descendant of the Prophet, was the target of many barbs.

By the early 1990s, the mujahidin parties had not only resorted more consistently to strategies of ethnic mobilization but had also begun to rely on images of the heroic figure as the embodiment of each party. In key respects, this shift mirrored the politics of the DRA. Its politics were dominated by a succession of highly publicized leaders, first Nur Muhammad Taraki, then Hafizullah Amin, Babrak Karmal, and finally Dr. Najibullah, whose early revolutionary career had been marked by an arrest for protesting U.S. vice president Spiro Agnew's visit to Kabul in 1970. Najibullah became general secretary in 1986.[50]

Among their opponents, Gulbuddin Hekmatyar had been the first to insist on this cult of the party leader, combining the roles of guerrilla commander, geopolitical strategist, and Islamist intellectual. Rivaling the media strategies of Massoud's backers, Hekmatyar's propaganda touted his pronouncements on wide-ranging subjects and credited his leadership of the jihad with far more than the liberation of Afghanistan. Hekmatyar's party, Hizb-i Islami, was the favorite of key factions in Islamabad and Washington. It published its own English-language glossy, the *Mujahideen Monthly*. Celebrating the cult of the party's "amir," it delivered news of mujahidin victories and presented profiles, together with individual photographs, of the martyrs who laid their lives down for the cause. Its editors claimed distribution via vendors in India, Denmark, Belgium, France, Britain, Malaysia, Holland, West Germany, France, Australia, and two outlets in the United States—in Flushing, New York, as well as Van Nuys, California. In seeking to influence the Afghan diaspora and foreign patrons and supporters, it offered detailed refutation of specific articles about Afghanistan in the international media. To deflect criticism from feminist and humanitarian voices, some articles highlighted respect for women's rights; others featured photographs of wounded children.

At the same time, Hekmatyar's *Mujahideen Monthly* presented a forum for Muslims from around the world to voice solidarity with their cause. One letter, identified as coming from Taha Farid from Lagos, Nigeria, requested permission to share its articles with Muslims there, since it had taught him "why Imperialists would generally not allow any Muslim nation to stand on its feet and would go at any length in blackmailing and destroying those so called Islamic Fundamentalists in Western ideological terminologies."[51] The editors invited submissions from all those who could "wield a facile pen" in the service of "the Muslim Ummah in particular and the whole humanity in general."[52] In their own work, the Hizb-i Islami writers identified their cause as a fundamental part of a unique conjuncture in the history of Muslims as a whole. For instance, commenting on the Babri Masjid controversy of 1986 in India that erupted when a court ruling opened up the mosque site to Hindus, one of these authors put this development in global perspective, arguing that "in Afghanistan the Russians are commiting genocide, butchering Muslims in their thirst for power. In Palestine and Lebanon the Zionists and American imperialists are decimating our people. Likewise systematic measures are being taken in Syria, the Philippines, Indonesia and Libya to suffocate the Ummah." It cited approvingly a sermon by the imam of the Shahi mosque in Delhi warning that "the Muslims of the world were asleep and were not helping the downtrodden Muslims of India against the Hindu onslaught."[53]

In the aftermath of the collapse of the Soviet bloc in Eastern Europe in autumn 1989, the *Mujahideen Monthly* insisted that the Hekmatyar-led mujahidin had achieved nothing less than the defeat of communism, freeing Eastern Europe—and the world—from its godless tyranny, thereby affirming the world-historical significance of their struggle. In January 1990, the *Mujahideen Monthly* gave this narrative visual form in a colored illustration of an Afghan fighter raising his rifle in the air in a defiant gesture that struck the Kremlin itself. Hekmatyar recalled that at the moment of the Soviet invasion a verse from the Quran had "flashed" before his eyes, convincing him that God had "willed that the fall of the Soviet empire would be initiated in Afghanistan." "The Afghan Jihad," he insisted, "exposed the false face of Communist expansion in the world and thus loosened the chain around the necks of the captive nations of Eastern Europe." "Gorbachev did not lead the Soviets to a new policy," Hekmatyar concluded, "the Afghan Jihad did."[54]

Hekmatyar was not content to rest on his laurels. He rebuked those in the West who took credit for the Soviet defeat. The future belonged to Islam, and the faithful would have to continue to "struggle against anti-Islamic forces, whether they be from the Wast [*sic*] or the East." Echoing many of the arguments of contemporary conservative critics within American and European societies, Hekmatyar warned that "their materialistic economy has no future, their moral fiber is torn by divorce and abortion, and their health is threatened by the spectres of drugs and the epidemic of AIDS."[55] By 1991, the year of the demise of the USSR, the magazine had collapsed the Soviets and Americans together into a single enemy with a common future. The mujahidin had ended Moscow's empire; the American "new world order," a slogan introduced by George H. W. Bush, would inevitably follow suit. "The only challenge to the supremacy of American imperialism and its New World Order," it argued, "is nothing but Islam."[56]

8 | AT THE CENTER
OF HUMANITY

AFGHANISTAN'S CENTRALITY TO global politics outlived the socialist bloc and the Cold War. From the 1990s, and particularly after the attacks of September 11, 2001, on targets in New York and Washington, diverse actors ranging from the Afghan mujahidin to Osama bin Laden and even the Pentagon imagined the country as the crucial front of global jihad—as the space where humanity was to be redeemed or destroyed. In 1998, bin Laden called on Muslims to aid Afghanistan "with all their might, their ideas, their charitable donations and funds," because, he explained, "with God's will it represents the banner of Islam today."[1] On the evening of September 11, George W. Bush addressed a grief-stricken public to argue that "America was targeted for attack because we're the brightest beacon for freedom and opportunity in the world."[2] The U.S. secretary of defense regretted that there were few "high-value targets" in Afghanistan, insisting that the conditions of this war would be so novel as to require a new vocabulary altogether. The American First Lady, Laura Bush, cast the war as a humanitarian and feminist cause, a point echoed by Cherie Blair, the spouse of the British prime minister Tony Blair.

The war had a territorial dimension, routing the Taliban regime in Afghanistan, and an extraterritorial one. The Bush administration's "Global War on Terror" would mirror its foes in operating beyond all borders. The two fronts intersected in Afghanistan, which the Americans would treat as a space where neither existing Afghan nor international law would apply. The United States would not honor the Geneva Conventions in Afghanistan. In 2002, the Soviet-built Bagram air base would emerge as the hub of a global network of penal facilities that included Abu Ghraib in Iraq and Guantánamo Bay in Cuba, to which American officials transferred from Bagram what they called "enhanced interrogation techniques," themselves a jumble of Stalin-era Soviet police tactics, American prison culture, and a reliance on academic writing that fetishized Muslims' (and especially Arabs') supposed obsession with sexual humiliation. All of this was justified, the American authorities argued, because the enemy could strike anywhere. As one of the main architects of this system, Condoleezza Rice, put it in May 2006, if the Bush administration were to put an end to the indefinite imprisonment at Guantánamo of those it deemed terrorists, then the whole world might suffer. People around the globe would then ask, " 'Why didn't you make provisions to keep dangerous criminals, dangerous terrorists, that you knew were terrorists, out of America's neighborhoods or London's neighborhoods or the neighborhoods of Amman, Jordan?' "[3]

By 2014, the United States alone had spent some $700 billion on the war in Afghanistan, a commitment that dwarfed even the Marshall Plan that followed the Second World War in Europe. These funds paid for a vast technological infrastructure to collect nearly all electronic and telephone communications in the country as well as an ambitious program to collect biometric data on millions of Afghans. Over a million Americans cycled through the country on combat missions or in supportive roles in the sprawling kaleidoscope of state and private enterprises that managed logistics for the American military. Dozens of other countries committed personnel and resources as well.

The Americans played an essential role in placing an Afghan diaspora figure who had spent considerable time in the United States and who spoke fluent English at the head of the government they created, first in 2002, with Hamid Karzai, and again in 2014, with Ashraf Ghani Ahmadzai. The mutual dependence of Washington and the U.S.-backed government in Kabul proved impossible to disentangle, despite President Barack Obama's pledge to end American involvement in Afghanistan by the end of 2014. In fact, the Americans conceded, a "secret war" continued after this deadline.[4]

Moreover, the delicate edifice of Afghan state institutions continued to be both sustained and undermined by international patrons. Whole sectors of the economy were inextricably tied to global financial flows. Foreign aid frequently departed as quickly as it landed, diverted not just by Afghan elites but by the foreign nationals attached to nongovernmental organizations (NGOs) and government institutions that had provided the aid in the first place. Afghan opium was the domestic mainstay of the Afghan social order, rivaled only by cannabis. Traffickers and consumers from West Africa to China formed a vast web with Afghan farmers at the center. The global and the local had been knitted together in an illicit bond. The war proved to be a catalyst for processes of globalization that could not easily be undone.

The American project in Afghanistan hinged on the idea that now Afghans were to become, at the center of the world's attention, the object of a beneficent humanitarianism. However, this idea, as we shall see, would be buffeted by a grueling military campaign. Always fragile and contradictory, the notion that Afghans could be redeemed proved to have a short life. Within a decade of 9/11, other, more enduring ideas about Afghans had resurfaced.

The Afghan beyond the borders of Afghanistan—whether aboard a smuggler's ship in the waters of the Mediterranean Sea or the Indian Ocean in search of safe harbors in Italy or Australia, or the bricklayer working his trade on the outskirts of Tehran—was more likely to be taken as a threat. Afghans who made their way secreted in freight containers from the European continent to England via the Chunnel found themselves in another kind of cosmopolitan milieu that was in many respects similar to that of their ancestors a century before who took the steamship on hajj: their travel compansions were Africans, Arabs, Indians, Pakistanis, a cross-section of global society whose movement had become an object of European policing and public anxiety. As of 2012, Afghans remained the largest refugee population in the world (estimated by the United Nations at over two and a half million people). Indeed one in four of the world's refugees was Afghan. Tragically, in 2014, Syria's civil war produced a refugee total that surpassed the Afghan numbers, though this Syrian refugee population, too, included Afghans who had migrated there in search of a reprieve from volatile political and economic conditions in Afghanistan: some two thousand Afghans, mostly Hazaras, were displaced yet again by fighting among Syrian armed factions.[5] Thus several million Afghans, the victims of more than three decades of fighting, continued to face an unsettled existence in locales across the globe. Their homeland, in turn, remained wracked by instability, its political crises only deepened by more than a decade of international intervention on a grand scale. Nonetheless, Afghans mapped out new forms of globalism in ways that would, once again, fundamentally reshape Afghan society.

The Afghan jihad against the Soviets had ended with the likes of Gulbuddin Hekmatyar and other mujahidin making bold claims about Islam as a bulwark against a post–Cold War world dominated by the Americans. In reality, the mujahidin struggled to gain control of their own country after the Red Army withdrew in February 1989. They managed to defeat the government of Dr. Najibullah only in 1992, when their rivalries, always just below the surface, simultaneously came to the fore. Meanwhile, vast swathes of the countryside, including the Helmand Valley, the jewel in the crown of Cold War-era American investment, had come to be dominated by poppies and hashish. Millions of Afghans remained displaced or strategically in transit between neighboring countries and their home districts and towns, while mujahidin commanders such as Ahmad Shah Massoud and Gulbuddin Hekmatyar were among the main protagonists whose forces destroyed much of Kabul in their fight for the capital. Their rivalries were a catastrophe for the two million Afghans who inhabited the city, several hundred thousand of whom had migrated from other regions to seek refuge from violence and chaos.

Despite near universal condemnation of the conduct of the mujahidin factions and of the deepening humanitarian crisis in the country, one figure, Ahmad Shah Massoud, managed to preserve his international renown as a figure of global significance, whose commitment to humanitarian values would put an end to the turmoil left in the wake of the Soviet war. Massoud's fame owed much to his stunning successes on the battlefield that pitted his ragtag fighters against the Soviet Goliath. More important, though, was his portrayal in Afghan and international media that had cast him as a universal hero. His struggle was not merely of the people inhabiting the Panjshir Valley or of a parochial religious militant, but of a cosmopolitan intellectual whose cause was the defense of all humanity. The notion that Massoud was not simply a brilliant military tactician but also a profound thinker on the world stage was very much the work of his Panjshiri entourage. Like other activists in the frantic mediascape of Peshawar, the savvy autodidacts and budding intellectuals deployed an iconography that was at once eclectic and disciplined, drawing on training by media experts provided by the United States to realize their own ambitions to remake Afghan society.[6]

Initially, Massoud had appealed most to European journalists and humanitarian aid workers. Dubbed the "Lion of the Panjshir," he was the subject of documentary films and the Ken Follet novel *Lie Down with Lions* (1985). His foreign admirers frequently compared him to Che Guevara, suggesting that he evoked associations that were amenable to the left. That he knew some French from studying at Istiqlal high school in Kabul was another advantage. It was probably not by accident that the Soviet intelligence file on Massoud mentioned his iconic Nuristani headgear, a flat woolen hat with a rounded border, as "a kind of beret." His supporters made effective use of photographs of the commander, clad in his "beret" and scarf and beaming a broad smile from his mountain redoubts.[7]

The American journalist Robert Kaplan credited Massoud's "thoroughly Westernized" spokesmen in Peshawar, who "spoke foreign languages and actually arrived on time for appointments," with securing him favorable coverage and generous amounts of aid. Kaplan's account offers another insight into the international reception of Massoud and his rivals by showing how many foreigners saw the mujahidin parties through a highly racialized lens. Kaplan was not just derisive of Afghan punctuality. He faulted Massoud for employing a tactic (a cease-fire), calling it "a very Tajik thing to do," contrasting this with "the wild, quixotic, completely unreasonable mentality of the Pathans, to whom the whole notion of tactics was anathema because it implied distinctions, and Pathans at war thought only in black and white." Thus, while Europeans favored Massoud, the American community in Peshawar—spies and journalists alike—continued to prefer Abdul Haq, a Pashtun commander, with, as Kaplan put it, "substance." If in Kaplan's version of events, Abdul Haq became a casualty of American neglect, in the American writer Steve Coll's telling, Massoud fell victim to the Pakistani and Saudi forces that gave rise to the Taliban movement, which took

Kabul in September 1996, and to Osama bin Laden, who had moved to Afghanistan (though not to an area under Taliban control) in May of the same year.[8]

Massoud was the last major commander to hold out successfully against the Taliban as they advanced from their base in Kandahar toward the north, ultimately taking control of some 90 percent of Afghan territory. Massoud's death at the hands of al-Qaeda assassins posing as journalists just two days before September 11, 2001, convinced many observers in the West that they had been on the same side all along—that Massoud had died in almost Christlike fashion (the angular face and slight beard may have cemented the subconscious connection for many Americans) as the first victim of 9/11.

When Massoud's men captured Kabul, steaming ahead of the American commandos and air power, they built on this global legacy—of martyr for the world—to make a claim to political power. Besides taking over key ministries overseeing the military and security forces, they established the Massoud Foundation (Bunyād-i Shahīd Mas'ūd), which served as an institutional repository and purveyor of Ahmad Shah Massoud's status as national martyr and global icon. His devotees published speeches and interviews. They reconstructed his childhood—the games he played in Kart-i Parwan in Kabul, his studiousness, and his devotion to his mother—and emphasized his refined image as a lover of the poet Fardowsi and as a fighter for the "homeland and Islam" on behalf of all communities (qawms). In one of the tributes offered at a 2002 "International Conference on Massoud Studies (Mas'ūd'shināsī)," one contributor offered praise to "a martyr who fought for years in his own country for the triumph of freedom and humanity and who is even remembered by the whole world for the fruits of his selflessness." "Ahmad Shah Massoud devoted his being," he continued, "for the destruction of the royal palaces that were built on the bones of people and the skulls and graves of the weak, and accordingly it was thus his greatest goal to be martyred." Another tribute claimed that his death had reverberated throughout construction sites and bazaars in both Russia and Tajikistan, "for all Tajiks." A Russian profile would praise him as "an Islamic humanist and internationalist."[9]

Among Afghans, though, there was much less of a consensus about this portrayal of Massoud. Calling him "the icon of the north," Michael Barry observed that from 2001 posters of Massoud disappeared an hour south of Kabul, marking an ethnic fault line between north and south. The events of September 11, 2001, were not the caesura that many in the West imagined. The recent past remained very much alive. One line of critique thus came from the Shia population of the Afshar district in the west of Kabul, where in February 1993 forces under the control of Abd (Rabb) al-Rasul Sayyaf and Ahmad Shah Massoud killed some seven hundred civilians, consigning their bodies to mass graves.[10] And while Massoud did draw support from supporters of different ethnic groups, it became more difficult for him to retain the loyalties of Hazaras, Pashtuns, and Uzbeks.

Despite his wife's glowing portrait of her husband, published in French (and in a large-print edition), women were another constituency who questioned Massoud's global legacy.[11] The Revolutionary Association of the Women of Afghanistan (RAWA) was particularly outspoken in its criticism. Founded in 1977 by Mina, a woman born, like Massoud, in 1956, RAWA countered that nothing distinguished the Taliban from "their traitor 'Jehadi brothers,'" which included "Rabbani, Gulbaddin, Khalili, Masud, Sayyaf and their accomplice Rashid Dostum." They were "criminal fundamentalists" who were "all equally responsible for the on-going tragedy in Afghanistan."

From its Pakistani exile, the RAWA leadership countered the propaganda of the mujahidin by also claiming to speak to a global public, but in this instance on behalf of women's rights. In 1997, one of their flyers accused Massoud's men of raping foreigners. In asking the world to remember the "desperate plight of Afghan women" under the Taliban and mujahidin, another communiqué conveyed RAWA's "deep support for and solidarity with the heroic struggle of women and freedom-loving forces in Iran, Palestine, Kashmir, Kurdistan and throughout the world against reactionary and oppressive forces and states."

At the same time, RAWA highlighted American complicity in the history of the Afghan jihad. "The United States, as the master player in this Great Chess Game and posing as the prime defender of democracy and human rights, replaced her Jihadi chessmen in our country with the mercenary Taliban band to further promote her regional interests," read another RAWA declaration. "Foreign interference is not the cause but the effect," it argued, "of the traitorous essence of criminal fundamentalists and mercenary warlords who with unparalleled insolence are ever ready and willing to put on the dog's collar of whatever foreign power who outdoes the others in its largesse of arms and dollars." When the United States launched cruise missile strikes in Afghanistan and Sudan in response to al-Qaeda's attacks on the American embassies in Kenya and Tanzania in August 1998, RAWA condemned them, calling the United States "terrorism-sponsoring" and maintaining:

> Even if the US somehow manages to get Osama bin Laden she will in no way be immune to the sting and poison of hundreds of other Afghan or non-Afghan Osamas lurking to strike in different parts of the world. When the US was frantically busy arming and training fundamentalist groupings in Afghanistan she did not give the slightest thought to the fallout for the people of Afghanistan nor for a moment paused to think what those very same anti-democracy and anti-women

criminal protégés would do to the Afghan people once they had achieved their aim of coming to political power in Afghanistan.

In its glossy magazine *Woman's Message (Payām-i zan)*, RAWA mapped out a distinctively feminist perspective, to be sure. Yet it shared certain rhetorical strategies in common with the mujahidin in that its editors prominently featured often graphic images of atrocities and devoted extensive space to commemorating martyrs—including Mina herself, who was killed by unknown assassins in Quetta, Pakistan, in 1987. *Woman's Message* also carried dozens of letters (in translation) that the organization received from women all over the world, from small-town America to Europe and beyond. A flyer for a Human Rights Day RAWA demonstration in Islamabad in 1999 showcased a poem in English by Sue Silvermarie, identified as "an American supporter of RAWA."[12]

An essential aspect of RAWA's appeal was that these women posed a challenge to the Taliban, a movement that seized Kabul in September 1996 and that seemed to many outsiders bent on using brute force to drag Afghans back to a more primitive time. Indeed, an Afghan who worked in one of the Taliban offices recalled an awkward joke by a German diplomat working for the UN: when he arrived for a Taliban meeting and found a broken clock on the wall, he quipped, "Time has stopped here."[13] Their hostility to technology and symbolic execution (by hanging) of televisions and audio- and videocassettes after they stormed Kabul was another striking feature of their rule. Above all, though, the Taliban attitude toward women seemed to mark them as enemies of the "modern" world.[14]

What such interpretations of the movement missed, of course, was that the Taliban had emerged in the mid-1990s out of a landscape molded by the superpowers and their clients, the most important being the Pakistani security establishment, which hoped a dependent regime in Kabul would aid in managing the contentious Afghan-Pakistani frontier and strengthen Pakistan's defensive capabilities in the event of war with India. In fact, for much of their history, the Taliban movement held a certain attraction to key international actors. They promised to reunite the country in a fashion that would allow Washington and oil companies to construct pipelines that would, skirting Iran and Russia, link Western consumers directly to energy resources in post-Soviet Central Asia.[15] At the same, they pledged to end the drug trade and reestablish commerce, which were American priorities as well. Some Taliban commanders may have been terrified of flying in airplanes and may have recoiled at particular kinds of technology, but like the mujahidin groups they challenged, the movement included self-educated intellectuals who imagined their own distinctive brand of globalism.[16]

For all of their aggressive piety, a number of Taliban officials were invested in the developmentalist rhetoric inherited from the Afghan regimes of the 1970s and 1980s. As "director general of the northern industries," Mullah Abdul Salam Zaeef, one of the movement's key leaders, recalled how he brought discipline to the decrepit factories in the north of the country, distributing radios and demanding "obligatory daily productivity reports." As a result, Mullah Zaeef boasted in his memoirs, "the brick-baking plant, ice factory and water plant were re-built. The engineers surveyed and repaired the existing wells. The gas network was extended from Sheberghan to Mazar-e Sharif; the production of cement increased; and industrial plants were rebuilt and became active throughout the north. Contracts were signed with foreign investors for new refineries." Mullah Zaeef's account is self-serving, of course, but it is a reminder that the Taliban actively courted international investors, multinational energy companies such as Unocal and Bridas among them. One can even identify the continued imprint of international labor legislation. Many of these principles were incorporated in a draft of the Taliban constitution, which included provisions for workers' rights, including a forty-hour work week, paid public holidays, and social security. In his own management of economic issues, Mullah Abdul Salam Zaeef claimed to have been quite critical of the private sector, alternating between nationalization and privatization to maximize efficiency. Though underresourced and anemic like the other ministries that the Taliban inherited, it is telling that the Ministry of Planning survived under the Taliban.[17]

Like previous Afghan governments, the Taliban craved international legitimacy. One of their first encounters with the world involved the detention of Russian pilots whose plane they forced to land in Kandahar. The Taliban were determined to be treated like a state in their negotiations with Moscow. The pilots were eventually allowed to leave, though the Russians claimed they executed a heroic escape (and a film was later made about the incident), but insiders said the Russians paid, in effect, a ransom.[18]

Given these international tensions, the Taliban were grateful to have the support of Muslims in other lands. In his memoirs, Mullah Zaeef tells the story of a particularly emotional encounter with a foreigner:

> One day an Arab-speaking Muslim called me many times, but after saying "hello" he always started crying, so eventually I hung up. Finally he managed to speak, asking me not to put down the phone. I promised to hear him out. In the background, I could hear his wife crying and it took him several minutes to speak clearly. He told me that his wife had become

agitated and emotional. She would not eat or drink and would cry all day. They were Palestinians. He asked me to speak to his wife and gave her the receiver. Even though she could not talk and all I could hear was her weeping, I tried my best to console her. I recited verses from the holy *Qur'an* and the *hadith* of the Prophet Mohammad (PBUH). Two or three days after this conversation, the man called again. He wanted to thank me. "My wife is well now, since you spoke with her," he said.

Even if apocryphal, the scene reveals how figures such as Mullah Zaeef understood their role as leaders whose charismatic authority and wisdom touched downtrodden Muslim men and, contrary to Western propaganda, they would insist, women across the globe.[19]

The Taliban were also interested in establishing relations with the United States as a crucial step toward having their government recognized internationally (beyond Pakistan, Saudi Arabia, and the United Arab Emirates) and gaining control of the Afghan seat at the General Assembly of the United Nations in New York. In meetings in Kandahar and Kabul in March 1997, Taliban and American officials discussed Osama bin Laden (who had arrived from Sudan the year before). The Taliban wanted to improve their standing with the United States but were not prepared to give up bin Laden, who, they explained, had been invited to territory not under their control and who had always maintained closer ties to the enemies of the Taliban: Gulbuddin Hekmatyar, Burhanuddin Rabbani, and Abd (Rabb) al-Rasul Sayyaf.

In place of expelling the Saudi, they suggested that American recognition of the Taliban government would lead to a resolution of the bin Laden question. The Americans concluded that the Taliban had sent "mixed signals." Despite their intransigence, it seemed, Mullah Ehsan, a member of the council under the principal leader

Mullah Muhammad Omar, wanted to "bargain," exchanging bin Laden for diplomatic recognition. Relations between the Taliban leadership and al-Qaeda were contentious.[20]

Mullah Omar even held talks by phone with the U.S. State Department after the Clinton administration launched cruise missile attacks on bin Laden in 1998. The Americans received reports that these events had estranged "many in the Taliban movement who considered themselves friends of the U.S." In seeking to establish some space for bargaining with the Americans, Taliban spokesmen were keen on showing their hostility toward Iran. And for their part, the U.S. officials were eager to establish some rapport with the group, not least of all by offering praise that they assumed the Taliban wanted to hear. In one communiqué to the group, an American official pointed to a long history of collaboration with the Afghans, including the Helmand River Valley Project, the construction of the Kandahar airport, and the creation of Kabul University, noting, too, that "we agree with your statement that the people of Afghanistan performed a major service to the world by defeating the forces of the Soviet Union and note the enormous sacrifices the Afghan people made in this effort." Phone conversations with Mullah Omar continued well into 2001, and the United States offered the Taliban government "humanitarian aid" in the summer, a move that was likely a step toward negotiations that may have been under way on the eve of the September 11 attacks by a group of al-Qaeda hijackers composed of young men from Saudi Arabia, Egypt, Lebanon, and the United Arab Emirates.[21]

The American-led invasion of Afghanistan in 2001 inaugurated a new era of Afghan globalism. The United States initially aimed at destroying the Taliban and al-Qaeda, assuming—in error, it would turn out—that political control of territory was absolutely essential to the functioning of both. However, the American project gradually evolved and expanded to offer the promise of liberating men and especially women from Taliban oppression. In addition to military personnel led mainly by Anglo-American forces, hundreds of international organizations and tens of billions of dollars descended on the country. Unwittingly, they revived many of the promises that the Afghan socialists, the People's Democratic Party of Afghanistan, had made in 1978 and even breathed new life into the prestige projects of the monarchy's Cold War patrons.

Beyond their immediate military objectives, the foreigners had arrived, they emphasized, to introduce enlightenment and health and to eradicate poverty, ignorance, and disease. Schools for girls became the preferred measure of Afghan reconstruction. Their construction was relatively easy. Photographs of these schools offered a narrative of progress for distant audiences in Europe and the United States. For instance, one American official described visiting a girls' school to deliver a bulletin board emblazoned with the pictures of "positive female role models that we hoped the children would emulate." It featured "Condoleezza Rice, Sandra Day O'Connor, Halle Berry, a female astronaut, and many other successful women." Most of these foreigners subscribed to the conventional wisdom that they were pioneers entering a "forbidden land," whose landscapes and people were reminiscent of biblical times, untouched by more than fifty years of American, Soviet, and other foreign advisory and development projects, not to mention nearly two billion dollars in foreign aid. Forgotten, of course, were the stories spanning the twentieth century of foreigners, harking back to the American envoy Cornelius Van H. Engert's secular missionaries, who had arrived to make Afghans "modern."[22]

The American agenda, then, was not merely altruistic. Reviving the outsiders' refrain about Afghanistan as an age-old cauldron of mayhem and violence that threatened to spew its toxic brew far beyond its borders, they had arrived in Afghanistan, first of all, to make Americans safe. Toward this end, in the months that followed September 11, the United States transformed Afghanistan into a central node in the circulation of detainees caught up in Washington's "Global War on Terror." Connected by U.S. military and privately contracted aircraft, a network of secret prisons and interrogation facilities would stretch from Poland to Somalia, Libya, Syria, and beyond. In November, the American president ordered the detention of any persons who have "engaged in, aided or abetted, or conspired to commit, acts of international terrorism" against the United States or had "knowingly harbored" such people. In January 2002, the president suspended the Geneva Conventions for the Afghan theater. Ignoring the most recent decades of American involvement in the country, the president's attorneys justified the decision by claiming that Afghanistan had been "a failed state" and that the Taliban were "in fact, not a government, but a militant, terrorist-like group." Suspected members of the Taliban, al-Qaeda, and their confederates were now labeled "enemy combatants." During the same month, the first men and boys started to arrive at the U.S. naval base in Guantánamo Bay, Cuba, for interrogation and detention.[23]

Within Afghanistan, the Soviet-built Bagram air base became the epicenter of America's global security campaign. Its detention facility was the key locale where American security forces improvised a regime of torture, abuse, and homicide, practices which then circulated to Guantánamo and, in 2003, the prison at Abu Ghraib in Iraq. It held prisoners not only from the Afghanistan and Pakistan theaters but from many other places where CIA and other American officials seized suspects. Men abducted in other countries such as the German citizen Khaled El-Masri were housed at Bagram and at another, more secret site, which was apparently not far away, known to some as the "Salt Pit" (and officially codenamed "COBALT"). In a case that resembled dozens of others, the CIA seized Muhammad Saad Iqbal, a Pakistani citizen, in Indonesia just a few months after 9/11. They transferred him to be interrogated in Egypt and then held him at Bagram for nearly a year. The Americans then sent him to Guantánamo Bay. In August 2008 they released him without filing charges.[24]

Bagram simultaneously grew into a vast base for U.S. forces, housing more than twenty thousand men and women. It quickly expanded to five thousand acres, accommodating institutions that would provide servicemen and women with a bit of American life: besides the Warrior and Enduring Faith Chapels, there was a Disney Drive, Burger King, Popeye's Chicken, two Subways, two Pizza Huts, two Green Beans Coffee shops, a Harley Davidson shop, an Afghan souvenir store, and more. American contracting firms brought some four thousand workers to the site from the Philippines, Russia, India, Pakistan, China, and elsewhere. Moreover, in accounts reminiscent of those describing the illicit traffic that surrounded the Red Army in Afghanistan, journalists pointed to Bagram and other bases as sites of transnational criminality. The American journalist Joshua Foust claimed:

> At most large U.S. bases in Afghanistan, you can find all of these things: construction workers cooking crystal meth in their isolated housing camp with the cheap and abundant pseudoephedrine cold medicine available at the Base Exchange, Korean prostitutes running a kimchi house on Disney Drive, Egyptian medical workers selling cocaine outside their hospital, and abused women at massage parlors trying, desperately, to make enough money in tips to make their years of indentured servitude somehow worth the stress to their families.

Beyond the comforts of this remarkably globalized complex, however, the war took a deadly toll, claiming over 3,300 fatalities among U.S. and coalition troops. An unknown number of militants and Afghan civilians and security forces died as well. The number was not determined because the principal parties involved, namely the U.S. government, its international allies, and the Afghan government, did not keep count. Only in 2007 did the United Nations Assistance Mission to Afghanistan begin compiling and making public Afghan civilian casualty statistics.[25]

Derisive of "nation building," the administration of President George W. Bush plotted a jagged strategic course that jettisoned its initial 2001 "light footprint" strategy and steadily increased American and allied investment in the form of troops and money. Barack Obama's antiwar positions in the campaign of 2008 focused squarely on condemning U.S. actions in Iraq and redirecting resources toward Afghanistan, where, in contrast to the debacle of Iraq, the United States would renew focus on "the good war." President Barack Obama followed suit, but with his own "surge," complete with a "counterinsurgency" plan adapted from Iraq. Personnel changed as quickly as the strategy. Meanwhile, Washington's more than forty coalition allies improvised their own, frequently conflicting, approaches, while coalition leaders offered constantly shifting rationales in pursuit of public support. The war might have been at one moment about preventing another 9/11. At another, it was in defense of women and education for girls. In July 2006, the British head of the International Security Assistance Force, General David Richards, ingeniously brought these two themes together in raising the alarm about the costs of NATO failure in Afghanistan: "I think of my own daughters in London and the risk they would be in."[26]

The problems of coordinating such a vast and complex multinational operation have been analyzed elsewhere. Perhaps no account

better captured the surrealism of this American-inspired internationalism than that of a British officer, Leo Docherty, who offered a vi-
gnette worthy of Rowan Atkinson's *Blackadder* in describing one of
the coalition military bases in the south of the country:

> In the cookhouse there are thirty different signing-in books:
> one for each nationality in the Coalition. I wonder what it is
> the Bulgarians do, and am entertained to see a solitary Ice-
> landic soldier guarding the front gate alongside some Italians.
> The French seem especially ornamental and pose absurdly in
> their too-short combat trousers. These over-clean staff officers
> are the physical opposite of the Afghans whose city they live
> in. As a body they are bloated and ineffectual. Their only value
> lies in the veneer of international inclusivity which they lend
> the Coalition. . . . Thankfully I'll be getting well away from
> them; there's no room for their sort in Helmand.

Concentrating almost exclusively on the actions of the foreigners,
many such critiques of the war assumed that better logistical coordi-
nation, funding, or public support would have turned the course of
the war and would have ended the stalemate with a dogged insurgency
that was present throughout the country and in control of whole
districts despite the combined military might of the United States
and NATO.[27]

Away from the U.S. military bases and the journalists who trailed
them from place to place, novel modes of Afghan globalism emerged.
Migrants and exiles returned from distant corners of the globe. Capital flowed in and out of the country at a dizzying pace. U.S. dollars,
Saudi riyals, Euros, UAE dirhams, Pakistani rupees, and British

pounds periodically streamed out of the country through numerous channels on the way to Dubai, where much of this cash went to purchase real estate. The chairman of Kabul Bank, Shir Khan Farnood, for example, was rumored to own some thirty-nine properties on the Palm Jumeirah in Dubai. Kabul International Airport was the epicenter of much of this traffic. By one insider's estimate, in a single day as much as $75 million might pass through the airport on the way to Dubai.[28] In 2007, the Afghan state signed a contract with China Metallurgical Group Corporation to excavate copper at Mes Aynak, the first major deal to exploit what some experts estimated to be $1 trillion in mineral resources in the country. An adviser at the U.S. Geological Survey, James Devine, spoke for many aid experts and Chinese investors when he expressed confidence that mining "will get Afghanistan out of the 14th century."[29]

Foreign aid and investment was one source of the money that flowed through Afghanistan. Drugs were another. Afghanistan's position as the leading producer both of opium (estimated at 6,400 tons in 2014) and cannabis (about 1,400 tons in 2012) connected Afghan farmers with consumers across the globe. But Afghans did more than cultivate these crops. Afghan men, women, and children increasingly became users of drugs themselves. And Afghans were active at nearly every phase of the global drug trade. The arrest of two Afghan nationals in October 2007 in the capital of Ghana, Accra, pointed to the important role of Afghan intermediaries in operating beyond Afghanistan's borders and adapting new transit routes through West Africa toward heroin markets in the United States.[30]

At the same time, new communications systems, including cell phones, satellite television, and the Internet spread throughout Afghan cities. Afghan media outlets sprang up in towns large and small. A TV singing competition, *Afghan Star,* riveted the attention of all age groups and ethnic communities.[31] Young Afghan men and women went abroad to study on scholarships by the thousands to countries such as Turkey and the United Kingdom. Domestically, new schools appeared, even if foreign donors inflated their number, or on many occasions built schools that would collapse not long after their departure. Protesters took to the streets to express outrage at the mistreatment of Muslims in Palestine, Denmark, Iraq, and Guantánamo, while militants took up arms, sometimes in defense of a village and at others on behalf of Muslims suffering a world away.

For their part, the Taliban took to the Internet to present themselves simultaneously as protectors of the Afghan nation and of Muslims everywhere. Likely reflecting pressure from the universalist pretensions of the Islamic State, the militant organization based in Syria and Iraq, an official biography published by the Taliban on their website in April 2015 celebrated Mullah Muhammad Omar as a defender of the al-Aqsa Mosque and "the vindicated claim of Palestinian Muslims." Indeed, the Taliban statement emphasized, Mullah Omar "has taken a clear stance and supported all issues of Muslims in all parts of the world" and "considers it the duty and obligation of every Muslim to liberate the al-Aqsa Mosque from the occupation of Zionist Jews." Contrasting Mullah Omar with other Afghan leaders, the text insisted that the head of the Taliban had no foreign bank accounts but that he shared "the sufferings of all Muslim people" and that Mullah Omar's "sincerity, sympathy, brotherhood and cooperation with the Muslim brothers of the world are not restricted only to slogans but rather he has proved it practically and in the real sense of all these terms."[32]

With Afghanistan at least, Mullah Omar's Taliban fighters backed up his words. Despite American and NATO declarations about ending the war in Afghanistan, fighting actually intensified. Indeed, the year 2014 was the most lethal yet for Afghan civilians since authorities began collecting statistics in 2007: 3,699 civilians, including

714 children and 298 women, were killed in insurgent attacks and fighting between some combination of foreign and Afghan security forces and insurgents. Moreover, American drone strikes continued. In February 2015, according to media accounts, one of them targeted a Taliban leader, once imprisoned at Guantánamo, who had recently begun recruiting for the Islamic State movement. Many Afghans interpreted the abduction of thirty-one Hazaras in Zabul Province in the same month as proof that the influence of the Islamic State had spread to Afghanistan and, in fact, that global forces were arrayed in yet another coalition against the Afghan nation. Ali Akbar Qasemi, a parliamentarian from Ghazni Province warned, "Those who are funded by Jews and Christians under the name of Daesh [Islamic State] are trying to create tensions between ethnic groups, which we will never allow." Demonstrations protesting this kidnapping stretched from Ghazni to the Afghan diaspora in Europe and Australia.[33]

Amid this violence, a desire for normalcy structured the everyday lives of millions of Afghans. After 2001, Kabul became a teeming city packed with automobile traffic, where brightly colored modernist glass wedding halls and weight-lifting gyms sat just a stone's throw from districts with pastel-colored villas shielded by armed men and others lined with begging women and small children adjacent to blocks encased in blast walls and armed checkpoints. Suicide bombers—perhaps the most shocking artifact of Afghanistan's post-9/11 globalization—circulated in the city despite the ubiquity of convoys of massive armored vehicles with menacing graffiti in foreign languages and electronic equipment that knocked out cell phone coverage as they snaked through this surrealist cityscape.

Of all the changes that the expanded foreign presence has made possible, the transformation of the Shia community has been among the most striking, particularly because this shift owed so much to such

7   Street scene, Kabul, November 2013. Photo by author.

diverse global forces. A relatively small minority (perhaps 15–25 percent of the total population), the Shia include Farsiwan in western Afghanistan, the Turkomans of Parwan Province northwest of Kabul, small pockets of Baluch in the north, the Qizilbash in Kabul and other cities, Tajik Ismailis concentrated in the northeastern province of Badakhshan, and the largest group, the Hazaras, who reside in the central region of the Hazarajat as well as in numerous urban centers.

In the last quarter century, the Shia have acquired a political significance far beyond their numbers. The year 1979 was a major turning point. The Iranian revolution and Soviet invasion were watersheds that brought the Afghan Shia into contact with revolutionary ideologies that would utterly transform their politics and communal organizations. Exposure to Khomeinism and socialism, as well as to migration, exile, and civil war, unsettled an Afghan political order that had consigned the Shia, particularly the predominant Hazara ethnic minority among them, to the lowest rungs. The politics of the jihad and of the Soviet-backed government gave the Shia, for the first time in the history of the country, an avenue for substantive participation in Afghan politics at the national level. Brutal persecution at the hands of the Taliban movement strengthened Shia claims on political inclusion in 2001.

Having destroyed the anti-Shia Taliban regime and scattered its leaders, the United States and its allies brought about other far-reaching changes for the Shia and other Afghans by introducing popular elections. Although the post-2001 elections for parliament and president were flawed in numerous ways—and the United States and international community crudely stacked the deck in favor of Hamid Karzai in 2004 and again in 2009—Shia communities gained entrée to national politics, and Shia notables won seats in parliament. Karzai, in turn, was forced to court their votes to shore up his fragile legitimacy. Subject for generations to sectarian and ethnic discrimination and frequent persecution, Shia communities became a significant electoral constituency, and some entrepreneurs with connections from the diaspora brilliantly navigated the new terrain: Saad Mohseni, who returned from Australia to become the celebrated "Rupert Murdoch of Afghanistan," was the most successful example, parlaying investments from USAID and other international sponsors into the country's dominant media conglomerate that included Arman Radio and Tolo TV and its popular show, *Afghan Star*.[34] As the case of Mohseni also demonstrates, however, the Shia did not form a monolithic bloc. Competing jihadi parties jockeyed to reassert their authority in this new context, while many Hazara leaders mobilized to claim rights on the basis of ethnic affinity. Afghan Shia found themselves with new power and influence in the national politics inaugurated by the U.S.-led occupation, even as their transnational ties persisted through the diaspora as well as more structured refugee and clerical networks.

Many Afghan Shia came to characterize the post-2001 period as a kind of renaissance. By most accounts, they flourished under an American protectorate. They enjoyed religious toleration on an unprecedented scale and privileged access to the post-Taliban institutional landscape of NGOs, schools, state offices, and commercial enterprises. Though beneficiaries of the new order, Shia religious scholars emerged at the center of key controversies about the character of the Afghan political system, presenting forceful challenges to the liberal restructuring of Afghan politics and society advanced by the United States and its international and Afghan allies.

In contesting the marginality of Shiism and in seeking to transform the tradition and its relationship to Afghan understandings of nationhood, the Shia clerics have drawn deeply on transnational connections. For many Afghan and foreign observers, it has been precisely the global character of the Shia project in general and ties to Iran in particular that have attracted negative scrutiny. Domestic and international critics of Shia leaders interpreted their activism as a plot directed from an aggressively expansionist regime in Tehran, a transnational conspiracy intended both to extend Iran's power in Afghanistan, as in Lebanon and Iraq, and to make Afghan Shia religious institutions mirror those of Iran.

At the center of these controversies was the central institution of Shia religious authority, the person of the "source of imitation" *(marja-yi taqlid)*, the authoritative religious expert, typically bearing the title *ayatollah*, whose judgments about Islamic law and other matters individual Shia followers are meant to follow. For Shia everywhere, this institution had been in flux in recent decades. Following the deaths of Khomeini in 1989 and Abu-l-Qasim Khu'i in 1992, not to mention multiple executions and assassinations of these religious experts (marjas) based in Najaf, Iraq, the number of aspiring ayatollahs and marjas rapidly increased, sparking intense competition for followers and the influence, prestige, and taxes that come with them.

Afghan Shia elites were thus embroiled in the same contests and were indeed part of the global scholarly network of Shia scholars who studied, mostly in the 1970s and 1980s, in the seminaries of Najaf and Qum, Iran, where two of these Afghan figures still teach and reside permanently. Ties to these seminaries and to the global discourse of Shia religion and politics were essential to Afghan Shia scholars' efforts to establish their personal and institutional authority in Afghanistan.

Yet it is laypeople who choose their marjas, which gave this competition a particular dynamism and fluidity, especially in Afghanistan. These politics proved so controversial not only because they represented a mode of transnationalism that operated outside of American attempts to control global flows through Afghanistan, but also because they were very much about the regulation of sex, personal autonomy, and the divide between public and private, on the one hand, and citizenship, on the other. On each of these issues, Shia clerics made claims on guardianship—of the community, of the family, of women—that contested the liberal ideologies of various international organizations that flooded the country after 2001. These scholars have, for instance, engaged in a running critique of what they portrayed as "Western" gender norms and offered extensive commentary on what roles Muslim women should play in a "globalized" world, where conflicting norms are in competition. One of the most important of these clerics, Ayatollah Muhammad Asef Mohseni, has presented a relentlessly comparative argument, relying on a broad secular literature on social theory, and insisting that the modern and the global were irrefutable facts around which Muslims must craft their positions on gender and other topics.

These controversies ran through the works of these Afghan Shia scholars, including their responses to followers' requests for opinions about legal, ritual, political, and other matters *(istiftā'āt)*—remarkable sources, which offer a window into the imagination of the faithful, in this case, of Afghans from around the world. Men and women wrote to ask about paying alms and eating halal food while living in places such as Sweden and China. A sixteen-year-old boy sent a query from Afghanistan seeking guidance about how to deal with his passionate feelings for a girl who had caught his eye. Another inquired about the legal status of buying foreign-made leather shoes at one of the secondhand-clothing bazaars. Others asked for instruction about how to evaluate the morality of women in film and how to navigate the presence of women in gyms and the playing of music on public buses. Several focused on rules governing women and the hajj and wanted to know whether a woman needed her husband's permission (Ayatollah Mohaqeq Kabuli replied that she did not).[35]

The crucial medium that made these exchanges possible was the Internet, which Shia marjas had used brilliantly from the late 1990s to project their authority beyond traditional channels and across all kinds of boundaries. The spatial dimension was particularly significant, since Afghans enjoyed the right, in theory, to choose any of the dozen or more Internet marjas, whether they were based in Lebanon, Iraq, Iran, or elsewhere. The contest was not confined to Afghan territory because the ayatollahs asserted their authority over Afghan Shia everywhere. They sought extraterritorial power over the diaspora, and especially over Afghans in Iran, a terrain already rich with marjas.[36]

The lives of these senior Afghan clerics were defined not only by extraordinary mobility but also by deep connections to global Shia institutions, personnel, and ideas. They reflected the ambitious pursuit of the new possibilities of the mass politics and religious latitude of the post-2001 period. But another aspect of this political conjuncture formed a crucial part of their politics, though in varying degrees for each of them: the international politics of the country—namely, the expansive foreign presence—furnished multiple occasions for talking about the Afghan nation, sovereignty, Islam, "the West," and "tradition"—and for asserting claims to clerical leadership alongside demands for the political inclusion of Shia as brothers of the Sunnis. At the same time, their relationships with each other were marked by rivalry. This was especially striking in the construction of Shia institutions, not solely in the sense of the physical erection of imposing architectural monuments—as in the Khatam-al Nabiyin Islamic University and other schools and mosques that have transformed urban spaces in Kabul, Herat, and elsewhere—but in the sense of clerical organizations, large-scale ceremonial performances, and other competitive efforts aimed at establishing these figures as the preeminent marja, the source of emulation for Afghans and perhaps others.[37]

Cultural capital derived from transnational scholarly networks as well as from domestic patronage was the critical resource in this competition. It was on display in the architectural artifacts associated with each figure and carefully crafted by their retinues through websites and online communities, including Facebook. The sites of Grand Ayatollah Shaykh Muhammad Asef Mohseni, Grand Ayatollah Qurban ʿAli Mohaqeq Kabuli, Ayatollah Muhammad Hashem Salehi Mudaress, and Muhammad Ishaq al-Fayyaz have resembled those of prominent Shia clerics in Iran and elsewhere. Indeed their format and language appear to be derivative of those sites, likely reflecting their construction in Iran. They have allowed readers to learn about the biographies of the ayatollahs, to solicit fatwas and advice, and to read their pronouncements on politics, theology, law, and other matters. Photographs and videos have begun to play an important role as well in documenting aspects of their biographies, including their ties to important religious and political figures and the devotion of their followers.[38]

Consider the case of Ayatollah Muhammad Asef Mohseni. His official biography elides any mention of ethnic origin, but most accounts suggest his background is Pashtun. Born into a clerical family in Kandahar in 1936, he moved with his father to Pakistan at the age of thirteen and learned Urdu. As a teenager he began work at a trading firm in Kandahar, where he likely encountered some of the commercial institutions curated by the founder of the National Bank, Abdul Majid Zabuli. But Mohseni soon left this to pursue his religious studies, initially in Jaghori and then in 1953, at the age of eighteen, in Najaf, Iraq. He completed the first part of his education in two and a half years before moving on to study the Islamic legal sciences with the quietist Ayatollah Sayyid Mohsen Hakim, as well as with Ayatollah Husayn Hilli, Ayatollah Sayyid 'Abdul 'Ali Sebzevari, and the powerful Ayatollah al-Khoei. After twelve years in Najaf, he returned to Kandahar in about 1965, where he established a place for Shiite ceremonies (a *hosseiniya*) and madrasa. In 1977 he was one of several thousand Afghans (estimates ranged as high as eight thousand per year) who went on hajj. From Saudi Arabia, he continued on to Syria, stopping there for several months to teach at the seminary *(howza)* in Damascus.[39]

When the People's Democratic Party of Afghanistan seized power in April 1978, Mohseni was in Qum. Together with other Shia Afghan clerics at the howza, he responded to news from Afghanistan by forming the Islamic Movement Party (Hizb-i Harakat-i Islami) to mobilize resistance against the new regime. Under Mohseni's leadership, the party claimed thousands of fighters and more than a hundred bases in nineteen Afghan provinces. The ayatollah's biography has relatively little to say about the period of the jihad but resumes in roughly 1992 with a brief summary of his role as secretary and spokesman for the leadership council of the mujahidin government. It is also laconic about his role in the civil war, noting only that he left for Islamabad after the mujahidin turned on one another. In 1997, he relocated to Qum and returned to teaching. Mohseni's biography is silent about his reaction to the Taliban, noting only that he returned to Kabul after the collapse of their government. It was in the post-Taliban era that Mohseni flourished: his website credits him with gaining official recognition for Shia legal practices and highlights his founding of the Tamaddon ("Civilization") television station and the "great scholarly and cultural complex" Khatam al-Nabiyin, an institution "the likes of which Afghanistan has never had."[40]

His TV station became embroiled in conflict in 2008 when Mohseni's camp accused the staff of Emroz ("Today"), a rival station, of slandering the Shia. Apparently their programs suggested that Shia clerics were in the pockets of the Iranians. In October 2008, Mohseni's seminary became the staging ground for protests against the station. According to an Iranian press report that highlighted the invocation of Khomeini at the rally, one speaker proclaimed to the crowd, "Israel's servant, [the] Muslim's enemy and the enemy of fraternity comes and insults the great imam, the leader of the Islamic Revolution, the leader of Muslims, Imam Khomeini (People chanting: God is great), then mocks the great personality, Ayatollah Mohseni . . . and disrespects our values. Our people are not pharaoh's relatives, our people have forgotten the pharaohs one after the other, our people will defend their interests and the ideal of the world's great imam,

Khomeini."[41] In April 2009 the Emroz station manager was arrested for slandering Mohseni. The station also faced charges of undermining "national unity."[42]

In 2009, Ayatollah Mohseni oversaw the introduction of a new "Shia personal status law." Widely castigated in international circles as the "Afghan rape law," the legislation provoked a profound political crisis, sparking protests for and against the law, dividing Shia communities, and heightening sectarian tensions. Critics honed in on the articles discussing the wives' sexual duties, which they glossed as license to commit rape, an interpretation challenged by the authors of the legislation and many (but not all) of their Shia defenders. International media coverage linked it to more general frustrations with the Afghan war and with Karzai, who faced elections and who seemed to be focused more on courting Shia votes than on defending a universal human rights agenda. Thanks to WikiLeaks, we know that the U.S. embassy worked behind the scenes to have it scuttled and even visited Mohseni's seminary to try to dissuade him.[43]

Debates about the law became an occasion to comment on Khatam al-Nabiyin, Ayatollah Mohseni, and Iran's role in spreading "extremism." An Afghan commentator, Zia Zarak, contrasted Mohseni's seminary with nearby Kabul University, which he called "a symbol of modernization and a farewell to our old ways."

Why were those veiled women protesting in favour of the law and rallying on the streets? Did they want an anti-women law that makes the women a second-class human who needs permission of her husband to go out of her house? Like other religious leaders, Mr. Mohseni needs to develop hatred among his followers. Most interestingly, such religious movements are ethically based on morality and human values. But one of the slogans the followers of Mr. Mohseni were using in their protest was the word "prostitute" to describe women rallying against the law. Those hurling stones and swear words at the protesters against the law will kill, terrorize or imprison anyone who demonstrates against their opinions if they gain political power. . . . Mr. Mohseni is a part of fundamentalist movement in Afghanistan. The other arm of this movement is the Sunni Taleban. They both have the same values of being against modernism, freedom, humanism, democracy, human rights, progress, pluralism and religious reform. They consider all above values as against religion and will try to demolish them using hatred. . . . Resisting the movement of Mr Mohseni and the Taleban is our responsibility as citizens. They may try to use all possible means to exert pressure on the government to impose their thoughts on the public and personal affairs of the people.[44]

But a parliamentarian from the north, Sayyid Hussain Alemi Balkhi, wrote an open letter to President Obama calling foreign criticism of the law an insult to the views of 1.5 billion Muslims. On June 28, *Rah-e Nejat* published an editorial countering criticism of the law by charging that women were treated as objects in the West and calling on the government to resist foreign requests to change the law. During the same period, an editorial in *Shahadat*, a Peshawar-based Pashto newspaper aligned with Gulbuddin Hekmatyar, criticized Western pressure on Muslim leaders to permit Muslim women to dress in any imaginable way and noted that French president Sarkozy had acted hypocritically by banning the veil in France. Amid the controversy, editors of *8 AM (Hasht-e Sobh)* accused Mohseni's followers of hacking the newspaper's website.[45]

At issue was how to interpret a provision of the law that laid out the different rights and obligations that Shia men and women would have in marriage. The controversy mobilized women on all sides, though it also exposed generational and sectarian differences (young Shia women appeared to make up most of the protesters, and American officials complained that they could not identify more established female Shia notables to condemn the proposal). Karzai eventually signed the bill, though apparently with some modifications, and Mohseni touted the law as one of the crowning achievements of his leadership. For Mohseni, it was at once a rebuke to foreign powers who would seek to violate the Afghan constitution (which, in his reading, gave the Shia the authority to define their personal status law) and a landmark event in the inclusion of the Shia into an expanded framework of citizenship in Afghanistan, one that reserved considerable space for the clerical regulation of sex and personal autonomy in a polity whose institutions had otherwise been cast, to a great extent, in the American liberal mold.

Mohseni has himself couched his ideology as one of the fruits of globalization, a process that he has examined at length. He has stressed that "in the twentieth century as a result of the discovery of means of transportation (the automobile, the airplane, the locomotive) and means of communication (the telephone, telegraph, fax, radio, television and the Internet) man entered a new era of complex and rapid social interactions." All of this yielded "larger social entities." Drawing on authors ranging from Margaret Mead to Anthony Giddens and Samuel Huntington and pointing to new entities like the European Union and the World Bank, the ayatollah concluded that "these institutions—especially international organizations—have limited the authority of states over their nations and countries to an extent that much of this authority has devolved, in part, to international organizations and to other transnational institutions." "From the point of view of technology," he continued, "man is progressing in intellectual, scientific, and artistic fields, and modernity [*modernite*] continues to search for itself, the latest manifestation of which is the Internet. In our age the distance of time and space has become extremely short and the world has become one country."[46] For this Internet-savvy cosmopolitan, hyperconnectivity was an undeniable reality for Muslims and non-Muslims, for Sunni and Shia, and for Afghans and non-Afghans alike. The challenge, then, was not to deny or escape this globalized modernity but to bend the world to one's will.

EPILOGUE

AFTER SPENDING FOUR years in American captivity, mostly at the prison at Guantánamo Bay, Cuba, an Afghan doctor resolved to write about his experience for his fellow countrymen. In the introduction to his memoir, Dr. Muhammad 'Ali Shah Musavi Gardezi enumerated the many ways that foreign involvement has harmed the long-suffering Afghan people. He wrote that it was difficult to write about such a subject because it involved

> the story of a land whose people have been thrown alive into graves by domestic oppressors, whose basis of life has been destroyed by tyranny, injustice, ignorance and poverty, and where under various names foreign military powers have ruined their foundation, foreign powers, who have arrived under various names and with different goals, at times coming in the name of helping the people and friendship and for making peace and prosperity and colonization, and at times in the name of internationalist and workers' assistance and sometimes in the name of religion and faith and now in the name of democracy, peace, security and freedom, who are killing and committing slaughter and building prisons filled with the innocent and fighters and who answer to no person, no power and no authority.

Armed with an intelligence report that he had returned to Gardez, in Paktia Province, from Iran with $150,000 to aid al-Qaeda and the Taliban, American soldiers arrested him in August 2003. His nightmare began at a local U.S. camp and then continued at Bagram air base and then in Cuba, a path followed by more than two hundred Afghan detainees, including those who, according to subsequent U.S. investigations, were murdered in American custody.[1]

To Gardezi's captors, his personal history seemed suspicious. His life story was one of mobility, border-crossing, and an itinerant quest for knowledge. He had been forced to interrupt his medical studies at Kabul and then resume them in Iran. In between his studies he took on shifts in a taxi and other odd jobs after a period of exile in Pakistan and time waging jihad against the Red Army. All of this made plausible the denunciation that someone, presumably an acquaintance with a grievance or an interest in collecting a bounty, lodged against him. It guaranteed his arrest and detention halfway around the globe, even if the notion of a Persian-speaking Shia assisting a Sunni militant outfit that had abused and murdered en masse his brethren defied logic, as Gardezi himself tried to argue in his court proceedings. A Muslim who crossed borders prompted anxieties about unknown numbers of the faithful acting in stealth and in concert against the Westerners who had recently arrived in the country. In defying outsiders' expectations about a supposedly immobile, static, and inward-looking population, Gardezi's case resembles that of many others whom U.S. forces seized because the Americans associated Afghan strategies for coping with war and displacement with illicit border crossing, smuggling, and, they assumed, militancy.[2]

Such itinerant lives seemed threatening. Given official thinking about the country, they appeared to be suspiciously out of place. What were Afghans doing mixing with Iranians and attending Pakistani schools? What were those suspect-looking Arabic books about? Assuming Afghans to be primitive, parochial, and ignorant of the world beyond their mud compounds, foreign forces were wary of Afghans who did not fit the mold they had cast for them. Even in dealing with figures from the diaspora who had advanced degrees and who had mastered a half dozen languages, the international community tended to see them as little more than stand-ins for whole ethnic groups whose internal cohesion and uniformity they took for granted. In 2001, the notion that an ethnic Pashtun had to be in charge of the country was treated as an article of faith. After routing the Taliban, Washington was determined to find one. Subsequently, the development of state institutions was almost an afterthought. As several scholars have shown, the jumble of international agencies and state actors working at cross-purposes hampered the building of an effective bureaucracy and other institutions. Elections gave cover for heavily centralized rule.[3] But the foreigners were also happy to bypass state institutions, passing funds on to other NGOS or hiring local militias, for a host of reasons, one of the most important, but little noticed, being the mistaken belief that no Afghans really wanted a strong state anyway. They were, after all, essentially "tribal."

This was the idea at the heart of American counterinsurgency doctrine, which relied on ideas first developed about the Afghans in the eighteenth and nineteenth centuries and which foreign observers recycled in the 1980s. Robert Kaplan's influential account of the mujahidin stood out neither for its racism nor for its condescension: "Afghanistan existed without bridges to the twentieth century. The country was mired in medievalism; a 'mass of mountains and peaks and glaciers,' as Kipling noted; a place where terrible things always happened to people." They defeated the Soviets, Kaplan argued, "precisely, and only, because they were so primitive." Echoing nineteenth-century British colonial language, Kaplan insisted that evolution had made them "arguably the physically toughest people on earth. . . . They seemed an extension of an impossible landscape that had ground up one foreign invader after another." In a statement that could have applied to all Afghans seen through this distorted lens, Kaplan alleged that the mujahidin were "a movement without rhetoric or ideology" and that "they had no politics."[4] Some twenty years later, these ideas remained largely unchallenged in official circles. The top commander in Afghanistan in 2010–2011, General David Petraeus would draw inspiration from a Special Forces major, Jim Gant, the author of an essay called *One Tribe at a Time: A Strategy for Success in Afghanistan,* in which he pointed out "the absolute necessity of working with and bonding with the tribal leader—man-to-man, warrior-to-warrior."[5]

A chief architect of General Petraeus's counterinsurgency project, the Australian anthropologist David Kilcullen, called for investment in "cultural and ethnographic intelligence." Kilcullen endorsed the proposition that would become axiomatic for American doctrine: most of the fighters the United States faced in Iraq, Afghanistan, or in other "tribal societies" were actually "accidental guerrillas." They might fight alongside "extremist forces" such as al-Qaeda, but they do so "not because they support the *takfiri* ideology but because they oppose outside interference in their affairs, because they are rallied to support local tribal or community interests, or because they are alienated by heavy-handed actions of the intervening force." To Kilcullen and his acolytes, inhabitants of "traditional societies" were stamped by a parochial localism. Unchanging social structures and timeless isolation, not politics, ideas, or ideology, defined the lives of these populations: "local people in tribal societies will always tend to side with closer against more distant relatives, with local against external actors, and with coreligionists against people of other faiths."[6]

With respect to the Taliban, Kilcullen concluded that 90 percent were "reconcilable under some circumstances" and "actually or potentially co-optable," though he added the caveat that "any such attempt at cooption would have to be conducted from a position of

strength lest insurgent leaders (or, more importantly, local communities) interpret this as a Taliban victory."[7] In engaging these
populations, which are "unlike Western societies," Kilcullen cautioned, "we must also recognize that in a tribal, traditional society,
choices are made collectively (by family, section, clan, tribal, or village units), not by single individuals." "If we focus on winning over
key traditional leaders," he argued, "we can win the support of an
entire village or lineage group at one time, rather than piecemeal."[8]
By this account, the Taliban were like any other "tribal" guerrillas,
essentially apolitical and collectivist. This notion, in turn, inspired
research by Pentagon contractors and Human Terrain System specialists aimed at unpacking the tribal genealogies of the Pashtuns. Formerly of interest only to historians, British colonial ethnography
enjoyed a renaissance.[9] At the same time, senior officers' frequent
references to "$10 Taliban" reflected confidence that Taliban fighters
were little more than mercenaries who could easily be "flipped" if
offered more attractive financial and other incentives. Meanwhile,
counterinsurgency specialists and most other observers of Afghan affairs dismissed a growing body of Taliban communications issued
via the Internet and sophisticated video productions as little more
than "propaganda" rather than seek to interpret them as clues to
shifting Taliban ideology and their engagement with international
media and an Afghan public.

A similar myopia has plagued the international approach to the
state. Here, too, many observers pointed to the ostensible incompat-
ibility of Afghan notions of the state and nation with modern forms
of government. Only after 2008, when the United States created a
Special Inspector General for Afghanistan Reconstruction, did substantial documentation begin to emerge to challenge claims to the
effect that the Afghans were mired in a "culture of corruption."
Dozens of criminal prosecutions of American officials, military per-

sonnel, and contractors who diverted millions in reconstruction funds from Afghanistan have supplied convincing proof that it was the American-designed procurement system that generated a staggering degree of fraud that enriched so many Afghans and Americans alike. Contractors even participated in human trafficking to supply workers from third countries to work on American military bases. Soldiers and officers engaged in bribery, often making payments to militants to secure transportation routes. In one notable case, a U.S. Army sergeant stationed at Bagram received $250,000 in kickbacks from Afghan contractors, which he smuggled back into the United States in toy trucks.[10]

Refusing to see such activities as part of a global web of interdependence is but one example of the ways that misreadings of the spatial, intellectual, and ethical horizons of Afghans have had a profound impact on the policy choices of international actors, perpetuating a war that has taken an increasingly lethal toll on Afghan soldiers and civilians alike. Clinging to the "graveyard of empires" narrative or blaming the outcome of the U.S.-led intervention on Afghan "culture" are distractions from the more challenging task of grasping the current conjuncture through a wider framework in which Afghan globalism is entangled with our own modern condition.

The Afghan past serves as a guide. The story of the emergence of Afghanistan played out across a vast space. As traders, pilgrims, students, scholars, poets, mercenaries, workers, and political exiles, Afghans set out in all directions. For generations, Afghan lives have been defined by extraordinary mobility. From China to Africa and Australia, Afghans adapted to foreign millieus, gaining exposure to intellectual and cultural resources that then circulated throughout the diaspora and back to these migrants' points of origin in what is now Afghanistan. By the early twentieth century, the Afghan state could be counted among these resources. Leaving Afghanistan frequently meant bringing the state along. Yet this meant more than access to consular officials, a passport, or the prospect of state intervention on behalf of Afghans abroad. For many, it was the idea of an Afghan nation with a distinctive role to play on the world stage that fired their imagination beyond the borders of the country.

Indeed, the diaspora played a crucial role in the contest for political power in Afghanistan. The circulation and return of exiles was a constant of nineteenth-century politics. In the twentieth century, from the era of Muhammad Nadir Shah, who returned from France to seize power in 1929, every Afghan leader has come from, or at least had to seriously contend with, Afghan communities abroad. Like Nadir Shah, Muhammad Zahir Shah had to maintain his guard against the deposed Amanullah. Liberal and radical movements in the diaspora were another perennial concern. In the 1980s, the opponents of the Democratic Republic of Afghanistan were based in Iran and Pakistan, where they drew on the support of a dozen or more nations, the United States, Saudi Arabia, and China among them. After 2001, three Afghans, Hamid Karzai, Zalmay Khalilzad, and Ashraf Ghani Ahmadzai (the latter two alumni of the American University of Beirut), returned from lengthy periods of residency in the United States to claim positions at the pinnacle of power in Afghanistan. Several million more Afghans migrated strategically in the last decades of the twentieth and first decades of the twenty-first century. Families frequently placed members in different locales to maximize their prospects for security and economic success. These transnational families were linked, in turn, by various kinds of technologies, ranging from handwritten letters to the Internet. For many of them, cutting across lines of ethnicity, geography, class, religious orientation, and gender, the sense of belonging to a global Afghan nation had become a firmly held ideological commitment.

Against the backdrop of hundreds of years of shifting interconnections that Afghans have forged with different parts of the globe, the violent revolution launched in 1978 stands out in that it unleashed an irreversible process of global dispersal and integration. In its wake, despite the persistence among foreigners of the trope of Afghan isolation and total otherness, Afghans were more globalized than ever before and more simultaneously invested in Afghan nationalism and universalism. The primary brakes on Afghan globalism have come, though, from without.

Seen from Europe and the United States, drugs were the most alarming source of danger emanating from the country. In 2014, poppy cultivation spanned over 224,000 hectares, an all-time high. This was despite the fact that the United States had since 2001 spent more than $7 billion to combat opium production in Afghanistan. A vicious cycle had descended on these communities: fighting between insurgents and NATO and U.S. forces had created conditions that made the cultivation of these commodities a necessary survival strategy—one that the foreign powers simultaneously criminalized. Provinces in the south that were the least secure produced the most. But this was hardly a local story, of course. Shifts in demand in places like Berlin, Moscow, or even Nairobi could affect how much Afghan families had to spend at the market in Helmand.

But drugs were not the only threat to haunt the imagination of Western governments. Increasingly since 2001 and, in particular, as the United States sought an exit strategy from the war, the Americans and their partners in Europe and Australia, and even some of their rivals, namely Iran, have adopted aggressive policies to keep Afghans in place. The American dreams of transforming Afghans, of making them more "modern" and less dangerous—only the most recent iteration of revolutionary projects that targeted the Afghan

population from the 1920s to the present—were deflated by the war
and the waning enthusiasm of the American public. As of 2015, it
seemed that all that was left was to attempt to manage the Taliban
insurgents with a smaller contingent of American forces and to throw
up a cordon sanitaire around the country, stemming the movement
of Afghan migrants. To the Americans and others in the West, the
"hermit kingdom" had become too global, its population too mobile and interconnected. Afghans topped the list, next to Syrians
and Iraqis, of asylum-seekers in Europe and the United States. Yet
the American policy was to keep Afghans out. In 2013, for example,
more Albanians than Afghans received U.S. visas. Afghans who had
served as interpreters or worked in intelligence for the military fared
little better than others. In fact, it proved far easier for Afghan dogs,
strays rescued by American soldiers or other foreigners, to gain access to the United States.[11]

Despite these impediments to Afghan mobility, other forms of
connectivity showed few signs of losing their strength or dynamism.
Global flows of money and commodities and trafficking in smuggled
goods and people were poised to persist and perhaps even expand
under more restrictive (and thus profitable) conditions. And in spite
of disillusionment with the post-2001 international project in Afghanistan and the looming sense of betrayal at the hands of the retreating foreigners, distant shores continued to hold the imaginations
of Afghans young and old. Film, television, radio, the Internet, and
print media presented opportunities for engaging in novel ways with
global news and politics. From rap music to new architectural designs and commercial advertising, Afghans managed to draw on multiple cosmopolitan repertoires, making these ideas and aesthetic
styles their own. At the same time, events such as the tragic mob
killing of a woman, Farkhunda, outside a central Kabul mosque in
March 2015 served as catalysts for Afghan mobilization in protests

around the globe in the name of national solidarity and an Afghanistan without such violence.

Afghans of various backgrounds also expressed a deeply held conviction that what lay ahead for Afghanistan would have an immense impact on the world. This notion has persisted as one of the central threads of modern Afghan nationalist ideology. Recognizing it as a core feature of Afghan nationalism, as an artifact of our modern times, is not to dismiss it, however. Indeed, the world would be well advised to listen to this strand of Afghan globalism and to recognize the many ways global processes have made Afghanistan what it is today, a place that occupies a pivotal position in the highly interconnected world we all share.

NOTES

INTRODUCTION

1. James Darmesteter, *Chants populaires des afghans* (Paris: Imprimerie nationale, 1888–1890), CLII. Unless otherwise noted, all translations of non-English texts are my own. In transliterating Persian and other foreign words I have simplified some spellings. Where feasible, I have converted dates to the Gregorian calendar.

2. See, to name just a few, the important studies in the field of anthropology and related disciplines by Pierre Centlivres, *Un bazar d'Asie Centrale: Forme et organisation du bazar de Tashqurghan (Afghanistan)* (Wiesbaden: Dr. Ludwig Reichert Verlag, 1972); M. Nazif Shahrani and Robert L. Canfield, eds., *Revolutions and Rebellions in Afghanistan: Anthropological Perspectives* (Berkeley: Institute of International Studies, University of California, Berkeley, 1984); and Margaret A. Mills, *Rhetorics and Politics in Afghan Traditional Storytelling* (Philadelphia: University of Pennsylvania Press, 1991). An insightful survey and critique of anthropological thinking about Afghanistan may be found in Alessandro Monsutti, "Anthropologizing Afghanistan: Colonial and Postcolonial Encounters," *Annual Review of Anthropology* 42 (2013): 269–285. One of the most valuable treatments of Afghanistan in a national context remains Vartan Gregorian, *The Emergence of Modern Afghanistan: Politics of Reform and Modernization, 1880–1946* (Stanford, CA: Stanford University Press, 1969).

3. See Lutz Rzehak, "Ethnic Minorities in Search of Political Consolidation," in *Under the Drones: Modern Lives in the Afghanistan-Pakistan Borderlands*, ed. Shahzad Bashir and Robert D. Crews (Cambridge, MA: Harvard University Press, 2012), 136–152; Magnus Marsden, "Being a Diplomat on the Frontier of South and Central Asia: Trade and Traders in Afghanistan," in

Beyond Swat: History, Society, and Economy along the Afghanistan-Pakistan Frontier, ed. Benjamin D. Hopkins and Magnus Marsden (New York: Columbia University Press, 2013), 93–103; and Hopkins and Marsden, *Fragments of the Afghan Frontier* (London: Hurst and Co., 2011).

4. Trevor R. Getz, *Cosmopolitan Africa, c. 1700–1875* (Oxford: Oxford University Press, 2013), xv; Charles Piot, *Remotely Global: Village Modernity in West Africa* (Chicago: University of Chicago Press, 1999); and Akhil Gupta and James Ferguson, eds., *Culture, Power, Place: Explorations in Critical Anthropology* (Durham, NC: Duke University Press, 1997). For a different anthropological approach that focuses on the problem of Afghan political legitimacy, with ethnic and tribal groups at the center of these contests for power, see Thomas Barfield, *Afghanistan: A Cultural and Political History* (Princeton, NJ: Princeton University Press, 2010). Important new interpretations and promising directions for future study have recently been mapped out in "The Future of Afghan History," special issue of *International Journal of Middle East Studies* 45, no. 1 (2013), in contributions by Nile Green, "Introduction" and "Locating Afghan History," 127–128 and 132–134; Amin Tarzi, "The Maturation of Afghan Historiography," 129–131; R. D. McChesney, "On Mobility in Afghan History," 135–137; James Caron, "Elite Pasts and Subaltern Potentialities," 138–141; Christine Noelle-Karimi, "Maps and Spaces," 142–145; Robert Nichols, "Afghan Histories beyond the State, War, and Tribe," 146–148; Shah Mahmoud Hanifi, *Connecting Histories in Afghanistan: Market Relations and State Formation on a Colonial Frontier* (Stanford, CA: Stanford University Press, 2011); Hopkins and Marsden, *Fragments of the Afghan Frontier*; and Nile Green and Nushin Arbabzadah, *Afghanistan in Ink: Literature Between Diaspora and Nation* (New York: Columbia University Press, 2013).

1. IMPERIAL COSMOPOLITANS

1. Bernhard Dorn, trans., *History of the Afghans: Translated from the Persian of Neamat Ullah,* part 1 (London: J. Murray, 1829; repr., Cambridge: Cambridge University Press, 2013), 5–25, here, 25.

2. Ibid., 38–42. On the Ghaznavids, see Clifford Edmund Bosworth, *The Ghaznavids: Their Empire in Afghanistan and Eastern Iran, 994–1040* (Edinburgh: Edinburgh University Press, 1963); and Bosworth, *The Later*

Ghaznavids: Splendour and Decay; The Dynasty in Afghanistan and Northern India, 1040–1186 (New York: Columbia University Press, 1977).

3. C. E. Bosworth, "Kandahar" and "Kabul," in *Encyclopaedia of Islam,* 2nd ed., ed. P. Bearman et al., Brill Online, 2014. The saying was "Turk wa Kabul." See also "Bada<u>khsh</u>ān," in *Encyclopaedia of Islam;* Arezou Azad, *Sacred Landscape in Medieval Afghanistan: Revisiting the* Faḍā'il-i Balkh (Oxford: Oxford University Press, 2013); and Christine Noelle-Karimi, *The Pearl in Its Midst: Herat and the Mapping of Khurasan (15th–19th Centuries)* (Vienna: Verlag der Österreichischen Akademie der Wissenschaften, 2014).

4. I. N. Allen, *Diary of a March through Sinde and Affghanistan* (London: J. Hatchard and Son, 1843), 3; and Waldo Drake, "Afghanistan Past Story of Conquest," *Los Angeles Times,* October 23, 1947, p. 6. These images were a feature of earlier British works such as Percy Sykes, *A History of Afghanistan,* 2 vols. (London: Macmillan, 1940). Many in the U.S. military as well in policy and journalistic circles internalized them after 2001. See, for example, Daniel P. Bolger, *Why We Lost: A General's Inside Account of the Iraq and Afghanistan Wars* (Boston: Houghton Mifflin Harcourt, 2014), xiii, xxix, 51, 73, 95, and elsewhere.

5. See Jos J. L. Gommans, *The Rise of the Indo-Afghan Empire, c. 1710–1780* (Delhi: Oxford University Press, 1999), on this text, 160–163; Nile Green, "Tribe, Diaspora, and Sainthood," *Journal of Asian Studies* 67, no. 1 (February 2008): 171–211.

6. See Jane Burbank and Frederick Cooper, *Empires in World History: Power and the Politics of Difference* (Princeton, NJ: Princeton University Press, 2010).

7. Dorn, trans., *History of the Afghans,* v–vi. The British Orientalist scholar William Jones thought Pashto resembled Chaldaic, thus showing a link between Afghans and Jews. See ibid., viii.

8. H. W. Bellew, *An Inquiry into the Ethnography of Afghanistan* (1891; repr., Graz: Akademische Druck-u. Verlagsanstalt, 1973), iii–iv and 5.

9. D. W. MacDowall and M. Taddei, "The Early Historic Period: Achaemenids and Greeks," in *The Archaeology of Afghanistan from Earliest Times to the Timurid Period,* ed. F. R. Allchin and Norman Hammond (London: Academic Press, 1978), 187–232; on lapis lazuli, see Lionel Casson, trans., *The Periplus Maris Erythraei: Text with Introduction, Translation and Commentary*

(Princeton, NJ: Princeton University Press, 2012), 16–17 and 194; Morris Rossabi, "A Translation of Ch'en Ch'eng's *Hsi-yü fan-kuo chih*," *Ming Studies* 17 (1983): 49–59, here, 54. See also Ralph Kauz, *Politik und Handel zwischen Ming und Timuriden: China, Iran und Zentralasien im Spätmittelalter* (Wiesbaden: Reichert Verlag, 2005), 106–108; Joseph F. Fletcher, "China and Central Asia, 1368–1884," in *The Chinese World Order*, ed. J. K. Fairbank (Cambridge, MA: Harvard University Press, 1968), 208; and *The Baburnama: Memoirs of Babur, Prince and Emperor*, trans. and ed. Wheeler M. Thackston (New York: Modern Library, 2002), 153.

10. Richard C. Foltz, *Mughal India and Central Asia* (Oxford: Oxford University Press, 1998), 6–7.

11. Sayyidī 'Alī Ra'īs, *Mir'āt al-mamālik: Safar'nāmah'ī bih Khalīj-i Fārs, Hind, Mā Varā' al-nahr va Īrān*, trans. Maḥmūd Tafazzulī and 'Alī Ganjih'lī (Tehran: Bunyād-i Farhang-i Īrān, 2535 [1976 or 1977]), 123–124; H. C. Verma, *Medieval Routes to India: Baghdad to Delhi: A Study of Trade and Military Routes* (Calcutta: Naya Prokash, 1978), 30–34; and C. Wessels, *Early Jesuit Travellers in Central Asia, 1603–1721* (The Hague: Martinus Nijhoff, 1924), 1–41.

12. Scott C. Levi, *Caravans: Indian Merchants on the Silk Road* (New York: Penguin, 2015); Levi, "Objects in Motion," in *A Companion to World History*, ed. Douglas Northrop (Hoboken, NJ: Wiley-Blackwell, 2012), 321–338; Levi, *The Indian Diaspora in Central Asia and Its Trade, 1550–1900* (Leiden: Brill, 2002); R. D. McChesney, *Central Asia: Foundations of Change* (Princeton, NJ: Darwin Press, 1997), 41–44; see also Niels Steensgaard, "The Route through Quandahar: The Significance of the Overland Trade from India to the West in the Seventeenth Century," in *Merchants, Companies and Trade: Europe and Asia in the Early Modern Era*, ed. Sushil Chaudhury and Michel Morineau (Cambridge: Cambridge University Press, 1999), 55–73; Muzaffar Alam and Sanjay Subrahmanyam, *Indo-Persian Travels in the Age of Discoveries, 1400–1800* (Cambridge: Cambridge University Press, 2007); Stephen Frederic Dale, "Indo-Russian Trade in the Eighteenth Century," in *South Asia and World Capitalism*, ed. Sugata Bose (Delhi: Oxford University Press, 1990); and John F. Richards, *The Mughal Empire* (Cambridge: Cambridge University Press, 1993), 50.

13. K. A. Antonova, N. M. Gol'dberg, and T. D. Lavrentsova, eds., *Russkoindiiskie otnosheniia v XVII v.: Sbornik dokumentov* (Moscow: Izdatel'stvo

vostochnoi literatury, 1958), 19, 92, 169, 219; B. A. Akhmedov, *Istoriia Balkha (XVI–pervaia polovina XVIII v.)* (Tashkent: Izdatel'stvo "FAN" Uzbekskoi SSR, 1982), 206–217; and Daniel R. Headrick, *The Tentacles of Progress: Technology Transfer in the Age of Imperialism, 1850–1940* (Oxford: Oxford University Press, 1988), 20.

14. A. Sh. Shamansurova, "Novye dannye po istorii Afganistana," in *Ocherki po novoi istorii Afganistana*, ed. M. G. Pikulin (Tashkent: Izdatel'stvo "FAN" Uzbekskoi SSR, 1966), 105–116; N. Khanykov, *Opisanie Bukharskogo khanstva* (St. Petersburg: V tipografii Imperatorskoi Akademii Nauk, 1843); Calvin H. Allen, Jr., "The Indian Merchant Community of Masqat," *Bulletin of the School of Oriental and African Studies, University of London* 44, no. 1 (1981): 39–53; and J. R. Wellsted, *Travels in Arabia*, vol. 1 (London: John Murray, 1838), 15; Joseph Barlow Felt Osgood, *Notes of Travel; or, Recollections of Majunga, Zanzibar, Muscat, Aden, Mocha, and Other Eastern Ports* (Salem, MA: George Creamer, 1854), 94; and Muhammad Hayat Khan, *Afghanistan and Its Inhabitants: Translated from the "Hayat-i-Afghan,"* trans. Henry Priestley (Lahore, 1874; repr., Lahore: Sange-e-Meel Publications, 1981), 18.

15. Fletcher, "China and Central Asia," 206–224. See also Kauz, *Politik und Handel*, 47–50 and 185–186; and Iu. V. Gankovskii, ed., *Rossiia i Afganistan* (Moscow: Glavnaia redaktsiia vostochnoi literatury, 1989), 12–23.

16. Halim Baki Kunter, "Tarsus'taki Türkistan Yavizelerinin Vakfiyeleri," *Vakıflar Dergisi* 6 (1965): 31–50.

17. Muḥammad Riẓā Barnābādī, *Tazkire ("Pamiatnnye zapiski")*, ed. N. N. Tumanovich (Moscow: Izdatel'stvo "Nauka," Glavnaia redaktsiia vostochnoi literatury, 1984), 16, 25, 64–65, 202–203; and ʻAlī Karīmiyān, ed., *Asnād-i mawqūfāt-i Āstān-i Quds-i Raẓavī dar Harāt, 1181–1360 Q.* (Tehran: Intishārāt-i Sāzmān-i Asnād-i Millī-i Īrān, 2000).

18. R. D. McChesney, *Waqf in Central Asia: Four Hundred Years in the History of a Muslim Shrine, 1480–1889* (Princeton, NJ: Princeton University Press, 1991), especially 26–36; Lutz Rzehak, "Narrative Strukturen des Erzählens über Heilige und ihre Gräber in Afghanistan," *Asiatische Studien* 58, no. 1 (2004): 195–229; Richard Tapper, "Peasant's Pilgrimage: A Ballad from Afghan Turkistan," *Asian Music* 18, no. 1 (Autumn–Winter, 1986): 20–34; and

Muḥammad ʿAzīz Bakhtiyārī, *Shīʿiyān-i Afghānistān* (Qum: Shīʿahʾshināsī, 1385 [2006]), 380–381.

19. Robert D. McChesney, "ʿBarrier of Heterodoxy'? Rethinking the Ties between Iran and Central Asia in the Seventeenth Century," in *Safavid Persia: The History and Politics of an Islamic Society,* ed. Charles Melville (London: I. B. Tauris, 1996), 231–267, here, 236. See, too, the list of manuscripts surveyed in repositories in Herat and Kabul in Serge de Beaurecueil, *Manuscrits d'Afghanistan* (Cairo: Imprimerie de l'Institut français d'archéologie orientale, 1964).

20. Jo-Ann Gross, "Naqshbandi Appeals to the Herat Court: A Preliminary Study of Trade and Property Issues," in *India and Central Asia*, ed. Xinru Liu (Ranikhet: Permanent Black, 2012), 326–342; Gross, "The Naqshbandiya Connection: From Central Asia to India and Back (16th–19th Centuries)," and Stephen F. Dale and Alam Payind, "The Ahrari *Waqf* in Kabul in the Year 1546 and the Mughul Naqshbandiyyah," in *India and Central Asia: Commerce and Culture, 1500–1800,* ed. Scott C. Levi (New Delhi: Oxford University Press, 2007), 232–259 and 200–231; Anke von Kügelgen, "Die Entfaltung der Naqšbandīya Muǧaddidīya im mittleren Transoxien vom 18. bis zum Beginn des 19. Jahrhunderts: Ein Stück Detektivarbeit," in *Muslim Culture in Russia and Central Asia,* ed. Anke von Kügelgen, Michael Kemper, and Allen Frank, vol. 2 (Berlin: Klaus Schwarz Verlag, 1998), 101–151; and Jürgen Paul, ed., *Katalog sufiiskikh proizvedenii XVIII–XX vv. iz sobranii Instituta Vostokovedeniia im. Abu Raikhana al-Biruni Akademii Nauk Respubliki Uzbekistan* (Stuttgart: Franz Steiner Verlag, 2002), 134–138 and 153–158.

21. Joseph F. Fletcher, "Central Asian Sufism and Ma Ming-hsin's New Teaching," in *Proceedings of the Fourth East Asian Altaistic Conference,* ed. Ch'en Chieh-hsien (Taipei: National Taiwan University), 75–96, here, 87; and Almut Wieland-Karimi, *Islamische Mystik in Afghanistan: Die strukturelle Einbindung der Sufik in die Gesellschaft* (Stuttgart: Franz Steiner Verlag, 1998), 21–32. Afghans also had ties to Meccan scholars and a few may have established themselves as teachers. See Joseph Fletcher, "The Naqshbandiyya in Northwest China," in *Studies on Chinese and Islamic Inner Asia,* ed. Beatrice Forbes Manz (Burlington, VT: Ashgate, 1995), 25; M. A. Usmanov, "Knigi-ʿputeshestvennitsy,ʾ" in *Dagestan i musul'manskii Vostok: sbornik statei,*

ed. A. K. Alikberov and V. O. Bobrovnikov (Moscow: Izdatel'skii dom Mardzhani, 2010), 273–279.

22. V. V. Kushev, *Afganskaia rukopisnaia kniga (ocherki afganskoi pis'mennoi kul'tury)* (Moscow: Izdatel'stvo "Nauka," Glavnaia redaktsiia vostochnoi literatury, 1980), 119.

23. Malik Shah Khusain Sistani, *Khronika voskresheniia tsarei (ta'rikh-i ikhia al-muluk)*, trans. and ed. L. P. Smirnova (Moscow: Izdatel'skaia firma "Vostochnaia literatura" RAN, 2000), 351–352.

24. B. V. Norik, *Biobibliograficheskii slovar' sredneaziatskoi poezii (XVI–pervaia tret' XVII v.)* (Moscow: Izdatel'skii dom Mardzhani, 2011), 720–729; V. V. Kushev, "Kandagarskii poet v Bukhare," in *Blizhnii i Srednii Vostok (Istoriia, kul'tura, istochnikovedenie)*, ed. Iu. A. Petrosian and V. A. Romodin (Moscow: Izdatel'stvo "Nauka," Glavnaia redaktsiia vostochnoi literatury, 1968), 67–72. On Sufism, Shahzad Bashir, *Sufi Bodies: Religion and Society in Medieval Islam* (New York: Columbia University Press, 2011).

25. Talaqani achieved fame among Shia intellecutals who were expert in the discipline of *'irfān*, or gnosis, and became a counselor to Nadir Shah Afshar. 'Abd al-Majīd Nāṣirī Dāvūdī, *Mashāhīr-i Tashayyu' dar Afghānistān* (Qum: Mu'assasah-i Āmūzishī va Pizhūhishī-i Imām Khumaynī, 1379– [2000–]), vol. 3, 133–134. This Talaqan is not to be confused with the place of the same name in the northeast of Afghanistan today.

26. Munis D. Faruqui, *The Princes of the Mughal Empire, 1504–1719* (Cambridge: Cambridge University Press, 2012), 49; see also Richards, *The Mughal Empire.*

27. Faruqui, *The Princes of the Mughal Empire,* 85, 150, 153–154, 171, 174, 225.

28. Muzaffar Alam and Sanjay Subrahmanyam, *Writing the Mughal World: Studies on Culture and Politics* (New York: Columbia University Press, 2012), 356–357, 368, 374, and 393–394; and Sinnappah Arasaratnam, *Merchants, Companies and Commerce on the Coromandel Coast, 1650–1740* (Delhi: Oxford University Press, 1986), 169–171.

29. Faruqui, *The Princes of the Mughal Empire,* 214–215, 229. See also Rita Joshi, *The Afghan Nobility and the Mughals (1526–1707)* (New Delhi: Vikas, 1985).

30. *The Baburnama*, 152–153. See also Stephen F. Dale, *The Muslim Empires of the Ottomans, Safavids, and Mughals* (Cambridge: Cambridge University Press, 2010), 73–74.

31. *The Jahangirnama: Memoirs of Jahangir, Emperor of India*, trans. and ed. Wheeler M. Thackston (New York: Oxford University Press, 1999), 75–77 and 83. See also Foltz, *Mughal India and Central Asia*, 31.

32. Noelle-Karimi, *The Pearl in Its Midst;* and Sheila S. Blair, *A Compendium of Chronicles: Rashid al-Din's Illustrated History of the World* (London: Nour Foundation, 1995).

33. Noelle-Karimi, *The Pearl in Its Midst;* Oleg Grabar, *Mostly Miniatures: An Introduction to Persian Painting* (Princeton, NJ: Princeton University Press, 2000), 21–23, 52–62; Maria Szuppe, *Entre Timourides, Uzbeks et Safavides: Questions d'histoire politique et sociale de Hérat dans la première moitié du XXVIe siècle* (Paris: Association pour l'Avancement des Études Iraniennes, 1992), 69–77; Szuppe, "The Female Intellectual Milieu in Timurid and Post-Timurid Herat: Faxri Heravi's Biography of Poetesses, *Javaher al-'Ajayeb*," *Oriente Moderno* 15, no. 2 (1996): 119–137, here, 132; *The Baburnama*, 215.

34. Antoni de Montserrat, *Embajador en la corte del Gran Mogol: Viajes de un jesuita catalán del siglo XVI por la India, Paquistán, Afganistán y el Himalaya*, ed. Josep Lluís Alay and trans. Ramon Sala (Lleida: Milenio, 2006), 162 and 178; C. Wessels, *Early Jesuit Travellers in Central Asia, 1603–1721* (The Hague: Martinus Nijhoff, 1924), 1–41; and Foltz, *Mughal India and Central Asia*, 30.

35. Levi, *The Indian Diaspora*, 32–35; Foltz, *Mughal India and Central Asia*, 8–9; Malik Shah Khusain Sistani, *Khronika voskresheniia tsarei*, 146 and 381; Richards, *The Mughal Empire*, 132–135; and Akhmedov, *Istoriia Balkha*, 15–16, 188–193.

36. On Kandahar as a bordertown, see Michael H. Fisher, ed., *Visions of Mughal India: An Anthology of European Travel Writing* (London: I. B. Tauris, 2007), 136; Antonova, Gol'dberg, and Lavrentsova, *Russko-indiiskie otnosheniia v XVII v.*, 74–75 and 79–80; and Birgitt Hoffmann, trans. and ed., *Persische Geschichte 1694–1835 erlebt, errinert und erfunden: Das Rustam at-tawarih in deutscher Bearbeitung*, vol. 1 (Bamberg: Aku GmbH, 1986), 253.

37. Abdolqasem Ferdowsi, *Shahnameh: The Persian Book of Kings*, trans. Dick Davis (New York: Penguin Classics, 2007), 71.

38. Joshi, *The Afghan Nobility and the Mughals*, 2; on migrations, 1–20.

39. *The Akbarnāmā of Abu-l-Fazl*, trans. H. Beveridge (Calcutta: The Asiatic Society, 1907), 327–328 and 342.

40. Gankovskii, *Rossiia i Afganistan,* 12–23.

41. Quoted in I. M. Reisner, *Razvitie feodalizma i obrazovanie gosudarstva u Afgantsev* (Moscow: Izdatel'stvo Akademii nauk SSSR, 1954), 308.

42. Christine Noelle-Karimi, "The Abdali Afghans between Multan, Qandahar and Herat in the Sixteenth and Seventeenth Centuries," in *Beyond Swat: History, Society and Economy along the Afghanistan-Pakistan Frontier*, ed. Benjamin D. Hopkins and Magnus Marsden (New York: Columbia University Press, 2013), 31–38; Reisner, *Razvitie feodalizma i obrazovanie gosudarstva u Afgantsev*, 310; Gankovskii, *Rossiia i Afganistan.*

43. Muhammad Hayat Khan, *Afghanistan and Its Inhabitants*, 53; Gommans, *The Rise of the Indo-Afghan Empire,* 160–161; and Green, "Tribe, Diaspora, and Sainthood," 185.

44. See C. A. Bayly, *Imperial Meridian: The British Empire and the World, 1780–1830* (New York: Longman, 1989).

2. FORGING AN AFGHAN EMPIRE

1. Rudi Matthee, *Persia in Crisis: Safavid Decline and the Fall of Isfahan* (London: I. B. Tauris, 2012), 162; I. M. Reisner, *Razvitie feodalizma i obrazovanie gosudarstva u Afgantsev* (Moscow: Izdatel'stvo Akademii nauk SSSR, 1954), 308; S. A. Makarian, "Georgii XI i kandagarskoe vosstanie 1709 g.," *Vostok* 5 (2009): 41–45, here, 43–44.

2. Laurence Lockhart, *The Fall of the Safavi Dynasty and the Afghan Occupation of Persia* (Cambridge: Cambridge University Press, 1958), 86–87; Peter Avery, "Nadir Shah and the Afsharid Legacy," in *The Cambridge History of Iran*, ed. Peter Avery, Gavin Hambly, and Charles Melville, vol. 7 (Cambridge: Cambridge University Press, 1991), 11–14.

3. Willem Floor, ed. and trans., *The Afghan Occupation of Safavid Persia, 1721–1729* (Paris: Association pour l'Avancement des Études Iraniennes, 1998), 51.

4. Ibid., 46, 49, 51, 119–120, 139; Lockhart, *The Fall of the Safavi Dynasty,* 130; and *The Chronicle of Petros di Sarkis Gilanetz,* trans. Caro Owen Minasian (Lisbon: Imprensa nacional, 1959), 40–41.

5. Floor, *The Afghan Occupation,* 86, 90, 154, 157, 173–176; and Sebouh David Aslanian, *From the Indian Ocean to the Mediterranean: The Global Trade Networks of Armenian Merchants from New Julfa* (Berkeley: University of California Press, 2011), 203–204.

6. Jürgen Osterhammel, *Die Entzauberung Asiens: Europa und die asiatischen Reiche im 18. Jahrhundert* (Munich: C. H. Beck, 1998), 104; Orlin Sabev, "The First Ottoman Turkish Printing Enterprise: Success or Failure?," in *Ottoman Tulips, Ottoman Coffee: Leisure and Lifestyle in the Eighteenth Century,* ed. Dana Sajdi (London: I. B. Tauris, 2007), 63–89.

7. Judas Thaddaeus Krusínski, *The History of the Revolution of Persia,* vol. 1 (London: Printed [by S. Aris] for J. Pemberton, 1728), 137; John Barrow, *A New Geographical Dictionary* (London: Printed for J. Coote, at the King's Arms in Pater-Noster-Row, 1760); and George Newnham Mitford, ed. and trans., *The Chronicles of a Traveller; or, A History of the Afghan Wars with Persia* (London: James Ridgway, 1840).

8. Krusínski, *History of the Revolution of Persia,* 138–149.

9. Robert W. Olson, *The Siege of Mosul and Ottoman-Perisan Relations 1718–1743: A Study of Rebellion in the Capital and War in the Provinces of the Ottoman Empire* (Bloomington, IN: Indiana University Publications, 1975), 46–49, quote at 48.

10. Reisner, *Razvitie feodalizma i obrazovanie gosudarstva u Afgantsev,* 315.

11. Details in V. M. Masson and V. A. Romodin, *Istoriia Afganistana,* vol. 2 (Moscow: Izdatel'stvo "Nauka" Glavnaia redaktsiia vostochnoi literatury, 1965), 100 and 95–102; and J. L. Lee, *The 'Ancient Supremacy': Bukhara, Afghanistan and the Battle for Balkh, 1731–1901* (Leiden: E. J. Brill, 2006).

12. For an important critique of nationalist scholarship, see Shah Mahmoud Hanifi, "Quandaries of the Afghan Nation," in *Under the Drones: Modern Lives in the Afghanistan-Pakistan Borderlands,* ed. Shahzad Bashir and Robert D. Crews (Cambridge, MA: Harvard University Press, 2012), 83–101.

13. John R. Perry, *Karim Khan Zand: A History of Iran, 1747–1779* (Chicago: University of Chicago Press, 1979), chap. 3 and elsewhere; and Jos J. L. Gommans, "Indian Warfare and Afghan Innovation during the Eighteenth Century," in *Warfare and Weaponry in South Asia, 1000–1800*, ed. Jos J. L. Gommans and Dirk H. A. Kolff (Oxford: Oxford University Press, 2001), 369.

14. Gommans, "Indian Warfare and Afghan Innovation," 365–386.

15. Ibid., 371.

16. Iu. V. Gankovskii, "Nezavisimoe afganskoe gosudartvo Akhmad-Shakha Durrani i ego preemnikov (1747–1819)," in *Nezavisimyi Afganistan: sbornik statei*, ed. R. T. Akhramovich (Moscow: Izdatel'stvo vostochnoi literatury, 1958), 52–57.

17. D. Saidmuradov, "Vvedenie," in Makhmud al-Khusaini al-Munshi ibn Ibrakhim al-Dzhami, *Ta'rikh-i Akhmad-Shakhi ("Akhmadshakhova istoriia")*, ed. D. Saidmuradov, vol. 1 (Moscow: Glavnaia redaktsiia vostochnoi literatury izdatel'stva "Nauka," 1974), 21–28; Maḥmūd ibn Ibrāhīm al-Ḥusaynī, ed., *Tārīkh-i Ahmad Shāhī: Tārīkh-i tashkīl-i avvalīn ḥukūmat-i Afghānistān* (Tehran: Mu'assasah-i Intishārāt va Chāp-i Dānishgāh-'i Tihrān, 1384 [2005]), 50–51.

18. M. Longworth Dames, "The Coins of the Durranis," *The Numismatic Chronicle and Journal of the Numismatic Society* 8, 3rd ser. (1888): 325–363. Compare Figure 2 with the oil painting of Nadir Shah at the Victoria and Albert Museum, http://collections.vam.ac.uk/item/O81782/portrait-of-nadir-shah -painting-muhammad-riza-hindi/.

19. Pirouz Mojtahed-Zadeh, *Small Players of the Great Game: The Settlement of Iran's Eastern Borderlands and the Creation of Afghanistan* (London: Routledge-Curzon, 2004), 124.

20. "Farmān-i Aḥmad Shāh Durrānī," Digital Persian Archive Asnad.org, http://www.asnad.org/fa/document/195/.

21. Ayesha Jalal, *Partisans of Allah: Jihad in South Asia* (Cambridge, MA: Harvard University Press, 2008), 53–57.

22. Joseph F. Fletcher, "China and Central Asia, 1368–1884," in *The Chinese World Order*, ed. J. K. Fairbank (Cambridge, MA: Harvard University Press, 1968), 220. See also Matthew M. Mosca, *From Frontier Policy to Foreign Policy:*

The Question of India and the Transformation of Geopolitics in Qing China (Stanford, CA: Stanford University Press, 2013).

23. Ghulām Jīlānī Jalālī, ed., *Nāmah-'i Ahmad Shāh Bābā bih' nām-i Sulṭān Muṣṭafā' ṣāliṣ-i 'Uṣmānī kih as rū-yi nuskhah-'i vāḥid-i khaṭṭi ārshīf-i salṭanatī-yi Istanbūl tartīb shudah ast* (Kabul: Anjuman-i Tārīkh-i Afghānistān, 1346 [1967]), for example, 68–81.

24. Hamid Algar, "*Ṭarīqat* and *Ṭarīq*: Central Asian Naqshbandîs on the Roads to the Haramayn," in *Central Asian Pilgrims: Hajj Routes and Pious Visits between Central Asia and the Hijaz,* ed. Alexandre Papas, Thomas Welsford, and Thierry Zarcone (Berlin: Klaus Schwarz Verlag, 2012), 59; Ömer Koçyğit, "Üsküdar Afganîler Tekkesi ve Haziresindeki Mezartaşları," *Uluslararası Üsküdar Sempozyumu VI: 6–9 Kasım 2008,* vol. 2 (Üsküdar, İstanbul: Üsküdar Belediyesi, 2008), 665–688.

25. On non-Muslim traders, see B. D. Hopkins, *The Making of Modern Afghanistan* (New York: Palgrave Macmillan, 2008), especially 117–118.

26. Lewin B. Bowring, *Haidar Ali and Tipu Sultan and the Struggle with the Musalman Powers of the South* (Oxford: Clarendon, 1899), 175; Bowring refers to Afghans as an "eminently treacherous race" (77).

27. Masson and Romodin, *Istoriia Afganistana,* 139–145.

28. Ibid., 145.

29. C. U. Aitchison, ed., *A Collection of Treaties, Engagements and Sanads Relating to India and Neighbouring Countries,* vol. 13 (Calcutta: Government of India Central Publication Branch, 1933), 233–234. See also Hopkins, *The Making of Modern Afghanistan.*

30. Jean-Marie Lafont, *La présence française dans le royaume sikh du Penjab, 1822–1849* (Paris: École française d'Extrême-Orient, 1992), 117–123. See, too, Stefano Malatesta, *Il napoletano che domò gli afghani* (Vicenza: Neri Pozza Editore, 2002).

31. R. D. McChesney, trans. and ed., *The History of Afghanistan: Fayz Muhammad Katib Hazarah's Siraj al-tawarikh* (Leiden: Brill, 2013), 1:145 [hereafter Fayz Muhammad, *History of Afghanistan*]; Shir Muhammad Mirab Munis and Muhammad Riza Mirab Agahi, *Firdaws al-Iqbāl,* trans. and ed. Yuri Bregel (Leiden: Brill, 1999), 536; Sakartvelos sakhelmtsipo saistorio akhivi [Cen-

tral State Historical Archive of the Republic of Georgia], f. 11, op. 1, d. 438 and 731; "Poslantsy iz Avganistana v Rossiiu v 1833–1836 gg.," *Russkaia starina* (August 1880): 784–791; M. G. Pikulin, ed., *Ocherki po novoi istorii Afganistana* (Tashkent: Izdatel'stvo "FAN" Uzbekskoi SSR, 1966).

32. Muḥammad ʿAlī Bahmanī Qājār, ed., *Īrān va Afghānistān, az Yagānagī tā Taʿyīn-i Marz'hā-yi Siyāsī* (Tehran: Markaz-i Chāp va Intishārāt-i Vizārat-i Umūr-i Khārijah, 1386/2006), 226–227.

33. Aitchison, *A Collection of Treaties*, 236. For more on this conflict, but with a different focus and interpretation, see William Dalrymple, *Return of a King: The Battle for Afghanistan, 1839–1842* (New York: Knopf, 2013); and Ben Macintyre, *The Man Who Would Be King: The First American in Afghanistan* (New York: Farrar, Straus and Giroux, 2004).

34. India Office Records, British Library, London [hereafter IOR], F/4/1915/820-015, Translation of letter from "the Principal Sultana of Kamran Shah," attached to letter from J. Rawlinson, February 27, 1841.

35. Fayz Muhammad, *History of Afghanistan*, 1:280.

36. Ibid., 263.

37. Ibid., 276.

38. Conrad Malte-Brun, *Universal Geography; or, A Description of All Parts of the World on a New Plan according to the Great Natural Divisions of the Globe*, vol. 1 (Philadelphia: A. Finley, 1827), 398–399 and 445–450; *Foreign Missionary Chronicle* 3 (1835): 44, 139, 151, and 183.

39. Masson and Romodin, *Istoriia Afganistana*, 221–230.

40. ʿAbd al-Qādir Khān, *Tuḥfat al-ʿUlamā'* ([Kabul]: Maṭbaʿ-i Amīr Shīr ʿAlī Khān, 1292 [1875]); S. E. Grigor'ev, "Nachalo litograficheskogo dela v Afganistane," in *Afganistan: Ekonomika, politika, istoriia* (Moscow: Izdatel'stvo "Nauka" Glavnaia redaktsiia vostochnoi literatury, 1984), 248–259.

41. *Shams al-nahār-i Kābul*, February 3, 1874; Grigor'ev, "Nachalo litograficheskogo dela v Afganistane"; and R. R. Sikoev, "Ocherk istorii afganskoi pressy," in *Stranitsy istorii i istoriografii Indii i Afganistana*, ed. R. B. Rybakov et al. (Moscow: Izdatel'skaia firma "Vostochnaia literatura" RAN, 2000), 341–366.

42. Fayz Muhammad, *History of Afghanistan*, 2:268.

43. Charles Gray Robertson, *Kurum, Kabul and Kandahar* (Edinburgh: David Douglas, 1881), 102. For the wider context with an important focus on commerce, see Shah Mahmoud Hanifi, *Connecting Histories in Afghanistan: Market Relations and State Formation on a Colonial Frontier* (Stanford, CA: Stanford University Press, 2011).

44. V. A. Romodin, *Ocherki po istorii i istorii kul'tury Afganistana seredina XIX—pervaia tret' XX v.* (Moscow: Glavnaia redaktsiia vostochoi literatury izdatel'stva "Nauka," 1983), 143–144.

45. *The Life of Abdur Rahman, Amir of Afghanistan,* ed. Sultan Mahomed Khan (London: John Murray, 1900), 1:230.

3. BODIES IN MOTION

1. Colonial Office, The National Archives, Kew [hereafter, CO] 886/9, Secretary of State J. H. Thomas to Governor-General in Pretoria [enclosure of May 22, 1924]; J. C. Smuts responded that the bill would not be going forward due to dissolution of the House of the Assembly.

2. Ludwig W. Adamec, *Historical Dictionary of Afghanistan,* 3rd ed. (New Delhi: Manas Publications, 2006), 371; and Adamec, *Afghanistan, 1900–1923: A Diplomatic History* (Berkeley: University of California Press, 1967), 110.

3. See David Blackbourn, *The Long Nineteenth Century: A History of Germany, 1780–1918* (Oxford: Oxford University Press, 1998), 259–269; Eugen Weber, *Peasants into Frenchmen: The Modernization of Rural France, 1870–1914* (Stanford, CA: Stanford University Press, 1976); and Christopher Clark, *Iron Kingdom: The Rise and Fall of Prussia, 1600–1947* (Cambridge, MA: Harvard University Press, 2006), xvi.

4. *Navajivan,* May 29, 1921, in *The Collected Works of Mahatma Gandhi,* vol. 20 ([Delhi]: Publications Division, Ministry of Information and Broadcasting, Government of India, 1966), 102–103; and Faisal Devji, *The Terrorist in Search of Humanity: Militant Islam and Global Politics* (New York: Columbia University Press, 2008), 1–23.

5. For population estimates, see Erwin Grötzbach, *Afghanistan: Eine geographische Landeskunde* (Darmstadt: Wissenschaftliche Buchgesellschaft, 1990), 56–57.

6. "Report of the Medical Officer of the Privy Council," *Annals of British Leg-islation,* n.s., ed. Leone Levi, vol. 4 (London: Elder, Smith, 1868), 111–140, here, 135; T. N. Zagorodnikova and P. M. Shastitko, eds., *Russko-indiiskie otnosheniia v 1900–1917 gg.: Sbornik arkhivnykh dokumentov i materialov* (Moscow: Izdatel'skaia firma "Vostochnaia literatura" RAN, 1999), 196; Eileen Kane, "Odessa as a Hajj Hub, 1880s–1910s," in John Randolph and Eugene M. Avrutin, eds., *Russia in Motion: Cultures of Human Mobility since 1850* (Urbana: University of Illinois Press, 2012), 107; and Foreign Office, The National Archives, Kew [hereafter, FO] 416/42, "Affairs of Persia. Further Corre-spondence Part XX, 1909 October–December."

7. Hafez F. Farmayan and Elton L. Daniel, trans. and ed., *A Shi'ite Pilgrimage to Mecca (1885–1886): The Safarnâmeh of Mirzâ Moḥammad Ḥosayn Farâhânî* (Austin: University of Texas Press, 1990), 189. They were exceeded only by the Malayans (29,604), Javanese (39,704), Indians (26,496), and Egyptians (15,547). See FO 406/60, "Eastern Affairs. Further Correspondence Part XXI, 1927 July–December."

8. *Abstract of Sanitary Reports* 6, no. 25 (June 19, 1891): 287; Adar Arnon, "The Quarters of Jerusalem in the Ottoman Period," *Middle Eastern Studies* 28, no. 1 (January 1992): 1–65; and Mordechai Eliav, *Österreich und das Heilige Land: Ausgewählte Konsulatsdokumente aus Jerusalem 1849–1917* (Vienna: Verlag der Österreichischen Akademie der Wissenschaften, 2000), 479; A. G. Ravān Farhādī and Ghulām Sakhī Ghayrat, eds., *Khāṭirāt-i Maḥmūd Ṭarzī* (Kabul: Anstītūt-i Dīplūmāsī-i Vizārat-i Umūr-i Khārijah, 1389 [2010 or 2011]), 188; J. G. Lorimer, *Gazetteer of the Persian Gulf, Oman and Central Arabia* (Calcutta, 1908 and 1915; repr., Oxford: Archive Editions, 1986), 2369.

9. FO 424/224, "Asiatic Turkey and Arabia, Further Correspondence, 1910 July–September," Consul General Lorimer to Government of India, August 20, 1910, pp. 102–103; Grace Martin Smith, "The Özbek Tekkes of Istanbul," *Der Islam* 57, no. 1 (1980): 132; Lale Can, "Connecting People: A Central Asian Sufi Network in Turn-of-the-Century Istanbul," *Modern Asian Studies* 46, special issue 2 (2012): 373–401; FO 424/97, Affairs of Turkey, "Fur-ther Correspondence, Part 48," p. 114, Consul Zohrab to the Marquis of Salisbury, March 22, 1880. For more, see Ş. Tufan Buzpinar, "The Hijaz, Abdulhamid II and Amir Hussein's Secret Dealings with the British, 1877–80," *Middle Eastern Studies* 31, no. 1 (January 1995): 99–123; FO 406/44,

"Eastern Affairs, Further Correspondence, Part 5, 1920 July–December," Note by Captain Nasiruddin Ahmed on the Status of British Subjects in the Hedjaz (October 14, 1920); FO 402/16, "Further correspondence respecting Afghanistan: parts XVI-XVII. Further correspondence respecting Afghanistan and Nepal: part XVIII," Diary no. 49 for the week ending December 2, 1932.

10. Ikbal Ali Shah, *Westward to Mecca: A Journey of Adventure through Afghanistan, Bolshevik Asia, Persia, Iraq & Hijaz to the Cradle of Islam* (London: H. F. & G. Witherby, 1928), 211–215.

11. Mahmud Tarzi, "What Is to Be Done?," trans. Helena Malikyar, in *Modernist Islam, 1840–1940: A Sourcebook,* ed. Charles Kurzman (Oxford: Oxford University Press, 2002), 129. On other Afghan travel narratives, see Nile Green, "The Afghan Afterlife of Phileas Fogg," in *Afghanistan in Ink: Literature between Diaspora and Nation,* ed. Nile Green and Nushin Arbabzadah (New York: Columbia University Press, 2013), 67–90; and Green, "The Trans-Border Traffic of Afghan Modernism and the Indian 'Urdusphere,'" *Comparative Studies in Society and History* 53, no. 3 (2011): 497–508.

12. Heinrich Karl Brugsch, *Reise der K. Preussichen Gesandschaft nach Persien 1860 und 1861,* vol. 1 (Leipzig: J. C. Hinrichs'sche Buchhandlung, 1862), 218; Hamid Algar, "*Tarîqat* and *Tarîq:* Central Asian Naqshbandîs on the Roads to the Haramayn," in *Central Asian Pilgrims: Hajj Routes and Pious Visits between Central Asia and the Hijaz,* ed. Alexandre Papas, Thomas Welsford, and Thierry Zarcone (Berlin: Klaus Schwarz Verlag, 2012), 74. This lodge at Torbat-i Jam remained a hub of transnational Sufi activity at least until the early 1970s. Mīrzā Qahramān Amīn-i Lashkar, *Rūznāmah-'i safar-i Khurāsān: bih hamrāhī-yi Nāṣir al-Dīn Shāh,* ed. Īraj Afshār and Muḥammad Rasūl Daryāgasht (Tehran: Asāṭīr, 1374 [1995]), 196; C. E. Yate, *Khurasan and Sistan* (Edinburgh: William Blackwood and Sons, 1900), 397–399; O. I. Zhigalina, *Kurdskie khanstva Khorasana pri poslednikh Kadzharakh: Konets XIX–nachalo XX veka* (Moscow: "Vostochnaia literatura," RAN, 2002), 36–37.

13. O. N. Seniutkina and I. K. Zagidullin, *Nizhegorodskaia iarmarochania mechet'—tsentr obshcheniia rossiiskikh i zarubezhnikh musul'man (XIX–nachalo XX vv)* (Nizhnii Novgorod: Izd-vo Nizhegorodskogo islamskogo medrese "Makhinur," 2006). At Makar'ev there was both a Sunni and a Shia mosque. A. P.

Mel'nikov, *Ocherki bytovoi istorii Nizhegorodskoi iarmarki (1817–1917)*, 2nd ed. (Nizhnii Novgorod: Izdatel'stvo AO "Nizhegorodskii komp'iuternyi tsentr pol'zovatelei, 1993), 200–203; and Catherine Evtuhov, "Nizhnii Novgorod in the Nineteenth Century: Portrait of a City," in *The Cambridge History of Russia*, vol. 2, *Imperial Russia, 1689–1917,* ed. Dominic Lieven (Cambridge: Cambridge University Press, 2006), 264–283.

14. See, for example, Rossiiskii gosudarstvennyi istoricheskii arkhiv, f. 1396, op. 1, d. 264, ll. 223–226, http://zerrspiegel.orientphil.uni-halle.de/t895.html.

15. On the expansion of the Afghan state toward the north, see J. L. Lee, *The 'Ancient Supremacy': Bukhara, Afghanistan and the Battle for Balkh, 1731–1901* (Leiden: E. J. Brill, 2006).

16. V. I. Masal'skii, ed., *Rossiia: Polnoe geograficheskoe opisanie nashego otechestva,* series ed. V. P. Semenov-Tian-Shanskii, vol. 19 (St. Petersburg: Izdanie A. F. Devriena, 1913), 412–413 and 651; Iu. V. Gankovskii, ed., *Rossiia i Afganistan* (Moscow: Glavnaia redaktsiia vostochnoi literatury, 1989), 59–60, 71–82, 114–120, and 166–167.

17. Ḥāfiz Farmān-Farmāyān, ed., *Safarnāmah-'i Ḥājjī Pīrzādah,* vol. 1 (Tehran: Intishārāt-i Bābak, 1360 [1981]), 119; William Sheowring, ed., *The British Empire Series,* vol. 1, *India* (London: Kegan Paul, Trench, Trübner, 1899), 87–88; and Edward Hamilton Aitken, *Gazetteer of the Province of Sind* (Karachi: "Mercantile" Steam Press, 1907), 156, 168–169.

18. 'Abd al-Nāṣir Zalmay, *Mazārāt-i Parvān* (Kabul: 'Abd al-Nāṣir Zalmī, 1389 [2010]), 30–33. See also Amin Tarzi, "Political Struggles over the Afghanistan-Pakistan Borderlands," in *Under the Drones: Modern Lives in the Afghanistan-Pakistan Borderlands,* ed. Shahzad Bashir and Robert D. Crews (Cambridge, MA: Harvard University Press, 2012), 17–29.

19. Rolf Bindemann, *Religion und Politik bei den schi'itischen Hazara in Afghanistan, Iran und Pakistan,* Ethnizität und Gesellschaft Occasional Papers no. 7 (Berlin: Das Arabische Buch, 1987), 31; Charles Townshend, *Desert Hell: The British Invasion of Mesopotamia* (Cambridge, MA: Harvard University Press, 2011), 71; Sarah Jones, "The Hazaras and the British in the Nineteenth Century," *Afghanistan Journal* 5, no. 1 (1978): 3–5; and Muḥammad 'Alī Bahmanī Qājār, ed., *Īrān va Afghānistān, az Yagānagī tā Ta'yīn-i Marz'hā-yi*

Siyāsī (Tehran: Markaz-i Chāp va Intishārāt-i Vizārat-i Umūr-i Khārijah, 1386/2006).

20. Shah Mahmoud Hanifi, *Connecting Histories in Afghanistan: Market Relations and State Formation on a Colonial Frontier* (Stanford, CA: Stanford University Press, 2011); and Hasan Kawun Kakar, *Government and Society in Afghanistan: The Reign of Amir 'Abd al-Rahman Khan* (Austin: University of Texas Press, 1979), 123–131.

21. C. M. Enriquez, *The Pathan Borderland*, 2nd ed. (Calcutta: Thacker, Spink, 1921), 53. See also Scott C. Levi, *Caravans: Indian Merchants on the Silk Road* (New York: Penguin, 2015).

22. John Ferguson, *Mohammedanism in Ceylon: Moormen, Malay, Afghan and Bengali Mohammedans* (Colombo: Observer Printing Works, 1897), 7; *The Punjab Record, or Reference Book for Civil Officers,* vol. 19 (Lahore: W. Ball, 1884), 48–49; Raymond Chickrie, "The Afghan Muslims of Guyana and Suriname," *Journal of Muslim Minority Affairs* 22, no. 2 (2002): 381–399; and Goolam H. Vahed, "Mosques, Mawlanas and Muharram: Indian Islam in Colonial Natal, 1860–1910," *Journal of Religion in Africa* 31, no. 3 (August 2001): 305–335.

23. "Savage and Semi-Barbarous Chiefs and Rulers," available at http://library .duke.edu/digitalcollections/eaa_D0152/#info; "American Women Attacked by Fanatical Afghans," *Los Angeles Herald,* March 11, 1910. Two American women were supposedly injured by gunfire from Afghans near a mosque in Jerusalem.

24. "Hindu Women Next to Swarm California," *San Francisco Call,* May 15, 1910.

25. "Immigration File for Golab Deen," South Asian American Digital Archive, http://www.saadigitalarchive.org/item/20131031-3239.

26. CO 886/9, Secretary of State J. H. Thomas to Governor-General in Pretoria [enclosure of May 22, 1924]; IOR/L/P&S/11/277–2091, "Afghanistan: Prohibition against Afghan subjects visiting Nepal, Australia, and South Africa, February 1927."

27. R. C. Banerjee's letter and Gandhi's reply in *Young India,* November 3, 1921 in *The Collected Works of Mahatma Gandhi,* vol. 21 ([Delhi]: Publications Division, Ministry of Information and Broadcasting, Government of

India, 1966), 394–395; and Gandhi in *Young India,* May 18, 1921, in *Collected Works,* vol. 20, 109.

28. Rabindranath Tagore, *Stories from Tagore* (New York: Macmillan, 1918), 3–17. I thank Parna Sengupta for drawing my attention to this text.

29. There was an Afghan Consulate General at the Headquarters of the Government of India; there were also consulates at Calcutta, Karachi, and Bombay and Afghan Trade Agents at Peshawar, Quetta, and Parchinar. See C. U. Aitchison, ed., *A Collection of Treaties, Engagements and Sanads Relating to India and Neighbouring Countries,* vol. 13 (Calcutta: Government of India Central Publication Branch, 1933), 225–226; and National Archives of India, Foreign and Political Department, File No. 986-F 1932.

30. National Archives of India, Foreign and Political Department, File No. 176-F.

31. Abdul Ghofur, Officiating Consul General for Afghanistan, to Mount Stewart, dated Simla, July 12, 1930, National Archives of India, Foreign and Political Department, File No. 436-F.

32. National Archives of India, External Affairs, File No. 366-F (1939).

33. *The Life of Abdur Rahman, Amir of Afghanistan,* ed. Sultan Mahomed Khan (London: John Murray, 1900), 2:14–19 and 70–71; Masʿūd Pūhanyār, *Ẕuhūr-i Mashrūṭīyat va Qurbāniyān-i Istibdād dar Afghānistān* (Peshawar: Sabā Kitābkhānah, 1376 [1997]), 100; Sana Haroon, "Religious Revivalism across the Durand Line," in Bashir and Crews, *Under the Drones,* 45–59; and Zagorodnikova and Shastitko, *Russko-indiiskie otnosheniia,* 343–355.

34. A. C. Jewett, *An American Engineer in Afghanistan,* ed. Marjorie Jewett Bell (Minneapolis: University of Minnesota Press, 1948), 229–231 and 253–255.

35. Ibid., 317–319.

36. His name also appears as Sayyid Hasan al-Jilani, and he was known as the Naqib Sahib of Chaharbagh and Pir Naqib of Baghdad. See Helena Malikyar and Amin Tarzi, "The Jilani Family in Afghanistan," *Journal of the History of Sufism* 1–2 (2000): 93–102; Adamec, *Historical Dictionary of Afghanistan,* 126–127; Almut Wieland-Karimi, *Islamische Mystik in Afghanistan: Die strukturelle Einbindung der Sufik in die Gesellschaft* (Stuttgart: Franz Steiner Verlag, 1998), 24.

37. Augustus Le Messurier, *Kandahar in 1879* (London: W. H. Allen, 1880), 78; N. M. Gurevich, *Vneshniaia torgovlia Afganistana v noveishee vremia* (Moscow: Glavnaia redaktsiia vostochnoi literatury izdatel'stva "Nauka," 1981), 7; Abdul Ghani, *A Review of the Political Situation in Central Asia* (Lahore: Aziz Publishers, 1980), 69; Jewett, *An American Engineer in Afghanistan,* 4, 48, 71–72, 170.

38. See Robert D. Crews, "Trafficking in Evil? The Global Arms Trade and the Politics of Disorder," in *Global Muslims in the Age of Steam and Print, 1850–1930,* ed. James Gelvin and Nile Green (Berkeley: University of California Press, 2014), 121–142.

39. Gurevich, *Vneshniaia torgovlia Afganistana,* 68.

40. Ibid., 70–71.

41. Ibid., 11.

42. Gurevich, *Vneshniaia torgovlia Afganistana,* 14–15; M. A. Babakhodzhaev, *Russko-afganskie torgovo-ekonomicheskie otnosheniia vo vtoroi polovine XVIII–nachale XX v.* (Tashkent: Izdatel'stvo "Nauka" Uzbekskoi SSR, 1965), 60–66; and Fayz Muhammad, *The History of Afghanistan,* vol. 3, pt. 3, 1285.

43. *The Life of Abdur Rahman,* 1:200–202.

44. S. Shokhumorov, *"Akhkam-i kuzur" kak istochnik po istorii Afganistana nachala XX v.* (Moscow: Izdatel'stvo "Nauka," Glavnaia redaktsiia vostochnoi literatury, 1980), especially 136–137, 141, 147, 152, and 230. See also Saidanvar Shokhumorov, "Princely Archive of Court Decrees: A Rare Insight into the History of Afghanistan (End 19th–Beg. 20th C.)," in *Écrit et culture en Asie centrale et dans le monde turco-iranien, Xe–XIXe siècles/Writing and Culture in Central Asia and the Turko-Iranian World, 10th–19th Centuries,* ed. Francis Richard and Maria Szuppe (Paris: Association pour l'Avencement des Études iraniennes, 2009), 111–126.

45. Rossiiskii gosudarstvennyi voenno-isoricheskii arkhiv [RGVIA], f. 400, op. 1, d. 3873, "Svodka svedeniia o sopredeliannykh stranakh, dobytykh razvedkoi," January 1–February 1, 1910, ll. 13–13 ob., and July 1–October 1, 1910, ll. 152–159.

46. "Svodka svedeniia o sopredeliannykh stranakh, dobytykh razvedkoi," July 1–October 1, 1910, ll. 168 ob.–170.

47. Ibid., ll. 168 ob.–170, 173–174, and 249 and 249 ob. For a similar phenomenon in the 1920s, see Rossiiskii gosudarstvennyi arkhiv sotsial'noi-politicheskoi istorii [hereafter, RGASPI], f. 62, op. 2, d. 71. On the history of opium smuggling in the region, see David Bello, "Opium in Xinjiang and Beyond," in *Opium Regimes: China, Britain, and Japan, 1839–1952*, ed. Timothy Brook and Bob Tadashi Wakabayashi (Berkeley: University of California Press, 2000), 127–151.

48. *The Life of Abdur Rahman*, 294–295.

49. V. A. Romodin, *Ocherki po istorii i istorii kul'tury Afganistana seredina XIX–pervaia tret' XX v.* (Moscow: Glavnaia redaktsiia vostochoi literatury izdatel'stva "Nauka," 1983), 140–150.

50. *Iran Political Diaries*, ed. R. M. Burrell (Oxford: Archive Editions, 1997), 2:132 and 434 [November 17, 1905]; Yate, *Khurasan and Sistan*, 31 and 402–403; and George N. Curzon, *Persia and the Persian Question* (London: Longmans, Green, 1892), 1:173–174.

51. Mir Hashim to Col. Sir Robert Sandeman, June 22, 1885, *Kandahar Newsletters* [hereafter, KN], 2nd ed. (Quetta: Directorate of Archives Department, Government of Baluchistan, 1990), vol. 2 (1884–1885), 192–193.

52. See James Darmesteter, *Chants populaires des afghans* (Paris: Imprimerie nationale, 1888–1890); and Lutz Rzehak, "Remembering the Taliban," in *The Taliban and the Crisis of Afghanistan*, ed. Robert D. Crews and Amin Tarzi (Cambridge, MA: Harvard University Press, 2008), 182–211.

53. See C. A. Bayly, *Empire and Information: Intelligence Gathering and Social Communication in India, 1780–1870* (Cambridge: Cambridge University Press, 1996).

54. IOR/L/P&S/7/58, Peshawar Confidential Diary, August 24, 1889.

55. IOR/L/P&S/7/58, translation of Kabul newsletter, September 28, 1889.

56. IOR/L/P&S/7/58, translation of Kabul newsletter, October 5, 1889.

57. KN, vol. 1.

58. KN, 4:17.

59. IOR/L/P&S/7/58, Peshawar Confidential Diary, October 26, 1889.

60. Khan Bahadur Mirza Muhammad Taki Khan to Quetta, October 24, 1888, KN, 4:18.

61. IOR/L/P&S/7/55, translation of Herat newsletter, October 11, 1888.

62. KN, 4:15.

63. Khan Bahadur Mirza Muhammad Taki Khan to Quetta, October 24, 1888, KN, 4:18.

64. KN, 4:66.

65. Yate, *Khurasan and Sistan*, 3–4. On Afghans in Australia and the camel trade, see Robert Nichols, *A History of Pashtun Migration, 1775–2006* (Oxford: Oxford University Press, 2008), 111; and Christine Stevens, *Tin Mosques and Ghantowns: A History of Afghan Cameldrivers in Australia* (Melbourne: Oxford University Press, 1989).

66. Yate, *Khurasan and Sistan*, 27.

67. See IOR/L/P&S/7/58.

68. Yate, *Khurasan and Sistan*, 10–11. On the longer history of such legends in the region, see C. M. Naim, "'Prophecies' in South Asian Muslim Discourse: The Poems of Shah Ni'matullah Wali," *Economic and Political Weekly* 46, no. 28 (July 9, 2011): 49–58. I thank Shahzad Bashir for sharing this reference with me.

69. *Iran Political Diaries*, 2:140–141.

70. IOR/L/P&S/7/58, translation of Herat newsletter from Khan Bahadur Mirza Muhammad Yakub Ali Khan, British news-writer at Herat, no. 39, dated September 26, 1889.

71. Tsentral'nyi gosudarstvennyi arkhiv respubliki Uzbekistan, f. I-1, op. 31, d. 726/19, http://zerrspiegel.orientphil.uni-halle.de/t1148.html; IOR L/PS/10/200, Herat Diary, week of February 15, 1912.

4. THE STAR OF ASIA

1. IOR/L/PS/10/200, Herat Diary, week of January 25; Kandahar Diary, January 1912; Kabul Diary, February 1912, Kabul Diary, week of July 12, 1912; FO 424/229, Counsel Satow to Sir G. Lowther, October 14, 1911 (Jerusalem), p. 30 [Asiatic Turkey and Arabia, Further Correspondence, Part 4].

2. Mas'ūd Pūhanyār, *Ẓuhūr-i Mashrūṭīyat va Qurbāniyān-i Istibdād dar Afghānistān* (Peshawar: Sabā Kitābkhānah, 1376 [1997]), 100.

3. Touraj Atabaki, "Constitutionalism in Iran and Its Asian Interdependencies," *Comparative Studies of South Asia, Africa and the Middle East* 28, no. 1 (2008): 142–153; and V. G. Korgun, *Intelligentsiia v politicheskoi zhizni Afganistana* (Moscow: Izdatel'stvo "Nauka," Glavnaia redaktsiia vostochnoi literatury, 1983), 22–27.

4. A. G. Ravān Farhādī and Ghulām Sakhī Ghayrat, eds., *Khāṭirāt-i Maḥmūd Ṭarzī* (Kabul: Anstītūt-i Dīplūmāsī-i Vizārat-i Umūr-i Khārijah, 1389 [2010 or 2011]), 36–39; Cemil Aydin, *The Politics of Anti-Westernism in Asia: Visions of World Order in Pan-Islamic and Pan-Asian Thought* (New York: Columbia University Press, 2007), 71–72.

5. Maḥmūd Ṭarzī, *Vaṭan va Maʿānī-yi Mutanavviʿah va Muḥākamāt-i Ḥukmiyah-'i ān, Aṣar-i Maḥmūd Ṭarzī* (Kabul: Maṭbaʿah-'i Ḥurūfī, 1335 [1917]), 2–3 and 91.

6. Mahmud Tarzi, "What Is to Be Done?," trans. Helena Malikyar, in *Modernist Islam, 1840–1940: A Sourcebook*, ed. Charles Kurzman (Oxford: Oxford University Press, 2002), 126–129.

7. IOR/L/P&S/10/200, Afghan and Northwest Frontier Diaries, July 21, 1912; "Ameer of Afghanistan Has Fifty-Eight Motors," *Popular Mechanics*, February 1914, 177.

8. IOR/L/P&S/10/200, January 20, 1912.

9. Ibid., January 21, 1912.

10. See Erika Knabe, *Frauenemanzipation in Afghanistan* (Meisenheim am Glan: Hain, 1977); and Vartan Gregorian, *The Emergence of Modern Afghanistan: Politics of Reform and Modernization, 1880–1946* (Stanford, CA: Stanford University Press, 1969), 239–244.

11. ʿAbd al-Rabb, [Dīniyāt] [n.p., n.d.], 1; *Khulāṣah-'i Tārīkh-i anbiyā: Barā-yi ṣinf-i sivvum-i ibtidā'ī* (Lahore: Salīm Prīs, 1304 [1925]); *Jughrāfiyā-yi kūchak: Barā-yi ṣinf-i sivvūm-i ibtidā'ī; Bi-qarār-i prūgrām-i maʿārif-i Afghānistān* ([Kabul]: Maṭbaʿah-'i Shirkat-i Rafīq, 1307 [1928]); Tarzi, "What Is to Be Done?"; and see, for example, *Siraj al-ʿaqāʾid* ([Kabul]: 1340 [1922]).

12. "Az Ustraliyā," *Sirāj al-akhbār*, no. 6, November 20, 1914 [1 Muharram 1333], p. 8.

13. Iu. N. Tikhonov, *Afganskaia voina Stalina: Bitva za Tsentral'nuiu Aziiu* (Moscow: Eksmo; Iauza, 2008); T. N. Zagorodnikova and P. M. Shastitko,

eds., *Russko-indiiskie otnosheniia v 1900–1917 gg.: Sbornik arkhivnykh dokumentov i materialov* (Moscow: Izdatel'skaia firma "Vostochnaia literatura" RAN, 1999), 123–127.

14. Nikki R. Keddie, *Sayyid Jamal ad-Din "al-Afghani"* (Berkeley: University of California Press, 1972), 11, 37–57, 135–136, 206; Thomas L. Hughes, "The German Mission to Afghanistan, 1915–1916," in *Germany and the Middle East, 1871–1945,* ed. Wolfgang G. Schwanitz (Madrid: Iberoamericana, 2004), 25–63; Werner Otto von Hentig, *Ins verschlossene Land: Ein Kampf mit Mensch und Meile* (Potsdam: Ludwig Voggenreiter, 1928), 22; and Stefan M. Kreutzer, *Dschihad für den deutschen Kaiser: Max von Oppenheim und die Neuordnung des Orients (1914–1918)* (Graz: Ares Verlag, 2012).

15. Renate Vogel, *Die Persien- und Afghanistanexpedition Oskar Ritter v. Niedermayers, 1915/16* (Osnabrück: Biblio Verlag, 1976), 81–82, 94–95, 177–178.

16. Abdullah Khan, *Mawlana 'Ubayd Allah Sindhi's Mission to Afghanistan and Soviet Russia,* ed. Ross Masood Hussain (Peshawar: Area Study Centre, 2000); Maia Ramnath, *Haj to Utopia: How the Ghadar Movement Charted Global Radicalism and Attempted to Overthrow the British Empire* (Berkeley: University of California Press, 2011); Seema Sohi, "Race, Surveillance, and Indian Anticolonialism in the Transnational Western U.S.-Canadian Borderlands," *Journal of American History* 98, no. 2 (2011): 420–436; Touraj Atabaki, "Going East: The Ottomans' Secret Service Activities in Iran," in *Iran and the First World War: Battleground of the Great Powers,* ed. Touraj Atabaki (London: Tauris, 2006), 38–39; Saul Kelly, " 'Crazy in the Extreme'?: The Silk Letters Conspiracy," *Middle Eastern Studies* 49, no. 2 (2013): 162–178; and Sana Haroon, *Frontier of Faith: Islam in the Indo-Afghan Borderland* (New York: Columbia University Press, 2007).

17. Zagorodnikova and Shastitko, *Russko-indiiskie otnosheniia,* 444.

18. Iu. N. Tikhonov, "Bor'ba sovetskoi diplomatii za 'afganskii koridor' v zonu pushtunskikh plemen v 1919–1921 gg. (po arkhivnym materialam)," in *Afganistan i bezopasnost' Tsentral'noi Azii,* ed. A. A. Kniazev. (Bishkek: Ilim, 2005), 2:32–51.

19. Solidarity among Muslims had drawn tens of thousands to the "Khilafat" movement protesting British policy toward the Ottoman sultan, but increasingly Muslim intellectuals in India and along its frontiers turned their gaze

to the plight of their coreligionists in Palestine. Following meetings at which activists drew up petitions against British policy in numerous towns, including Peshawar and Kohat on the Afghan frontier in fall 1929, Muslims organized the celebration of "Palestine Day" on May 16, 1930, marked by gatherings, processions, and the sending of telegrams to protest the mistreatment of their coreligionists at the hands of the Zionists and the British. In the following decade, Afghans would follow events in Palestine closely. See Sandeep Chawla, "The Palestine Issue in Indian Politics in the 1920s," in *Communal and Pan-Islamic Trends in Colonial India,* ed. Mushirul Hasan, rev. ed. (New Delhi: Manohar, 1985), 43–58.

20. FO 402/16, "Leading Personalities in Afghanistan," (January 12, 1933), pp. 15–16 and 29.

21. FO 371/9209, Reference Diary for October 6, 1922, from Kashgar; FO 293/278/10, Kashgar Diary, July 1923; David Bello, "Opium in Xinjiang and Beyond," in *Opium Regimes: China, Britain and Japan, 1839–1952,* ed. Timothy Brook and Bob Tadashi Wakabayashi (Berkeley: University of California Press, 2000), 127–151; Lars-Erik Nyman, *Great Britain and Chinese, Russian and Japanese Interests in Sinkiang, 1918–1934* (Stockholm: Esselte Studium, 1977), 52–53.

22. RGASPI, f. 62, op. 2, d. 71, ll. 13–16.

23. RGASPI f. 62, op. 2, d. 243, ll. 53–61 and 135–145 ob.

24. IOR/L/PS/11/250-3607, "Persecution of Ahmadiyya Sect," September 1924–April 1925.

25. FO 402/10, "Diary of the Secretary, British Legation, Kabul, for the Week ending November 10, 1928," p. 7; 'Abd al-Ghafūr Khān, *Uṣūlnāmah-'i Futbāl: Barā-yi Ṭalabah'i Ma'ārif* (Kabul: Maṭba'ah-'i Anīs, [1930?]); *Varzish va Fava'id-i ān* ([Kabul]: Maṭba'ah-i Shirkat-i Rafīq, 1307 [1928]), 2 and 23.

26. For example, FO 402/16, "Diary no. 49 for the Week ending December 2, 1932," describing the travel of Bibi Aisha Begum, daughter of Muhammad Aziz Khan, to Europe for medical care, p. 111.

27. See, for example, IOR L/P&S/10/984, Sd. E. B. Howell to Sardar Mohamed Haidar Khan, Consul General for Afghanistan, Simla, July 11, 1923.

28. FO 402/16, "Leading Personalities in Afghanistan," p. 12.

29. Ibid., 13.

30. Ibid., 13–23.

31. Some material for his biography may be found in Isḥāq Shujāʿī, *Sitārah-i Shab-i Dījvar: Yādmān-i ʿAllāmah Shahīd Sayyid Ismāʿīl Balkhī* (Tehran: Sūrah-i Mihr, 1383 [2004]), 25–41.

32. Nancy Hatch Dupree, "King Amanullah's Building Boom," in *L'art d'Af-ghanistan de la préhistoire à nos jours* (Paris: Centre d'Études et de Recherches Documentaires sur l'Afghanistan, 2007), 157–167.

33. Sirdar Ikbal Ali Shah, *Afghanistan of the Afghans* (London: Diamond Press, 1928), 240; Ikbal Ali Shah, *Westward to Mecca: A Journey of Adventure through Afghanistan, Bolshevik Asia, Persia, Iraq, & Hijaz to the Cradle of Islam* (London: H. F. & G. Witherby, 1928), 82–83, 86, 91; and May Schinasi, *Kaboul, 1773–1948: Naissance et croissance d'une capitale royale* (Naples: Università degli Studi di Napoli "L'Orientale," 2008).

34. Soviet authorities suspected the governor of Herat, in particular, of seeking to coax Soviet émigrés to his territory. See RGASPI f. 62, op. 2, d. 2540.

35. Gregorian, *The Emergence of Modern Afghanistan*, 283–284.

36. V. Boiko, "Sovetsko-afganskaia voennaia ekspeditsiia v Afganistan 1929 goda," *Aziia i Afrika segodnia,* July 1, 2001, 31–57, here, 31.

37. Ibid., 31–32.

38. Ibid., 32–37.

39. Mahendra Pratap, *Afghanistan: The Heart of Aryan* (Peping: World Federation, n.d.), 12–41.

40. IOR/L/P&S/12/1659; *Islah* excerpt is in translation of *Al-Mujahid*, published April 15, 1934, in Chamarkand.

5. SEDUCED BY CAPITAL

1. "Old School Altered for Business Use," *New York Times*, March 9, 1947, p. R1.

2. On Abdul Majid Zabuli's biography, see Leon B. Poullada and Leila D. J. Poullada, *The Kingdom of Afghanistan and the United States: 1828–1973* (Omaha, NE: Dageforde, 1995), 162–163; Ludwig W. Adamec, *A Biograph-

ical Dictionary of Contemporary Afghanistan (Graz, Austria: Akademische Druck-u. Verlagsanstalt, 1987), 201.

3. "'Arabah-i Mutursikl," *Anīs,* April 10, 1931 [2 Saur 1310], p. 8. See also *Da Kabul kalanay* (Kabul, 1319 [1940–1941]), especially 382–385.

4. See Wahīd Muzhdah, ed., *Yād'dāsht'hā-yi 'Abd al-Majīd Zābulī: Sābiq Vazīr-i Iqtiṣād-i Millī-i Afghānistān* (n.p.: 1380 [2001]). Note the structural parallels with German finance in Harold James, *The Nazi Dictatorship and the Deutsche Bank* (Cambridge: Cambridge University Press, 2004).

5. FO 402/16, Sir R. Maconachie to Sir John Simon, September 16, 1933.

6. Iu. V. Gankovskii, ed., *Istoriia vooruzhennykh sil Afganistana, 1747–1977* (Moscow: Izdatel'stvo "Nauka" Glavnaia redaktsiia vostochnoi literatury, 1985), 100–104.

7. Gurevich, *Vneshniaia torgovlia Afganistana v noveishee vremia* (Moscow: Glavnaia redaktsiia vostochnoi literatury izdatel'stva "Nauka," 1981), 25.

8. Ibid., 23–25; Adamec, *Biographical Dictionary,* 66.

9. FO 402/16, Agent to the Governor-General, North-West Frontier Province, to Viceroy of India, Peshawar, November 14, 1933.

10. FO 402/16, Maconachie to Simon, July 22, 1933.

11. FO 402/16, Maconachie to Simon (received January 3, 1934).

12. IOR/R/12/41, British Legation in Kabul to Secretary of State for Foreign Affairs, August 21, 1930.

13. FO 402/16, British Legation Diary no. 37 for week ending September 15, 1933; diary no. 31, for week ending August 1, 1935; diary of September 29, 1933, p. 195. Rudolf Stuckert, *Erinnerungen an Afghanistan, 1940–1946* (Liestal: Stiftung Bibliotheca Afghanica, 1994), 9, 35, 49; W. K. Fraser-Tytler, *Afghanistan: A Study of Political Developments in Central and Southern Asia,* 3rd ed. (London: Oxford University Press, 1967), 253.

14. Poullada and Poullada, *The Kingdom of Afghanistan,* 164–165; FO 402/16, Diary no. 42 for the week ending October 20, 1933, December 21, 1933, and August 1, 1935.

15. Ernest F. Fox, *Travels in Afghanistan* (New York: Macmillan, 1943), 261; Kurt Ziemke, *Als Deutscher Gesandter in Afghanistan* (Stuttgart: Deutsche Verlags-Anstalt, 1939), 164–171.

16. *Fur Trade Review,* April 1922, p. 132.

17. "Diverse Trends Likely at $1,000,000 Fur Show," *New York Times,* June 4, 1939, p. F7; "Use of Fur in a Wide Variety Is Shown; Neckline, Hats and Even Bags Bedecked," *New York Times,* September 11, 1940, p. 26; display ad, *New York Times,* August 9, 1939, p. 14. Other retails advertised "grey" as well.

18. V. S. Boiko, *Vlast' i oppozitsiia v Afganistane: Osobennosti politicheskoi bor'by v 1919–1953 gg.* (Moscow: Institut vostokovedeniia RAN; Barnaul: Altaiskaia gos. pedagogicheskaia akademiia, 2010), 175; Terry Martin, "Origins of Soviet Ethnic Cleansing," *Journal of Modern History* 70, no. 4 (1998): 832; Adrienne Lynn Edgar, *Tribal Nation: The Making of Soviet Turkmenistan* (Princeton, NJ: Princeton University Press, 2004), 67; RGASPI f. 62, op. 2, d. 3037, ll. 30–33.

19. RGASPI, f. 62, op. 2, d. 2540; K. N. Abdullaev, *Ot Sin'tsziana do Khorasana: Iz istorii sredneaziatskoi emigratsii XX veka* (Dushanbe: Irfon, 2009); Edgar, *Tribal Nation,* 193; S. B. Panin, "Sovetskaia emigratsionnaia i reemigratsionnaia politika v Srednei Azii (20-30-e gg. XX v.)," *Vostok* 6 (2003): 12–20; and Dzh. Annaorazov, "Vosstanie turkmenskikh kochevnikov v 1931 g.," *Voprosy istorii* 5 (2013): 36–53.

20. RGASPI, f. 62, op. 2, d. 3037, l. 141.

21. Oleg V. Khlevniuk, *The History of the Gulag: From Collectivization to the Great Terror,* trans. Vadim Staklo (New Haven, CT: Yale University Press, 2004), 319–320; they may have included Afghans attached to the consulates (p. 160).

22. Alisher Latypov, "The Opium War at the 'Roof of the World': The 'Elimination' of Addiction in Soviet Badakhshan," *Central Asian Survey* 32, no. 1 (2013): 19–36.

23. RGASPI, f. 62, op. 2, d. 2740, l. 59.

24. Sara Koplik, "The Demise of Afghanistan's Jewish Community and the Soviet Refugee Crisis (1932–1936)," *Iranian Studies* 36, no. 3 (2003): 353–379, here, 362.

25. Ibid., 369.

26. "Mawqi'īyat -i Ṭabī'ī-yi Iqtiṣādī-yi Afghānistān," *Anīs,* no. 42, February 1932, pp. 2–6.

27. *Sar'rishtah-'i Islāmīyah Rūm* (1886?), available at http://afghanistandl.nyu.edu /books/adl0003/adl0003_000002.html.

28. Mohammed Ali, *Guide to Afghanistan* (Kabul, 1938), 5–6 and 50–55.

29. Richard N. Frye, "Oriental Studies in Afghanistan," *Journal of the American Oriental Society* 64, no. 3 (1944): 144–145.

30. FO 402/19, Fraser-Tytler to Viscount Halifax, June 28, 1938.

31. Siegfried Rohmeder, "Deutsche in Afghanistan," *Wir Deutsche in der Welt* (1938): 105–110.

32. FO 402/20, "Further correspondence respecting Afghanistan: part 22 (1939)," pp. 89–92 and elsewhere.

33. Generaloberst Halder, *Kriegstagebuch: Tägliche Aufzeichnungen des Chefs des Generalstabes des Heeres, 1939–1942,* ed. Hans-Adolf Jacobsen, vol. 3 (Stuttgart: W. Kohlhammer Verlag, 1964), 29, 250, 254, 268.

34. Johannes Glasneck and Inge Kircheisen, *Türkei und Afghanistan—Brennpunkte der Orientpolitik im Zweiten Weltkrieg* (Berlin: VEB Deutscher Verlag der Wissenschaften, 1968), 266–268; Iurii Tikhonov, *Afganskaia voina tret'ego reikha: NKVD protiv Abvera* (Moscow: Olma-Press, 2003), 323–324; Engert to the Secretary of State, May 24, 1943, *Foreign Relations of the United States* (hereafter FRUS), 1943, vol. 4, *The Near East and Africa* (Washington, D.C.: Government Printing Office, 1964), 35–36.

35. Tikhonov, *Afganskaia voina tret'ego reikha,* 325–327.

36. See Glasneck and Kircheisen, *Türkei und Afghanistan,* 238–274.

37. IOR/L/P&S/12/1879, secret extract from Intelligence Summary no. 49 for week ending December 4, 1942, p. 22.

38. Glasneck and Kircheisen, *Türkei und Afghanistan,* 259.

39. Engert to the Secretary of State, June 17, 1942, FRUS, 1942 4:51–52 (Washington, D.C.: Government Printing Office, 1963), 4:51–57, 63.

40. Engert to the Secretary of State, August 5 and 7, 1942, in ibid., 53–54.

41. Engert to the Secretary of State, January 27, 1943, and Memorandum of Conversation by Calvin H. Oakes, August 3, 1943, FRUS, 1943, 4:21, 27–29.

42. Engert to the Secretary of State, January 24, 1943, in ibid., 53.

43. Engert to the Secretary of State, March 31, 1943, in ibid., 56.

44. Engert to the Secretary of State, April 20, 1943, in ibid., 57.

45. Engert to the Secretary of State, August 25, 1944, FRUS, 1944, 5:48–50.

6. THE ATOMIC AGE

1. "'Aṣr-i atūmik," *Anīs*, January 1, 1946, p. 3; Marvin Brant, "Recent Economic Developments," in *Afghanistan in the 1970s,* ed. Louis Dupree and Linette Albert (New York: Praeger, 1974), 94.

2. Brant, "Recent Economic Development," 94; *Afghanistan Strategic Intelligence: British Records, 1919–1970* [hereafter, ASI], ed. Anita L. P. Burdett, vol. 4, *1948–1970: The Post-War Years* ([London?]: Archive Editions, 2002), 173.

3. FO 402/24, "Further correspondence respecting Afghanistan: part 2 (1948)."

4. U.S. National Archives, "Enclosure to Kabul Despatch No. 45," April 7, 1948, Central File: Decimal File 890H.4016, Records of the Department of State relating to Internal Affairs: Afghanistan, 1945–1949; Paul Grimes, "Americans Aloof in Afghan 'Exile,'" *New York Times*, March 12, 1960, p. 7. See also "U.S. 'Town' Nestles Behind Afghan Walls," *Christian Science Monitor*, November 6, 1957, p. 3.

5. The Chargé in Afghanistan (Horner) to the Department of State, September 9, 1952, FRUS, 1952–1954 (Washington, D.C.: United States Government Printing Office, 1983), vol. 11, pt. 2:1449–1450.

6. Max Klimburg, *Afghanistan: Das Land im historischen Spannugsfeld Mittelasiens* (Vienna and Munich: Österreichischer Bundesverlag, 1966), 74–75; R. T. Akhramovich, *Afganistan posle vtoroi mirovoi voiny* (Moscow: Izadatel'stvo Vostochnoi literatury, 1961); Eric Newby, *A Short Walk: A Preposterous Adventure* (Garden City, New York: Doubleday, 1959), 74; Nick Cullather, "Damming Afghanistan: Modernization in a Buffer State," *Journal of American History* 89, no. 2 (2002): 512–537; and Rajiv Chandrasekaran, *Little America: The War within the War for Afghanistan* (New York: Alfred A. Knopf, 2012).

7. On this contested frontier linking Afghanistan and Pakistan, see the excellent studies by Amin Tarzi, "Political Struggles over the Afghanistan-Pakistan Borderlands," in *Under the Drones: Modern Lives in the Afghanistan-Pakistan Borderlands,* ed. Shahzad Bashir and Robert D. Crews (Cambridge, MA: Harvard University Press, 2012), 17–29; and Sana Haroon, *Frontier of*

Faith: Islam in the Indo-Afghan Borderland (New York: Columbia University Press, 2007).

8. ASI, 4:157 and 173–179.

9. Ibid., 164, for example.

10. Ibid., 162.

11. Telegram from the Embassy in Afghanistan to the Department of State, September 20, 1961, FRUS, 1961–1963 (Washington, D.C.: United States Government Printing Office, 1996), 19:104–106.

12. Memorandum of Conversation, by the Acting Officer in Charge of Pakistan-Afghanistan Affairs (Metcalf), January 5, 1954, FRUS, 1952–1954, vol. 11, pt. 2:1407–1411.

13. FO 402/31, "Further correspondence respecting Afghanistan: part 9 (1955)," 12–16.

14. Ibid., 18–21.

15. Cited in M. G. Pikulin, *Razvitie natsional'noi ekonomiki i kul'tury Afganistana, 1955–1960* (Tashkent: Izdatel'stvo Akademii Nauk Uzbekskoi SSR, 1961), 137; and Sohail Daulatzai, *Black Star, Crescent Moon: The Muslim International and Black Freedom beyond America* (Minneapolis: University of Minnesota Press, 2012), 27–28.

16. "Qatl va khūnrīzī dar sarzamīn-i Filistīn," *Anīs,* May 15, 1948, p. 1; "Az i'lāmīyah-'i Balfor," *Anīs,* May 16, 1948, p. 1; ASI, 4:141; "Mulāqāt-i kumīshīnir-i 'āli-yi Filistin," *Anīs,* January 1, 1946, p. 1.; another on violence in Palestine, *Anīs,* May 15, 1948.

17. ASI, 4:492.

18. Ibid., 490.

19. Ibid., 490. The Afghan press reported that Afghans took up collections for Egypt. See Pikulin, *Razvitie natsional'noi ekonomiki,* 137.

20. National Security Council Report, "Statement of Policy on U.S. Policy toward South Asia," January 10, 1957, FRUS, 1955–1957 (Washington, D.C.: United States Government Printing Office, 1987), vol. 8, *South Asia,* 29–43.

21. See the untitled album of their trip in Delmas H. Nucker miscellaneous papers, Hoover Institution Archives.

22. Erwin Grötzbach, *Afghanistan: Eine geographische Landeskunde* (Darmstadt: Wissenschaftliche Buchgesellschaft, 1990), 123–129.

23. Ibid., 144–145.

24. Drew Pearson, "Moslems Nearly Kill Americans," *Washington Post*, January 9, 1960, p. B15. Lower casualty figures appear in "50 Afghan Dead Reported in Kandahar," *Times* (London), December 29, 1959, p. 6; "Reported Revolt in Afghanistan," *Times* (London), January 7, 1960, p. 10. "Afghanistan Hope of Friendship," *Times* (London), January 11, 1960, p. 11; "Renewed Fighting in Afghanistan," *Times* (London), January 26, 1960, p. 8.; "Plebiscite Call by Afghan Pathans," *Times* (London), March 21, 1960, p. 11; Narayan Swamy, "Austrian Consul & ICA Officer among Injured: Kandahar Disturbances," *Times of India* (New Delhi), January 5 1960, p. 1. See also Jenifer Van Vleck, "An Airline at the Crossroads of the World: Ariana Afghan Airlines, Modernization, and the Global Cold War," *History and Technology* 25, no. 1 (2009): 3–24.

25. Grötzbach, *Afghanistan,* 157; "Educational Progress in Afghanistan," *Asia Foundation Program Bulletin* (June 1962): 5–7.

26. See Grötzbach, *Afghanistan,* 157–158 for details; and Louis Dupree, *Afghanistan* (Princeton, NJ: Princeton University Press, 1980), 598–600 and 639–640.

27. Horst Büscher, *Die Industriearbeiter in Afghanistan: Eine Studie zur gesellschaftspolitischen Problematik sozial schwacher Bevölkerungsschichten in Entwicklungsländern* (Meisenheim am Glan: Verlag Anton Hain, 1969), 161; Wilma Oksendahl, "Business Education for Afghan Women," *Asia Foundation Program Bulletin* (June 1961): 5–7; and Foreign and Commonwealth Office, The National Archives, Kew [hereafter, FCO], 37/1009 "Afghan Representation at Women's International Democratic Federation Conferences," appendix to May 9, 1972, H. J. Spence, to J.R. James.

28. Digital National Security Archive, U.S. Agency for International Development, "Retrospective Review of U.S. Assistance to Afghanistan, 1950–1979," October 31, 1988, p. 146.

29. "Soviet Press Comment, 1 April–30 June 1965," *Central Asian Review* 13, no. 3 (1965): 282–283; Grötzbach, *Afghanistan,* 83.

30. Grötzbach, *Afghanistan,* 151; "3,364 Haj Pilgrims Take Ariana Home in Last 2 Weeks," *Kabul Times,* March 12, 1970, p. 1.

31. Prita K. Shalizi, *Here and There in Afghanistan* (Kabul: Department of Translation and Compilation, 1966), 2, 13, and 15.

32. Grötzbach, *Afghanistan*, 198–202; May Schinasi, *Kaboul 1773–1948: Naissance et croissance d'une capitale royale* (Naples: Università degli Studi di Napoli "L'Orientale," 2008), 176–180.

33. Dari-language transcript of Fariba Nawa's interview with Shabnam, Fremont, CA, April 2011.

34. Abdullah Aziz, *Essai sure les catégories dirigeantes de l'Afghanistan, 1945–1963: Mode de vie et comportement politique* (Berne: Peter Lang, 1987), 180–198 and 227–241; Harrison Forman Collection, Afghanistan, 1953, available at http://collections.lib.uwm.edu/cdm/singleitem/collection/af/id/622/rec/7 and http://collections.lib.uwm.edu/cdm/singleitem/collection/af/id/553/rec /1; U.S. National Archives, U.S. Embassy in Kabul to the Secretary of State, September 1, 1960, Records of the Department of State relating to Internal Affairs: Afghanistan, 1960–1963: Decimal File 889.00; Herbert Penzl, "Western Loanwords in Modern Pashto," *Journal of the American Oriental Society* 81, no. 1 (January–March 1961): 43–52; on new naming practices, see Muhammad Khan Jalallar, *Rumi Tomato: Autobiography of an Afghan Minister*, ed. Babur Rashidzada (n.p., 2011), 54.

35. Interviews with Mohammad Asef Soltanzadeh in Copenhagen, Aziz Arianfar in Munich, August 2013, and Abdul Zuhur Razmjo in Kabul, November 2013; Sulṭān ʿAlī Kishtmand, *Yād'dāsht'hā-yi Siyāsī va Rūydād'hā-yi Tārīkhī* ([n.p.]: Najīb-i Kabīr, 2002), 83–84; and Ṣurayyā Bahāʾ, *Rahā dar bād* (Kabul: Intishārāt-i Tāk, 1392 [2013]), 25–26, 37–38, and elsewhere. See also Jinrāl ʿAbd al-Qādir, *Khāṭirāt-i siyāsī-yi Jinrāl ʿAbd al-Qādir: Dar guftogū bā Dāktur Parviz Ārzū* (Kabul: Bunyād-i Khadamātī-Farhangī-i Hirāt, 1392 [2013]), 36.

36. A. S. Gerasimova, "Gor'kii v Afganistane," *M. Gor'kii i literatury zarubezhnogo Vostoka: sbornik statei,* ed. V. A. Keldysh, K. Rekho, E. P. Chelyshev, and M. E. Shneider (Moscow: Glavnaia redaktsiia vostochnoi literatury izdatel'stva "Nauka," 1968), 179–189; Gerasimova, "M. Gor'kii i sovetskaia literatura v Afganistane," *Literatura stran zarubezhnogo Vostoka i sovetskaia literatura,* ed. A. I. Borshchukov, V. I. Ivanova, S. N. Uturgauri, E. P. Chelyshev, and L. E. Cherkasskii (Moscow: Glavnaia redaktsiia vostochnoi literatury izdatel'stva "Nauka," 1977), 41–52. See also Wali Ahmadi, *Modern*

Persian Literature in Afghanistan: Anomalous Visions of History and Form (London: Routledge, 2008); Thomas Wade, "Demarcating Pashto: Cross-Border Pashto Literature and the Afghan State, 1880–1930," in *Afghanistan in Ink: Literature between Diaspora and Nation*, ed. Nile Green and Nushin Arbabzadah (New York: Columbia University Press, 2013), 91–112; and James Caron, "Ambiguities of Orality and Literacy, Territory and Border Crossings: Public Activism and Pashto Literature in Afghanistan, 1930–2010," in ibid., 113–139.

37. Vartan Gregorian, *The Emergence of Modern Afghanistan: Politics of Reform and Modernization, 1880–1946* (Stanford, CA: Stanford University Press, 1969), 357–361; N. A. Dvoriankov, *Sovremennyi Afganistan* (Moscow: Izdatel'stvo vostochnoi literatury, 1960), 361–364; *Kabul Times,* April 10, 1962, p. 4; for cinema notices see, for example, *Kabul Times,* December 29, 1963, p. 4; *Kabul Times,* April 10, 1962, p. 4; on Habibia High School students singing Elvis Presley songs, see "Benefit Held to Help Blind," *Kabul Times,* August 9, 1966, p. 1; and Linette Albert, "Afghanistan: A Perspective," in *Afghanistan in the 1970s,* ed. Louis Dupree and Linette Albert (New York: Praeger, 1974), 249–259.

38. Grötzbach, *Afghanistan,* 199 and 228–230; Mark Slobin, *Music in the Culture of Northern Afghanistan* (Tucson: University of Arizona Press, 1976), 157; and Heribert Strathmann, *Händler und Handwerker als soziales Segment in Afghanistan* (Meisenheim: Anton Hain, 1980), 272–275.

39. FCO 37/1689, B. W. V. Tomsett [Kabul Embassy] to G. K. Woodfield, November 20, 1976.

40. V. G. Korgun, *Intelligentsiia v politicheskoi zhizni Afganistana* (Moscow: Glavnaia redaktsiia vostochnoi literatury izdatel'stva "Nauka," 1983), especially 49–85; Aleksandr Liakhovskii, *Tragediia i doblest' Afgana: Informatsiia, analiz, vyvody* (Iaroslavl': "Nord," 2004), 38; FCO 37/2077, "Afghanistan: military coup, 27 April 1978 (Folder 2)."

41. Amān al-Dīn Amīn, *Khāṭirāt: 1318–1371* (Peshawar: Markaz-i Nashrāt-i Saʿīd, 2005), 106 and elsewhere.

42. On Hafizullah Amin's claims and American officials' commentary on them, see the embassy cable reproduced in *Asnād-i lānah-i jāsūsī* vol. 30 ([Tehran]: Dānishjūyān-i Musalmān-i Payruv-i Khaṭṭ-i Imām, 1979), 59; and on the

students in California, "How the CIA Turns Foreign Students into Traitors," *Ramparts* (April 1967): 22–24; these contrasting views of the American and Soviet military establishments emerged from my interview with Nur ul-Haq Ulumi, Kabul, November 2013; for positive assessments of Ulumi by Soviet authors, see, for example, M. A. Gareev, *Afganskaia strada (s sovetskimi voiskami i bez nikh)*, 2nd rev. ed. (Moscow: "Insan," 1999), 254–258; and V. Khristoforov, *Afganistan: Praviashchaia partiia i armiia 1978–1989* (Moscow: Granitsa, 2009), 198–199.

43. Dominions Office, The National Archives, Kew, 201/11, United Kingdom High Commissioner in Pakistan, A. C. B. Symon, to the Secretary of State for Commonwealth Relations, March 10, 1960; Hasan Kakar, "The Fall of the Afghan Monarchy in 1973," *International Journal of Middle East Studies* 9, no. 2 (1978): 195–214, here, 197; see also David Edwards, *Before Taliban: Genealogies of the Afghan Jihad* (Berkeley: University of California Press, 1992).

44. ASI, 4:885–887.

45. Babrak Karmal, "Zur Strategie und Taktik der Volksdemokratischen Partei Afghanistans," in *Afghanistan seit dem Sturz der Monarchie: Dokumentation zur Politik, Wirtschaft und Bevölkerung*, Aktueller Informationsdienst Moderner Orient: Sondernummer (Hamburg: Deutsches Orient-Institut, 1981), 47–52.

46. Digital National Security Archive, U.S. Agency for International Development, "Retrospective Review of U.S. Assistance to Afghanistan, 1950–1979," October 31, 1988, p. 6; and FCO 37/1686, J. A. Birch (British embassy in Kabul) to DJ Holder, South Asian Department, July 13, 1976, pp. 15–16.

47. Albert, "Afghanistan: A Perspective," 251–257; see also Karl Otto Hondrich, "Die Einstellung afghanischer Studenten zum sozialen Wandel," *Kölner Zeitschrift für Soziologie und Sozialpsychologie* 16 (1964): 703–726.

48. "Memorandum of Conversation," Washington, D.C., March 28, 1967, FRUS, 1964–1968, vol. 25, *South Asia*, doc. 539.

49. "Protestors Try but Fail to Stop Agnew Motorcade," *Boston Globe*, January 7, 1970, p. 2. Members of the Peace Corps apparently delivered letters of protest for Agnew via the embassy criticizing the Vietnam War, but it remains unclear how much contact the young Americans had with the Afghan student activists. See also Lemmy Pinna, "Agnew Encounters Protestors on

Tour," *Atlanta Daily World,* January 9, 1970, p. 2; and William Reeves, "Dr Najibullah," *Independent* (London), September 28, 1996, p. 16.

50. Michael Kelly, "Afghans Learned UCLA's Tactics," *Omaha World-Herald,* June 8, 2010. I thank Bob McCabe for sharing this article with me.

51. Erika Knabe, "Afghan Women: Does Their Role Change?," in *Afghanistan in the 1970s,* ed. Louis Dupree and Linette Albert (New York: Praeger, 1974), 144–166; and Hans Hopfinger, "Geographische Aspekte des internationalen Handels mit gebrauchter Bekleidung: Perfektes Recycling oder Verlängerung asymmetrischer Handelsbeziehungen mit der Dritten Welt am Fallbeispiel Syrien," *Erdkunde* 39, no. 3 (September 1985): 206–217.

52. Shannon Caroline Stack, "Herat: A Political and Social Study" (PhD diss., University of California Los Angeles, 1975), 527; Erika Knabe, *Frauenemanzipation in Afghanistan* (Meisenheim am Glan: Hain, 1977), 325 and 375.

53. On fashionable middle- and upper-class gathering places in Kabul, see Nasrine Abou-Bakre Gross, ed., *Qaṣārikh-i Malālay yā Khāṭirāt-i Avvalīn Līsah'ī Dukhtarān-i Afghānistān* (Falls Church, VA: Kabultec, 1998), 252–253.

54. Abou-Bakre Gross, *Qaṣārikh-i Malālay*; Mári Saeed, *Mein Kabul—mein Deutschland: Máris mutiger Weg zwischen den Kulturen* (Rüsselsheim: Göttert, 2008), 91–92; Nadia Qani, *Ich bin eine Deutsche aus Afghanistan* (Frankfurt am Main: Krüger, 2010), 70; translation of *The Caravan,* May 2, 1971 in FCO 37/767. Gulzar was in Shar-i nau. It advertised a Christmas dinner and music program, *Kabul Times,* December 17, 1970, p. 4.

55. Gross, *Qaṣārikh-i Malālay,* 253; Stack, "Herat," 520–521; for a snapshot of marriage and mobility, see Wolfram Eberhard, "Afghanistan's Young Elite," *Asian Survey* 1, no. 12 (February 1962): 3–22.

56. *Anīs,* July 1, 1968; John Baily, "Cross-Cultural Perspectives in Popular Music: The Case of Afghanistan," *Popular Music* 1 (1981): 105–122, here, 111.

57. Slobin, *Music in the Culture of Northern Afghanistan,* 38 and 52; Baily, "Cross-Cultural Perspectives"; and John Baily, *Music of Afghanistan: Professional Musicians in the City of Herat* (Cambridge: Cambridge University Press, 1988), 30–33 and 83–84.

58. Baily, "Cross-Cultural Perspectives."

59. Slobin, *Music in the Culture,* 37.

60. Baily, "Cross-Cultural Perspectives," 117–120; Baily, *Music of Afghanistan,* 151; and Slobin, *Music in the Culture,* 50.

61. Slobin, *Music in the Culture,* 38, 44, 51; "Best Actors, Actresses of the Year Chosen," *Kabul Times,* May 25, 1969; Gross, *Qaṣārikh-i Malālay,* 252; Saeed, *Mein Kabul,* 40.

62. Louis Dupree, "Free Enterprise in Afghanistan, Part 1: The Private Sector and the New Investment Law," *American Universities Field Staff Reports,* South Asia Series, vol. 14, no. 3 (1970): 1–3.

63. Richard S. Newell, "Afghanistan: The Dangers of Cold War Generosity," *Middle East Journal* 23, no. 2 (Spring 1969): 168–176. See also Peter Franck, *Afghanistan between East and West* ([Washington, D.C.]: National Planning Association, 1960), 50–51. Germans echoed many of these complaints. See Hermann Röhrs and Volker Lenhart, *Deutsche Entwicklungshelfer in der Lehrausbildung Afghanistans: Eine Evaluationsstudie* (Meisenheim am Glan: Hain, 1978), 103–105 and 126.

64. Jan-Heeren Grevemeyer, *Afghanistan: Sozialer Wandel und Staat im 20. Jahrhundert* (Berlin: Verlag für Wissenschaft und Bildung, 1990), 102–103.

65. Dupree, "Free Enterprise in Afghanistan, Part 1," 5.

66. Tony Wheeler, *Across Asia on the Cheap* (1973; repr., Oakland, CA: Lonely Planet, 2013), 112.

67. FCO 37/1227, "Afghanistan: The Hippy Trail."

68. FCO 37/1227, Summary of "Afghanistan: The Hippy Trail."

69. [London Times Service], "Ruin Comes to Hippies in Afghanistan," *Milwaukee Journal,* August 27, 1971.

70. Morris Kaplan, "Hashish Valued at $1.5-Million Seized in a Federal-State Raid," *New York Times,* February 4, 1971, p. 58.

71. Nicholas Schou, *Orange Sunshine: The Brotherhood of Eternal Love and Its Quest to Spread Peace, Love, and Acid to the World* (New York: Thomas Dunne Books, 2010); Peter Maguire and Mike Ritter, *Thai Stick: Surfers, Scammers, and the Untold Story of the Marijuana Trade* (New York: Columbia University Press, 2014); Ryan Gingeras, *Heroin, Organized Crime and the Making of Modern Turkey* (Oxford: Oxford University Press, 2014).

72. Nixon in FCO 37/1014, pp. 22–23.

73. "Nucker, Director of USAID, Describes Major Areas of Afghanistan Programme," *Kabul Times,* March 6, 1965, p. 3; David Zurick, *Errant Journeys: Adventure Travel in a Modern Age* (Austin: University of Texas Press, 1995), 46–48; FCO 37/1014, pp. 4–6; Bernd Schäfer, "Schmuggel in Afghanistan," *Afghanistan Journal* 1, no. 2 (1974): 27–31.

74. FCO 37/1014, "Afghan narcotics trade (1972)."

75. Telegram 4948 From the Embassy in Afghanistan to the Department of State, July 6, 1973, FRUS, 1969–1976, vol. E-8, *Documents on South Asia, 1973– 1976,* (Washington, D.C.: Government Printing Office, 2007), 2–13.

76. Ibid.

77. Paul Theroux, *The Great Railway Bazaar: By Train through Asia* (Boston: Houghton Mifflin, 1975), 71–72.

78. U.S. Embassy in Kabul to Secretary of State, "Afghan Request for Further U.S. Assistance in the Helmand-Arghandab Valleys," November 26, 1974, available at http://aad.archives.gov/aad/createpdf?rid=256364&dt=2474 &dl=1345; and FCO 37/1227, "Narcotics in Afghanistan (Folder 2)," British Embassy in Kabul to P. J. Radley, UN Department, FCO, August 22, 1973.

79. U.S. Embassy in Kabul to Secretary of State, October 30, 1974, https:// wikileaks.org/plusd/cables/1974KABUL06836_b.html.

80. U.S. Mission in Geneva to Secretary of State, July 15, 1974, https://wikileaks .org/plusd/cables/1974GENEVA04490_b.html.

81. U.S. Embassy in Kabul to Secretary of State, September 14, 1974, https:// wikileaks.org/plusd/cables/1974KABUL05839_b.html.

82. U.S. Embassy to DEA, December 10, 1974, https://www.wikileaks.org/plusd /cables/1974KABUL07706_b.html; and Martin Booth, *Cannabis: A History* (New York: Picador, 2003), 289.

83. U.S. Embassy in Kabul to Secretary of State, January 30, 1975, https:// wikileaks.org/plusd/cables/1975KABUL00618_b.html.

84. U.S. Embassy in Kabul to DEA, November 28, 1976, https://wikileaks.org /plusd/cables/1976KABUL08726_b.html; U.S. Embassy in Kabul to DEA, November 17, 1976, https://wikileaks.org/plusd/cables/1976KABUL08494 _b.html; and FCO 37/1852, "Narcotics Control in Afghanistan (1977)."

85. Mathea Falco, "Hearings before a Subcommittee of the Committee on Appropriations, House of Representatives," April 5, 1878, available at http://nsarchive.chadwyck.com/nsa/documents/AF/00265/all.pdf. She projected that Afghan opium exports would reach about 270 tons in 1979.

86. FCO 37/1417, British Embassy in Kabul to J. D. Garner of South Asia Department of FCO, May 8, 1974; Dilip Mukherjee, "Afghanistan under Daud: Relations with Neighboring States," *Asian Survey* 15, no. 4 (April 1975): 301–312, here, 303.

7. REVOLUTIONARY DREAMS

1. "Film-i Ruts," *Mīsāq-i khūn* 1 (Haml 1370/1991): 40–43.

2. Martha Vogel, *Roter Teufel—mächtiger mugāhid: Widerstandsbilder im sowjetisch-afghanischen Krieg, 1979–1989* (Vienna: Böhlau Verlag, 2008), 135–136; and ['Abdul Alī Mazārī], *Ihyā-yi Huvvīyat (Majmū'ah-'i Sukhanrānī'hā-yi Shahīd-i Mazlūm Ustād 'Abd al-'Alī Mazārī)* ([Tehran?]: Intishārāt-i Sirāj, 1374 [1995]), 5–6.

3. The key text here is Olivier Roy, *Afghanistan: From Holy War to Civil War* (Princeton, NJ: Darwin Press, 1995). For a similar emphasis, but with a somewhat different interpretation, see Barnett R. Rubin, *The Fragmentation of Afghanistan: State Formation and Collapse in the International System* (New Haven, CT: Yale University Press, 1995).

4. Peter Holquist, *Making War, Forging Revolution: Russia's Continuum of Crisis, 1914–1921* (Cambridge, MA: Harvard University Press, 2002), 3.

5. Andreas Kohlschütter, "Kabuls neue Klasse," *Die Zeit*, June 9, 1978.

6. See Vasily Mitrokhin, "The KGB in Afghanistan," Cold War International History Project Working Paper no. 40, July 2009; Dastāgīr Panjshīrī, *Zuhūr va Zavāl-i Hizb-i Dimūkrātīk-i Khalq-i Afghānistān* part 2 (Peshawar: Markaz-i Nashrātī-i Fazl, 1999), 45–46.

7. On Marxian language, consider, for example, the work of the Afghan historian Ghulām Muhammad Ghubār, *Afghānistān dar masīr-i tārīkh,* 8th ed. (Tehran: Intishārāt-i Jumhūrī, 1383 [2004]); for accounts by socialists with rural backgrounds, see Sultān 'Alī Kishtmand, *Yād'dāsht'hā-yi Siyāsī va*

Rūydād'hā-yi Tārīkhī ([n.p.]: Najīb-i Kabīr, 2002); Jinrāl 'Abd al-Qādir, *Khāṭirāt-i siyāsī-yi Jinrāl 'Abd al-Qādir: Dar guftogū bā Duktur Parviz Ārzū* (Kābul: Bunyād-i Khadamātī-Farhangī-i Hirāt, 1392 [2013]); Shāh 'Alī Ākbar Shahristānī, *Yāddāsht'hā* (Delhi: Mu'assasah-i Nashrātī-i Zar-nivisht, 2000); and on the politics of the military, see Muḥammad Nabī 'Aẓīm, *Urdū va Siyāsat: dar Sih Dahah-'i Akhīr-i Afghānistān* (Peshawar: Markaz-i Nashrātī Mayvand, Sabā Kitābkhānah, 1378 [1999]), 64–65.

8. Miktrokhin, "The KGB in Afghanistan," 149.

9. Interviews with Aziz Arianfar, Munich, August 2013, Abdul Zuhur Razmjo, Kabul, August 2013, and others; Kishtmand, *Yād'dāsht'hā-yi Siyāsī*, 137; Jinrāl 'Abd al-Qādir, *Khāṭirāt-i siyāsī-yi Jinrāl 'Abd al-Qādir: Dar guftogū bā Dāktur Parviz Ārzū* (Kābul: Bunyād-i Khadamātī-Farhangī-i Hirāt, 1392 [2013]), 52.

10. "Babrakis and Ikhwanis Denounced" and "Shameful Crimes of Ikhwanul Muslimeen," *Kabul Times,* October 4, 1978, also references elsewhere to "Ikhwan-ul-shayateen"; "Afghan Delegation Back from Benghazi," *Kabul Times,* October 6, 1978; "First Group of Afghan Hajis Leaves for Mecca," *Kabul Times,* October 14, 1978.

11. "Vietnam Delegation Visits Nangarhar Valley Project," *Kabul Times,* October 1, 1978; "Katawazi Explains Saur Aims at New Delhi Meet" and "Struggle against Colonialism Common Bond between Afghan-Indian People," *Kabul Times,* October 4, 1978.

12. Leonid Bogdanov, *Afganskaia tetrad'* (Moscow: Natsional'noe obozrenie, 2004).

13. A. A. Zhemchugov, *Komu my obiazany "afganom"?* (Moscow: Veche, 2012), 335–342.

14. Ibid., 337–342.

15. V. A. Merimskii, *Zagadki afganskoi voiny* (Moscow: "Veche," 2006), 14.

16. On Kabul's population increase, see Erwin Grötzbach, *Afghanistan: Eine geographische Landeskunde* (Darmstadt: Wissenschaftliche Buchgesellschaft, 1990), 199–200.

17. "Grand Khalqi Marches Held to Condemn Reaction" and "Afghan Provinces," *Kabul Times,* October 9, 1978.

18. See the photographs in Makhmud Baryalai, ed., *Afghanistan: The Revolution Continues* (Moscow: Planeta Publishers, 1994). Their works began to appear in local languages in inexpensive Soviet-style editions.

19. Ibid., 214–219.

20. C.-J. Charpentier, "One Year after the Saur Revolution," *Afghanistan Journal* 6, no. 4 (1979): 117–120, here, 117.

21. Baryalai, *Afghanistan,* 142–143.

22. Ṣurayyā Bahā', *Rahā dar bād* (Kabul: Intishārāt-i Tāk, 1392 [2013]), 93–111.

23. "Anahita Ratebzad: Emergence of Afghan Women," *Times of India,* January 28, 1980. (This interview was apparently before her first exile, but published upon her return to power under Karmal; other sources claimed she studied in Chicago.)

24. Ibid.

25. Michael T. Kaufman, "Travelers Tell of Afghan Students' Bloody Protests," *New York Times,* May 11, 1981.

26. "Anahita Ratebzad on Afghan-Soviet Friendship," *Kabul New Times,* March 4 and 5, 1981 in *Afghanistan seit dem Sturz der Monarchie: Dokumentation zur Politik, Wirtschaft und Bevölkerung,* Aktueller Informationsdienst Moderner Orient: Sondernummer (Hamburg: Deutsches Orient-Institut, 1981), 233–238.

27. "2 More Women Freed on Anahita Ratebzad's Appeal" and "A Mass Rally of Militant Women," *Kabul New Times,* March 8, 1981, pp. 1 and 3.

28. Legacy Tobacco Documents Library, University of California, San Francisco, "Letter from Monica Lentino to Phillip Cunningham regarding duty free shopper's transparency rental agreement," May 1, 1985, available at http://legacy.library.ucsf.edu/tid/xuy87a99; also "Pakistan Visit by Messrs Coburn Aitken of Batuke, Mr. G. Graham of Sutl 22nd to 29th November 1984," available at http://legacy.library.ucsf.edu/tid/fsp17b00.

29. Iurii Krushinskii, *Afganskii dnevnik* (Kiev: Akademvidav, 2006), 13, 17–54, 277, 394.

30. Gilles Dorronsoro, *Revolution Unending: Afghanistan 1979 to the Present,* trans. John King (London: Hurst & Co., 2005); Dorronsoro, "The Transformation

of the Afghanistan-Pakistan Border," in *Under the Drones: Modern Lives in the Afghanistan-Pakistan Borderlands*, ed. Shahzad Bashir and Robert D. Crews (Cambridge, MA: Harvard University Press, 2012), 30–44; Conrad Schetter, "Flüchtling—Arbeitsmigrant—Dschihadist: Zur Rolle von Translokalität in Afghanistan," *Geographische Rundschau* 11 (2011): 18–24; and Alessandro Monsutti, "The Transnational Turn in Migration Studies and the Afghan Social Networks," trans. Helen Lackner, in *Dispossession and Displacement: Forced Migration in the Middle East and North Africa*, ed. Dawn Chatty and Bill Finlayson (Oxford: Oxford University Press, 2010), 45–67.

31. Michael Pohly, *Krieg und Widerstand in Afghanistan: Ursachen, Verlauf und Folgen seit 1978* (Berlin: Das Arabische Buch, 1992), 208.

32. Interview with Hussain Razaiat, Munich, August 2013 and Sayyid Muhammad Ali Javid, Kabul, November 2013.

33. FCO 37/2215, "Afghanistan: Opposition Groups."

34. The National Security Archive, The George Washington University [hereafter NSA], U.S. Embassy in Kabul to Secretary of State, "Merajuddin: Portrait of a Moslem Youth Extremist," available at http://nsarchive.gwu.edu /NSAEBB/NSAEBB59/zahir10.pdf.

35. Robert M. Gates, *From the Shadows: The Ultimate Insider's Story of Five Presidents and How They Won the Cold War* (New York: Simon & Schuster, 1996), 144–149, 178, 242. On the wider context, see Odd Arne Westad, *The Global Cold War: Third World Interventions and the Making of Our Times* (Cambridge: Cambridge University Press, 2005).

36. Neamatollah Nojumi, "The Rise and Fall of the Taliban," in *The Taliban and the Crisis of Afghanistan*, ed. Robert D. Crews and Amin Tarzi (Cambridge, MA: Harvard University Press, 2008), 90–117; Pohly, *Krieg und Widerstand*, 208–213.

37. Gates, *From the Shadows*, 252; see, also, Steve Coll, *Ghost Wars: The Secret History of the CIA, Afghanistan and bin Laden, from the Soviet Invasion to September 10, 2001* (New York: Penguin Books, 2005).

38. See Aleksandr Liakhovskii, *Tragediia i doblest' Afgana: Informatsiia, analiz, vyvody* (Iaroslavl': "Nord," 2004), 462–463 and 472–473; Laurent Gayer, *Karachi: Ordered Disorder and the Struggle for the City* (London: Hurst and Co.,

2014), 19; and Alfred W. McCoy, *The Politics of Heroin: CIA Complicity in the Global Drug Trade*, 2nd rev. ed. (Chicago: Lawrence Hill Books, 2003), 470–487.

39. "Text of the President's Address to the Nation," January 4, 1980, available at http://nsarchive.chadwyck.com/nsa/documents/AF/00756/all.pdf.

40. Joe Stephens and David B. Ottaway, "From U.S., the ABC's of Jihad: Violent Soviet-Era Textbooks Complicate Afghan Education Efforts," *Washington Post*, March 23, 2002, p. A01; Yahia Baiza, *Education in Afghanistan: Developments, Influences and Legacies since 1901* (London: Routledge, 2013), 150.

41. Pohly, *Krieg und Widerstand*, 454–459.

42. Ḥamzah Vāʻiẓī, ed., *Maydān-i havāyī-yi Gardīz* (Tehran: Ḥawzah-i Hunarī, 1375 [1996]); and, for similar emphases, Sayyed Mohammed Akbar Agha, *I Am Akbar Agha: Memories of the Afghan Jihad and the Taliban* (Berlin: First Draft Publishing, 2014), 89.

43. Vahid Brown and Don Rassler, *Fountainhead of Jihad: The Haqqani Nexus, 1973–2012* (New York: Columbia University Press, 2013); Thomas Hegghammer, *Jihad in Saudi Arabia: Violence and Pan-Islamism since 1979* (Cambridge: Cambridge University Press, 2010), 25–28; Stéphane Lacroix, *Awakening Islam: The Politics of Religious Dissent in Contemporary Saudi Arabia* (Cambridge, MA: Harvard University Press, 2011), 110–113.

44. Hegghammer, *Jihad in Saudi Arabia*, 25, 27–28, 38.

45. FCO 37/2215, "Afghanistan: Opposition Groups"; McCoy, *The Politics of Heroin*, 480–487.

46. Ronald Reagan, "Proclamation 5034–Afghanistan Day, 1983," March 21, 1983, available at http://www.reagan.utexas.edu/archives/speeches/1983/32183d.htm.

47. "Radio Address to the Nation on the Soviet Occupation of Afghanistan, December 28, 1985," available at http://www.reagan.utexas.edu/search/speeches/speech_srch.html.

48. "Biased Afghan Coverage at CBS," *Extra!* (October–November 1989), available at http://fair.org/extra-online-articles/biased-afghan-coverage-at-cbs/19/?media_outlet_id=10; David Barboza and Narendra Nandoe, "University Seeks to Expand Its Role in Afghan Media Project," *Daily Free Press*,

December 10, 1986, p. A3; Richard Bernstein, "For Journalism Dean, Questions about Objectivity," *New York Times*, November 3, 1987, p. A14.

49. FCO 37/2214, "Leading Personalities in Afghanistan, July 1980," pp. 10 and 13.

50. For an example of accounts that downplay ethnic antagonisms in earlier time periods, see the testimony in Ṣafā Akhavān, *Tārīkh-i shafāhī-i Afghānistān: 1900–1992 Mīlādī* (Tehran: Vizārat-i Umūr-i Khārijah, Markaz-i Chāp va Intishārāt, 2002), 118–120.

51. "Letters to the Editor," *Mujahideen Monthly,* October–November 1991, p. 47.

52. Ibid., p. 48.

53. Q. M. Saeed, "Hindu Lust for Muslims Bleeding," *Mujahideen Monthly,* March 1986, pp. 13–14 and 19, quotes at 19.

54. "Editorial: Reverberation of Afghan Jihad Echoes around the Globe," *Mujahideen Monthly,* January 1990, pp. 3–4. This editorial likened the iconoclasm of the East European uprisings to the destruction of statues in Mecca in 632, arguing that in both instances "symbols representing repressive and pagan systems were destroyed as a consequence of an Islamic Jihad and the accompanying act of migration." The same issue includes a story about the martyrdom of Abdullah Azzam in November 1989. See also "Hekmatyar Links Changes in E. Europe to Afghan Jihad," *Mujahideen Monthly,* January 1990, pp. 5–9, quotes at 6–7.

55. "Hekmatyar Links Changes in E. Europe to Afghan Jihad," p. 7.

56. "Solution Lies in Jihad," *Mujahideen Monthly,* July–August 1991, p. 3.

8. AT THE CENTER OF HUMANITY

1. Bruce Lawrence, ed., *Messages to the World: The Statements of Osama bin Laden,* trans. James Howarth (London: Verso, 2005), 85.

2. "Address to the Nation on the Terrorist Attacks," September 11, 2001, available at http://www.presidency.ucsb.edu/ws/?pid=58057.

3. See her remarks at http://www.defense.gov/news/newsarticle.aspx?id=15706; see also Jasbir K. Puar, "On Torture: Abu Ghraib," *Radical History Review* 93

(2005): 13–38; and Philip Gourevitch and Errol Morris, *Standard Operating Procedure* (New York: Penguin, 2008).

4. Matthew Rosenberg and Eric Schmitt, "U.S. Is Escalating a Secretive War in Afghanistan," *New York Times*, February 13, 2015, p. A1.

5. Interviews with Afghan workers and students in London, July 2013; "New UNHCR Report Says Global Forced Displacement at 18-Year High," June 19, 2013, available at http://www.unhcr.org/51c071816.html; Ahmad Shuja, "Syria's Afghan Refugees Trapped in a Double Crisis," *UN Dispatch*, January 28, 2013, available at http://www.undispatch.com/syrias-afghan -refugees-trapped-in-a-double-crisis/.

6. Interview with Hafiz Mansour, Kabul, November 2013.

7. Michael Barry, *Massoud: De l'islamisme à la liberté* (Paris: Editions Louis Audibert, 2002), 9–14; Aleksandr Liakhovskii, *Tragediia i doblest' Afgana: Informatsiia, analiz, vyvody* (Iaroslavl': "Nord," 2004), 458; Robert D. Kaplan, *Soldiers of God: With the Mujahidin in Afghanistan* (Boston: Houghton Mifflin, 1990), 41.

8. Kaplan, *Soldiers of God,* 39–44; Steve Coll, *Ghost Wars: The Secret History of the CIA, Afghanistan and bin Laden, from the Soviet Invasion to September 10, 2001* (New York: Penguin Books, 2005), 569–570.

9. Aḥmād Shāh Farzān, *'Uqāb'hā-yi Pāmīr: Zindagī va Mabārizāt-i Aḥmad Shāh Mas'ūd* (Iran: Kitābkhānah'-i Millī-yi Iran, 1383 [2004]), 74–75 and 201; Akbar Zīvarī, ed., *Mas'ūd farātar az marz'hā* (Kabul: Bunyād-i Shahīd-i Mas'ūd, 1382 [2003]), 4; Aleksandr Liakhovskii and Viacheslav Nekrasov, *Grazhdanin, politik, voin: Pamiati Akhmad Shakha Masuda* (Moscow: published by authors, 2007), 300 and 327.

10. Sayed Askar Mousavi, *The Hazaras of Afghanistan: An Historial, Cultural, Economic and Political Study* (Richmond, Surrey: Curzon, 1998), 198–199.

11. For his wife's account, see Sediqa Massoud, Marie-Françoise Colombani, Chékéba Hachemi, *Pour l'amour de Massoud* (Paris: XO Editions, 2005).

12. Revolutionary Association of the Women of Afghanistan Issuances, Hoover Institution Archives, issues of *Payām-i zan* in Box 1 and "Masou'd Men Rape Foreigners," *Burst of the 'Islamic Government' Bubble in Afghanistan* 2 (1997):

21; and material dated December 10, 1996, March 8, 1999, April 18, 1999, and November 18, 1999 in Box 2.

13. Waḥīd Muzhdah, *Afghānistān va Panj Sāl-i Sulṭah-'i Ṭālibān* (Tehrān: Nashr-i Nay, 1382 [2003]), 117.

14. See Juan R. I. Cole, "The Taliban, Women, and the Hegelian Private Sphere," and Robert L. Canfield, "Fraternity, Power, and Time in Central Asia," in *The Taliban and the Crisis of Afghanistan,* ed. Robert D. Crews and Amin Tarzi (Cambridge, MA: Harvard University Press, 2008), 118–154, 212–237.

15. The classic work on the geopolitical and energy context for the rise of the Taliban is Ahmed Rashid, *Taliban: Militant Islam, Oil and Fundamentalism in Central Asia* (New Haven, CT: Yale University Press, 2000). See also Abdulkader Sinno, "Explaining the Taliban's Ability to Mobilize the Pashtuns" and Neamatollah Nojumi, "The Rise and Fall of the Taliban," in Crews and Tarzi, *The Taliban and the Crisis of Afghanistan,* 59–89 and 90–117.

16. I owe this anecdote to Hamidullah Tarzi. See also Robert D. Crews, "The Taliban and Nationalist Militancy in Afghanistan," in *Contextualizing Jihadi Thought,* ed. Jeevan Deol and Zaheer Kazmi (New York: Columbia University Press, 2012), 343–368.

17. Abdul Salam Zaeef, *My Life with the Taliban,* ed. Alex Strick van Linschoten and Felix Kuehn (New York: Columbia University Press, 2010), 94–95; and "The Labor Law of Afghanistan," November 1, 1999 available at http://www.asianlii.org/af/legis/laws/lloaogn790p19991101142007222a443/.

18. Muzhdah, *Afghānistān va Panj Sāl-i Sulṭah-'i Ṭālibān,* 117–118.

19. Zaeef, *My Life with the Taliban,* 160–161.

20. NSA, U.S. Embassy (Islamabad), Cable, "Afghanistan: Raising Bin Ladin With the Taliban," March 4, 1997, available at http://www2.gwu.edu /~nsarchiv/NSAEBB/NSAEBB134/Doc%201.pdf.

21. NSA, U.S. Embassy (Islamabad), Cable, "SITREP 6: Pakistan/Afghanistan Reaction to U.S. Strikes," August 25, 1998, available at http://www2.gwu .edu/~nsarchiv/NSAEBB/NSAEBB134/Doc%204.pdf; U.S. Embassy (Islamabad), Cable, "Afghanistan: Demarche to Taliban on New Bin Laden Threat," September 14, 1998, available at http://www2.gwu.edu/~nsarchiv

/NSAEBB/NSAEBB134/Doc%206.pdf; and U.S. Department of State, Cable, "Message to Mullah Omar," October 1, 1998, available at http://www2 .gwu.edu/~nsarchiv/NSAEBB/NSAEBB134/Doc%207.pdf.

22. Daniel R. Green, *The Valley's Edge: A Year with the Pashtuns in the Heartland of the Taliban* (Washington, D.C.: Potomac Books, 2012), 49–50.

23. Gourevitch and Morris, *Standard Operating Procedure,* 29–30.

24. Jane Perlez, Raymond Bonner, and Salman Masood, "An Ex-Detainee of the U.S. Describes a 6-Year Ordeal," *New York Times,* January 6, 2009, p. A1.

25. John Ehrenberg, J. Patrice McSherry, José Ramón Sánchez, and Caroleen Marji Sayej, eds., *The Iraq Papers* (Oxford: Oxford University Press, 2010), 427–431, 451–453. On the "Salt Pit" facility, see, inter alia, Dana Priest, "CIA Avoids Scrutiny of Detainee Treatment," *Washington Post,* March 3, 2005, p. A01; Adam Goldman and Kathy Gannon, "Death Shed Light on CIA 'Salt Pit' near Kabul," March 28, 2010, available at http://www.msnbc.msn.com /id/36071994/ns/us_news-security/#.UMocfqVS01c; on Bagram, Seymour M. Hersh, *Chain of Command: The Road from 9/11 to Abu Ghraib* (New York: HarperCollins, 2004), 155; Joshua Foust, "End Contractor Mistreatment," *Registan,* June 4, 2011, available at http://registan.net/2011/06/04/end -contractor-mistreatment/; Sarah Stillman, "The Invisible Army," *New Yorker,* June 6, 2011; and Anthony H. Cordesman, "The US Cost of the Afghan War: FY2002–FY2013: Cost in Military Operating Expenditure and Aid and Prospects for 'Transition,'" May 14, 2012, Center for Strategic and International Studies, http://csis.org/files/publication/120515_US_Spending _Afghan_War_SIGAR.pdf.

26. Cited in Astri Suhrke, *When More Is Less: The International Project in Afghanistan* (London: Hurst, 2011), 49.

27. Leo Docherty, *Desert of Death: A Soldier's Journey from Iraq to Afghanistan* (London: Faber and Faber, 2007), 58. See also Suhrke, *When More Is Less;* and Tim Bird and Alex Marshall, *Afghanistan: How the West Lost Its Way* (New Haven, CT: Yale University Press, 2011).

28. Karl Eikenberry, U.S. Embassy in Kabul to Secretary of State and others, "Afghanistan: Capital Flight and Its Impact on Future Stability," October 19, 2009, available at https://wikileaks.org/plusd/cables/09KABUL3364_a.html.

See also Edwina A. Thompson, *Trust is the Coin of the Realm: Lessons from the Money Men in Afghanistan* (Oxford: Oxford University Press, 2011).

29. Richard Stone, "Mother of All Lodes," *Science*, August 15, 2014, pp. 725–727.

30. U.S. Embassy in Accra to Secretary of State, October 23, 2007, available at http://wikileaks.org/cable/2007/10/07ACCRA2244.html. On women's role in Afghanistan's drug economy, see Fariba Nawa, "Women and the Drug Trade in Afghanistan," in *Under the Drones: Modern Lives in the Afghanistan-Pakistan Borderlands*, ed. Shahzad Bashir and Robert D. Crews (Cambridge, MA: Harvard University Press, 2012), 236–256.

31. See the documentary film *Afghan Star*, directed by Havana Marking ([New York]: Zeitgeist Films, [2010]).

32. "Commemorating the Nineteenth Anniversary of the Historical Gathering and Selection of Ameer-ul-Momineen on 4th April 1996 in Kandahar," April 4, 2015, Islamic Emirate of Afghanistan, *Voice of Jihad*, available at http://shahamat-english.com/index.php/paighamoona/53792-commemorating-the-nineteenth-anniversary-of-the-historical-gathering-and-selection-of-ameer-ul-momineen-on-4th-april-1996-in-kandahar; for more on this global sensibility among militants, see Canfield, "Fraternity, Power, and Time in Central Asia," in 212–237.

33. Sune Engel Rasmussen, "Afghan Civilian Deaths Reach Record High," *The Guardian*, February 18, 2015; Dan Lamothe, "Meet the Shadowy Figure Recruiting for the Islamic State in Afghanistan," *The Washington Post,* January 13, 2015; Rateb Noori, "Protests in Ghazni over 31 Hazara Hostages," *Tolo News*, March 17, 2015, available at http://www.tolonews.com/en/afghanistan/18659-protests-in-ghazni-over-31-hazara-hostages.

34. See Ken Auletta, "Afghanistan's First Media Mogul," *New Yorker*, July 5, 2010.

35. These examples are drawn from Muhammad Ishaq al-Fayyaz's website, http://alfayadh.org/fa/#questions; and from 'Alī Moḥaqeq Kābulī, *Istiftā'āt-i jadīd-i ḥazrat-i Āyat Allāh al-'Uẓmā Moḥaqeq Kābulī* vol. 1 (Kabul: n.p., 1381 [2002]), 185–195 and 458–468.

36. There is now a very rich literature on Afghans in Iran. See "Afghan Refugees," special issue of *Iranian Studies* 40, no. 2 (April 2007), particularly in

essays by Fariba Adelkhah and Zuzanna Olszewska, "The Iranian Afghans," 137–165; Alessandro Monsutti, "Migration as a Rite of Passage: Young Afghans Building Masculinity and Adulthood in Iran," 167–185; Diana Glazebrook and Mohammad Jalal Abbasi-Shavazi, "Being Neighbors to Imam Reza: Pilgrimage Practices and Return Intentions of Hazara Afghans Living in Mashhad, Iran," 187–201; Olszewska, "'A Desolate Voice': Poetry and Identity among Young Afghan Refugees in Iran," 203–224; Elaheh Rostami-Povey, "Afghan Refugees in Iran, Pakistan, the U.K., and the U.S. and Life after Return: A Comparative Gender Analysis," 241–261; Diane Tober, "'My Body Is Broken like My Country': Identity, Nation, and Repatriation among Afghan Refugees in Iran," 263–285.

37. For more on the history of competition among Shia clerics for this status, see Linda S. Walbridge, ed., *The Most Learned of the Shi'a: The Institution of the Marja' Taqlid* (Oxford: Oxford University Press, 2001).

38. See, for instance, the websites of Ayatollah Mohaqeq Kabuli, http://www .mohaqeq.org/fa/ and Ayatollah Muhammad Ishaq Fayyaz, http://alfayadh .org/fa/#main.

39. Mohseni's autobiography *(zindigī'nāmah)* was available in Dari on his now defunct website, http://almohseni.com/index.php/component/content /article/111-z.html?tmpl=component&print=1&page=. Much, but not all, of this original website material has migrated to a new address, http://mohseny .com/da/. On the hajj, see Erwin Grötzbach *Afghanistan: Eine geographische Landeskunde* (Darmstadt: Wissenschaftliche Buchgesellschaft, 1990), 151.

40. Mohseni's autobiography at almohseni.com.

41. "Iranian Radio: Protesters in Afghanistan's Kabul Denounce Private Television," Voice of the Islamic Republic of Iran External Service, Friday, October 24, 2008.

42. "Afghan TV Chief to Be Prosecuted for 'Slander,'" *Kabul Weekly,* April 7, 2009.

43. "Pressing Ayatollah Mohseni on Human Rights for All Afghans," U.S. Embassy in Kabul to Secretary of State, April 21, 2009, available at https:// wikileaks.org/plusd/cables/09KABUL1012_a.html.

44. "Afghan daily urges people to oppose spread of religious extremism," *Hasht-e Sobh,* April 23, 2009.

45. "Afghan paper accuses government of Internet censorship," *Hasht-e Sobh,* June 2, 2009.

46. Muḥammad Āsaf Muḥsinī, *Jahānī Shudan va Jahānī'sāzī* ([Afghanistan]: Maṭbaʿah-'i Ṣanʿatī-yi Iʿtiṣām, 1387 [2008]), 11–12.

EPILOGUE

1. Muḥammad ʿAlī Shāh Mūsavī Gardīzī, *Ḥaqāyiq-i nāguftah az Guvāntānāmū: Sarguzasht-i Yik Dāktur-i Zindānī* (Kabul: Maṭbaʿah-i Mayvand, 1386 [2007]), i–ii.

2. See his hearing transcripts at http://media.mcclatchydc.com/smedia/2008/06 /02/12/ISN-1154.source.prod_affiliate.91.pdf. See also the case of Sabar Lal Melma, who was sent to Guantánamo in October 2002. He was released in 2005, but coalition forces killed him at his home in a night raid in September 2011, suspecting that he had lent financial backing to insurgents. "The Guantánamo Docket: Sabar Lal Melma," at http://projects.nytimes.com/guantanamo /detainees/801-sabar-lal-melma. For valuable surveys of various kinds of Afghan mobility and their political contexts, see Conrad Schetter, "Flüchtling—Arbeitsmigrant—Dschihadist: Zur Rolle von Translokalität in Afghanistan," *Geographische Rundschau* 11 (2011): 18–24; and Robert Nichols, *A History of Pashtun Migration, 1775–2006* (Oxford: Oxford University Press, 2008).

3. See Astri Suhrke, *When More Is Less: The International Project in Afghanistan* (London: Hurst and Co., 2011); Thomas Barfield, *Afghanistan: A Cultural and Political History* (Princeton, NJ: Princeton University Press, 2010); Rajiv Chandrasekaran, *Little America: The War within the War for Afghanistan* (New York: Alfred A. Knopf, 2012); Tim Bird and Alex Marshall, *Afghanistan: How the West Lost Its Way* (New Haven, CT: Yale University Press, 2011); Anand Gopal, *No Good Men among the Living: America, the Taliban, and the War through Afghan Eyes* (New York: Metropolitan Books, 2014); Daniel P. Bolger, *Why We Lost: A General's Inside Account of the Iraq and Afghanistan Wars* (Boston: Houghton Mifflin Harcourt, 2014); and Jack Fairweather, *The Good War: Why We Couldn't Win the War or the Peace in Afghanistan* (New York: Basic Books, 2014).

4. Robert D. Kaplan, *Soldiers of God: With the Mujahidin in Afghanistan* (Boston: Houghton Mifflin, 1990), 15–17.

5. Paula Broadwell, *All In: The Education of General David Petraeus* (New York: Penguin, 2012), 62–63.

6. David Kilcullen, *The Accidental Guerrilla: Fighting Small Wars in the Midst of a Big One* (Oxford: Oxford University Press, 2009), 38 and 299.

7. Ibid., 49.

8. Ibid., 68.

9. For a sophisticated analysis and critique of assumptions about the essentially "tribal" nature of the Taliban, see Thomas Ruttig, "How Tribal Are the Taliban?," in *Under the Drones: Modern Lives in the Afghanistan-Pakistan Borderlands*, ed. Shahzad Bashir and Robert D. Crews (Cambridge, MA: Harvard University Press, 2012), 102–135.

10. See the reports compiled by the Special Inspector General for Afghan Reconstruction, www.sigar.mil; U.S. Department of Justice, "Two Individuals Plead Guilty to Conspiring to Launder Bribes Received in Afghanistan," May 28, 2014, available at http://www.justice.gov/opa/pr/two-individuals-plead-guilty-conspiring-launder-bribes-received-afghanistan; see also Suhrke, *When More Is Less*, 117–136.

11. For visa data, see http://travel.state.gov/content/dam/visas/Statistics/AnnualReports/FY2013AnnualReport/FY13AnnualReport-TableIII.pdf. Stories about Afghan dogs became a staple of local news outlets covering the drawdown of U.S. forces in Afghanistan. See, for instance, Cristina Corbin, "Dogs Rescued in Afghanistan to be Reunited with Comrades," available at http://www.foxnews.com/world/2014/07/21/dogs-rescued-in-afghanistan-and-raised-as-us-comrades-to-be-reunited-with/.

ACKNOWLEDGMENTS

IN WRITING THIS BOOK I have benefited from the generous support of a great number of people. It is a privilege to acknowledge the many debts I have accumulated here.

An invitation to speak in the Leon B. Poullada Memorial Lecture Series of the Program in Near Eastern Studies at Princeton University provided the initial impetus for taking on this project. For their encouragement and insightful feedback at a critical stage, I am most grateful to the entire Poullada family. I would also like to thank colleagues at Princeton, especially Molly Greene, Şükrü Hanioğlu, and Muhammad Qasim Zaman, for making this opportunity so productive. A grant from the Carnegie Corporation of New York afforded me time to engage in further research and writing.

This book would have been unthinkable without the wit and wisdom of the inimitable Scott Levi, who first introduced me in 1997 to our Afghan friends in Tashkent, and whose pioneering work on Central and South Asia has been such a revelation and source of inspiration. His incisive comments on the manuscript improved it considerably. Another veteran of the Tashkent scene, Amin Tarzi, was the other truly indispensable figure whose erudition, generosity, friendship, and humor shaped this project. My unfailing tutor and guide to Afghan history and politics, Amin kindly shared his vast learning and made numerous introductions to figures who were enormously helpful in conducting my research. Among these contacts, Mr. Hamidullah Tarzi, a man who has lived much of the history that I have tried to reconstruct in this book, was particularly gracious in assisting me in Kabul, not least of all by giving me a ride around the city in his exquisite Cadillac.

Also in the Afghan capital, I would like to thank the staff of the American Institute of Afghanistan Studies for aiding me in conducting interviews and for giving me an opportunity to try out some of my ideas before an audience there. I owe a special debt to the director of the institute, Dr. Rohullah Amin, a remarkable scholar from whom I have learned so much. He tirelessly went beyond the call of duty to facilitate my research, even tracking down books from local publishers.

Closer to home, I am grateful to Naeem Azizian and Fariba Nawa, who gathered oral histories of fascinating figures in the Afghan diaspora in California on my behalf. For aiding me with my own interviews in Europe and Turkey, I thank Liaquat Ali Hazara, Ali Ahmed Shahrestani, Hussain Yasa, and Imran Ali Yousifi. In helping to arrange these conversations—and for their insights, I am especially indebted to Nasim Fekrat and Mohammad Mahdi Mohebbi. In Denmark, it was my very good fortune to make the acquaintance of Mohammad Asef Soltanzadeh, a brilliant writer and most generous intellectual, to whom I express my deepest gratitude.

I would also like to thank librarians and archivists at the Afghanistan Center at Kabul University, the Afghanistan Digital Collections of the University of Arizona, the Afghanistan Digital Library of New York University, the British Library, the Hoover Institution, the National Archives (in the United Kingdom), the National Archives of India, the Russian State Archive of Social and Political History, the Russian State Military History Archive, the San Carlos Public Library, and Stanford University's Green Library.

For very insightful comments on presentations and drafts of earlier versions of this work, I thank Madihah Akhter, Nicholas Breyfogle, Diana Dakhlallah, Peter Holquist, Eileen Kane, Mejgan Massoumi, Ahoo Najafian, Mohammad Qayoumi, Will Sherman, Yuri Slezkine, and audiences at George Mason University, Ohio State University, and the University of California at Berkeley. At talks at the University of North Carolina at Chapel Hill and Yale University I was grateful to receive encouragement from Laura Engelstein, Donald J. Raleigh, and Richard Wortman, exemplary scholars who remain major sources of inspiration for me and so many others.

In various conversations tied to research for this project I have been fortunate to draw on the expertise of a long list of friends and colleagues. In this connection, I thank in particular Mariam Amini, Nushin Arbabzadah, Aziz Arianfar, Dr. Azim, Joel Beinin, Albert Camarillo, James Caron, Dean Chahim, Gilles Dorronsoro, Stéphane Dudoignon, Parwana Fayyaz, Nile Green, Shah Mahmoud Hanifi, Sana Haroon, David Holloway, Mohammad Isaqzadeh, Mary Javaheri, Stephen Kotkin, Magnus Marsden, Mark Mazower, Robert McChesney, Razi Mohebi, Sayed Askar Mousavi, Norman Naimark, Neamatolluh Nojumi, Jeremy Prestholdt, Hussain Razaiat, Thomas Ruttig, Lutz Rzehak, Somaye Sarvarzade, Nazif Shahrani, and Frank Trentmann.

At Harvard University Press, Brian Distelberg was exceptionally effective in keeping this project on track. For expert editing I thank Edward Wade and Jennifer Shenk. Joyce Seltzer brilliantly intervened at crucial points to sharpen my thinking and to offer precisely the right advice about structuring the book. Her critical eye and enthusiastic backing were absolutely essential.

I have drawn inspiration and courage from friends who have left their own distinctive imprints on this book—and who have diminished my ignorance in innumerable ways. Shahzad Bashir, an always reliable source of original ideas and wisdom, helped me figure out how to approach this topic. Conversations with the singular Aishwary

Kumar and Parna Sengupta have been unfailingly stimulating, exciting, and, most important, fun. They may not recognize their influence in what I have written, but my debt could not be greater or more heartfelt. Ken Petersen was there at the outset and knows his esteemed place in my education about all things related to the region. In his humility and gentle patience, Atiq Sarwari sparked my interest in this subject long ago. In this same spirit, I thank the selfless Kavous Barghi, a talented tutor who has helped me with the Persian language along the way. As an unrivalled scholar, humorist, and friend, Olga Litvak remains a model for my entire family. I have also absorbed more than I can acknowledge here from very learned friends, who, buoyed by a keen sense of humor and a reassuringly clear grasp of the world, include Dominic Parviz Brookshaw, David Como, J. P. Daughton, Zephyr Frank, Sean Hanretta, David Jesitus, and Uğur Zekeriya Peçe.

Above all, though, I must thank my family for patiently supporting this project. My sisters, Kathleen, Loretta, Cynthia, and Susan, have always encouraged me. My parents, Kay and Denny Crews, are not easily intimidated. They backed my forays to distant research locales, as did Margaret Sena, for whom the word 'intimidated' does not exist. She remains the most talented and thoughtful historian in the family, by far, though she faces challengers from the next generation. Christopher and Reina, to whom I dedicate this book with love and gratitude, have added their own contagious energy and hilarious (but wise) sense of right and wrong.

INDEX